DO SOMETHING!

Ken

With best wishes and

many thanks for all your

contributions to Canada

Pierre M

DO SOMETHING!

365 Ways You Can Strengthen Canada

PRESTON MANNING

sh.
SUTHERLAND
HOUSE

TORONTO, 2020

Sutherland House
416 Moore Ave., Suite 205
Toronto, ON M4G 1C9

First edition, February 2020

If you are interested in inviting one of our authors to a live event or
media appearance, please contact publicity@sutherlandhousebooks.com
and visit our website at sutherlandhousebooks.com for more
information about our authors and their schedules.

Manufactured in the United States
Cover designed by Greg Tabor
Book composed by Karl Hunt

Library and Archives Canada Cataloguing in Publication
Title: Do something! : 365 ways you can strengthen Canada / Preston Manning.
Names: Manning, Preston, 1942- author.
Description: Includes index.
Identifiers: Canadiana 20200154575 | ISBN 9781989555255 (softcover)
Subjects: LCSH: Political participation—Canada. |
LCSH: Social participation—Canada. | LCSH: Canada—
Politics and government—21st century.
Classification: LCC JL186.5 .M36 2020 |
DDC 323/.0420971—dc23

ISBN 978-1-989555-25-5

DEDICATION

Among all those whose lives are affected by the processes and institutions of democracy in Canada, there is a group of unsung heroes who deserve recognition and appreciation above and beyond what it is humanly possible to convey by words alone.

That group is composed of the wives, husbands, partners, children, and grandchildren of those who are democratically elected to public office, be it the parliament of Canada, the legislatures of the provinces and territories, or local municipal councils.

The holders of public office too often find themselves "missing in action" when it comes to the home life and needs of their loved ones, called away time and time again by public business, missing birthdays, anniversaries, graduations, and other special occasions, distracted by public worries and political pressures even when physically present, and exposing the family to scrutiny and abuse by opponents and hostile media from which family members have no means of defending themselves.

In my case, this band of unsung heroes includes my dear wife Sandra, our children—Andrea, Avryll, Mary Joy, Nathan, and David—and our twelve grandchildren.

It is to them, and the members of all the other political families of which they are representative, that this book on strengthening democracy and conservatism in Canada is respectfully dedicated.

Preston Manning
Calgary, Alberta
January, 2020

FOREWORD

Can we merge the politician and the citizen, into a single category: the politician-citizen or the citizen-politician? In other words, can we have a person who even when active, and a national leader in the political arena, retains the instincts and idealism of a citizen? That is my reckoning of Preston Manning. He was always tethered to fundamental ideas—ideas of our democracy, a bedrock notion of real citizenship—even as he exercised leadership in the House of Commons. Not incidentally, he was and is a high example of that "civility" so many now report as missing in Canadian politics.

In this new work Mr. Manning is back, or still at what he was always about. Going to the core of our system of government. Emphasizing citizen involvement. Reinforcing the need for thought in politics. He is also writing during a time in Canadian politics when disenchantment with how our system runs deep, and the engagement of citizens from politics is at a disastrously low ebb.

Do Something! is Manning's imperative of a title. It signals his sense of urgency but the arguments and illustrations of what could and should be done are both practical and genuinely encouraging. He is a decent man with a fine mind and, oh Lord, how we need both.

—Rex Murphy, 2020

INTRODUCTION

"Every citizen of Canada has the right to vote in an election of members of the House of Commons or of a legislative assembly."[1] This, according to the Canadian Charter of Rights and Freedoms, is one of our most basic democratic rights.

So how did Canadians exercise this basic right in the nine most recent elections held in 2018-19, including the federal election of October 21, 2019? The results are summarized below.

Ontario, June 7, 2018: Voter turnout was 57%. The Progressive Conservative Party of Ontario, led by populist Doug Ford, won a majority government with 76 of the 124 seats in the legislature. The NDP formed the official opposition. The Liberals, who formed the previous government, recorded the worst election result in their 161-year history, losing official party status.

New Brunswick, September 24, 2018: Voter turnout was 67%. Four parties won seats in the 49-seat legislature: 22 by the Progressive Conservatives; 21 by the Liberals; three each by the People's Alliance and the Greens, with the NDP failing to elect a single member. Former Liberal Premier Brian Gallant attempted to form a government but was defeated on a confidence vote. On November 9, Progressive Conservative leader Blaine Higgs was sworn in as premier with a minority government.

Quebec, October 1, 2018: Voter turnout was 66%. The Coalition Avenir Quebec (CAQ) led by Francois Legault won a majority government with 74 of 125 seats, unseating the previous Liberal government. The Liberals, with 31 seats, became the official opposition. The Parti Quebecois and Quebec Solidaire each won 10 seats.

Alberta, April 16, 2019. Voter turnout was 64%. The United Conservative Party, led by Jason Kenney and formed by the union of the Wildrose and Progressive Conservative parties two years earlier, won a majority government with 63 seats in the 87-seat legislature. The previous NDP government won only 24 seats and was reduced to official

1   Constitution Act, 1982, s.3

opposition after only one term in office, experiencing the shortest term in office of any governing party in Alberta's history.

Prince Edward Island, April 23, 2019: Voter turnout was 76%. The Progressive Conservative Party under Dennis King won 12 seats in the 27-seat legislature to form a minority government. The Greens won eight seats to form the Official Opposition. The previous Liberal government won only six seats with the Liberal leader losing his own seat, and the NDP failed to elect a single member.

Newfoundland and Labrador, May 16, 2019: Voter turnout was 61%. While the Progressive Conservative Party under leader Ches Crosbie led in the opinion polls by as much as 9 points, the governing Liberal Party led by Dwight Ball won re-election with 20 seats, one short of a majority in the 40-seat legislature. The Progressive Conservatives with fifteen seats form the official opposition. Three seats were won by the NDP and two by independents.

Manitoba, September 10, 2019: Voter turnout was 55%. The Progressive Conservative Party led by Brian Pallister won its second majority government with 36 seats in the 57-seat legislature. The NDP led by Wab Kinew retained its position as the official opposition with 18 seats, with the Liberals holding three seats.

Northwest Territories, October 1, 2019: Voter turnout was 54%. Nineteen MLA's, only four of them incumbents, were elected to the NWT legislature as independents. Nine of these were women, thus giving the NWT assembly the highest percentage of female representation of any Canadian legislature. Under the NWT's "consensus government system," the MLA's select the premier, and Yellowknife MLA Caroline Cochrane was chosen to fill this position.

Canada, October 21, 2019: Voter turnout was 66%. The Liberal government led by Justin Trudeau was reduced to minority status with 157 seats. The Conservative Party of Canada under Andrew Scheer, with 121 seats, increased its seat total but remained the official opposition. A resurgent Bloc Quebecois won 32 seats, the NDP was reduced to 24 seats from 39 in the previous parliament, the Greens won three seats, and there was one independent. With the Liberals losing every seat in Alberta and Saskatchewan, and the Bloc winning 43% of the Quebec seats, Canada's parliament is now seriously divided ideologically and geographically. National unity–completely ignored as an issue during the election campaign–emerges once again as a major national concern. On December 12, 2019, while the British Conservatives under Boris Johnson were winning a resounding electoral victory,

Andrew Scheer resigned as the leader of the Conservative Party of Canada.

What can Canadian democrats of all political stripes learn from these exercises in democracy? What can be done to better address the issues which dominated or failed to register in these election campaigns? What can be done to strengthen democracy and party performances in the years going forward? This book endeavors to provide answers to precisely such questions.

The democracy challenge

The holding of free elections, by itself, is not necessarily a sign that democracy in Canada is in good health. In fact, democracy in Canada, defined as government of the people, by the people, and for the people, is in deep trouble.[2]

Low voter turnouts are one obvious symptom. In the last elections in Manitoba and the Northwest Territories, for example, 45% of eligible electors did not vote. In the October 2019 federal election, one third of those eligible to vote did not bother to do so.

The average voter turnout in the thirty federal elections held in the twentieth century was 72.8%.[3] Despite all the subsequent improvements in communications, transportation, and political organization, which ought to have increased voter participation, the average voter turnout in the first five federal elections in the twenty-first century was 62.8%, a 10% decline.

Citizen dissatisfaction with democratic politics as currently practiced in Canada is further evidenced by:

2   When this definition of democracy, taken from Abraham Lincoln's Gettysburg Address, is quoted verbally today, we often put the emphasis on the prepositions . . . *of* the people, *by* the people, and *for* the people. But as Professor David Zarefsky has pointed out in his monumental series of lectures on Lincoln's speeches, when Lincoln actually spoke these words he personally put the emphasis on the *people* . . . of the *people*, by the *people*, and for the *people*. Democracy is ultimately about the *people*. (Zarefsky, David, *Abraham Lincoln in His Own Words, Lecture 23: "Lincoln at Gettysburg,"* The Teaching Company, 1999.

3   Source: Current and past elections section of Elections Canada website, https:// www.elections.ca/. The average voter turnout in the nine elections summarized in Table 1 is also 63%, more than one third of eligible Canadian voters declining to participate in the electoral process over the 2018-19 period.

- Declining respect for and trust in the political process. Politicians, the day-to-day practitioners of democracy, and the institutions that employ them (political parties, municipal councils, legislatures, and parliament) are increasingly disrespected and mistrusted by the public as they fail to come to grips with the issues and concerns of the people they are elected to serve.
- Incompetence in high office, which further erodes voter confidence in elected officials. The biggest single reason given by Albertans for the rejection of its one and only NDP government after one term in office, was incompetence. A party that had been thrust into office unexpectedly in 2015 was unprepared to govern.
- The rise of populism and populist leadership, increasingly drawn from outside the traditional political establishments, as reflected in the election of Doug Ford and company in Ontario and the growth of the populist-rooted separatist movement in Alberta and Saskatchewan.
- The increasing difficulties in recruiting quality candidates for public office. The federal NDP, whose representation in the House of Commons fell from 39 to 24 seats in the recent federal election, failed to find more than token candidates in dozens of federal ridings.
- The nastiness and polarization of public discourse in the political arena, expanded and amplified by social media.

The polarization of public political discourse has reached the point where democratic debate, as illustrated by recent leaders' debates at both the federal and provincial levels, is often little more than content-free exchanges of simplistic one-liners or shouting matches between those deaf to all opinions but their own. And much of the so-called debate in our elected assemblies has become little more than exchanges of highly-partisan opinions often written by professional speechwriters or unknown partisan subordinates behind the scenes.

Internationally, citizen-directed democracy as practiced in most western countries faces an unprecedented challenge from state-directed democracy as practiced and promoted worldwide by the Communist Party and government of China. It is deeply disturbing that in recent times, it is the Chinese model, not the western model, that is receiving increased admiration and acceptance in many parts of Africa, South America, and Asia.

And so, one of the main purposes of this book is to identify, based on the author's personal experience in the democratic arena, what must be done to strengthen democracy in Canada, especially for the benefit of next-generation Canadians. In particular, proposals are offered for:

- Strengthening the intellectual capital available to small-d democrats.
- Increasing the knowledge and skills of democratic practitioners, regardless of their party label, so that they enter the political arena better prepared.
- Understanding the root causes of populism and directing the political energy it represents toward constructive rather than negative ends.
- Making use of issue campaigns and financial incentives to encourage political innovation and to stimulate greater voter participation in elections.
- Redefining political space for disengaged Canadians, especially millennials.
- Encouraging periodic political realignments among political parties in response to the changing needs and demands of electorates.
- Balancing the needs and interests of minorities and majorities through unity politics rather than the practice of identity politics.
- Strengthening relations between the political and scientific communities.
- Assisting faith-oriented Canadians to participate wisely and graciously in democratic political processes.
- Raising the ethical tone of political discourse and the conduct of elected officials in office.
- Employing social media more effectively and responsibly for democratic purposes.
- Constructively responding to the challenge of populism and addressing the roots and current expression of western alienation.
- Wining the global competition between citizen-directed democracy and state-directed democracy as practiced and promoted by the Communist Party and government of China.

Each chapter includes action lists for strengthening democracy on all these fronts and specific pleas for the reader to *Do Something!* In response. For those of us of the older generation, many of the action items on these lists constitute unfinished business, things we had hoped to achieve but were unable to do so. And thus we pass them on, plus some important additions, as a challenge to the next generation.

Strengthening democracy in Canada is in the interest of all of us, young and old regardless of where we live in the county or whatever else may divide us into competing political camps.

The conservative challenge

In a democratic political system in which political parties are very major players, strengthening democracy includes improving the performance and contributions of whatever political party one chooses to support. It is my personal conviction that conservatism–the political tradition that played such a pivotal role in the founding of Canada and which currently guides many members of governing or opposition parties at both the federal and provincial levels–has a particularly important role to play in addressing the democracy challenge. Conservatism in Canada, however, also needs renewal and strengthening in order to provide the leadership the country requires.

Conservative oriented political parties now form the governments in seven of ten provinces: Alberta, Saskatchewan, Manitoba, Ontario, New Brunswick, Quebec, and Prince Edward Island. And while successful in winning their recent elections, these conservative or near-conservative governments now face unprecedented challenges on a host of fronts, not just the democracy front.

Most, for example, have inherited the fiscal legacy of their financially irresponsible, left-leaning predecessors, governments which consistently spent more dollars than they collected in taxes, constantly increasing deficits and public debts that next-generation Canadians will be obligated to pay.

In Ontario, for example, the new Progressive Conservative government under Doug Ford inherited a provincial deficit of $3.7 billion[4] and

4   See https://www.ontario.ca/page/public-accounts-2017-18-annual-report. The difficulties of a new government immediately reducing such a deficit are compounded by the additional costs of extricating a province from expensive long-term commitments made by its predecessor. Thus in the case of the Ford government, the deficit for 2018-19 ballooned to $7.4 billion due in part to the need to pay penalties associated with the cancellation of the Wynne governments climate-change initiatives and the need to provide relief through subsidies to electricity consumers from the astronomical hydro bills resulting from the Wynne government's policies.

a public debt of \$323.8 billion[5] from the fiscally irresponsible Wynne government which preceded it. A similar situation exists in Alberta, a province which once prided itself on being able to balance its budgets. There, the newly-elected United Conservative government under Jason Kenny has inherited a provincial deficit of \$6.7 billion[6] and a public debt of \$63 billion[7], the fiscal legacy of the fiscally-irresponsible one-term NDP government that preceded it and the fiscally-weak Progressive Conservative governments of Premiers Stelmach and Redford before that.

The three largest expenditure commitments of most provincial governments are in the areas of health, education, and social services, all vitally important to the quality of life of Canadians. Yet today, investments in these services are passing the point of diminishing returns—the point where more money spent on them produces less and poorer service, not more and better service. Thus conservative governments at the provincial level face the daunting challenges of reforming, not simply managing and perpetuating, the traditional institutions and programs of the welfare state.

"Conservation" and "conservative" come from the same root. There is nothing incompatible between the principles of environmental conservation and political conservatism. Yet conservative political parties on both the federal and provincial levels have been slow to develop and promote a positive, pro-active conservative position on environmental protection and instead have largely adopted a default position characterized by opposition to the environmental positions of liberals, social democrats, and greens. This posture seriously damaged the Conservative Party of Canada's chances of winning support in the 2019 federal election, especially support among young people and electors in our largest cities. Thus one of the major challenges facing Canadian conservatism going forward is that of rethinking and repositioning itself on the issue of environmental protection, including that of climate change.

And as if the list of challenges facing the country and conservatives is not already long enough, as previously mentioned, national unity, completely ignored as an issue during the recent federal election campaign, has emerged once again as a major national concern.

---

5   Ibid
6   See https://open.alberta.ca/dataset/7714457c-7527-443a-a7db-dd8c1c8ead86/
     resource/b4cf321b-4b11-4b1b-a269-88f5828274ab/download/2018-19-goa-
     annual-report.pdf
7   Ibid

Structural inequities in our federal system and the ill-advised polices of the Trudeau administration on the fiscal, trade, transportation, energy, and environmental fronts have completely alienated millions of western Canadian voters, especially in Alberta and Saskatchewan, and have given rise to a surge of separatist sentiment which cannot be ignored.

The challenge this presents to the conservative governments of Alberta and Saskatchewan is one of preparing and vigorously impressing upon the federal government the key elements of a Fair Deal Now package for their provinces. Such a Fair Deal Now package is expected to include justifiable demands for reform of the equalization formula, unobstructed transportation corridors to the Atlantic and Pacific, immediate construction of the Trans Mountain pipeline expansion, and an administrative agreement limiting federal spending and taxation in areas of provincial and joint jurisdiction (such as environmental protection) without the consent of the affected provinces.

If these demands, which are perfectly understandable and reasonable, are not responded to quickly and affirmatively by the Trudeau minority government and the other provinces, the outcome is likely to be a further escalation of demands that the west pursue political independence from the Canadian federation.

The challenge which all this presents to federal conservatives is that of entering into solidarity (an informal coalition) with governing conservative provincial parties, pressuring the federal parliament to respond quickly and positively to the Fair Deal Now demands, and to offer constructive alternatives to the inactions and policies of the Liberal Party of Canada on the national unity front.

And thus the second major purpose of this book is to develop and present a series of action lists aimed specifically at conservatives for the purpose of renewing and strengthening the capacity of Canadian conservatism to better serve the people of Canada. In responding to the many challenges facing Canadian conservatives, these action lists include proposals for:

- Scouting and recruiting conservative candidates and leaders of exceptional ability and experience, and providing them with in-depth training for political participation and governance.
- Revitalizing conservatism through extensive networking, periodic political realignments, coalition building, and a vigorous effort to relate conservative principles and policies to municipal politics.

- Giving the highest priority to affirming and protecting the exercise of fundamental rights as purportedly guaranteed by our constitution–i.e., freedom of expression, freedom of religion, freedom of thought, freedom of belief, freedom of peaceful assembly, and freedom of association.
- Refreshing traditional conservative commitments to budget balancing, tax relief, economic rights, and economic freedoms by refreshing the language in which these positions are expressed and the means whereby they are to be achieved.
- Pursuing domestic free trade and using the constitutional powers of the federal government to provide unobstructed transportation corridors to the Atlantic, Pacific, and Arctic.
- Providing more freedom of choice in health, educational, and social services through a mixed (public and private) social services sector.
- Cultivating a green conservatism offering market-based approaches to environmental protection as an alternative to bureaucratic, politicized, regulation-based approaches.
- Offering a unity politics based on those characteristics which Canadians share in common as an alternative to the divisive identity politics offered by those who primarily focus on our differences.
- Addressing poverty through a better distribution of the tools of wealth creation rather than relying exclusively on income redistribution through progressive taxation.

Internationally, these action lists for conservatives also propose measures to address the challenge to market-directed capitalism, which free market liberals and conservatives have long championed, by state-directed capitalism as promoted by the Communist Party and government of China.

Once again, these action lists are not presented merely for the purpose of stimulating discussion. They are accompanied by specific pleas for the conservatively inclined reader to *Do Something!* To analyze, support, and implement the measures these lists prescribe.

These action lists for conservatives will, of course, be criticized and attacked by those who oppose conservative principles and policies. Nevertheless, my challenge to such critics, especially liberals and social democrats, is to move beyond tiresome and predictable negative criticism and come up with better alternatives to the problems and challenges these action lists address, alternatives which can and should be openly and honestly debated in the public arena, allowing the best ideas and public policy proposals to succeed in winning public support. At the end of the day, isn't that what genuine democratic debate and decision-making in a free society is supposed to be about?

Common sense and optimism

Political discourse framed in the "policy speak" of the political and media establishments, and laced with the sermons of the politically correct, can be especially dull and boring. But among the rank and file of the public, the grass roots and ordinary folk who have so informed and supported most of my own political work, there is an abundance of stories, practical analogies and humorous anecdotes sufficient to enrich any discussion of our politics and political options.

One gains access to such resources by simply meeting with and listening to (rather than lecturing) such people. Often you will find them trying to say back to you what you were trying to say to them but in language and with nuances and illustrations, drawn from their own experience, which are highly insightful and instructive. With the advent of the social media these stories, analogies, and humorous illustrations are now even more accessible than in the past, and the reader will find the following pages infused time and time again with nuggets of common sense drawn from these sources.

There is also an old saying that a Canadian optimist is someone who believes things could be worse. I am a Canadian optimist who believes the future can be better if enough of us resolve to make it so.

Thus while Canadian democracy is definitely in trouble and Canadian conservatism faces daunting challenges, please be assured that this book is not all doom and gloom.

Yes, Canadian conservatism has suffered its setbacks and Canadian democracy is flawed. But notwithstanding its imperfections, the Canadian democratic arena still provided me and a small group of friends with the tools and opportunities that enabled us to create a new federal political party, the Reform Party.[8] We went on to win increasing representation in the House of Commons and lay the foundations for the formation of a conservative majority government under Stephen Harper.

---

8   See Manning, Preston, *Think Big: My Adventures in Life and Democracy.* McClelland and Stewart Ltd., 2002.

Whether you agree or disagree with what the Reform movement or the Harper government did or didn't do is not the point. The fact that a movement started with five people, using the tools which democracy offers to us all—freedom of speech, freedom of association, and opportunities to persuade electors to vote this way or that—could change the national government and policy agenda in this way, ought to be a source of encouragement to all small-d democrats regardless of whatever else divides us.

Given the political freedoms and opportunities that each of us enjoy, is it not the obligation of each of us to *Do Something!* in the democratic political arena to strengthen Canada going forward? If your answer is yes, read on!

Preston Manning
Calgary, Alberta
January, 2020,

TABLE OF CONTENTS

PART 5: STRENGTHEN DEMOCRACY   327

APPENDICES

PART 1

BUILD THE MOVEMENT

It is useful to distinguish between political parties and the movements that undergird, surround, and support them. The movements are comprised of think tanks, interest groups, advocacy groups, political action committees (PACs), mentors, training programs, political investors, communicators, and networkers who are generally supportive of a particular party but not legally or structurally bound to it.

Most modern political parties have become almost exclusively marketing mechanisms for fighting elections. That is their primary preoccupation and they devote almost all of their resources to it. The role of the movement is to finance and perform those other necessary functions which the parties tends to neglect but which are essential to their long run credibility and effectiveness. These functions include:

- The generation and communication of ideas and policies
- The training of political participants, from leaders and political executives, to employees, members, and volunteers of party and movement organizations
- The raising of funds for investment in political institutions and processes other than the party and elections
- The provision of "ladders" for political aspirants and "landing pads" for veteran political warriors
- The networking and communications activities necessary to sustain or rebuild party strength and capacity between elections

The role of the movement is to build and maintain what I call democratic infrastructure beneath and around the parties in order to improve the knowledge, skills, ethics, communications, leadership capacities,

FIGURE 1 The Political Infrastructure Pyramid

and achievements of those who participate directly in our democratic political processes and institutions through those parties. See Figure 1.

As someone who has been directly and personally involved in partisan federal politics,[1] I appreciate and value the role political parties play and the functions they perform in our democratic system. But over the years, I also became aware of the limitations of party organizations and the way in which their necessary preoccupation with getting and staying elected crowds out other worthwhile pursuits essential to their long-term relevance and viability. These pursuits include: constantly developing their intellectual capital; enriching their human resources through education and training; and cultivating relationships outside the narrow partisan arena.

---

1   I have been involved in creating two new federal political parties, The Reform Party of Canada (1987–1998) and the Canadian Conservative Reform Alliance, (1998–2003) which led to the creation of a third federal party, the present day Conservative Party of Canada. For more on this, see Manning, *Think Big*.

This was the very reason that my friends and I set up two conservative-oriented infrastructure organizations when I left parliament, the Manning Foundation for Democratic Education and the Manning Centre for Building Democracy.[2] Both of these organizations, which are now in transition as I retire from public life, were tasked to assist within the movement in these broader functions that tend to be neglected by party organizations. It should be noted that supporters of both the Liberal and New Democratic Parties are also investing in the creation and support of similar infrastructure organizations, as rightly they should.[3]

This book describes what is required to build stronger and better democratic infrastructure in Canada. My particular focus is on building the infrastructure required to sustain and expand the influence and contributions of conservatism. But many of the principles and proposals discussed will be relevant to strengthening democratic infrastructure beneath and around whatever political cause or organization you support.

At the end of the day, strengthening democratic infrastructure through democratic movements is in everyone's interest. However, achieving this requires each of us to *Do Something!* As the anthropologist Ashley Montagu once wrote: "The only measure of what you believe is what you do. If you want to know what people believe, don't read what they write, don't ask them what they believe, just observe what they do."[4]

---

2   Founded in 2005, the Manning Centre's original mission was to support Canada's conservative movement, primarily through research, training, and networking. In more recent years, it has narrowed its focus to concentrate almost exclusively on networking the various diverse and separate components of the conservative movement through regional and national networking conferences and related activities. For more information, visit www.manningcentre.ca. The Manning Foundation is a registered charity through which I provide my advice on strengthening democracy to those seeking it. The foundation also publishes the online journal, C2C. Please visit c2cjournal.ca.

3   Politicos of other ideological persuasions have also seen the need to develop their own movement organizations as distinct from the formal parties. In 2011, former NDP Leader Ed Broadbent set up the Broadbent Institute, similar in structure to the Manning Centre, and, more recently, liberal-oriented Canadians have organized Canada 2020. These developments, to the extent that they contribute to strengthening the democratic process, are welcome additions to Canada's political landscape.

4   Malloy, Merrit & Shauna Sorenson, *The Quotable Quote Book*, Carol Publishing Group, 1990.

1.1 Know Thyself

In 1965, I made my first attempt to run for Canada's parliament in the federal riding of Edmonton East. With little chance of winning, I ran primarily to gain experience. I eventually finished a distant second. At the time, Edmonton East was one of Canada's most multicultural ridings, recognized and valued as such long before Toronto appreciated multiculturalism. Its electorate consisted of a colorful mixture of Canadians of Ukrainian, German, Italian, French, Polish, Latvian, Estonian, Lithuanian, and Russian origins, to give only a sample of its diversity.

If you were a new candidate for election in Edmonton East, and especially if you were a young one, you were expected to pay a courtesy call to all the various ethnic and religious leaders of the community. At these meetings, it was the custom for your host to offer you a drink of whatever constituted the strongest and most favorite beverage of that particular ethnic group. You were most definitely expected to drink it, for courtesy's sake.

I was taken on this initial round of courtesy calls by a provincial cabinet minister (my father Ernest Manning was Alberta's Premier at the time) whose provincial riding included part of Edmonton East. At the time, I did not drink alcohol so when we were offered the customary drinks at these meetings, my cabinet minister friend would drink his, for courtesy's sake, and then he would also drink mine, again for courtesy's sake. By the time we had completed our fifth call, he was three sheets to the wind and our meetings rapidly passed the point of diminishing returns from a political standpoint.

Of more practical use to me was my association with a Latvian business friend, August Osis, who seemed to be on good terms with virtually every ethnic group in the riding. As August explained, there were deep political tensions between almost all the other ethnic groups in Edmonton East based on who had done what to whom in the various European wars going back three centuries. But since Latvia had usually been on the receiving rather than the delivery end of military aggression, he as a Latvian was in a better position than most to act as a go-between, and Edmonton East constituents were more likely to accept an invitation from him to attend a political gathering than from anyone else.

One such meeting which I was invited to attend was to honor the importance of political freedom by commemorating Latvia's brief period of independence prior to its decades-long subjugation by the Soviet Union. The highlight was to be a speech by a prominent member of the Edmonton Latvian community, Dr. Anna Rudovics. Growing up in a political family[5] and having participated in Canadian politics one way or another all my life, I have listened to hundreds and hundreds of political speeches, most of which I have forgotten and many of which (including many of my own) deserve to be forgotten. But the political speech given in 1965 by Dr. Rudovics is indelibly impressed on my mind.

Her theme was "The Three Great Commandments of Western Civilization" which she urged the members of her audience to remember and practice, particularly if we were in the political arena. The Three Great Commandments, which she eloquently described and elaborated upon, were:

- Know Thyself, from Socrates and the Greeks;[6]
- Control Thyself, from the Hebrew leader Moses and the lawmakers of Rome;[7] and
- Give Thyself, from Jesus of Nazareth and the Christians.[8]

5   My father, Ernest C. Manning, became Premier of Alberta in 1943 when I was a year old and served in that position and various other Alberta cabinet positions until I was 26 years of age.

6   Know Thyself is one of the Delphic maxims allegedly given by the Greek god Apollo's oracle at Delphi and expounded upon by the philosopher Socrates in Plato's *Charmides* and other works.

7   The rule of law was embodied in the legal system of ancient Rome, developed over a thousand years, championed by Roman statesmen such as Cato the Younger, Cicero, and Justinian, and formed the basis of civil law in most European countries and their colonies. Centuries earlier, the Law of Moses, reportedly received by him from the hand of God on Mount Sinai, governed every aspect of the economic, political, social, and personal lives of the ancient Hebrews. Even the Hebrew rulers were to be subject to the Law.

8   "Give Thyself" is derived from the Christian conception of self-sacrificial love as taught and demonstrated by Jesus of Nazareth (e.g., see the 3rd chapter of the Gospel of John) and expounded by the Apostle Paul (e.g., see the 13th chapter of his first Letter to the Corinthians).

She urged politicians to remember that public service, not service to self or faction or party, should be the ultimate aim of seeking election. She maintained that political freedom could be preserved and expanded only to the extent that its practitioners exercised self-control, in particular, through adherence to the rule of law. She argued that for the political class knowing yourself and knowing your personal strengths and weaknesses and those of your class, your ideology, and your party was more important to practicing self-control and rendering public service than simply knowing the political landscape, your constituents, the issues, or the techniques of political campaigning.

Part of the unfinished business for Canadian politicians and especially conservatives, includes strengthening our capacities to make good laws and provide genuine public service. But here let me simply emphasize the importance to Canadians in general, and to political parties and political movements in particular, of making a more conscious and deliberate effort to *Know Ourselves*.

DO SOMETHING!

Canadian democracy would be strengthened if every Canadian family and citizen resolved to "get to know Canada better," compiling a short "to do" list of activities to achieve that objective, and acted upon it over the next few years. In particular:

- Read to broaden your knowledge on Canadian history, geography, demography, culture, science, religion, economy, sport, politics, etc., and discuss these subjects with others
- Visit other provinces and cities in Canada, with the aim of eventually visiting every province and territory of our country, the second-largest geographically on the face of the earth
- Make the acquaintance of other Canadians outside your traditional circle of acquaintances, whatever that may be. For many this might mean making a special effort to become better acquainted with indigenous people (Canada's first inhabitants), and recently arrived immigrants

Somewhere out there among Canada's talented and diverse population is that special someone who will write the definitive text or produce the definitive radio, TV, or web-based series for the next generation on "Knowing Canada" or knowing some particular aspect of our politicis such as Canadian Conservatism. Could it be you?

Knowing yourself personally

There is one further and most important dimension to knowing ourselves as Canadians or as adherents to a particular political philosophy or group, and that is to simply know ourselves personally. Do we know or have we reflected upon how our own personal circumstances, upbringing, associations, experiences, fears and hopes influence our perspective on Canada, democracy, and politics? Each of us view these things through a different lens and it a good idea to know what that lens we are looking through is and how it shapes our perceptions, what it magnifies or ignores, what it sharpens our focus on, or what it blurs.

None of us are without blind spots. Each of us should be aware of ours when we view and react to the political world. Know yourself as a Canadian. Know yourself as a Democrat. But be sure to know yourself in this personal sense which shapes our perspective on everything else.[9]

---

9   In reading a book of this type, it is worth taking a few moments to know more about the background, associations, experiences, biases, and aspirations that the author brings to the subject. For a brief summary of my personal background and experience see my profile on Wikipedia which (as of 2018) is reasonably accurate.

1.2 Respect the Past and Learn From It

Political philosophers and practitioners from bygone days have repeatedly articulated and taught the wisdom of respecting the past and learning from it:

> *"People will not look forward to posterity who never look backwards to their ancestors"*
>
> *– Edmund Burke*[10]

> *"The past is the cause of the present and the present is the cause of the future."*
>
> *– Abraham Lincoln*[11]

> *"Those who cannot remember the past are condemned to repeat it."*
> *– George Santayana*[12]

And yet it seems necessary for this precept to be retaught and relearned by each generation of citizens and politicians. An example from my own experience began in the late 1960s with my father's interpretation of the Quiet Revolution in Quebec.[13] "It will lead to a full-blown attempt by Quebec to secede from Canada," he told me. "So if you're going to get

---

10   Burke, Edmund, *Reflections on the Revolution in France*, London, J.M. Dent & Sons Ltd., 1790, 18–19.
11   Herndon, William Henry, *Herndon's Life of Lincoln: The history and personal recollections of Abraham Lincoln*, 1889.
12   Santayana, George, *The Life of Reason Or The Phases of Human Progress: Reason in Religion, Volume VII, Book Three*. Vol. 7. MIT Press, 2014.
13   With the election of Jean Lesage's Liberal government, the Quiet Revolution represented the secularization and ascent of the welfare state in Quebec, which in turn stimulated a new surge of Quebec nationalism.

involved in federal politics, you'd better study up on how to deal with a secession attempt."

It was this advice which led me to thoroughly study the most famous (or infamous) secession case in North American history, the secession of the southern states from the American union which led to the American civil war. The focus of my studies was not on the war itself but on the various strategies and compromises proposed and pursued in the thirty years preceding it in efforts to avoid the breakup of the country.[14] Little did I know in the late 1960s that I would be a member of the Canadian parliament in the 1990s that would be forced to wrestle with this very same issue, driving home the importance of the old adage to *respect the past and learn from it.*

Broad jumping

Years ago, there was an event in the summer Olympics called the standing broad jump. Contestants competed to see who could jump forward the farthest from a standing position. The event was discontinued after the 1912 Olympics with the world record established at 3.47 meters. Today there is still a broad jump event at the Olympics, the "running" broad jump. The current world record for it is 8.95 meters.

The lesson in this? You can leap forward further when you get a run at it than when you start from the stationary position.

And so it is in the political world. You can get ahead further when you get a run at it, when you know the political history of your country, your people, your party, and your constituency, than when you start from where you're presently standing, as if politics did not really begin until the day you discovered it and entered the field.

---

14   It was this endeavor which caused me to thoroughly study the career and words of Abraham Lincoln, in particular, his activities and proposals for handling the impending secession crisis before his election as president. I became a lifelong Lincoln fan and suffer melancholy every April 14 on the anniversary of his tragic assassination. More recently, I penned a fictional piece entitled *A Horse for Mr. Lincoln*, Octavia Book Bindery, Calgary, Alberta, 2017, speculating on how much more united the United States would be today if Lincoln had not gone to the Ford theatre that fateful night.

Two American books

In the United States, if someone shows an interest in supporting or running for office on the Republican ticket, they can be handed a huge, well-documented book entitled *The Grand Old Party: The History of the Republicans* by Lewis L. Gould.[15] It tells them almost everything they need to know about the history, origins, personalities, adventures, and misadventures of the party through which they have chosen to participate in the democratic process.

If someone thinks they want to support or run for the Democratic Party, they can likewise be handed another huge and comprehensive volume entitled *Party of the People: A History of the Democrats* by Jules Witcover.[16]

In Canada there are no such comprehensive, definitive histories of our principal political parties and movements but there should be. Not just for the benefit of political partisans, but, more importantly, for the benefit of Canadians generally. Such histories would better enable us to understand the political options presented to us on election day and how they evolved, why they take their present form and positions, and how they might be reshaped in the future to better serve Canada.

Unfinished political business

Is there not, therefore, some unfinished political business here which some person or institution, perhaps some historical society, university history department, or research council, with the cooperation of the political parties themselves, should undertake?

This effort would involve the preparation and completion of at least four definitive histories of the four major political traditions in Canada. Not only would they need to describe and interpret the expression of these political traditions at the national level, but also at the provincial level in ten provinces and several territories since the stories of our provincial, territorial, and federal parties are very much intertwined.

15   Gould, Lewis, L., *Grand Old Party: The History of the Republicans*, New York, Random House, 2003.
16   Witcover, Jules, *Party of the People: A History of the Democrats,* New York, Random House, 2003.

The completion of this particular unfinished political business would involve commissioning, financing, and publishing:

- *The Liberal Political Tradition in Canada*: a definitive political history of the liberal political tradition in Canada from pre-Confederation days, through the first genuinely liberal parties, to its present incarnation in the Liberal Party of Canada and Liberal provincial parties.
- *The Conservative Political Tradition in Canada*: again tracing the conservative political tradition from pre-Confederation days, through the first genuinely conservative parties, to its present incarnation in the Conservative Party of Canada, Progressive Conservative provincial parties, and other conservative-oriented provincial parties like the Saskatchewan Party and the United Conservative Party of Alberta.
- *The Social-Democratic Tradition in Canada*: tracing the social-democratic tradition in Canada through the labour movement, the Antigonish movement in Atlantic Canada, its various incarnations in Quebec, its embodiment in agrarian socialism on the Prairies through the Progressive Party of Canada and the Cooperative Commonwealth Federation (CCF), to its present incarnation in the New Democratic Party of Canada and the New Democratic provincial parties.
- *The Reform Tradition in Canada* (my own interest is showing here): tracing the activities of the reformers throughout Canadian history who have challenged the status quo and sought to change the system by organizing politically to do so. This volume would trace this tradition from the efforts of the early Reform Parties of Nova Scotia and Upper and Lower Canada to achieve responsible government, to the alliance of Reformer George Brown with Conservative John A. Macdonald in the Great Coalition that brought Confederation into being. It would also include in-depth descriptions of the two great regional branches of the reform tradition, the third-party traditions of Quebec and the West, and describe the genesis and progress of the environmental movement and the Green Party.

If there was interest in and support for undertaking such a project, I am certain that reputable historians and political scientists could be found who would be willing to advise and participate. The involvement of political practitioners would also be vitally important so that the stories of the parties would be told from both an academic and participant perspective.

I would also hope that some of the traditional financial donors to these parties who can no longer make large contributions under existing party and election financing laws could be approached for major financial support, particularly if the effort could be organized as a charitable endeavor.

DO SOMETHING!

- If you're an academic historian, prepare a party history project proposal and submit it to an appropriate funding body
- If you're a political practitioner, urge the cooperation and support of your party in having its history properly researched and recorded
- If you're an executive of, or a donor to, a potential funding body, offer your enthusiastic support
- If you're a Canadian who appreciates the value of political history in shaping our future, buy and read one or more of these party histories once they are published

1.3 Undertake Periodic Political Realignments

The dictionary defines the concept of realignment as the action of changing or restoring something to a different or former position or state. Since we live in an ever-changing world, both democracy and conservatism need to be periodically realigned in order to adapt to different conditions but in such a way as to conserve, not abandon, the core values and principles on which both are based. In order for democracy and conservatism to better serve the next generation of Canadians, the actions required to bring about such realignments constitute part of our unfinished political business and ought to occupy a prominent place on our political *Action Lists*.

Realigning Canadian democracy

The principles of democracy include: the recognition of the inherent worth of the individual human being; the equality of all before the law; freedom of expression and association; the right of the people to govern themselves by electing and dismissing their representatives and leaders; decision-making by majorities while respecting the rights of minorities; adherence to the rule of law;[17] and pursuing the objective of "government by, for, and of the people" to the greatest extent possible. But the conservation and expression of such principles for the benefit of each generation often requires changes in the laws, policies, and institutions that express them.

17 Defined as the principle that all people and institutions are subject to and accountable to law that is fairly applied and enforced. Includes not only just laws, but also adherence to the principles of accountability, open government, and accessible and impartial dispute resolution.

The British parliamentarian Edmund Burke once declared that the principles of conservation and correction (change) need to be applied *simultaneously* in order to conserve inviolate the original design and rationale of valued institutions and principles while adapting to changing conditions.

At first blush, recommending the simultaneous pursuit of conservation and change appears to be contradictory, but according to Burke:

> "A state without the means of some change is without the means of its conservation. Without such means it might even risk the loss of that part of the constitution that it wished the most religiously to preserve. The two principles of conservation and correction operated strongly [in concert] at the two critical periods of the Restoration and Revolution. . ."[18]

In Canada, for example, in the 1860s, just prior to Confederation, the parliament of the United Province of Canada needed to be realigned to accommodate the demand by Upper Canada for "representation by population" while conserving the principle of equality between the French and English segments of the population insisted upon by Lower Canada. This realignment, accomplished by the passage of the 1867 BNA Act, involved the creation of a bicameral parliament with representation by population in the lower House (the House of Commons) and equal representation of Ontario and Quebec in the upper house (the Senate). Legislation was only to become law after it was passed by both chambers. A democratic institution, the parliament of Upper and Lower Canada, had to be realigned in order to conserve and express two democratic principles of great importance to the people of each province.

During my time in federal politics in the 1980s and 1990s, as the leader of the newly created Reform Party of Canada I argued that the conservation and strengthening of Canadian democracy required three major reforms:

- Greater freedom for elected members of parliament to represent their own views and those of their constituents via free votes rather than being compelled to always vote the party line[19]

---

18   Burke, Edmund, *Select Works of Edmund Burke Vol.3*, A New Imprint of the Payne Edition, Indianapolis, Liberty Fund, 1999 Vol. 3. 2/17/2019.

19   Reform Party of Canada, *Blue Sheet: Principles, Policies & Election Platform*, Calgary,

- Adoption of a policy that the defeat of a government bill or motion in parliament should not automatically mean the defeat of the government but should be immediately followed by a confidence motion. The House would then need to decide whether it actually desired to defeat the government or simply wanted to reject or modify some government measure[20]
- Reform of the Senate to make it elected, with equal representation from each province, thereby enabling it to more effectively represent and advance regional interests (the so-called Triple-E Senate proposal)[21]

Regardless of whether you agree or disagree with these particular democratic reforms, every democratic political party should have a section in its platform in which it proposes democratic reforms designed to realign democratic institutions and practices for the benefit of the current generation. The objectives of such realignments should be to more faithfully practice and conserve democratic principles, to correct any deviations from democratic principles and practices that may have developed, and to adapt democratic institutions and practices to changing conditions in order to better serve the people of Canada.

DO SOMETHING!

- If you are a member of a political party, encourage your party to develop and promote a specific section of its platform to promoting agreed upon democratic reforms.
- If you are a citizen and voter, demand that the political parties and candidates seeking your support present and commit to implementing reforms to strengthen democracy as part of their platforms.

Reform Party of Canada, 1993. The text used comes from the collection of political texts made available at www.poltext.org by Lisa Birch, Jean Crête, Louis M. Imbeau, Steve Jacob and François Pétry, with the financial support of the *Fonds de recherche du Québec—Société et culture* (FRQSC).

20   Ibid.
21   Ibid.

Correcting deficiencies

I want to briefly mention three significant challenges which will require major adjustments to our democratic institutions and practices if we wish to conserve the principles and values on which they are based. I will elaborate more on each in later chapters, but let me just introduce them here.

The first challenge to full, free, and fair democratic discourse is that represented by the advent and growth of social media. On the one hand, these platforms provide incredibly effective tools for allowing large numbers of individuals to inform and express themselves and to connect with others for political purposes. On the other hand, these same tools can be used to generate and distribute misinformation and fake news on a vast scale, and to quickly and easily mobilize financial and human resources in pursuit of anti-democratic objectives and causes.

How do we preserve the values and principles of democracy in a political world dominated by social media? What adjustments to democratic practices and realignments of democratic institutions are required to adapt to this fundamental change in how democratic discourse is conducted?[22]

Secondly, there is the challenge to democracy, in particular, to the rights and responsibilities of majorities, represented by state-supported identity politics. When a governing political party practices identity politics, it begins by identifying a group of voters, whose support it desires, in terms of some fundamental characteristic such as gender, ethnicity, sexual orientation, or political status (immigrant, refugee, etc.). It then confers, or offers to confer, some benefit or right upon members of the selected group in return for their political support, with the implication that this right or benefit will be lost if the group supports any other political party. Critics of identity politics are quickly and vehemently labeled as bigots motivated by prejudice against the identified group, thus insulating the policy itself from serious analysis or criticism of any kind.

In analyzing and critiquing identity politics, it is important to first of all recognize that there *are* various groups of Canadians who are or have been marginalized, victimized, and prejudicially treated by the majority of Canadians with the concurrence of the state: women and children, indigenous people, immigrants, members of the LGBTQ

22   These questions are more fully addressed in chapter 4.3.

community, and, most recently, people of religious faith. Both justice and compassion demand that such wrongs be recognized and rectified to the maximum extent possible. The challenge, however, is to do so by ways and means that foster acceptance of members of such groups at the most fundamental level, as human beings deserving of respect and fair treatment *regardless* of their distinguishing characteristics rather than because of them.

The weakness and danger of state-supported identity politics as currently practiced by the Trudeau administration and others is that it divides the population and electorate into an increasing number of minority groups distinguished mainly by their differences rather than their commonalities, making the reconciliation of conflicting interests and the achievement of a national consensus on anything increasingly difficult to attain.

How do we preserve the unity of a democratic state in which divisive identity politics is carried to extremes? What adjustments to democratic practices and realignments of democratic institutions are required to effectively balance minority and majority rights and responsibilities? Yet another formidable challenge to democracy in our times.[23]

The third contemporary challenge to democracy is at the macro-political level, the challenge to citizen-directed democracy as practiced, however imperfectly, in much of the western world, by state-directed democracy as practiced and promoted world-wide by the Communist party and government of China. In my judgement, this challenge represents the greatest ideological competition of the twenty-first century.

How do we preserve the values and principles of citizen-directed democracy? What adjustments to our democratic practices and institutions are required to compete effectively in this ideological contest?[24]

Realigning Canadian conservatism

Edmund Burke's advocacy of the simultaneous pursuit of conservation and correction as a means of simultaneously conserving and advancing democracy is equally applicable to conserving and advancing conservatism. It could be paraphrased as follows:

23 These questions are more fully addressed in chapter 5.4.
24 These questions are addressed more fully in chapter 5.5.

A conservative party without the means of changing itself from time to time is without the means of its own conservation. Without such means it might even risk the loss of those principles and policy commitments it wishes most religiously to conserve. These two principles of conservation and change (reform) can be seen to have been operating at critical times in the evolution of Canadian conservatism.

These "critical times" of political realignment for Canadian conservatism have included:

- The Confederation period when John A. Macdonald's Conservatives entered into the Great Coalition with George Brown's Reformers to bring Canadian Confederation into being.[25] Macdonald not only saw fit to bring reformers into his first cabinet but also (for a time) chose to rename his party the Liberal-Conservative party
- The period during and immediately after the first World War (1917–1921) when Conservative Prime Minister Robert Borden was obliged to create the Unionist Party, primarily to deal with the conscription issue[26]
- The period beginning in 1942 when the Conservative Party of Canada renamed itself the Progressive Conservative Party and reformed its platform to include social security benefits (for veterans and workers), and a stronger emphasis on agricultural policy. This was done primarily to attract members of the Progressive Party of Canada, including its leader, John Bracken, who eventually became the leader of the renamed party[27]
- The 1966 to 1969 period, during which I was personally involved in two unsuccessful political realignment efforts. These involved the attempt to unite the governing Social Credit Party of Alberta under my father's leadership with the up-and-coming Progressive

25 Cornell, Paul G. *The Great Coalition*, Canadian Historical Association, 1971.
26 He won the ensuing fall election amidst controversy and fierce recriminations, maneuvering many Liberals into supporting his Unionist ticket by making the conscription issue a test of loyalty to King and country. https://www.warmuseum. ca/firstworldwar/history/people/canadian-leaders/sir-robert-borden/
27 In 1943 Bracken reluctantly became Leader of the federal Conservative Party, insisting that it add the word "Progressive" to its name. http://www.mhs.mb.ca/ docs/people/bracken_j.shtml

Conservative Party of Alberta under Peter Lougheed,[28] and the attempt to unite the federal Social Credit Party with the Progressive Conservative Party of Canada under Robert Stanfield.[29] The definition of conservative principles developed in these attempts played a key role in the realignment of conservative forces at the federal level in the 1990s and was later incorporated into the founding documents of the Reform Party of Canada, the Canadian Reform Conservative Alliance, and the Conservative Party of Canada;

- The years between 1997 and 2003 when leaders and members of the federal Reform Party, the federal Reform Conservative Alliance, and the Progressive Conservative Party of Canada came together to form the present-day Conservative Party of Canada[30]

- The 1997 to 2007 period in Saskatchewan when a small group of provincial Progressive Conservatives, Liberal MLAs, and federal Reformers created the Saskatchewan Party. In 2007 it formed a government "committed to change" and continues to govern the province under the leadership of Premier Scott Moe.[31]

- The 2008 to 2017 period in Alberta when provincial conservatism was first split between the old Progressive Conservative Party and the newly created Wildrose Party, and then reassembled by the union of the two parties to form the United Conservative Party in

---

28 The proposal for this realignment was drafted by a small committee consisting of Dr. Erick Schmidt, then Executive Secretary to the Alberta Cabinet, Preston Manning (later to become Leader of the Opposition in the Canadian Parliament), Merv Leitch (later to become Attorney General for Alberta), and Joe Clark (later to become Prime Minister of Canada). See a summary of this exercise entitled *Political Realignment and Principled Conservatism* by John Whittaker, January, 2017, available in the archives of the Manning Centre for Building Democracy.

29 See Manning, Ernest, C. *Political Realignment: A Challenge to Thoughtful Canadians*, McClelland and Stewart, 1967.

30 Plamondon, Bob, *Full Circle: Death and Resurrection in Canadian Conservative Politics*, Key Porter Books, 2006.

   Manning, Preston, *The New Canada*, McClelland & Stewart, 1992.

   Manning, Preston, *Think Big: Adventures in Life & Democracy*, McClelland & Stewart, 2002.

   Carson, Bruce, *14 Days: Making the Conservative Movement in Canada*, McGill-Queen's University Press, 2014.

31 Wishlow, Kevin, "Rethinking the polarization thesis: The formation and growth of the Saskatchewan party, 1997–2001," *Saskatchewan Politics: Into the Twenty-First Century* (2001): 169–98.

2016. This party, under the leadership of Jason Kenney, became the governing party in Alberta in 2019.

It should be noted that in each of these instances of realignment, the changes involved were bitterly and vehemently opposed at the outset by the defenders of the status quo, only to be grudgingly accepted with the passage of time. Much needless expenditure of political energy and internal bickering could be avoided in the future if conservatives were to accept that these periodic realignments are not eccentric "one off" disruptions of the political status quo to be feared and resisted but an essential feature of the evolution of Canadian conservatism to be cautiously welcomed, carefully managed, and gradually embraced.

If the supporters and adherents of traditional parties could set aside blind partisanship and seek to understand and accommodate challenges to established orthodoxies, the change agents might be more inclined to work within the traditional structures rather than being forced to work outside through the creation of new parties. As one nineteenth-century commentator on this phenomenon nostalgically asked: how long will it be until the guardians of old principles and the advocates of new ideas, the keepers of the old wine and the champions of the new, learn to bear with one another and to recognize, each in the other, the necessary complements to their own one-sidedness?[32]

By carefully analyzing these past realignments of Canadian conservatism, we can identify principles and procedures to conserve the best of our political and cultural heritage as conservatives, while simultaneously adapting to changing conditions and the changing demands of electorates in an ever changing society.

The bare listing of past conservative realignments may leave you with the impression that political realignment is a boring, mechanical, procedural activity of interest or meaning only to political insiders and political wonks. Nothing could be further from the reality. We need to remember that democratic politics itself and the evolution of conservatism within a democracy are intensely human and social activities. As with any other human endeavour, aspirations and disappointments,

32   Bruce, Alexander Balmain. *The Training of the Twelve, Or, Passages Out of the Gospels, Exhibiting the Twelve Disciples of Jesus Under Discipline for the Apostleship.* T. & T. Clark, 1916.

egos and reputations, friendships and enmities, intellect and emotions, humour and pathos, play a huge part.[33]

To Illustrate, the first political realignment activity with which I was involved, the attempt in the 1960's in Alberta to put the governing Social Credit Party and the opposition Progressive Conservative Party together into a new entity, was a failure and thus a disappointment. And yet it had some very funny aspects that some of us involved in it remember and laugh about to this day. For example, when it was all over and our realignment proposal was rejected by the leadership of both parties, we, the realignment task force composed of Erick Schmidt, Merv Leitch, Joe Clark and myself, were ordered to destroy all the documentation. We decided that the best way to destroy all the paper evidence was to burn it, but where?

At that time, my parents lived on our dairy farm just outside of Edmonton in a ranch style house with a large fireplace. So Joe Clark and I drove there with a car load of political realignment drafts, correspondence, and papers and patiently fed them into that fireplace one by one. Nearly twenty years later, on the evening of May 22, 1979, my parents and I were watching the results of the 1979 federal election on television. When the television cameras focused on Joe Clark and the commentators declared him to be the winner and the next Prime Minister of Canada, my mother asked: "Isn't that the young fellow who sat in my living room years ago throwing papers of some sort into the fireplace?" "Yes Mother, that's the same Joe Clark. He's come a long way and is now Canada's 16th Prime Minister."

When participants in these realignment processes get together years later, they exchange colorful memories and stories just like those remembered and exchanged when old hockey players or business partners get together. And the only way to fully appreciate this dimension of political realignments is not merely to read about them or to study commentaries on them, but to become personally involved in whatever political realignment activity may be in process during your lifetime. If the need for a political realignment is a characteristic of your political environment, then *Do Something!* to support and advance it.

---

33   I am indebted for this observation to science writer David Quammen (*The Tangled Tree: A Radical New History of Life;* Simon & Schuster, 2018) who makes the point that science—which many lay people consider dry, procedural and dominated by cold facts and numbers—is also an intensely human and social activity which needs to be understood and appreciated more from that perspective.

DO SOMETHING!

- Study the past re-alignments of conservatism in Canada to assure yourself that this is a fundamental characteristic of the political evolution of conservatism
- If you are a member or executive or a conservative party, urge the periodic (say every eight years) establishment of a Political Realignment Task Force and conference to ascertain whether such a realignment is necessary and, if so, to make recommendations for its exercise
- Be open and welcoming to proposals for those changes which the political realignment of conservatism may necessitate rather than inherently suspicious and resistant

Avoiding extremes

A full exploration of the principles which should guide conservatism during a period of realignment is not possible here due to limitations of time and space. One principle, however, that deserves special emphasis is that of avoiding extremes. In particular, the necessity of avoiding the extremes of tradition-bound reactionary conservatism, on the one hand, and unprincipled pragmatic conservatism on the other.

Reactionary conservatism

The conservative political family may include those whose conception of conservatism is essentially reactionary and backward-looking, once described by William F. Buckley as those "who stand athwart history, yelling 'Stop.'"[34] Such conservatives seek to conserve conservative values and principles by determinedly keeping things as they are or were

---

34   This is the mission statement of the *National Review*, which Buckley founded in 1955. https://www.nationalreview.com/1955/11/our-mission-statement-william-f-buckley-jr/

and resisting change of any kind.[35] But as Burke observed, in taking such a position it is more than likely that the very values and principles such conservatives seek to conserve will be lost rather than preserved or enhanced.

There is a stark difference between the conservative and the reactionary (although detractors love to equate the two). The reactionary mind is one that is reflexively backward-looking, yearning (idealistically, in a perverse sort of way) for some non-existent past-paradise. The archetypical conservative, while temperamentally resisting rapid and wholesale change, nevertheless appreciates the long centuries of gradual corrective change that produced our present society.

Many years ago when I was engaged in community development work in north central Alberta, I heard tell of a sign east of the town of Slave Lake that was a tangible example of how failure to change the message and direction of a signpost became a source of error rather than a means of preserving its original intent.

The sign in question consisted of a large post, firmly set in the ground, with a solid plank bolted to it. On the plank was inscribed the word "Sawridge" with an arrow beneath it pointing west. That sign did not change in over fifty years. No matter how hard the winds blew or how hard the rain and snow beat upon it, that sign remained stubbornly steadfast in pointing travelers toward "Sawridge." A most reliable guide, some might say, and yet, if you followed the directions on that sign you would never actually get to the town of Sawridge. Why? Because although the intent, message, and direction of that sign were all once true and reliable and had never changed, everything else around it had.

During the lifetime of the sign, the town of Sawridge changed its name. It also changed its location, moving to higher ground after a flood in the 1930s. In addition, the roads leading to it were rerouted half a

---

35 An even more extreme version of this type of conservatism is a conservatism that not only rejects the status quo but seeks to return to some idealized past. For an insightful commentary on the extreme version of the conservative revolutionary position, see Stern, Fritz, *The Politics of Cultural Despair: A Study in the Rise of the Germanic Ideology*, Berkeley, University of California Press, 1961. In this work, Stern investigates the nineteenth-century ideological roots of twentieth-century fascism in Germany. He describes the "conservative revolutionaries" of that day as those who "sought to destroy the despised present in order to recapture an idealized past in an imaginary future."

dozen times after the signpost had been planted. It was the very fact that the sign had not changed while everything else around it had, that made it an unreliable guide to anyone travelling that road. To conserve the real purpose of that original signpost, both its message and the direction in which it pointed should have been changed or, as I would say, realigned.

DO SOMETHING!

If you are a leader or a member of the executive of a conservative-oriented party, or a member or supporter of such a party:

- Recognize that periodic realignments of conservatism are a positive and essential feature of the evolution of conservatism, to be welcomed and supported rather than resisted
- Resist the temptation to adopt a purely negative, reactionary position in response to the need for constructive change
- If you are opposed to the positions of your political adversaries, reflect on what a constructive alternative to the object of your aversion would be, rather than simply opposing and retrenching purely in the past

Pragmatic conservatism

The conservative family also includes people who, because they wish to distance themselves from reactionary conservatives, adopt a pragmatic conservatism without any guiding principles. A kind of conservatism that in its sensitivity to shifting electoral preferences, changes in direction with every political wind that blows.

The temptation to pursue the completely pragmatic course most often comes when conservatives have lost consecutive elections to centrist and left-of-center opponents and the strategy of "if you can't beat 'em, join 'em" becomes highly attractive. Some of the so-called progressive conservatism of the twentieth century was of this nature. Conservatives, particularly at the provincial level, failed to develop any real alternatives to the continuous expansion of the welfare state. Accepting that such expansion was inevitable, they were then reduced to simply declaring (unconvincingly) that conservatives could manage the welfare state better than liberals or socialists.

Similarly, when pragmatic conservatives witness the temporary successes of their political opponents in winning support through the practice of identity politics, the temptation is to follow suit rather than to challenge this deviation on the grounds of both democratic and conservative principles.

A realigned conservatism, in order to be truly progressive, should be neither reactionary nor pragmatic, but rather principled and forward-looking, conserving the heritage of the past while responding to the needs of the present and the future.

1.4 Redefine Political Space for Disengaged Canadians

In the previous chapter, we discussed the need to periodically realign democratic institutions and practices in order to keep them relevant under changing conditions while still conserving their core values. We particularly discussed the role of the realignment principle in the constructive evolution of conservatism.

But there is an even broader and more radical application of the re-alignment principle requiring discussion, research, and supportive action. It involves nothing less than redefining political space itself in order to make democracy and the ideological options it offers more relevant to segments of the Canadian electorate who are increasingly alienated and disengaged from our political processes altogether. Most worrisome is the fact that a high percentage of these disengaged citizens are next-generation Canadians.

After the 1997 federal election, I became involved in a major effort to unite the Reform Party of Canada, which then formed the Official Opposition in parliament, with the Progressive Conservative Party of Canada which had previously been a governing party under Brian Mulroney.[36] The aim was to create a principled, viable, national alternative to the federal Liberals which would appeal to a majority of Canadian voters.

The media immediately labelled this as an effort to "unite the right," a label which was both unfortunate and inappropriate, because, as I was becoming increasingly aware, a growing number of Canadians, including a majority of conservatives, simply do not identify with the left-centre-right conceptualization of political space.[37]

---

36   Manning, Preston, *Think Big,* pp. 275–76.
37   Where did this conceptualization come from anyway? Does it not come from the seating arrangements in the French Assembly after the French Revolution

In the spring of 1998, I asked our pollster, Dr. Andre Turcotte of Carleton University, to conduct a national public opinion survey asking Canadians to try to position themselves on the "left-centre-right" spectrum. Of those polled, 34% were unable or unwilling to do so. Another 39% positioned themselves at the centre (neither left nor right), a clear indication that they found the choices expressed this way quite meaningless. Of the remainder, 17% placed themselves "on the left," and only 10% located themselves "on the right." Even among our own supporters, 45% of Reformers could not or would not position themselves on the axis at all, and only 9% placed themselves on the right, while only 15% of PC supporters positioned themselves on the right. As Dr. Turcotte observed, "When political commentators refer to uniting the right, they are unknowingly referring to uniting the 10% of the electorate who consider themselves on the right of the political spectrum, surely not a strategically profitable exercise for either the Reform Party or the federal PCs".[38]

Twenty years later, the numbers of Canadians who fail to find the left-centre-right conceptualization of political space meaningful has further increased.[39] This is particularly true among next-generation Canadians[40] who, if they all ever voted, would constitute the largest voting block by age among the Canadian electorate.

In 2016, the Manning Centre for Democratic Education commissioned a national opinion survey of 2200 Canadian millennials.[41] Among other things, it asked respondents to position themselves on the traditional "left-centre-right" axis. See Figure 2.

Some of the responses to this request were quite predictable. For example:

in which the landowners and traditionalists sat on the right and the radicals sat on the left? If so, why on earth are we still using such an outmoded conceptualization?

38   Manning, *Think Big*, pp. 275–76. Even our national game, hockey, mixes left and right in odd combinations since right-handed players usually shoot left, i.e, shoot from the left-hand side, whereas left-handed players usually shoot right. Go figure.

39   https://reason.com/assets/db/2014-millennials-report.pdf

40   Generation Y (born between 1980–2000) and Generation Z (born between 2000-present).

41   Turcotte, Andre, *Millennials and the Conservative Movement: 2016 Political Values Study*, Mission Research & Manning Centre, November 2016.

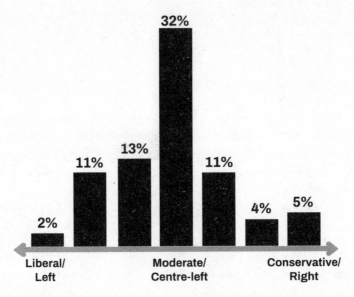

FIGURE 2 Millennial positioning on the traditional left-centre-right axis

- A majority of the millennials surveyed saw themselves as more lib-eral/centrist than conservative.
- When asked to define "the centre," the most frequent response was "neither left nor right," again, a largely meaningless default position to which respondents could supply little content.
- A plurality of respondents took a bifurcated position, defining them-selves as fiscally conservative but socially liberal.

But what was more interesting and significant was the number of respondents who made it clear that they did not like this archaic, one dimensional, left-centre-right axis at all, that it failed to define their personal political positions or preferences or to present them with political options meaningful to them and their friends.

Because so much of Canadian political reporting and discourse is conducted within this traditional framework, it would appear that such discourse actually tends to discourage rather than encourage many next-generation Canadians from engaging at all in Canada's democratic processes.

If Canadian democrats, of all political stripes, want to politically re-engage those Canadians, there is therefore a need to redefine political space in such a way as to better accommodate their conceptual frameworks, interests, concerns, and preferences.

Political engagement receptions

One approach to doing this, which the Manning Centre has experimented with and is encouraging other organizations to take up, is to hold informal "Political Engagement Receptions" at which the invited participants are presented with alternative axes posted on the walls of the reception room.

One such axis might be a *trust axis*. At one end is trust in big governments, companies, and unions to make and implement decisions affecting your life and society. At the other end is trust in yourself, your family, your friends, and small-scale organizations. Attendees are then asked to indicate where they would place themselves on this axis, using a sticker provided for that purpose.

There could be an *environmental axis*. At one end is securing environmental protection through political action and government regulation. At the other end is securing environmental protection by harnessing entrepreneurship, consumer responsibility, and market mechanisms to the task. And again, invitees are asked to place themselves on this axis using the sticker provided.

Of particular importance is where invitees place themselves on a *democratic axis*. Do they prefer bottom-up public decision-making involving consultation of and participation by large numbers of people? Or do they prefer more top-down, expert-led, executive type decision-making? Where respondents place themselves on this democratic axis actually gives us a clue as to whether they are predisposed to join or oppose a populist movement on some issue of importance to them.

This exercise can then be expanded by asking attendees to place themselves on a variety of other axes, for example, those defining alternative positions with respect to the Economy, Values, Health, Education, Poverty Alleviation, Lifestyle Choices, Responsibility for Lifestyle Choices, Communications, Jurisdictions, Identity, and so on. See Figure 3.

Finally, such receptions may be concluded by asking attendees to answer and discuss two more questions essential to focusing and effectively communicating the redefinition of political space. These are:

- If you could only choose three of these axes to define your preferred political space, which ones would they be?
- If you had to put a label on that political space, what would that be?

Decentralized Authority Citizens & Elected Officials	Democracy Axis	Centralized Authority Appointed Experts
Governments, Regulated Markets	Economy Axis	Individuals, Entrepreneurs, Free Market
Established Principles, Traditions	Values Axis	Pragmatism, Accommodations
By a 'Mixed' (Public & Private) System	Health Axis	Primarily by a Public (Taxpayer-Funded) System
By a Public (Taxpayer-Funded) System	Education Axis	Primarily by a Mixed (Public & Private) System
Improved Distribution of the Tools of Wealth Creation	Poverty Alleviation Axis	Redistribution of Income Through Progressive Taxation
Limited by Traditions, Religious Principles, Cultural Norms	Lifestyle Axis	Completely Unrestricted Except by Your Own Moral Code
The Government (Taxpayers)	Responsibility Axis	Those Individuals and Their Families
Individuals, Market Mechanisms	Environment Axis	Government Regulation
Yourself, Small Businesses, NGOs	Trust Axis	Government Corporations, Unions
Local/National	Jurisdiction Axis	Global/International
Building on Shared Values and Traditions	Identity Axis	Promoting Increased Diversity

FIGURE 3 Twelve alternative axis for redefining political space for millennials

DO SOMETHING!

- If you're interested in securing greater political involvement on the part of Canadians, including members of your own family and social circle, conduct an informal survey yourself
- Ask them where they would place themselves on the left-centre-right axis and note the percentage who are uncomfortable with that conceptual framework
- If the percentage is high, join in efforts to redefine political space for such Canadians by:

continued

- Organize one or more of these political Engagement Sessions yourself.
- Placing results in the public domain for others to see
- Communicating the results to political parties and political commentators who tend to shape political discourse
- Offering to participate in the development of policies and communications pieces for think tanks and political parties which focus on those nodal points on the alternative axes where the currently disengaged congregate in the largest numbers.

A task for non-partisan researchers

Ideally the type of research required to redefine political space for disengaged Canadians should be conducted by organizations and researchers completely independent of the political parties,[42]whose sponsorship and participation would raise suspicions of bias. But a strenuous effort should then be made to present the results to the parties, the media, and anyone else involved in leading political discourse in this country with a plea that more and more political discourse be conducted within the parameters and in the language of the redefined space as described.

DO SOMETHING!

If you are a member or on the executive of a non-partisan think tank or research body:

- Conduct your own Political Engagement Sessions for the purposes of redefining political space
- Communicate the results to political parties and media commentators in an effort to change the nature and language of political discourse so as to make it more attractive to millennials.

---

42   This is why the Manning Centre has sought to hand its Millennial Engagement Research Project to others with no close connection to any political party.

Uptake by political parties

The redefinition of political space for millennials in the real political world will eventually require some sympathetic and proactive work on the part of the political parties. This will involve at least three things:

- Identifying those nodal points on the alternative political axes where millennials congregate in the greatest numbers, but which are also most compatible with the party's principles and current orientation.
- Offering and effectively communicating platform positions and policies focused on those nodal points.
- Doing so using next-generation, not old-generation, language and communication media.

DO SOMETHING!

If you are a member or executive of a political party or political organization:

- Obtain and study the results of Political Engagement Receptions held by others
- Establish a party task force or working group to plan and carry out your party's effort to redefine political space for millennials
- Develop and communicate platform/policy positions on those nodal points on the alternative axes where next-generation Canadians congregate in the largest numbers and where there is the most compatibility with your party's principles and orientation.

Labels matter

By challenging the traditional, one-dimensional flat earth model of the left-centre-right axis, we are facing a challenge somewhat analogous to that facing Christopher Columbus as he set sail for the New World. The conventional wisdom of his day was that the earth was flat and that the greatest danger of sailing off into the unknown was falling over the edge.

Our proposed Political Engagement Receptions, like Columbus's Santa Maria, are the vehicle whereby we test the hypothesis that perhaps the political world is not flat, perhaps it is round, or three dimensional, or even n-dimensional as Stephen Hawking might have contended.

Aboard the Santa Maria there will be those who will find it difficult if not impossible to discuss the nature and destination of the voyage except in traditional terms. But hopefully, there will be enough others who share the faith of their captain that there is a better and more realistic model of the world than the traditional one, a model and a world yet to be discovered.

Columbus has been maligned by those who contend that when he started out he did not know where he was going, when he got there he did not know where he was, when he returned he did not know where he had been and, like today's politicians, he did it all using someone else's money. Columbus, bold adventurer that he was, did make some serious mistakes and we must be careful to avoid what was perhaps his greatest and most lasting mistake which was to mislabel the newly-discovered world and its inhabitants.

When the Santa Maria reached the Bahamas, Columbus apparently thought he had arrived in the East Indies and labeled those he found there "Indians".[43] He could not speak the language of the new world people he encountered. He could not or did not inquire who they were or what they called themselves or their homeland. And thus he attached a label to them and their location, drawn from incomplete prior conceptions,[44] which proved to be erroneous.

When people who no longer identify with the old left-centre-right definitions of political space are asked to label that alternative space they currently inhabit or wish to inhabit, it is unlikely that they will use such terms as social democratic, liberal, or conservative. But what terms will be used or should be used? Will those terms be anchored in any historical or philosophical foundations with substantial policy manifestations that address the major issues of the day? Will they merely

43 It should be noted that some historians dispute this interpretation as unfair to Columbus as a word resembling "Indian" may have been the word used by the indigenous people Columbus encountered to refer to themselves. Whichever is the correct interpretation, labeling a new discovery is a tricky business to be approached carefully.

44 By mistaking North America for Asia, he also thought the mainland must be China, that Cuba must be Japan, and so on.

be "brands" that temporarily resonate with the issue of the hour or appeal to the emotions of the moment, like the "post-political brand" of "Hope" that was employed so successfully in Barack Obama's 2008 presidential campaign? Or will they be something else?[45] And of particular importance, will the mass media accept and use any new nomenclature, or will they insist on continuing to conduct political discourse in the same old left-centre-right terms that they have been using for decades?[46]

It cannot be emphasized strongly enough that an integral aspect of redefining political space for the benefit of Canadians alienated and disengaged from democratic processes is that of finding and using better language for conducting democratic discourse within that space.

A direct appeal to Canadian millennials

If you are a next-generation Canadian and find yourself uninterested in and disengaged from Canada's political processes, I hope you will take a moment even now to reflect on what the long run consequences of such disengagement could be. The iron law of democratic politics is this: *that those who choose not to involve themselves in the politics of their society will be governed by those who do.*

If you find the left-centre-right positioning and language of those currently engaged in politics, uninteresting and irrelevant, why would you then consent by default to be governed by them? Why would you consent by default to let those with that traditional left-centre-right perspective have the ultimate say on how much you will pay in taxes, how those monies will be used, what services you will be offered, what freedoms you may or may not have, or what lifestyle options you may or may not be free to enjoy?

As someone not yet shaped or heavily influenced by politics as currently conceived and practiced, you have an opportunity to develop a

---

45   It is significant that the vague realization by some conservatives that old ideological terms are now less appropriate in naming political parties than they once were, has led to using geographical designations such as the Yukon Party and the Saskatchewan Party.

46   There is a challengé here for next-generation journalists and political commentators: to be in the forefront of developing and using a new and better vocabulary for the conduct of political discourse.

broader and more meaningful perspective by helping to redefine the
political space we all share.

At the same time, as a next-generation Canadian in search of more
meaningful alternatives, you will need to resist limiting yourself to the
kind of ideological homogeneity fostered by the social media, consuming only information that reinforces your existing beliefs and associating
only with "friends" who share those beliefs. It is these patterns of behaviour which can lead to the extreme polarization of communities and
societies, ultimately narrowing political space rather than enlarging it.

DO SOMETHING!

If you are a politically-disengaged millennial:

- Resolve to help redefine political space in Canada to make it
  more meaningful to your generation
- Resist the temptation to have that political space defined solely
  by information and associations which merely reinforce your existing beliefs
- Participate in the Political Engagement receptions and research
  processes described above and/or conduct your own

1.5 Survey Strengths and Weaknesses

Any organization that wishes to be sustainable and effective needs to be constantly aware of its strengths and weaknesses so that it can build on the former and remedy the latter. But it seems particularly easy for those of us who are leaders or members of democratic political parties, to delude ourselves on these points, to hold false and exaggerated opinions of our strengths and to be blind to weaknesses and deficiencies that are often quite obvious to others, especially voters.

The New Democratic Party, for example, both provincially and federally, blithely presents itself to voters as being quite capable of responsibly managing governments with multi-billion dollar budgets. But the stark reality is that the NDP is chronically weak on managing public finances. As a consequence, it has given the country a number of disastrous one term provincial governments such as the Barrett government in British Columbia (1972–75), the Rae government in Ontario (1990–95), and more recently, the Notley government in Alberta (2015–2019).

On the conservative side, we pride ourselves on being better at managing public finances and stimulating economic growth than our liberal or socialist competitors. But at the provincial level, where the three biggest spending areas of a provincial government are those of health, education, and social services, we (as previously noted) often have little more to offer than the dubious assertion that we can manage the institutions of the welfare state better than our competitors.

From the standpoint of strengthening the practice of democracy there is obviously merit in constantly surveying the strengths and weaknesses of the political class in general and political parties in particular so that actions can be proposed and taken to remedy the deficiencies. Let's start with the general weaknesses of the political class.

Weak on trust

Perhaps the most serious weakness of Canada's political class, one requiring our most urgent attention, is our declining ability to command the trust of those in whose name we purport to govern, namely the people of Canada. The Edelman public relations firm, through its Trust Barometer, has been monitoring the trust level of Canadians in business, the mass media, non-governmental organizations, governments, and political institutions for years.[47] See Table 1 below.

TABLE 1 Edleman Trust Barometer (Canada)

Level of Trust in...	2013	2014	2015	2016	2017	2018
NGO's	73	67	57	61	59	50
Media	61	58	52	55	45	49
Businesses	58	62	51	56	50	49
Governments	58	51	47	53	43	46

As Table 1 indicates, public trust in all major institutions in Canada has been declining. Between 2016 and 2017 alone, the first full year of the newly-elected federal government under Justin Trudeau, trust in government dropped almost ten percent, to below the 50% level for the first time in our history. In other words, more Canadians mistrust than trust, governments and the politicians that run them, a vote of non-confidence more serious in the long run than any non-confidence motion moved in parliament or the legislatures.

There is, of course, a symbiotic relationship between the trust of the people in politicians, and the trust of politicians in the people, as illustrated by the rise of so-called populism throughout the western world.

---

47   For a brief description of Edelman and its Trust Barometer, see https://www.edelman.com/trust-barometer.

When our political and media elites increasingly mistrust the voters, considering them to be intellectually challenged, generally misinformed, infected with detestable prejudices, and easily led astray by demagogues – then it should not surprise us when this mistrust is reciprocated.

"Why", asks the voter of the politician, "should I respect and trust you, when you don't respect and trust me?"

One obvious approach therefore to strengthening public trust in the political class is to strengthen the character and trustworthiness of politicians themselves and the political parties through which they operate.[48]

Weak on science and technology

We live in an age in which science and technology are two of the strongest and most dynamic forces influencing our lives and society. And yet one of the most pronounced intellectual weaknesses of Canada's political class in general is our relative ignorance of science and its application to the economic, social, environmental, and international challenges that face us.

In Canada, very few scientists or science administrators actively participate in the political arena and when they do, it is usually for the singular purpose of securing more and better funding for their own activities. At the same time, very few active politicians have a science background, and most speeches and comments by politicians on science and technology are pathetically shallow. This is a weakness to be acknowledged and urgently addressed.[49]

Weak on competence

Surely it goes without saying, that in a democracy the more competent our elected representatives and legislators are, the higher will be our quality of government, with immense benefits to the governed and the

---

48   More on how to accomplish this in chapter 1.5. And for ways and means of overcoming the mistrust between political elites and rank and file voters represented by populism, see chapter 5.2.

49   More on ways and means of strengthening relations between the scientific and political communities, to the benefit of both, in chapter 2.3.

nation. But, conversely, do we really appreciate the high price we pay in terms of misspent tax money, poorly framed laws, inferior public services, and unwise policy decisions when *incompetence* is a distinguishing characteristic of a legislature, a cabinet, a leader, and a government? I don't think so, but we should not only realize the price paid for such incompetence but fear it to the point where we insist that competence must be an essential characteristic of anyone we consider for elected office.

This point was brought home to me with particular force by an exchange I once had with a Canadian military hero and Canada's first democratically selected Senator, Stanley Charles Waters.

Stan Waters joined the Canadian military in 1941 and fought valiantly in Italy and Germany as part of a joint American and Canadian commando unit called The Devil's Brigade. He remained in the military after the war, rising to the position of Lieutenant-General and Commander of the Canadian Forces Mobile Command (1973–75). By the time I got to know him, Stan was a prominent member of the Calgary business community who had become disillusioned with the federal Progressive Conservatives. He joined the Reform Party and became our candidate in a special province-wide election to recommend to the Prime Minister the best person to fill a vacant Alberta seat in the Canadian Senate[50]. Stan subsequently became Canada's first democratically-selected Senator and an outspoken champion of Senate reform.

During the many hours Stan and I spent traveling together campaigning for that Senate seat, I got him to talk about his military adventures, and one night I asked him what he had *feared* the most as a soldier. I had read that in 1943, as a member of the Devil's Brigade, Stan had led his unit at night, up sheer cliffs using ropes, to overwhelm the German defenses of Monte de Difensa in Italy. I also knew that in 1944 he had been part of the amphibious landing at Anzio, an operation in which Allied losses were so heavy that Stan was obliged to temporarily assume command of a whole battalion.

So when I asked, what he had most feared as a soldier, I expected him to say something like coming under machine gun fire while dangling from a rope on Monte de Difessa, or being blown to bits by German artillery fire on the beaches of Anzio.

---

50 For a description of the 1989 Alberta senate selection campaign and results, see Manning, *Think Big*, pp. 37–39.

Instead, Stan's answer completely surprised me. He paused for a moment, then simply said: "What I feared most as a soldier was incompetence in high places." As we talked further, I got the distinct impression that he still very much feared the same thing, this time, incompetence on the part of people in high political office.

At the time of this writing, Canada is currently suffering from such incompetence, a Prime Minister, who may be well-meaning and charismatic on a superficial level, but who lacks the knowledge, experience, and judgment required to effectively lead a government challenged on the fiscal, economic, trade, energy, environment, unity, and international fronts.

The mishandling of the SNC Lavalin affair,[51] resulting in the resignations of two of his most competent cabinet ministers, further illustrates the point that the 2015 election ad run by the Conservative Party of Canada and completely ignored by the electorate was basically true. From an experience and competence standpoint, Justin Trudeau was simply "not ready for the job."

Provinces like Alberta have recently suffered from the same affliction. The distinguishing feature of the last seven years (2017–2014) of its aging Progressive Conservative administration was incompetence. And incompetence on the part of the Alberta NDP, which never expected to

---

51   In 2015, criminal charges were laid against Quebec based SNC-Lavalin for allegedly paying $48 million in bribes to government officials in Libya and defrauding Libyan organizations of $130 million. If convicted, the company would be banned from bidding on federal government contracts for ten years. In 2018, the company sought a deferred prosecution agreement from the Trudeau government and other measures which would allow it to escape the ten-year bidding ban. The decision as to how to deal with the criminal charges rested with Attorney General and Justice Minister Jody Wilson-Raybould who subsequently alleged political interference from the office of the Prime Minister, pressuring her to abandon the prosecution of the company. When she refused, she was demoted. She later resigned. Subsequently, both she and fellow minister Jane Philpott were expelled from the Liberal caucus and party. As of the publication of this book, controversy continues to swirl around the unresolved issue of interference by the Prime Minister in the judicial system and the efforts by the government to block a thorough investigation of the matter. In December 2018, SNC Lavalin pleaded guilty to a single count of fraud in relation to the activities of its construction division in Libya. The company must pay a $280-million fine over five years and be subject to a three-year probation, but appears to have escaped the damaging prospect of being banned from federal contract bidding as a result of its illegal international activities.

be thrust into government as a result of the 2015 provincial election, was a major reason why that government was turfed from office after only one disastrous term.

How can the frequency and extent of incompetence in high political office be reduced? By all political parties adopting higher standards of candidate recruitment; by the media paying much more attention to examining and publicizing the knowledge, experience, and skill levels of leaders and candidates for public office; by the provision of more extensive and higher quality training to those intending to seek public office; and, most importantly, as a voter assessing candidates for public office, making competence and trustworthiness your two most important evaluative criteria.

Weak on training

To become a barista at Starbucks you need at least twenty hours of training so that you know the difference between a latte and a cappuccino and can intelligently serve a demanding clientele. But you can become a lawmaker in the parliament of Canada, a provincial legislature, or a municipal council without a single hour of training in lawmaking, or democratic representation, or public finance, or many of the other specialized functions that elected officials are now required to perform. Is this acceptable? I don't think so. And does this not point to yet another general weakness of our political class: lack of adequate training for the jobs its members so assiduously seek?

The old idea was that you could learn the practical side of politics and government "on the job." But in this fast moving age of instant communications, not to mention the bewildering complexity of government and the political process itself, this method of acquiring the requisite skills to represent, legislate, manage and govern public affairs is obviously inadequate. Ideally, specific training in the performance of these functions is required before you ever arrive at elected office.

One of the skills most lacking among political partisans is the ability to carry on a civil and constructive dialogue with those with whom we fundamentally disagree.

The physical layout and symbols of our democratic assemblies contribute to this problem. Following the British Parliament, we foster confrontation by positioning the government and opposition benches opposite each other and "two swords lengths" apart. Then we place between them on the assembly table a mace: a weapon for clubbing your enemy over the head. This fosters civil and constructive dialogue?

How can we encourage the politicians of the future to conduct public discourse in a more civilized and constructive way? How can we give them the skills and the will to acquire those skills?[52]

Identifying specific strengths and weaknesses

One simple but effective tool for identifying the specific strengths and weaknesses of the political class is objective, third party public opinion surveying on this subject. For example:

- What does the general public believe are the strengths and weaknesses of the political class and particular political parties?
- What do specific groups within Canadian society, the media, the science community, the business community, the immigrant community, the first nations community, the religious community, the financial community, and so on, believe are the strengths and weaknesses of the political class and particular parties?
- How do they assess the performance of particular politicians and parties in particular areas?

The first challenge in conducting such surveys is to secure the necessary objectivity. Better therefore for such surveying to be financed and conducted by genuinely non-partisan institutes than by the parties themselves or others such as media and academic faculties with vested interests in particular outcomes.

The second challenge, even more daunting, is to get the political class and particular parties to accept the results and act upon them. This requires leaders who truly believe that the only worthwhile poll is the one that tells us what we need to hear, as distinct from want we want to hear."

---

52   More on how to significantly raise the knowledge and skills level of political practitioners through a major increase in attention and commitment to the development of human resources for the political sector in chapters 3.1 to 3.6.

DO SOMETHING!

Whatever your political persuasion, ask and answer these questions:

- What are the greatest weaknesses of Canada's political class and the political philosophy or party that you most strongly support?
- What might I do to help remedy those weaknesses and thereby strengthen Canada's democratic processes?
- Support, through advocacy, financing, and participation, the conduct of objective, third-party surveys designed to ascertain the strengths and weaknesses of Canada's political class and parties from a variety of perspectives.
- Communicate your opinions on this subject to your MP, MLA, and municipal councilor.

Calibrating the caucuses

When my father was Premier of Alberta, in the early days of political polling in that province, he once used the following technique to get his caucus members to better appreciate their own strengths and weaknesses as democratic representatives. He took the questionnaire which his pollster had prepared to get the opinions of Albertans on a number of current concerns and asked the members of his caucus to complete it themselves, not by expressing their own opinions on the issues but how they, as elected representatives, believed their constituents would respond. He would then collect and collate the questionnaires completed by caucus and compare the results with those obtained by the pollster in administering the same questionnaire to Albertans at large.

And what did he and his caucus learn from this exercise which might be called "calibrating the caucus"?

On some issues (and the Alberta government caucus in the 1950s and 1960s was a politically experienced group), the assessments of the caucus as to what the public was thinking were within 3% of what the pollster found to be the case. On those issues, the government caucus was truly representative of Albertans at large.

But on some other issues, usually issues on which the public and the legislature were polarized, the assessments of the caucus as to what the public was thinking were off by a considerable margin. On those issues, the caucus itself was functioning more as an interest group than as a representative body.

It was my father's contention that the leader, the cabinet, and the caucus itself needed to know and understand on what issues their views were truly representative of Albertans and on which issues they were not. Objective, third-party surveying was effectively used to ascertain their strengths and weaknesses as democratically elected representatives.

DO SOMETHING!

- If you are the leader or a member of a legislative caucus persuade your caucus to periodically conduct this "calibrating exercise"
- Identify steps you can take to secure a more accurate assessment of public thinking on those issues on which your caucus acts more like an interest group than a representative body.

Recognizing and combating the political lie

On the occasion when I first ran for Parliament in 1963 in the federal riding of Edmonton East, a very peculiar gentleman attached himself peripherally to our campaign. His name was Frank and he had spent most of his working life in the insurance business. He professed to be a lifelong Liberal, but for some reason he disliked the Liberal candidate in Edmonton East and had therefore decided to join our campaign. "Join" is not really the right word, because Frank didn't really do anything for us other than frequent the campaign office once or twice a week and offer unsolicited advice, often on "here's what we Liberals would or would not have done" in this or that situation.

One Saturday he offered the unsolicited opinion, based on his long-time Liberal campaigning experience, that it was sometimes necessary to "lie" in order to win an election. This he considered regrettable, but since it was sometimes required, the strategic question which had to be addressed was "out of whose mouth would the necessary lie be most credible?" With respect to this question, he then suggested that a campaign had two choices.

One choice was to utilize the services of those he called "the professional liars from downtown." By this he meant utilizing the services of certain young and ambitious Liberal lawyers from the downtown law offices who would say or do anything to get patronage work or appointments from the winning candidate and party. But the trouble with this kind of spokesperson, according to Frank, was that they generally aroused more suspicion than trust among grassroots voters, and therefore were inappropriate propagators of the lie that had to be communicated.

The second choice, and by far the most preferable one according to Frank, was to find some sincere souls who actually believed the lie to be true and who could therefore communicate it vigorously and effectively without any moral qualms or arousing any suspicion of prevarication among the electorate.

Why Frank chose to share this bit of political wisdom we could never ascertain, as it produced a negative reaction on the part of those who heard him and really had no apparent relevance to our campaign or anybody else's in Edmonton East.

Sadly, however, this strategy for misleading the public, in particular the voters, during an election campaign has become an integral part of the communications tool kit of both unscrupulous politicians and advocacy groups. Its deployment has been made even easier and more effective by the practice of data mining and the use of social media. For example, it is now easier than ever to find people who already believe the lie which the campaign wishes to propagate, to feed such people additional information to reinforce their erroneous belief, and to vigorously encourage them to sincerely share that erroneous belief with others.

If you are a recipient of political messages, the source from which you are receiving the message may well be a sincere person and a paragon of integrity. But today that does not at all guarantee that the message itself is true, if behind the scene the original source of the messaging is unscrupulous and employing the lying strategy described above.

The antidote? *Do Something!* to identify and combat the political lie!

DO SOMETHING!

- Check out the identity of the source behind any political message before believing it or communicating it to others
- Perform a "parity check" on any political message you consider important, checking its validity with at least two reliable sources outside your own circle
- Do not yourself inadvertently become the propagator of a political lie just because you have been led by others to believe that what you are saying is actually true

Conservative strengths and weaknesses

There is an organizational assumption held by many in the political arena that when you have identified the strengths and weaknesses of your constituency association, campaign, party, or caucus you should immediately give highest priority to addressing your weaknesses. I learned, particularly in starting a new political party whose weaknesses understandably outnumbered its strengths, that this is not always the wisest course to take. Better often to first identify your strengths and to do everything you can to build and capitalize upon them, which by so doing will often start to also remedy your weaknesses by giving you the knowledge and resources to do so.

The Reform Party, for example, had some very strong and well-researched positions on budget balancing and securing regional fairness in federal policies and decision-making. But we were conscious that, as a new party, we didn't have much to say or contribute in a host of other areas such as foreign policy, defense policy, social policy, aboriginal policy, immigration policy, etc. So we scrambled and devoted a lot of effort to bolstering ourselves as quickly as possible in those many policy areas where we perceived ourselves to be weak. We even produced a pamphlet entitled "64 Reasons to Support Reform" when, in retrospect, we probably would have been wiser to give voters three well-researched and strongly promoted reasons to vote for us, based on our strengths.

Even at the caucus level, if we had three or four members who were a source of trouble and disruption, I would devote hours trying to deal with them, while neglecting to cultivate and encourage stronger and more responsible members who were already doing a good job and could have done more if more recognized and empowered.

Conservative-oriented politicians, parties, and governments have their strengths, for example, a respect for history and traditional values, a commitment to individual freedom and responsibility, and a commitment to property rights and freer markets as keys to wealth creation and economic prosperity. And, of course, most conservatives are committed (at least in principle) to fiscal responsibility: balanced budgets, debt reduction, and tax relief, all of which are important priorities when conservatives are so often called upon to clean up the financial mess left by fiscally irresponsible liberals and social democrats.

Conservative parties would do well to develop and build upon these strengths and let the movement take a greater role in addressing perceived weaknesses and turning them into future strengths.

Identifying the specific strengths and weaknesses of conservatism

Each year from 2006 to 2016 the Manning Foundation for Democratic Education conducted surveys, including national public opinion surveys, which sought to identify some of the perceived weaknesses of conservatism in Canada so that they can be addressed and remedied.

Intellectual capital weaknesses

On the intellectual or policy front, these surveys indicate a particular need to strengthen conservative commitments, approaches, and policies with respect to:

- *Providing and managing social services, in particular health care, education, and social assistance.* Conservative parties are generally seen to be strong on the economy and fiscal issues but weak on the social side
- *Addressing the problems of poverty and economic inequality.* Conservatives are good at pointing out that attempting to solve these problems by income redistribution through progressive taxation has generally been unsuccessful. But we have not been creative and aggressive in offering alternative solutions

- *Championing and achieving environmental conservation and protection.* Conservative parties tend to be much more vocal and vigorous in opposing environmental conservation measures proposed by others, such as carbon taxes, than we are in proposing our own market-oriented solutions to environmental problems.
- *Addressing lifestyle issues involving the expansion or limitation of individual freedom of choice* such as beginning of life issues, end of life issues, LGBTQ issues, and issues surrounding the legalization and use of opioid. Divisions within conservatism, for example, between libertarian conservatives, social conservatives, and fiscal conservatives, significantly weaken our ability to address such issues.

Again, the key question becomes what to do to address the perceived weaknesses of conservatism on the intellectual front?[53]

Weakness on the jurisdictional front

Conservatives are visible and active in the federal and provincial political spheres, but much less so at the municipal level. This also is a weakness which needs to be addressed and remedied.

At present there are over 5,000 municipal or local governments in Canada, by far the most numerous governments in our country.[54] One of those municipalities, Toronto, has greater revenues than four of the provinces, and three of the other large municipal governments (Montreal, Ottawa, and Calgary), have greater combined revenues ($12.6 billion) than five of our provincial governments (see Table 2).[55]

While legally and constitutionally local governments are creatures of the provinces, in fact many of them predate the provincial governments which now have legislative jurisdiction over them and many in central

---

53 More in chapters 2.1 to 2.5 on addressing these weaknesses through increased efforts to develop conservative intellectual capital.
54 Statistics Canada uses the general term "Census Subdivision" (CSD) for municipalities (as determined by provincial/territorial legislation) or areas treated as municipal equivalents for statistical purposes (e.g., Indian reserves, Indian settlements, and unorganized territories). Municipal status is defined by laws in effect in each province and territory in Canada.
55 Financial information is from provincial and municipal 2016 financial statements.

TABLE 2 2018–19 revenues of the federal, provincial, and large municipal governments

Governments, By Jurisdiction	2018-19 Revenues (billions)
Canada	$332.2
Ontario	$153.7
Quebec	$114.7
British Columbia	$57.1
Alberta	$49.6
Manitoba	$16.9
Montreal + Ottawa + Calgary	$16.0
Saskatchewan	$14.4
Toronto	$13.7
Nova Scotia	$11.8
New Brunswick	$9.6
Montreal	$8.1
Newfoundland and Labrador	$7.8
Ottawa	$4.1
Calgary	$3.8
Edmonton	$3.0
Prince Edward Island	$2.0
Winnipeg	$1.9
Windsor	$0.8

and Atlantic Canada predate the federal government.[56] Moreover, many of our provincial and federal politicians actually got their political start at the municipal level. It is in the local government arena that they first learned and practiced the representation of constituents, the development and communication of public policy, lawmaking, and regulatory practice, and the budgeting and managing of public monies.

56   The First and Second Schedules to the BNA Act, 1867, Enactment no. 1, define the boundaries of the initial federal electoral districts for Ontario and Quebec in terms of pre-existing counties, townships, cities, and towns, all municipal entities.

In each of the 35th and 36th parliaments of which I was a member, fully one-third of the elected members got their political start at the municipal level. It is also worth recalling that even Sir John A. Macdonald, our first Prime Minister, got his political start at the local government level as a Kingston city councilor.

The textbooks usually describe local governments from a legal standpoint as being the third level of government. But in many respects, from a democratic standpoint, they are our first level of government, the one closest to the people by virtue of the practical, life-affecting issues they deal with and the relative ease with which the public can access local government officials.

Notwithstanding all of this, conservatives have tended to neglect the municipal field, particularly in the large urban municipalities where conservative-oriented councilors practicing fiscal prudence and offering market based solutions to municipal issues and service challenges are in a distinct minority.[57]

Weaknesses on the structural front

Both in the partisan arena and at the movement level, conservative organizations tend to keep themselves in silos, independent and remote from each other, rather than cooperatively linked for mutual support and collective action. In this respect we are worse than liberal, social democratic, and union organizations. The conservative think tanks and advocacy organizations, afraid of losing donors to each other or to the parties, or of running afoul of rules and regulations that separate charitable work from advocacy and political action, maintain a separate and independent existence which greatly hinders the free flow of conservative ideas and policy work from conception through communication to implementation.

The conservative-oriented provincial parties have little to do with the federal party or with each other in terms of meeting regularly, exchanging ideas, sharing research and training resources, or supporting each other's election campaigns.

---

57   More in chapter 5.1 on how to address the perceived weaknesses of conservatism on the municipal front through a vast expansion of conservative political organization and activism in that arena.

The net result is a failure to get maximum political results from the intellectual, human, and financial resources currently being invested in Canadian conservatism. Maximum results might be the election of principled and well-prepared conservative-oriented governments in two out of three elections.[58]

If the seven conservative oriented political parties currently governing at the provincial level were ever to act in concert with the conservative official opposition in Ottawa on a particular issue or in an election, they would be more than a match for the federal Liberal Party or the Liberal minority government. But to act in concert will require far more attention to silo dismantling, relationship building, and networking than in the past.

DO SOMETHING!

If you are a leader, executive, employee, or member of a conservative-oriented political party:

- Make a specific effort to periodically identify the strengths and weaknesses of your organization
- Resist the temptation to deny the existence of weaknesses
- Join in efforts to build on strengths and remedy weaknesses, rather than opposing them or pretending that the weaknesses don't exist
- Give specific attention to relationship building and networking with other components of the conservative movement, including other conservative parties, in order to strengthen the conservative community as a whole

58   More in chapters 4.1 to 4.4 on how to address the perceived weaknesses of conservatism on the structural front through greatly improved networking and cooperation.

1.6 Strengthen Character and Trustworthiness

One of the most disturbing political trends in all the western democracies is the declining public trust in politicians, elections, and elected assemblies such as parliaments and legislatures. This is evidenced, not only by the findings of the Edelman Trust Barometer referred to earlier (see Table 1), but by the continued downward trend in voter turnout in Canadian elections.[59] It is a trend that all democratic politicians and parties, including conservatives, must frankly acknowledge and address.

A major reason for this growing distrust of politicians by the public is the widespread perception that political players are unethical: dishonest, untruthful, manipulative, and primarily motivated by self-interest.[60]

When this mistrust manifests itself in lower voter turnouts, it becomes even easier for parties and candidates to identify and only cater to an increasingly narrow base of support, further undermining the confidence of the public at large in the democratic process.

In a 2014 public opinion survey conducted by the Manning Centre, and via frequent informal surveys since, we have asked Canadians the following questions:

---

59 As previously referenced, the average voter turnout in the thirty federal elections held in the twentieth-century was 72.8%. Despite all the improvements in communications and transportation which ought to have made voter participation easier, the average voter turnout in the five federal elections held thus far in the twenty-first century is 62.8%, a 10% decline.

60 The Gandalf Group, "Public Perceptions of the Ethics of Political Leadership," presentation at Ted Rogers School of Management, Ryerson University, November 5, 2014. http://www.gandalfgroup.ca/downloads/2014/Ryerson%20Ethics%20Survey %20-%20Final%20Report%20Nov%205%20-%20TC.PDF.

- How important is it to you that your elected officials be *knowledge-able,* that is, know a great deal about the issues and business of governing?
- How important is to you is it that your elected officials be *skillful,* that is, possess such skills as the ability to communicate, analyze, make decisions, legislate, manage public affairs, etc.?
- How important to you is it that your elected officials possess certain *character traits,* that is, that they be transparent, truthful, compassionate, responsible, etc.?

Predictably, *character* trumps knowledge and skills by a large margin. But how then does the public perceive the character of the political class?

To cite the findings of just one Manning Centre survey on this subject:[61]

- 77% of Canadians surveyed had an unfavorable view of elected officials from a character standpoint.
- 58% considered elected officials to be generally unprincipled.
- 90% saw elected officials as more concerned with making money than with the well-being of their constituents.

According to another survey on the same subject, one conducted by Ryerson University:[62]

- In terms of public trust levels, politicians, political staff, and lobbyists receive very low scores.
- Half of Canadians indicated they did not trust politicians and one in five indicated that political corruption has led them to stop voting.
- The unethical behaviors that respondents found most objectionable were the breaking of election promises (75%), with over 50% referring to the use of tax dollars to buy votes, and the tendency of politicians to only champion policies favorable to friendly interest groups, lobbyists, or family members.

In defining the character attributes most desirable in holders of political offices, I am reminded again of that speech by the Latvian scholar in

---

61   Ibid.
62   Ibid.

which she declared that the Second Great Commandment of Western Civilization after *Know Thyself* is *Control Thyself*. If we are going to give elected politicians the power to control the lives of others through law and executive decision making, should we not first insist that those politicians possess the character trait of self-control? Surely it is unwise to entrust the governing of others to those who have not yet learned to govern themselves.[63]

Strengthening the character and moral tone of society generally

In a majoritarian system like democracy, it would be surprising if the character and trustworthiness of the political class could rise significantly above the character and trustworthiness of the broader population from which it is drawn. If the primary preoccupations of a majority of the electorate are career advancement and "making money," should it really surprise us if these are the primary preoccupations of those whom we elect to govern us? If a majority of voters consider it fine to lie on occasion to protect themselves or to get ahead, should it surprise us if those we elect to govern us are also inclined to play fast and loose with the truth?

When I was just starting out in the consulting business and living in Edmonton, I would sometimes amuse myself and my friends by conducting a little public opinion survey of my own just before the civic elections. I would ask a random sample of Edmontonians the simple question, "Did you vote in the last civic election?" and usually about 50 to 60 percent would answer "yes." The worrisome thing about this result was that the actual turnout in the election referred to was usually around 25% to 30%. In other words (I am trying to find a diplomatic way of saying this) one out of two Edmontonians lied in response to my

---

63 We need to remind ourselves of John Milton's definition of a statesman as someone who first learned the government of themselves and only then became qualified to govern others. Referring to Oliver Cromwell, he wrote: "He first acquired the government of himself, and over himself acquired the most signal victories; so that on the first day he took the field against the external enemy, he was a veteran in arms, consummately practiced in the toils and exigencies of war." Milton, John, *The Poetical Works of John Milton*, ed. Egerton Brydges, London, William Tegg, 1862.

question. (I don't mean to pick on Edmontonians. I'm sure the results would be similar in other major cities.)

I would then have fun with this disturbing result in the subsequent civic election campaign when one of my friends or someone at a public forum would accuse one or more of the candidates of lying. "But," I would protest, "since one out of two of us are prepared to lie about political matters, don't we need to elect at least half a dozen liars to council in order to insure that it is truly representative?"

Before we get into proposals for *Doing Something* to strengthen the character and trustworthiness of the political class, on a broad front, not just with respect to telling the truth, there is merit in reflecting for just a moment on the need to strengthen the character and moral tone of society generally, that is, voters like you and me who elect those who govern us.

How to do this on such a broad front is beyond the scope of this book and my ability to prescribe. However, I suggest that we could begin by paying more serious attention to those among us, no matter how obnoxious we may find them, who try to identify the moral and ethical shortcomings of our society and call us to higher ethical and moral standards.[64]

Strengthening the character and trustworthiness of the political class

What needs to be recognized and done on the narrower front of strengthening the character and trustworthiness of Canada's political class, regardless of ideology or party? Here are a few suggestions, by no means comprehensive, but hopefully helpful in stimulating our thinking:

1. *Recognize that the ethical tone of a party or political organization is usually set by a few at the top.*

When I was younger and in the management consulting business I was skeptical that a few people in leadership positions at the top of a large organization with thousands of employees and shareholders,

---

64   See for example, Peterson, Jordan B., *12 Rules for Life: An Antidote for Chaos,* Random House Canada, 2018.

or thousands of members in the case of a political party, could significantly influence the ethical tone of the organization. But subsequent experience has convinced me that the ethical tone of an organization or group, *especially* a political party, is almost always set by just a few people, usually those at the top, and by no one else. Generally speaking, the ethics of an organization will never be stronger or better than those of its leadership.

Leaders in particular, whether in business, religious settings, politics, or in the home, need moral authority to be effective. That is, they need authority that comes not from their position or title but from their character and the morality of their actions. In selecting leaders, especially political leaders, the tendency is to look for someone who has the personality, image and skills to win. While all of these are important, it is character that is more important when the priority task is to regain and secure the trust of a demoralized party membership or a cynical and disillusioned electorate.

Personal integrity and personal ethics are dimensions of character which ought to be given at least as much weight as ideology, policy commitments, ability, and experience in selecting candidates for public office. But if you look at the criteria that candidate recruiters, nominating committees, or political headhunters use in recruiting people to run for public office, character is not very high on the list. It ought to be higher, much higher. [65]

When I attempted to push this view at the constituency level of the political parties I have been associated with, I sometimes encountered the contrary view that we have no business carefully examining or judging the personal lives and conduct of potential candidates, as this constitutes a violation of their privacy. For example, 68% of respondents in the Ryerson survey referenced previously agreed that "what politicians do on their own time is their own business, as long as it isn't against the law and doesn't affect their work."

On the other hand, and I think this is the more insightful opinion, over 50% of the respondents in the Ryerson survey also agreed that "a politician who is dishonest in his or her personal life cannot be trusted in their professional life."

---

65   Criteria such as name recognition, personal charm, charisma, communications skills, media smarts, relevant experience, and financial resources or access thereto.

For example, if you are prepared to lie to and deceive your spouse to whom you have made explicit and public commitments of faithfulness, you are unlikely to have many reservations about lying to or deceiving anybody else. At the end of the day, character matters if we want to win and retain the trust of others, and this should be kept uppermost in mind in recruiting people for public office. [66]

2.   *Recognize the limits to Codes of Ethics in ensuring ethical behaviour. Something more is required.*

Formal codes of ethics have their place in defining standards of conduct for politicians and the political class. But it has been the experience of humankind from time immemorial that such codes are insufficient by themselves to guarantee ethical conduct. Forty pages on ethical conduct in Enron's handbook for executives and employees did not safeguard that company from corrupt practices on a massive scale.[67] Proclamation of a Code of Ethics and the appointment of an Ethics Commissioner by the Liberal administration of Jean Chretien did not prevent officials at the highest level of the government from becoming embroiled in the Sponsorship Scandal during the Quebec referendum campaign.[68] Nor did the existence of a federal Code of Ethics, a federal Ethics Commissioner,[69] or the parliamentary Ethics Committee prevent unethical interference in the judicial process (including unethical suppression of testimony)

66   If we look to the social sciences, it is Professor Stanley Renshon who simply points out in his seminal work *Psychological Assessment of Presidential Candidates* (Routledge, 1998) that character matters.

67   Enron. *Code of Ethics. July 2000. Accessed, here: http://mishkenot.org.il/Hebrew/docs/ethics/קודיק%20אתיים%20של%20נוגרא%20סנעקיים/Enron%20Code%20Of%20Ethics.pdf*

68   The Sponsorship Scandal (also called AdScam or Sponsorgate) involved large scale corruption of a federal advertising program which operated in Quebec from 1996 to 2004 and involved the Liberal Party of Canada. Investigation of the program by the federal Auditor General forced the Martin government to establish the Gomery Commission inquiry which determined that at least $3.5 million in federal funds were either misappropriated or misused, and that numerous rules under the Financial Administration Act had been routinely broken. See LeBlanc, Daniel, *Nom de code: MaChouette*, Libre Expression, 2006.

69   Ironically, the federal Ethics Commissioner took a leave of absence for health reason at precisely the point in time when the ethical dimensions of the SNC Lavalin scandal were being drawn to public attention, leading to the unkind comment by one observer that it was ethical standards themselves that had long ago taken a leave of absence from Ottawa.

by the office of Prime Minister Trudeau in connection with the SNC Lavalin scandal.

The problem with Codes of Ethics is not with the codes themselves but with securing compliance, and this is a problem that organized religions, for example, have been wrestling with for ten thousand years. Thus the commentary on this subject that I have personally found most instructive is that contained in the Judeo Christian scriptures,[70] as relevant today on this subject as when they were originally written.

In the Hebrew scriptures you have the record of a four-hundred-year experiment to establish right (ethical) relationships and conduct by reliance on an ethical code, the Law of Moses. Promulgated by the highest authority known to the Hebrew people, it consisted of ten commandments and subsidiary legislation that governed every aspect of their political, social, economic, family, and personal lives. The Mosaic code promised great blessings and rewards for adherence to its demands and threatened the harshest of penalties and consequences for failure to comply.

But what was the conclusion of the latter-day Hebrew prophets concerning the use of a code of conduct to ensure ethical behaviour? It was that unless that code could be written "on the tables of the heart,"[71] internalized by some kind of inner moral transformation and commitment, it was not sufficient to merely have its demands proclaimed on tablets of stone, or parchment, or in statute books. Nor was it sufficient to try to secure compliance through external enforcement measures, no matter how comprehensive or draconian those enforcement measures might be.

Personal character is the product of the *internalization* of our Code of Ethics, no matter what that Code might be. Which is why attention to the character[72] of political leaders and participants is so important if we want to strengthen the ethical tone of democratic politics.

---

70   I have discussed this subject at considerable length in Manning, Preston, *Faith, Leadership, and Public Life,* Castle Quay Books, 2017. See especially pages 167–174.

71   Ezekiel 11: 19–20; Jeremiah 31: 31–33.

72   The moral life, according to theologian Stanley Haurerwas, one of America's most respected theologians, is "character shaped by virtues," in particular, prudence, justice, temperance, courage (or fortitude) faith, hope, and charity (self-sacrificial love). From a personal interview by the author with Haurerwas, March 21, 2018.

3. *Secure the help of an ethical guide or support group to help you maintain your ethical integrity.*

This is not the place to thoroughly discuss,[73] nor am I competent to prescribe, the alternatives and best means of internalizing codes of ethics, although I imagine that the psychologists would tell us this is best done in the home before we are three years old.

But of one thing I am certain: maintaining high ethical standards for ourselves, our family, our office or a government or political organization, will rarely be successful if it's a solo effort. We need others who share our ethical standards or even higher standards: a parent, a partner, a counsellor, a spiritual guide, an honest family member, an older and wiser colleague, a like-minded support group, who realizes the difficulties we are encountering in adhering to our standards, who will hold us accountable for doing so or failing to do so, but who will also be sympathetic and helpful, not overly censorious and judgmental when we stumble.

The famous Hebrew ruler, King David, had a faithful counsellor, Nathan, who was not afraid to speak ethical truth to power and to call the King to account when David perpetrated one of the most infamous cases of sexual harassment in history.[74] William Wilberforce had the "Clapham Circle,"[75] a group of like-minded and supportive friends and colleagues who supported each other and held each other to account in the conduct of one of the greatest moral crusades in the history of British democracy, the campaign to outlaw slavery.

I have been blessed by a faithful and insightful partner, my dear wife Sandra, who is more detached, clear-headed, and frank on the ethical challenges posed by my political engagements than are myself or my closest political friends.

My father, longtime Premier of Alberta, was also a great example to me in this regard. He never told me the following story, he was too

---

73 I have attempted to do so, from a Christian perspective, in *Faith, Leadership, and Public Life*, 2017. According to my understanding of the teachings of Jesus of Nazareth, the desired internal moral transformation comes about by faith in, adherence to, and a sense of accountability to, a Being morally superior to ourselves, God himself being presented as the ultimate moral being, and by becoming part of a "body" of believers who will support and hold us accountable for our commitments and actions.

74 II Samuel chapters 11 and 12.

75 *Faith, Leadership, and Public Life*, pp. 109–111.

modest, but my mother did. When my father was first elected to the Alberta legislature in 1935 in the middle of the Depression, he became, at 26 years of age, the youngest cabinet minister in the country. One day he was walking down the street in Edmonton when he encountered a supporter, let us call him Doctor W., with whom he stopped to talk. As they chatted, my father began to cough. Dr. W said he didn't like the sounds of the cough and insisted that my father follow him to his office for an examination. The examination revealed that my father had tuberculosis, a potentially life-threatening illness in those days, and he was ordered to cease all of his political and administrative activities and undergo weeks of bed rest and treatment. The rest and treatment worked, and my father fully recovered, but it was no exaggeration to say that he owed his life to Dr. W and his timely intervention.

Years passed. My father became premier in 1943, and one of the senior positions which his government had to fill was that of the Chairman of the Alberta Workmen's Compensation Board. And guess what? Dr. W., who was an excellent doctor, but definitely not an administrator or executive, very much wanted the job.

Dr. W. was apparently not at all shy in pressing his case. I, of course, wasn't privy to their actual discussions but no doubt Dr. W. could (and did) say to my father something to this effect: "You owe your life to me. You wouldn't even be alive, let alone be the Premier and in a position to make this appointment if it hadn't been for me. I want and deserve that appointment and you owe it to me!"

What was my father to do? He wrestled with the decision but in the end his government did not appoint Dr. W. to the position. In his judgment, it wasn't the right thing to do from the standpoint of the Workmen's Compensation Board or Albertans, whom my father had sworn to serve to the best of his ability. Dr. W., of course, was furious. He ceased coming to any political events, no longer supported the government, and wouldn't even speak to my father. However, many years later, he acknowledged that maybe not getting that appointment was the best thing for both himself and Alberta, and an old friendship was renewed. I am, of course, biased but I think my father pursued the ethical course in this instance,[76] at the price of considerable personal anguish for himself. His example in that regard has always stuck with me.

76 Of course there are those who will say that it depends on your ethical framework as to whether this was the most "ethical" course to take in this instance. I have

But now, what about you, if you are engaged in democratic politics at any level? Who is your example or model of ethical behaviour that you can look up to? Who is your counsellor, guide, or support group that will help you maintain your ethical integrity in the ethically-challenged environment of the political arena?

4. *Engage in, rather than avoid, the discussion of difficult ethical issues presented by political involvements and challenging political choices.*

We Canadians have an aversion to confrontation and disagreement over fundamental issues. We would rather avoid discussing difficult ethical issues than recognize them, address them, and come at least to some temporary conclusion until we see more clearly.

In the field of politics and governments, the initial discussion of such issues need not occur in public where the result of premature or incomplete disclosure is usually misunderstanding or misrepresentation by the media or opponents. But the discussion of difficult ethical issues among political people *does need to occur*, perhaps initially in private sessions, until a publicly-defensible position and rationale can be hammered out.

To give just one illustration of an ethical question with which I have wrestled and where I would have benefited from discussion with others more learned and experienced than me: is choosing "the lesser of two evils" an ethically defensible position?

Abraham Lincoln, for example, was confronted with two terrible options, both evil, but in his judgment, one less so than the other. Either he allowed the American Union to be broken up over the slavery issue, or he prosecuted a civil war to prevent its breakup. In his case, he did not rely so much on the "just war" argument to justify military action, as he did on the argument that civil war, terrible as it was and admittedly evil, was a lesser evil than allowing the breakup of the American Union and the perpetuation of slavery in the South.

discussed this with political people from cultures and societies where politics is inherently corrupt, the concept of the "public interest" is a sham, and where it is believed that your highest ethical commitment as an elected official is to those who helped get you to your position of influence. They would argue that your highest ethical obligation is to your family, friends, and supporters and that the ethical thing to do in this instance would have been to appoint Dr. W to the position and that to fail to do so would have been unethical.

Fortunately, Canada has never had to have an ethical dilemma of that nature, although we might have come close to it if the Quebec secession referendum of 1995 had turned out differently.[77] But still, we need to wrestle with the following question which was once put to me by a colleague: "What do you say to party supporters and voters when they are presented with political leadership which clearly has moral and ethical deficiencies on the personal front but whose policy positions are preferable and more in line with the party line and voter preferences than those of the alternative party?"

This question is being hotly debated in the United States in relation to the personal ethics and conservative policies of Donald Trump. But it can and does arise in Canada as well.

Suppose the country were to get a liberal or social democratic leader who was a vigorous and successful champion of liberal and socialist policies, but turned out to be unethical and reprehensible from a character standpoint? What should Liberal and NDP supporters do in such a situation: continue to support such leadership with its ethical shortcomings for the sake of maintaining its policy direction, or turn away from such leadership and run the risk of electing conservatives as an alternative? And what should conservatives do if faced with a similar situation in reverse?

Or suppose it is alleged that a Canadian based multinational company, employing thousands of Canadians, has engaged in bribery and other unethical practices abroad.[78] Should the government vigorously investigate and prosecute it if the evidence so warrants, running the risk that the company may move its operations (and the jobs, incomes, and taxes associated therewith) to another country? Or should the government turn a blind eye to the company's ethical failures, for the sake of preserving those jobs, incomes, and tax revenues?

My own inclination, in both cases, would be to choose the lesser of the two evils, to turn away from unethical leadership and to vigorously prosecute Canadian based multinationals guilty of unethical practices abroad, regardless of the fact that there would be negative and hurtful, as well as positive, consequences from so deciding.

---

77 The conscription crises in 1917 and 1944, with their potential for breaking up the country, might also qualify as such an issue.

78 This, of course, is the issue raised by the recent SNC Lavalin case, the mishandling of which led to the resignation of then Justice Minister and Attorney General Jody Wilson-Raybould.

My point here, however, is not so much to come up with a definitive prescription for handling such situations as to insist that these are the kinds of discussions which should occur much more frequently among our political class, initially within the inner circles of the parties, but eventually in the public arena, if we are going to more consistently and effectively bring ethical considerations to bear on political behavior and public policy.

5.   *In seeking to improve the ethics of the political class, avoid relying solely on the perceptions received through the mass media or social media.*

There is a difference between an individual's perception of the ethics of a politician that they have met and know personally and their perceptions of that politician solely based on what they have read or seen through the media.

When I was still a student, I came home one day vigorously denouncing an Alberta politician whose positions and attitude I disagreed with and disliked. My father asked the source of my knowledge of this person and I had to acknowledge it came mainly from the newspapers and the gossip mill. He then suggested an experiment.

I was to identify several local political figures I was interested in but didn't really know and to write down my current perceptions of them. He would then make an effort over the following weeks to enable me to meet each of them personally or at least to be able to observe them at close quarters. I was then to compare my impressions after meeting them with my previous perceptions and see if there was any significant difference.

To make a long story short, we carried out the experiment and, predictably, my latter impressions were different than my original ones. In three of the four cases, my latter impressions, after meeting the individuals in question, were more accurate and positive than my original impressions.

For most of us, it is not possible to personally meet the political players we learn about through newspapers, television newscasts, social media, and the rumor mill. But there is wisdom in recognizing that impressions about distant public figures, based on information from a few, likely biased, sources, are generally unreliable. Better to withhold judgment until we have been able to gain impressions from a variety of perspectives and sources, including some closer than ourselves to the political figures in question. This is particularly advisable in an age when our perceptions of political players can be so easily and dramatically influenced by social media and fake news.

6. *Avoid hypocrisy, the Achilles heel of overly zealous moralists.*

In calling for a strengthening of the character and trustworthiness of the political class, we need to be especially careful to avoid insisting that others adhere to ethical standards that we do not or cannot keep ourselves. All of us have our ethical shortcomings, and if we point the finger too fast and too hard at the perceived ethical failings of others, we can be certain that someone will eventually challenge our apparent claim to moral superiority.

For example, those practicing identity politics frequently express great pride in their professed tolerance and acceptance of diversity, and disparage anyone whom they judge to be less tolerant and accepting, as morally inferior. But in many cases, if one investigates below the surface, one finds that the practitioners of identity politics (increasingly referred to as "identitarians") are not really as prejudice-free and accepting as they profess. They simply have different prejudices and intolerances than those they disparage.

I once attended a dinner where one of the guests, to demonstrate his tolerance and acceptance of diversity, declared proudly to others at the table: "And if my son or daughter came home and said they wanted to marry someone of another race or of the same sex, I'd have no problem with that at all." Which prompted another guest to ask: "But what if they came home and said they were going to marry an evangelical Christian or a conservative Catholic, or a Muslim from the Middle East, what would you say then?" To which the first guest replied sharply, "That would never happen." Apparently his tolerance and acceptance was not nearly as universal or prejudice-free as he initially implied.

The most repugnant feature of identity politics is not its ultimate divisiveness but the hypocrisy of some of its most vocal and active proponents. Hypocrisy, more than anything else, robs those tainted by it of any moral authority they might wish to claim or assert.

To paraphrase (and slightly politicize) a story on this point told by Jesus of Nazareth: "Two men went down to the temple to pray. The first approached the altar (which was probably a mirror) and, worshipping his own image, began to pray proudly, 'I thank God that I am not like other men, bigoted, intolerant, and riddled with prejudices.' The second, eyes downcast, simply acknowledged his personal faults and asked only that he be delivered from them."

"Which," asked the great teacher, "do you think came away justified in his position and most respected in the eyes of those who knew them?"[79]

DO SOMETHING!

If we are participants in democratic politics and want to strengthen the character and trustworthiness of politicians and parties:

- Recognize that the ethical tone of a party or political organization is usually set by a few at the top
- Make the possession of character a priority, not only in recruiting leaders, but also in recruiting candidates, political staff, and volunteers
- Recognize the limits to Codes of Ethics in ensuring ethical behaviour; internalization of ethics is required
- Secure the help of an ethical guide or support group to help secure and maintain your own ethical integrity and that of your political circle
- Avoid relying solely on your perceptions as received through the mass media or social media
- Avoid hypocrisy, the Achilles heel of zealous moralists

Remember Sable Island

When I was a Member of Parliament and unable to sleep at night, I would sometimes read and reread the British North America Act, our original constitution, which was more conducive to inducing sleep than the counting of sheep.[80] In due course, I would come upon Section 91,

79 Luke 18:9-14.
80 Unlike the American or French constitutions, and in keeping with our more modest national character, the BNA Act does not abound with ringing declarations

the favorite section of federal politicians since it defines, under thirty heads, the principal powers of the national government. In reading Section 91, I would then come to sub-section nine which declares that the federal government is responsible for "Beacons, Buoys, Lighthouses, *and Sable Island.*"

But why Sable Island, I asked myself? There are thousands of islands along Canada's three coastlines. Why would our Constitution single out Sable Island, a sliver of sand forty-four kilometres long, protruding from the Atlantic ocean 160 kilometres east of Nova Scotia, for specific attention?

Because, in the nineteenth-century, Sable Island was rightly known as "the Graveyard of the Atlantic." It lies along the major maritime shipping route between Europe and North America. Underwater sandbars extend for many kilometres beyond the visible ends of the island, constituting a great hazard for passing ships. In addition, three great ocean currents converge in the vicinity, constantly shifting the location of the sandbars and creating dense fog which enshrouds the island for more than 125 days a year.

By the 1860s, when our constitution was being drafted, over 350 ships had been wrecked on or near Sable Island. And thus maritime delegates to the Confederation conferences insisted that the new national government be made specifically responsible for erecting and maintaining lighthouses and lifesaving stations on Sable Island's shores.

For me, the constitutional reference to Sable Island has become a reminder that there are other even more hazardous coastlines in our world today, morally hazardous coastlines. In every field of human endeavor, business, science, medicine, artistic activity, the academy, sport, and especially politics and government, there are places and situations where self-interest and public interests collide, where the sandbars of public and personal opinion as to what constitutes right and wrong shift with the currents, and where the fog of pretense and expediency obscures the moral hazards that lie beneath the surface. These are places and situations where human lives, families, careers, organizations, campaigns,

and memorable phrases. It was apparently drafted by British bureaucrats usually responsible for drafting municipal statutes. When it was introduced in the House of Lords it "shared the order paper with such forgotten measures as a proposed sugar tax and the Criminal Lunatics Bill. After a particularly somnolent reading of the Canada Bill, the House of Commons came alive as MPs flooded in to debate a proposed dog tax." *National Post, March 30, 2017.*

governments and even whole nations can be shipwrecked just as surely as the ships that foundered and sank off Sable Island years ago.

It is on the Sable Islands of the business world that companies like Enron, WorldCom, and the financial houses that marketed dodgy derivatives foundered and ruined thousands of lives. It is on the Sable Islands of the religious world (yes, even the religious world) where, tragically, many of the aboriginal orphanages and residential schools in Canada, originally intended for good in the name of Christ, foundered as well. It is on the Sable Islands of the political world where the Sponsorship Scandal once punched a hole in the hull of a Liberal federal government, where the unhealthy relationship between the Trudeau government and SNC Lavalin has done similar damage, and where the Trump administration is also in danger of foundering.

It is on the Sable Islands of the contemporary workplace and social scene that women's lives have been traumatized and shattered, and men's careers ruined, by failure to steer clear of the life-destroying hazards of sexual harassment and abuse.

It is on these morally hazardous coastlines that individuals, institutions, and even nations can be shipwrecked today unless forewarned, safeguarded, and directed away from the dangers that lurk there.

It is on these morally hazardous coastlines that we particularly need, not merely ethical codes, but ethical persons. Ethical persons who are willing and able, without pretense or hypocrisy, to serve as moral compasses, beacons and lighthouses on the hazardous coastlines of politics. Ethical persons capable of warning others, by example and advocacy, away from dangers that lurk there. Ethical persons capable of steering the enterprises and communities of which they and their colleagues are a part, away from the dangerous shoals of unethical practices and behaviours and toward safer and more honourable harbours.

In the world of democratic politics and government, it doesn't take many to perform this vitally important function but it requires the special few. Will you be one?

BE SOMETHING!

The person of unshakeable personal integrity who will strengthen the character and trustworthiness of any political arena, party, or democratic institution of which you are a part.

How just a few ethical people can raise or maintain the integrity of a government

In 1947, when oil was discovered at Leduc, Alberta, there was a danger that public officials would experience a repetition of what had transpired in several U.S. jurisdictions over the previous decades wherever and whenever an oil boom had occurred: the offering of bribes by private companies and their acceptance by politicians and civil servants, in order to procure drilling rights or regulatory exemptions for the offeror. The predictable result? The corruption of the regulatory system and the administration in power at the time.[81]

Oilmen with this background and experience, arriving in Edmonton, the seat of the provincial government, had only two questions. Where is Leduc? And, who do we pay? Fortunately for Alberta, two of the first people to whom this question of "who do we pay?" was put, were a civil servant named Hubert Somerville and a political executive and fundraiser named Orvis Kennedy.

Somerville was a junior civil servant who had been hired by the Alberta government in the depression at the princely salary of $700 per year. Although he later became one of the most respected and powerful Deputy Ministers in the Alberta government, at the time of the Leduc discovery he was the civil servant responsible, among other things, for administering drilling rights.

When offered thinly disguised bribes by oil interests accustomed to paying off bureaucrats, regulators, and politicians in the U.S. for such rights, Somerville simply said "No." To have accepted such offers was contrary to his ethics as a professional civil servant and he was determined to live by those ethics.

Orvis Kennedy was the president and chief fundraiser of the governing Social Credit party in Alberta at the time of the Leduc discovery. When offered the same inducements as had been offered to Somerville, he went one step further. He assured the offerors that if they ever made

---

81   One of most infamous cases of the use of bribery to secure petroleum drilling rights in the United States was the so-called Teapot Dome scandal which occurred during the administration of U.S. President W. G. Harding (1921–23). Harding's Secretary of the Interior, A. B. Fall, was convicted of receiving bribes for granting drilling rights on federal lands to private oil companies at low rates and without competitive bidding. Fall was the first federal cabinet member in the United States to go to jail.

such a proposal again, to himself or to any of his people, he would use his political influence to guarantee one thing: that the individual and company making the offer would never get drilling rights in the province of Alberta.

Kennedy's personal integrity and ethics were rooted in his Christian conviction[82] that he was morally accountable to God for his decisions and actions as well as to his employer and the people of Alberta. And those ethics stood both him and the province in good stead under severe testing.

Together, the ethical standards of just a few people like Somerville and Kennedy, in key positions at the right time, spared the government and people of Alberta all the tragedy and expense which corruption has brought to the governments and people of so many other petroleum-rich jurisdictions.

Ethical leadership, codes of ethics, rigorous enforcement mechanisms, and the support of an ethical community can all contribute to raising the ethical tone of our politics and governance. But there is no substitute for the personal character, integrity, and trustworthiness of individuals in key positions.

Just a few persons of such integrity, at the right place and the right time, can make all the difference between an ethical public sphere and a public sphere plagued and discredited by ethical failures. Are you such a person? Could you be such a person? Who can tell whether they are in such a position of ethical influence for just such a time and purpose as this?

---

82   The problem in most ethically-challenging situations is not one of not knowing what is the right thing to do. The challenge is to find the inner will and strength to do the right thing in the face of strong pressures and temptations to do otherwise. In Kennedy's case (and my father and I knew him well) it was his Christian conviction that Jesus of Nazareth did much more than lay down high ethical standards as in his Sermon on the Mount. Beyond the code of ethics embodied in the Mosaic law, Jesus offered, and Kennedy availed himself of two specific means of enabling morally frail human beings to adhere to high ethical standards: (1) Inner transformation of the human heart through seeking a personal relationship with a Being (God) morally superior to ourselves. (2) Fellowship in a moral community (the Church and a Christian organization named the Gideons to which Kennedy belonged), the members of which support and hold one another accountable to God and to each other for their behaviour.

1.7 Invest Your Time and Money

To build democratic infrastructure, to learn and apply the lessons from the past, to undertake periodic political realignments, to redefine political space, to survey strengths and weaknesses, to strengthen movement organizations, to strengthen the character and trustworthiness of political practitioners—all of this requires substantial and continuous investments of time and money.

Millions of Canadians daily enjoy the freedoms and benefits of our democratic system of governance but invest no thought, no time, and no money in maintaining it, strengthening it, or ensuring that its freedoms and benefits will continue to be enjoyed by their children and grandchildren. Surely this is shortsighted and unacceptable.

Hundreds of thousands of Canadian entrepreneurs and private sector enterprises depend for their opportunities, livelihood, and wealth on a free-market economy, supported rather than strangled and overtaxed by governments, but invest no thought, no time, and no money in maintaining and strengthening the political conditions upon which such an economy depends for its continued existence. Surely this, too, is shortsighted and unacceptable.

How can we expect our democratic system or a free market economy to survive and prosper in the face of such benign neglect? We cannot. Hence the importance of determinedly, systematically, and substantially increasing our investments of time and money in both.

Stark comparisons: investments in democratic institutions v. investments in parties

Two of the most important components of Canada's democratic political sector are:

- Democratically elected institutions such as our parliament, provincial and territorial legislatures, and municipal councils.
- The administrative offices of organizations such as Elections Canada and its provincial and municipal equivalents, established to conduct democratic elections.

However, the quality and effectiveness of these democratic institutions and processes will only be as good as our investments in the intellectual capital, human resources, structures and activities of the political parties and political movement organizations which populate, guide, and energize them.

At present, the magnitude of financial support provided by Canadians to federal and provincial political parties is minuscule in relation to our investments in these democratic institutions and processes.

To illustrate, in 2018 Canadian taxpayers invested $729 million in supporting the federal parliament (House of Commons and Senate) and an additional $752 million supporting the thirteen provincial and territorial legislative assemblies (see table 3). During the same year, the total contributions by Canadians to the four major federal political parties, whose resources and capacities directly affect the quality and productivity of those democratic institutions and processes, amounted to only $71 million, approximately 4.8% of our total investment in the federal parliament and the provincial and territorial legislatures.

The total contributions by Canadians in 2018 to the major conservative-oriented political parties and think tanks in Canada, dedicated to championing limited government, fiscal responsibility, and a free market economy, was $46 million, or 3.1% of our total expenditures on the federal parliament and the provincial and territorial legislatures. This figure is much smaller again than public investments in the political institutions conservatives seek to influence and control. It is also much smaller than the total investment by non-conservatives in political parties ambivalent about or hostile to limited government, fiscal responsibility, and a free market economy.

TABLE 3 2018 Investments in Canada's Political Sector

Investments in the operations of:	
• Parliament of Canada	$ 729,372,000
• 14 Provincial/Territory Legislatures	$ 752,297,000
2018 Total:	**$1,481,669,000**
Investments in the operations of four major FEDERAL political parties:	
• Conservative Party of Canada	$16,757,932
• Liberal Party of Canada	$10,223,478
• New Democratic Party of Canada	$ 6,537,436
• Green Party of Canada	$ 1,736,942
18 year annual average:	**$35,073,788**
Investments in the operations of five largest PROVINCIAL political parties:	
• Quebec Liberal Party	$ 9,236,754
• Liberal Party of BC	$ 8,078,479
• Parti Quebecois	$ 6,634,996
• New Democratic Party of BC	$ 4,558,521
• Liberal Party of Ontario	$ 3,848,681
18 year annual average:	**$32,357,431**
Investments in the operations of CONSERVATIVE major provincial political parties and think tanks:	
• Progressive Conservative Party of Ontario	$ 3,165,925
• United Conservative Party of Alberta (PC Party)	$ 2,695,917
• Wild Rose Party	$ 987,648
• Think Tanks	
· Fraser Institute & Foundation	$12,702,141
· C.D. Howe Institute	$ 3,965,582
· Canada West Foundation	$ 2,389,169
· Centre for Civic Engagement	$ 1,247,948
· Frontier Centre for Public Policy	$ 860,499
· Atlantic Institute for Market Studies	$ 769,766
· Manning Centre & Foundation	$ 574,094
· MacDonald Laurier Institute	$ 397,119
18 year annual average:	**$29,755,808**

Canadians increasingly profess to dislike political parties. Nevertheless, for better or for worse, they are an integral part of our democratic system. If we are committed to strengthening democracy in Canada, a major part of our unfinished political business is to vastly increase our investments of time and money in improving the partisan segment of the political sector and to increase the productivity of those investments.

If we are conservative-oriented and support limited government, fiscal responsibility, and a free-market economy, an additional part of our unfinished political business is to vastly increase our investments in conservative-oriented political parties and movement organizations and to significantly increase the productivity of those investments.

And if we need something more to incentivize such investments, consider the following "stark comparisons" between the revenues and expenditures of other non-governmental organizations (many of them American based), seeking to influence Canadian public policy and Canada's political parties.

Stark comparisons: investments by advocacy groups in political processes v. investments in parties.

Robert Lyman is an Ottawa-based energy policy consultant who was also a public servant for twenty-seven years and a diplomat for ten years prior to that. In a 2018 research report,[83] based on information provided to the Canada Revenue Agency by registered charities, he summarized the revenues collected and spent from 2000 to 2018 by the forty largest ENGO's operating in Canada. ENGO's are Environmental Non-Governmental Organizations highly active in seeking to influence government policy, especially in the area of environmental and energy policy.

He then compared those figures with the revenues and expenditures of Canada's major political parties of all stripes and conservative think tanks, also seeking to influence government energy and environment policy. Here is what he found:

- The top forty ENGOs[84] received about $11.2 billion over the period 2000 to 2018.
- The top five "EnviroLaw" organizations received about $167 million over that same period.
- The combined revenues of the ENGOs and their EnviroLaw counterparts was almost $11.4 billion over the period.

---

83 *Money Matters: The ENGO Political Advantage;* See https://blog.friendsofscience.org/2019/02/16/money-matters-the-engo-political-advantage/

84 It should be noted that two of the largest of these are Ducks Unlimited Canada and the Nature Conservancy Canada, both of which do much good work and are not ideologically at war with the energy sector. Together these annually receive higher revenues than all the major federal political parties, a major portion coming from the federal government.

By comparison with the revenues and expenditures of Canadian political parties and conservative think tanks:

- The total revenues received by all four main federal political parties over the period was about $631 million.
- The total revenues received by the major political parties at the federal level and the provinces of Ontario, Quebec, British Columbia and Alberta over the period were $1.5 billion.
- The total revenues received by Canada's market-oriented (conservative) institutes over the period was $412 million.

In comparison, therefore, the revenues received by the ENGOs and their EnviroLaw counterparts over the period was over eighteen times the revenues received by all federal political parties, and over twenty-seven times the revenues received by the market-oriented institutes. The revenues received by the U.S.-based Tides organization alone were more than the combined revenues of Canada's two largest federal political parties, the Liberal Party of Canada and the Conservative Party of Canada, over the period.

The bottom line? Billions more dollars are collected and invested by advocacy groups of this kind, organized as charities, authorized to issue charitable receipts for donations made to them, and seeking to influence Canadian public policy, in comparison to the revenues and expenditures of Canadian political parties. When the investments by these advocacy groups are compared with the investments being made in Canada's conservative parties and think tanks, the contrast is more stark.

The conclusion? Again, a major part of our unfinished political business in Canada must be to vastly increase our investments of time and money in improving the partisan segment of the political sector and to increase the productivity of those investments. And if we still need more incentive to do so, consider yet one more stark comparison which constitutes a further threat to Canadian sovereignty.

Stark comparisons: foreign investments in Canada's political processes versus domestic investments

Is there anything distinctive about Canadian democracy? Yes, there is. Canadian democracy is government of Canadians, by Canadians, and for Canadians, which means any foreign interference in Canada's electoral, legislative, or public-policy-making processes is not only a potential threat to Canadian democracy, it is a threat to Canadian sovereignty and needs to be strenuously guarded against.

In the United States, the Mueller investigation was established to investigate the suspicion that there had been foreign (Russian) interference in the 2016 American elections.[85] In the end, it found no conclusive evidence of such interference.

In Canada, however, there already exists a significant amount of *a priori* evidence of foreign interference in *our* political and policy-making processes, evidence sufficient to justify a major investigative effort here. In Canada's case, this interference comes from the activities of American interests in financing Canadian advocacy groups, in particular those opposed to Canadian petroleum and pipeline developments.

Much of this evidence has been assembled and published by B.C. based researcher Vivian Krause[86] and is too detailed and comprehensive to be repeated here. In summary, it documents:

- The transfer of American funds to Canadian anti-pipeline interest groups such as Tides Fund Canada,[87] the Pembina Institute, the David Suzuki Foundation, and World Wildlife Fund Canada, from U.S. organizations such as the Rockefeller Brothers Fund, the William & Flora Hewlett Foundation, the Marisla Foundation, and the Gordon and Betty Moore Foundation,[88] through such U.S.-based intermediaries as the Tides Foundation in San Francisco and the New Venture Fund in Washington, D.C.
- The involvement of key members of these Canadian anti-pipeline groups, funded at least in part by American interests, in the

---

85   Mueller, Robert S., *The Mueller Report: The Final Report of the Special Counsel into Donald Trump, Russia, and Collusion*, Special Counsel's Office U.S. Department of Justice, et al. Apr 30, 2019.

86   See testimony provided by B.C. researcher Vivian Krause to the Canadian Senate Transport Committee, November 1, 2016, and repeated and augmented in various articles and internet postings since. See https://fairquestions.typepad.com/rethink_campaigns/

87   See www.tidescanada.org and https://apps.cra-arc.gc.ca/ebci/haip/srch/t3010form22quickview-eng.action?&fpe=2018-03-31&b=868947797RR000

88   The Gordon and Betty Moore Foundation, founded by Intel co-founder Gordon E. Moore and his wife Betty, has granted at least US$192 million to organizations active in Canada, including US$ 70 million to Tides Canada and US$ 9 million to WWF Canada. See https://www.moore.org/grantee-detail?granteeId=956

Canadian federal elections of 2015 and 2019, and their subsequent involvement in key government positions and policy-making on the energy/environment front.

These individuals include:

- Gerald Butts, Principal Secretary to Prime Minister Justin Trudeau, who was obliged to resign over the SNC Lavalin scandal and was president of World Wildlife Fund Canada at the time when WWF Canada received U.S. funding to participate in the anti-pipeline Tar Sands Campaign[89]
- Sara Goodman, a Policy Advisor to the Prime Minister in 2017 and currently the Director, Policy in the Office of the Prime Minister, who served as a senior vice-president of the Tides Canada Foundation for almost five years[90]
- Zoe Caron, who became a Policy Advisor to the Prime Minister in 2016–17 and is currently Chief of Staff to the Minister for Natural Resources, who was formerly part of the U.S.-funded WWF leadership team and co-author of "Climate Change for Dummies" with Elizabeth May, Leader of the Green Party of Canada[91]
- Marlo Raynolds, an unsuccessful Liberal candidate in the 2015 federal election, who is currently Chief of Staff to the Minister of Environment and Climate Change, and was Executive Director of the Pembina Institute which has received extensive American financial backing as part of the anti-pipeline Tar Sand Campaign.[92]

The primary beneficiaries of this foreign interference in Canada's political and policy-making processes are not Canadians but American petroleum consumers. Political opposition to the expansion of Canadian pipeline

---

89 See "Gerald Butt's history with Trudeau," *The Ottawa Citizen*, 17 May 2014, page 12. https://www.newspapers.com/clip/28603602/. See also "Foreign Donations have skyrocketed," *Windsor Star*, 13 Dec 2016, page 24. https://www.newspapers.com/clip/28603711/

90 See https://www.c2cjournal.ca/2019/03/killing-the-tar-sands-with-american-money-and-canadian-saboteurs/ and https://ca.linkedin.com/in/sarahgoodman

91 https://www.citynews1130.com/2017/06/15/husky-energy-hired-natural-resource-minister-jim-carrs-former-chief-of-staff/

92 https://calgaryherald.com/news/local-news/alberta-liberal-candidate-takes-on-key-environment-role-in-ottawa

capacity to move Canadian petroleum resources to tidewater has meant that the U.S. becomes our only export market for these resources. We are thus compelled to sell them at heavily discounted prices to the benefit of American petroleum consumers.

In 2018 alone, as a result of these discounts, it is estimated that the financial benefit to the American economy (and cost to the Canadian economy) amounted to approximately $80 million per day or about $3.9 billion. Equally worrisome from Canada's standpoint is the fact that our inability to move petroleum resources to tidewater for sale at world prices continues to kill investment, businesses, and jobs in a vitally important sector of our economy.

Do Something! on the political investment front

So what is to be done to significantly increase needed investment in strengthening Canadian democracy and conservatism, to restore balance between investment in political parties and other players in the political arena, and to protect Canada' political processes from foreign interference?

In the following pages, I will discuss such measures as:

- Creating and investing in Political Investment Portfolios
- Addressing the usual excuses for not investing in party politics
- Investing in positive messaging
- Understanding the laws and regulations governing political investing,
- Understanding recent changes in charity law and the potential of legislative initiatives to facilitate political investing
- Investing in social enterprises
- Crowdsourcing for political projects
- Political Investment Clubs
- Investing in people
- Volunteering: investing our time

But let us begin with measures to shield Canadian political processes from foreign interference through foreign political investments.

Exposing and addressing foreign political investment

The *a priori* evidence of American interference in Canada's political and policy-making processes cited above is substantive and serious enough to warrant an objective, high-level investigation. One approach would be for the federal government to initiate a formal inquiry under the federal Inquiries Act, like the Gomery Inquiry[93] into the Sponsorship Scandal commissioned by Prime Minister Martin.

However it is done, the terms of reference for such an investigation need to be crystal clear so as to avoid any misdirection of the investigator or misunderstandings by the public. For example, the objective must *not* be to try to prove some conspiracy theory that U.S.-sponsored anti-pipeline activism in Canada is *de facto* economic protectionism organized for the benefit of U.S. petroleum interests. While some U.S. petroleum interests are no doubt amused that anti-oil foundations like the Tides Foundation are inadvertently enabling U.S. buyers to acquire large volumes of Canadian petroleum at discounted prices, this paradoxical coincidence is not in itself evidence of a conspiracy.

It should also be made clear that the primary objective of investigating these allegations is *not* simply to protect the commercial interests of Canadian oil and gas companies. The ultimate objective is to protect the interests of Canadian workers, investors, taxpayers, and voters in general from the adverse effects of foreign interference in Canada's political and policy-making processes, not just in the energy sector.

It is, of course, highly unlikely that any such investigation will be launched by the Trudeau administration since it is the federal Liberal Party and a number of key government staffers who would be the main subjects of any such investigation. But such an investigation could be launched by one of the Attorney's General in any number of provinces[94]

---

93 The Gomery Commission was established by Prime Minister Martin in 2004 to investigate allegations by the Auditor General of corruption within the Canadian government's Sponsorship Program, an advertising campaign to boost the federal government's profile in Quebec.

94 Alberta's Premier, Jason Kenney, pledged to conduct such an investigation in his victory speech on April 16, 2019. On December 12, 2019, in fulfilment of this promise, Kenney opened the new $30-million Canadian Energy Centre in Calgary to challenge misinformation on Alberta's energy sector. It's multi-pronged approach includes a $2.5-million public inquiry into foreign funding of anti-oil advocacy groups.

where Canadian interest groups accepting foreign donations for political advocacy purposes are incorporated and/or registered provincially for fundraising purposes.

The end result of such investigations should be clear and implementable recommendations as to how Canada should deal with foreign donations to Canadian charities and interest groups, in particular those engaging in elections and public policy dialogue.

The immediate temptation, of course, would be to prohibit such donations altogether, and certainly the already-existing ban on foreign donations to political parties, election campaigns, and candidates needs to be rigorously enforced and expanded to cover indirect[95] contributions.

But there are many legitimate Canadian charities who receive and benefit from foreign donations in order to carry out international work and to pursue genuine, non-political and non-partisan charitable purposes in Canada. It would be a shame and unacceptable to penalize these charities and their work just because a few charities and advocacy groups abuse their ability to receive foreign donations for political and partisan purposes. Hence a balanced submission to any federal or provincial inquiry established to investigate this issue might simply recommend:

- A complete and enforced ban on direct and indirect foreign contributions to political parties by foreign donors.
- Complete transparency in reporting contributions received by Canadian charities from foreign sources and the uses to which they are put.
- Welcoming donations to Canadian charities from foreign sources, provided they are made for genuinely charitable purposes and are used for those purposes.

---

95 An example of an indirect contribution would be when a Canadian charity or advocacy group, receiving substantial foreign donations, grants a generous severance package to one of its executives or staffers, so that they can work the following year free of charge or for very little compensation on a partisan political campaign.

DO SOMETHING!

If you are a Canadian elector concerned opposed to foreign interference in Canada's political affairs:

- Call upon your elected representative at the federal and provincial level to establish an official investigation into foreign investments and interventions in Canada's political affairs
- Based on the results of such investigations, demand that the federal and provincial governments institute remedial measures such as those proposed above
- If you are a member of a Canadian political party: Insist that your party adopt and enforce a policy of refusing to accept direct or indirect financial contributions from foreign interests
- If you are a donor to political parties or political movement organizations: Refuse to donate to any Canadian foundation or advocacy group that acts as a direct or indirect conduit for foreign investments and interventions in Canada's political affairs

Political investment portfolios

Every Canadian who can afford it, and every free market enterprise in a profitable position, should have a *Political Investment Portfolio* and invest annually, whether it is $100 in the case of an individual, $1000 in the case of a family or small business, or tens of thousands in the case of larger corporations, in those political activities and entities judged by the investor to be most worthy of financial support.

As with most investment portfolios, it is rarely advisable to put all one's eggs in one basket. So our political investor would be better advised to diversify his or her annual political investments among the categories suggested by Table 4 overleaf.

If the investor has no strong ideological preferences and wishes to be non-partisan, there is still need to support the democratic process via investment in small-p political organizations and activities such as

TABLE 4 Sample Political Investment Portfolio

Name of Investor: _____

Amount of annual investment: $ [_____]

Allocation of Investments to	%	$
Political Parties		
Election Campaigns (candidates)		
Intellectual Capital (think tanks, policy schools, etc.)		
Issue Campaigns		
Political Training (programs, trainees, interns)		
Advocacy (PACs, interest groups)		
Networking (sponsorship of conferences, attendees)		
Communications (publications, websites, blogs, etc.)		
Other?		

assisting new Canadians to understand Canada's political processes and "getting out the vote." But what is equally important is that political investors not shy away from investments in the partisan political arena since, for better or for worse, that is where much of our democratic governance is shaped and directed.

DO SOMETHING!

- If you are the head or co-head of a family, adjust your family budget to include a line for political investments and initiate periodic discussions as to how much should be invested and where

- If you are the owner or manager of a private business (small or large), adjust your budget to include provision for a *Political Investment Portfolio* and decide how much should be invested and where
- If you are in an executive with a public company, propose that the company develop a *Political Investment Portfolio* for implementation after discussion with shareholders
- If you are a financial planner or investment counsellor, advise your clients of their obligations and opportunities to invest in the democratic political process via a *Political Investment Portfolio*

Addressing the usual excuses for not investing in party politics

There are of course dozens of excuses which can be given, particularly by corporate executives, for not investing in the partisan arena but, in my judgment, most of these need to be revisited and rejected as neither valid nor prudent. Both private and public companies need a pro-market economic and political environment to survive and prosper. If their shareholders or customers do not realize or appreciate this, then they need to be persuaded by management and their more politically astute peers that this is the case.

If the objection is that, in the past, corporate political support has not been transparent enough, then increase the transparency, fully disclosing management's proposed *Political Investment Portfolio* in the information circular to shareholders prior to the annual meeting and if necessary, put it to a vote.

If the objection is that nobody else is doing it, then provide shareholders with overwhelming evidence that "somebody else is doing it." In particular, share the evidence (from the Wyman report previously cited) that vast amounts of money are being invested annually in Canada's political processes by investors (some of them foreign investors) resolutely opposed to free markets, debt and tax reduction, and infrastructure developments to move Canadian resources to tidewater and world markets.

Also, share the evidence[96] of substantial financial and human resource investments in Canada's political processes by public-service unions whose objective is to grow the public sector by taxing the private sector, expanding the public sector's regulatory role, and expanding the public sector in general. The leadership of these unions, though not necessarily their membership, often strongly promote anti-free-enterprise policies. They are capable of raising millions of dollars through compulsory union dues and donating them directly or indirectly to anti-market parties, ideologically compatible organizations, and campaigns. They are also capable of directing thousands of hours of "volunteer labor" by their members to political entities and causes of the leadership's choosing.

It is again worth reminding entrepreneurs, small business people, corporate managers and shareholders that if they choose, for whatever reason, to not invest in the politics of their community, province, or country, they will be governed by those who do. If those who do are opposed to freedom of enterprise and wish to strangle it via excessive regulation and taxation, it is the investors, managers, and workers of the market economy who will be the first to suffer the consequences.

Often the rationale for not investing significantly in the partisan political arena is that "we have staff, management, shareholders, and customers who support different political parties, so the safest thing for us to do is to support none of them. We must be non-partisan."

In addressing this excuse, I am reminded of an experience I had trying to secure funding for Canada's first graduate program in political management. When I was an MP in Ottawa, I had noticed that many of

96 For example, the Alberta Union of Public Employees (AUPE) had around 87,000 members in 2015 with revenues of around $43 million, expenses of $35 million, and assets of $120 million. A significant portion of these resources are available for supporting its political allies, as section 3.10 of the AUPE constitution empowers it: "To give, donate, transfer, mortgage or pledge property and assets of the Union; to borrow on behalf of the Union; and to give or loan Union funds to such societies, associations or other companies as may benefit, directly or indirectly, some or all of the members of the Union."

In Ontario, the Ontario Public Service Employees Union (OPSEU) had 155,000 members in 2017 and assets of $88.2 million, revenues of $106 million, and expenses $125.8 million. Section 8 of the OPSEU Constitution similarly empowers it: "to co-operate with labour unions and other organizations with similar objectives in strengthening the Canadian labour union movement as a means towards advancing the interests and improving the well-being of workers generally in Canada and internationally."

our universities had public administration programs for training future civil servants, but none of them had graduate programs for training the political staff who work in the partisan arena. So I presented the need to Dr. Roseann Runte, then President of Carleton University, who agreed to develop such a program if sufficient funding could be secured.

I arranged for Dr. Runte to come to Calgary and meet Clay Riddell, a very successful oilman and generous philanthropist who had endowed the faculty of the Environment, Earth, and Resources at the University of Manitoba. In describing the proposed program to Clay, Dr. Runte said: "Of course, this program we're asking you to fund will be non-partisan because we can't be in the pocket of any one party." To which Clay replied: "And what non-partisan legislature or parliament is it that you will be training these people for?" His point was that the political arena is partisan, whether we like it or not, and this needs to be fully recognized by any educator or investor supporting the preparation of young people to participate in it.

Carleton subsequently agreed to make the program *cross-partisan*, with each of the major partisan divisions recognized by the program but none being allowed to dominate it. And Clay, a generous and farsighted leader, God bless him, supplied the bulk of the financing through his family foundation.

In adopting, if necessary, a cross-partisan approach to political investing an investor may choose to adopt a "cross-partisan support formula" like those which many firms (banks, law firms, and accounting firms in particular) once followed when financially supporting democratic political parties was considered a responsibility of good corporate citizenship.

Investing in positive messaging

The political parties in Canada have become very successful at fundraising from their membership base through regular, persistent, online and telephone appeals for donations within the limits prescribed by party and election financing laws.

The one disturbing aspect of this approach from a movement perspective is that the messaging used to generate donations from the membership base, especially by conservative parties in opposition, is almost entirely reactionary and negative. Week after week, at the federal level, the fundraising messages of the conservative opposition to its membership base are a focused, negative reaction to some reprehensible thing the Prime Minister or his government has done.

The never-ending increases in federal spending and taxes, the discriminatory Canada Summer Jobs Program, the foolish photo-op trip to India, the self-righteous sermons on identity politics, the bungling of the energy/environment file, the SNC Lavalin scandal and political interference in the judicial process, the black-face, brown-face fiasco. The list goes on and on with the conservative donor base being asked repeatedly and insistently to contribute funds to expose, denounce, and oppose such behaviour.

All of these appeals may well be legitimate and justifiable criticisms of the policies and actions of the governing party, but they are all essentially reactive, simply reactive to something the government or Prime Minister has done or said, and they are all negative reactions. Scarcely ever is the plea for donations from the conservative party core based on a positive and substantive appeal for support for some positive policy or pro-active initiative that the conservative opposition itself wishes to pursue if elected to government.

When asked why this is the case, the perfectly logical and understandable explanation is this: if the party in opposition puts forward some positive alternative to the government's position or actions in some key area, the governing party, with media cooperation, can so easily make that conservative alternative the main subject of debate and controversy rather than the weaknesses and defects of the government's own position. Hence the wisdom, from the perspective of conservatives in opposition, of hammering away, especially during the pre-election period, with negative messaging attacking the weaknesses of the government, and only offering positive, proactive, conservative alternatives closer to election day.

While there is certainly logic to political parties taking this approach, especially if they are in opposition, this logic need not apply to conservative movement organizations. Movement organizations can and should endeavor to build a sustaining donor base beyond the party membership base and serve it with positive messaging urging support of positive and substantive conservative proposals. Let the parties, if they must, raise money from those who are motivated to invest by attack ads and negative messaging; let the movement raise money from those who are motivated to invest by positive advocacy and positive messaging. The net effect should be a broadening and expansion of the overall conservative support base from a financial standpoint.

DO SOMETHING!

If you are an executive or manager of a conservative-oriented move-ment organization:

- Initiate and support efforts to build a membership base via posi-tive rather than negative messaging

If you are a conservative oriented political supporter:

- Make sure you provide volunteer and financial support to those organizations offering positive conservative messages and alter-natives, not just to those offering negative messages and critiques

Understanding laws and regulations governing political investing

Investors in the democratic process need to be aware of the increasingly complex and limiting rules and regulations governing such investments. The assistance of a knowledgeable political investment counsellor, usu-ally a lawyer or an accountant, may be helpful in this regard.

At the federal level, for instance, investors should consult the Elections Canada website[97] to get the latest yearly donation limits for political parties, Electoral District Association (EDA's), and candidates. Table 5 overleaf shows those limits for 2019 and the current law calls for these limits to increase by $25 on January 1 in each subsequent year. Note that such donations are eligible for a tax credit.

Federal political parties are also limited by law[98] as to how much they can spend during the election campaign period, from when the election writ is dropped until election day itself. In 2019, these limits were approximately $28 million for a federal party that ran candidates in

97   Visit http://elections.ca/content.aspx?section=pol&dir=lim&document=index& lang=e
98   http://elections.ca/content.aspx?section=pol&dir=limits&document=index& lang=e

TABLE 5 Limits on individual contributions to federal political entities

Political entity	2019 annual limit
To each registered party	$1,600
In total to all the registered associations, nomination contestants and candidates of each registered party	$1,600
In total to all leadership contestants in a particular contest	$1,600

all federal ridings and about $100,000 for each individual riding depending on size and population.

These spending caps apply to all expenditures by a party or EDA during the writ period, including expenditures on research and training, although in reality very little research or training is actually done during this period. Recently the Trudeau government introduced a further spending cap, limiting federal political party spending on advertising to $2 million in the two months prior to an election.

"Third parties" such as political action groups (PACs) are also subject to election advertising expense limits for general elections and by-elections, but otherwise are generally less regulated than political parties and candidates.

At the provincial level, using Alberta as an example, there are a number of options with respect to donations[99] and the best sources for information on what registered parties and third-party advertisers can and cannot do are the Elections Alberta Handbooks.[100] In Alberta, individual may contribute up to a total of $4000 per year to a registered provincial party or its candidates and are eligible for a tax credit. Corporations or individuals may also contribute to independent or party-aligned third-party advertisers. Similar regulations and limitations exist in all the provinces, their provincial election authorities being the best sources of up to date information.

99 Visit https://www.elections.ab.ca/wp-content/uploads/A-Guide-for-Contributors. pdf).
100 For political parties/constituency associations/candidates, see https://www. elections.ab.ca/wp-content/uploads/Party-CA-and-Candidate-Guide-to-the-EFCDA.pdf. For third party advertisers, see https://www.elections.ab.ca/ wp-content/uploads/Third-Party-Advertiser-TPA-Guide.pdf

Understanding recent changes in charity law and the use of legislative initiatives to strengthen political investment

Legislation governing donations to political parties, candidates, election campaigns, and movement organizations needs to be constantly reviewed and improved to encourage an increase in such investments without sacrificing transparency or safeguards against influence-peddling and corruption. This is a tall order, but something which should be on the legislative agenda of our parliament, legislatures, and municipal councils.

At the same time, legislation governing the definition, organization, and financing of charities also needs to be constantly improved to facilitate and encourage an increase in investments in the activities of political movement organizations (often organized as charities) and social enterprises. Safeguards also need to be provided to prevent charitable organizations (including religious organizations) from abusing their charitable status for purely partisan purposes. This, too, is a tall order, but something which should also be on the legislative agenda of our parliament, legislatures, and municipal councils.

Under existing laws, a charity cannot devote any of its resources to partisan political activities. This prohibits a charity from: telling its social media followers to vote for the party whose views most closely matches the views of the charity; directly or indirectly supporting or opposing any political party or candidate for public office or their partisan activities; or even distributing literature identifying the positions of all political parties on a particular subject and indicating which align most closely with the positions of the charity. This has been the law and is still the law.

But recent changes to Canada's charity laws[101] have significantly broadened the range of activities which registered charities in Canada can undertake. These changes facilitate much greater participation by charities in Canada's political processes than heretofore. In particular, charities are now allowed to devote an unlimited amount of their

---

101 For an excellent summary of these changes, their general implications for charities, and their political implications, see a presentation on this subject by Ottawa-based charity lawyer Adam Optowitzer to the 2019 Manning Networking Conference. Copies of this presentation, entitled *Charities and Political Activities* are available from Drache Aptowitzer LLP, 226 Maclaren Street, Ottawa, Ontario K2P 0L6. T: 613.237.3300. F: 613.237.2786. Email adamapt@drache.com

resources to non-partisan public policy dialogue and development activities (PPDDAs), so long as these further their charitable purposes.[102] (In the past, a charity could not devote more than 10% of its resources to non-partisan political activities).

Public policy dialogue, as defined by the Canada Revenue Agency,[103] may include: providing information in order to inform or persuade the public in regards to public policy; disseminating researched opinions; engaging in advocacy to keep or change a law, policy, or decision of any level of government; mobilizing public support for, or opposition to, a particular law, policy, or decision of any level of government; making representation to elected official, public officials, parliamentary committees, political parties, and candidates; providing forums, convening conferences, and communicating via social media.

Public policy dialogue by charities, as defined by the Canada Revenue Agency, also includes the conduct of research into public policy, the distribution of such research, and discussion of such research with the media and others as the charity see fit.[104]

DO SOMETHING!

If you are a member of a parliament, legislature, or municipal council:

- Constantly review legislation governing donations to political parties, candidates, election campaigns, and movement organizations to encourage an increase in such investments without sacrificing transparency or safeguards against misuse
- Constantly review legislation governing the definition, organization, and financing of charities to facilitate increased investments in charitable activities without sacrificing transparency or accountability

102 Canada uses a common law definition of "charitable purposes": namely, purposes that fall within the four "heads" of charity, i.e., the relief of poverty, the advancement of education, the advancement of religion, or other purposes that benefit the community in a way the courts have ruled to be charitable.
103 Public-policy dialogue and development activities by charities, CG-027, January 21, 2019. https://www.canada.ca/en/revenue-agency/services/charities-giving/charities/policies-guidance/public-policy-dialogue-development-activities.html.
104 Note that to advance education as a charitable purpose, a charity's research must meet the criteria in Policy statement CPS-029, Research as a charitable activity.

The broadening of what registered charities can do in the area of public-policy dialogue vastly increases the capacity of such entities to contribute to the strengthening of democracy if they so choose, provided they do not abuse the prohibition against employing such dialogue for narrow, partisan purposes.

This broadening of what Canadian charities are now allowed to do in the area of public policy dialogue has significant implications for hundreds of Canadian charities and for the future conduct of public policy discourse in Canada. As charity lawyer Adam Aptowitzer points out[105], these rule changes tend to disadvantage conservative-oriented charities and favor left-of-centre charities, the latter being more numerous and more committed to public-policy dialogue and advocacy in such areas as education, health, poverty alleviation, and environmental protection, all clearly recognized in law as charitable heads.

Since advancement of religion is also recognized as a charitable head, social conservative advocacy may be less restricted by the new rules, but public-policy dialogue on such subjects as pipelines, trade, and the reduction of deficits, debts, and taxes can only be conducted as a charitable activity, under the current rules, on the basis of research being done on these subjects.

In the light of the continued need for reform of Canada's laws governing charitable giving, Aptowitzer has suggested that there would be merit in establishing a special charity[106] dedicated to improving the effectiveness and efficiency of other charities, especially those more devoted to public-policy dialogue and advocacy on conservative themes or from a conservative perspective.

In time, such a charity might become both a source of research and advocacy for more substantive changes in the allowable functions and governance of charities, such as:

- Separating the regulation of charities from the Canada Revenue Agency and putting that function into the hands of a completely independent agency with no conflict of interest.[107]

105 Ibid.
106 For more on this proposal contact Adam Aptowitzer at Drache Aptowitzer LLP 226 Maclaren Street, Ottawa, Ontario K2P 0L6. T: 613.237.3300 F: 613.237. 2786
107 In that the main function of the Canada Revenue Agency is to secure revenues for the government of Canada, and the granting of tax-deductibility status to

- Championing further reforms designed to increase and enhance the effectiveness of charitable giving, such as those advocated by long time charity reformers such as Donald K. Johnson.[108]
- Exploring a more positive and proactive role for the provinces in enhancing charitable activity and giving, in that ss. 7 of section 92 of the BNA Act puts "the establishment, maintenance, and management of hospitals, asylums, charities, and eleemosynary[109] institutions" under provincial jurisdiction.
- Exploring and promoting alternative ways of encouraging vastly increased investment in areas currently designated as charitable, such as reforms to corporate, charity, and tax laws to permit the earning of a limited but reasonable return on capital invested in social enterprises offering services in these areas.

DO SOMETHING!

If you are a board member, executive, or supporter of a conservative movement organization organized as a charity:

- Acquaint yourself and your organization with recent changes in charity law
- Plan to become more active and effective in the public policy dialogue which these changes facilitate
- Evaluate and support proposals to create a conservative support group to assist in the above

donations to Canadian charities reduces government revenues, it may be argued that the CRA has an inherent conflict of interest in performing both functions.

108 Donald K. Johnson is a generous Canadian philanthropist and an indefatigable crusader for measures to improve the financing capabilities of Canadian charities. In particular, he has lobbied the federal government to remove tax barriers for gifts of publicly-listed securities to registered charities. Successes include getting the government, in 1997, to cut the capital-gains tax for such gifts in half, and then to eliminate the tax entirely in 2006. He may be contacted at don.johnson@bmo.com

109 Eleemosynary means "of or related to alms, charity, or charitable donations; charitable."

If you are an executive or a researcher with a conservative-oriented charity:

- Acquaint yourself with the recent changes to charity and tax law and seek to take full advantage of them in conducting public-policy dialogues
- Consider supporting the creation of the Special Charity described above, to improve the effectiveness and efficiency of other conservative oriented charities

If you are an elected conservative in a position to propose and champion amendments to the laws and regulations governing charities:

- Advocate the development and promotion of a charity-law reform plank for your party's platform
- Consider supporting the creation of the Special Charity described above, to improve the effectiveness and efficiency of other conservative-oriented charities.

Investing in social enterprises

Besides constantly reviewing and amending charity law to facilitate an expansion of the service and financing capabilities of charities, legislative initiatives are required to expand the service and financing capabilities of social enterprises.

The term "social enterprise"[110] is used to refer to business ventures operated by non-profits, whether they are societies, charities, co-operatives, or corporations with a social purpose. These enterprises sell goods or provide services in the market for the purpose of creating a blended return on investment, both financial and social. Their profits may be divided between providing a modest (but not a maximum) financial

110 For samples of Canadian social enterprises see the SEontario website, a community-driven showcase of social enterprise and the social economy in Ontario https://seontario.org/directory/. For the case history of an Alberta social enterprise, Spruceland Developments Ltd., with which the author was involved as a founder and executive, see Appendix 3.

return to the suppliers of social capital and reinvesting in the enterprise for the attainment of a social purpose.

Democrats of all stripes have a vested interest in facilitating the creation and operation of social enterprises in that much of the work required to strengthen democratic infrastructure (a social objective) could be carried out by such enterprises if they were better financed.

Conservatives, in particular, should be in the forefront of facilitating the formation, operation and financing of social enterprises, including permitting them to earn a return on social capital invested even though they may be organized as charities, since these are also the kind of enterprises needed to provide cost effective and socially responsible private-sector based health, education, and social assistance services in parallel with those of the publicly-funded welfare state.

DO SOMETHING!

If you are a legislator, be in the forefront of initiating and supporting the review and improvement of:

- Legislation governing donations to political parties, candidates, election campaigns and movement organizations to encourage an increase in such investments without sacrificing transparency, accountability, and independence
- Legislation governing the definition, organization, and financing of charities and social enterprises to encourage an increase in investments in political movement organizations dedicated to the social objective of strengthening democracy

Crowdsourcing initiatives

Crowdsourcing or crowdfunding is defined as "the practice of funding a project or venture by raising small amounts of money from a large number of people via the Internet."[111]

---

111 For example, the crowdsourcing campaign to raise money for the victims of the Humboldt Broncos tragedy raised more than $15 million, over a very short time

With the expansion of the Internet, the creation of vast databases easily accessible by political fundraisers, and the development of algorithms and data mining techniques for identifying and targeting prospective donors with those messages most likely to generate a positive response, the goal of raising vast sums of money for political purposes by securing "small amounts from large numbers of people" has become eminently achievable.

While the political parties primarily employ crowdsourcing to fund party operations and election campaigns, small-d democrats, issue campaigners, and movement organizations can use crowdsourcing to fund a host of projects designed to achieve democratic reforms and strengthen democratic discourse, and movement conservatives can use crowdsourcing to finance the intellectual capital, human resources, and broader relationship-building required to generate genuine, principled, electoral and governing success.

DO SOMETHING!

If you are an executive or manager of a conservative oriented movement organization:

- Initiate and support efforts to develop a crowd sourcing capability

If you are a conservative oriented political supporter:

- Respond positively to crowdsourcing appeals in support of conservative organizations and initiatives

period, from 140,000 donors at an average contribution of around $107 per donor. A further example: retired army colonel Lee Hammond of Vancouver set up a GoFundMe account with a goal of raising $50,000 to help finance the legal defense of Admiral Mark Norman who was unfairly (in Colonel Hammond's opinion) accused of serious wrongdoing by the Government of Canada. See https://nationalpost.com/news/canada/retired-army-officer-sets-up-legal-defence-fund-for-fired-vice-admiral-mark-norman

Investing in political clubs

It is worth reflecting on the fact that political parties in England evolved out of the old "political clubs" which were much less structured and controlled than the modern political party. While the party structures proved to be much more efficient in fielding candidates and winning election campaigns, could it be that something important was lost with the demise of the clubs, such as, the informal and more cordial relationships which they fostered among politicos and the more open exchanges of ideas that occurred in the club environment?

Could it be that a modest revival of the political club concept might be a benefit and a complement to the party system? Might not a modest revival of the political club concept be an idea well worth considering as a benefit to democracy as well?

Many years ago, I was thinking along these lines on a political trip to London, England, when Ian Todd, my long-time associate and I paid a quick visit to the Reform Club. I liked its name and its history, the club having been founded in 1836 by members of the British parliament dedicated to the passage of the Reform Act of 1832. It was that act which dramatically broadened the voting rights of the people of England and Wales and corrected various abuses of the electoral system. The portrait of William Ewart Gladstone, four times British Prime Minister, four times Chancellor of the Exchequer, and one of my political heroes, hung on one of its walls. And as I vaguely remember, the club even had a copy of a letter from the fiscally-conservative Gladstone, protesting the high cost of his club membership.

I've often thought it would be a great idea to have a Reform Club in our nation's capital. Membership might be focused on elected and unelected persons who have advocated and supported democratic reforms and wish to meet together to socialize and advance those reforms. On the more partisan level, there would also be merit in encouraging those who consistently and substantially invest time and money in conservative movement organizations and conservative-oriented political parties to get together periodically on their own to:

- Receive and analyze reports on the state of the movement and the parties and the successes and failures experienced over the previous year.
- Receive and analyze summary reports on what has been invested in the movement and the parties over the previous year.

- Discuss ways and means of increasing the size of the political capital pool and improving the political returns on their investments, and suggestions for improvement to be passed on to movement and party leaders.

In other words, would there not also be merit in encouraging the formation and operation of Conservative Investor Clubs?

DO SOMETHING!

If you are a small d democrat interested in promoting democratic reforms:

- Consider promoting and investing in a Reform Club in Ottawa and/or your provincial capital

If you are a conservative oriented individual, corporation, or foundation interested in strengthening the movement financially:

- Initiate the formation of a "Conservative Investment Club" in your area and among your acquaintants
- Perhaps begin with the formation of a conservative book club or social club but eventually add the discussion and operationalizing of conservative investments to its agenda

Investing in people

As previously mentioned, in an effort to ensure that the wealthiest segments of society do not control the democratic process through their financial support, election and party financing laws and regulations have been enacted which make substantive donations by individuals, foundations, or companies in individual candidates, parties, or leaders virtually impossible. Almost the only way left to raise the larger amounts of money still required to run national, provincial, or municipal election campaigns is to raise small amounts of money from large numbers of people. This is a commendable, pro-democracy development.

Having said this, there are fewer restrictions on investing larger amounts of money in the less-partisan components of the democratic system, the think tanks, political education programs, advocacy groups, and issue campaigns. The recent changes in the laws governing charitable donations further expand the opportunities to invest in non-partisan political research and advocacy. And the opportunities to invest upstream of the partisan electoral arena in the development of individuals with political potential and ambition is the least restricted of all.

Some examples:

A publicly-spirited company of my acquaintance once offered a promising young lawyer with political ambitions and abilities a vice-presidential position with their company which enabled him to spend the majority of his time developing political contacts, refining his political ideas, and building a political organization. He later became the premier of his province, and contrary to what might have been expected, the company never abused its position as his founding benefactor. Its support was a genuine effort to simply address the political needs of the province and most of it was initially provided in the form of financial and organizational support upstream from and outside the formal political arena.

Another individual of my acquaintance with both ability and ambition aspired to become a member of parliament. But he wisely wished to get some advanced training in communications and public-policy making before seeking office. At the time, I was meeting with a donor capable of making a large donation to our party, but restricted from doing so by the election and party financing laws. I happened to mention the young man in question, and said that in my judgment he would someday make an excellent member of parliament, but that the graduate-school training he required and was seeking would cost many thousands of dollars which he did not have.

The donor asked to meet the individual in question, did so, and, suitably impressed, financed his attendance at graduate school. The young man eventually did become a member of parliament and put this investment in his advanced training, provided on a private basis entirely outside the party and electoral system, to good public use.

I know a family, let us call them the Smiths, the patriarch of which is politically astute and the younger members of which are highly-educated and very talented. At a lunch one day with the family, I put forward the idea that their family had benefited much from their business success in the province, that they were very knowledgeable and talented, that they were in a position to give back politically, and that one of their younger members should run for the legislature with the backing and support of the rest of the family. The suggestion was well-received and a lively discussion ensued as to which member of the family could and should serve their province in this way. I expect that one day there will be a Smith in the legislature and cabinet of that province.

Political movement organizations such as think tanks and advocacy groups often have internship programs which give young people exposure to public policy making and political organization in the hopes that they may pursue political service in some form themselves. These internships require sponsors, and I have found this to be one of the areas that substantial political investors find most attractive. All that is required is that applicants be identified, screened, and presented with their resume to a potential donor. The creation of a successful relationship between applicant and donor is facilitated if a third party proposes the financial arrangement between them and offers to provide the supervision and enrichment of the internship to make it mutually beneficial. Do this and *voila*, a talented and public-spirited young Canadian may well be on his or her way to a career of public political service.

The preceding examples need to be multiplied a hundred or a thousand-fold. This simply requires that the *Political Investment Portfolios* of individuals of means and private enterprises include provisions for making direct investments in developing the human resource components of political parties, movement organizations, municipal councils, legislatures, and parliaments. Does your *Political Investment Portfolio* include such a provision? Should it? Will it?

DO SOMETHING!

If you are an aspirant to political office conscious of your need for substantial preparation:

- Identify the type and cost of training that would adequately equip you

continued

- Prepare a one-page letter explaining your need and attach your resume
- Market your need to party/movement organizations who could assist in finding an investor
- Include a provision in your Political Investment Portfolio for Human Resource Development
- Advise party or movement organizations of your interest in sponsoring aspiring politicos who want to improve
- Review the applicants for assistance which they provide to you and make a supportive investment decision

Volunteering: investing our time

Many Canadians do not have the resources to make substantial financial donations to political organizations and causes, but most of us could donate our time on a volunteer basis to such organizations and causes if we believed them important.

As Canada's population ages and large numbers of us enter our retirement years, there is a huge and ever growing pool of people with experience and skills in a host of areas that could be employed on a volunteer basis to strengthen democracy and whatever political party or cause we choose to support. By all means, let us have our bucket lists to spend time with family and friends, to travel, to paint, to write, to visit, to golf, to fish, to engage in social service, or whatever. But is it too much to request that our bucket list include doing something, on a volunteer basis, to strengthen democracy and a free-market economy?

On the democracy front, there are numerous of organizations in Canada (see Appendix 1 for a partial list) that work to strengthen our democratic institutions and processes. All of them need more members, supporters, donors, and spokespersons. But all of them also need administrative personnel (from receptionists and meeting/conference organizers to communications, legal, and accounting support), positions which could be filled, at least in part, by skilled and enthusiastic volunteers. Could you be one? Will you be one?

DO SOMETHING!

- Compile and scrutinize a list (search the Internet or review Appendix 1) of organizations involved in strengthening Canadian democracy in your are
- Offer your services as a volunteer to the one whose objectives and leadership most appeals to you

On the conservative front, there are dozens of organizations in Canada (see Appendix 2 for a partial list) that work to create and strengthen the political conditions necessary to maintain and strengthen a free-market economy and/or to achieve conservative-oriented governments. These include the conservative political parties but they also include many conservative movement organizations, as well: think tanks, advocacy groups, PACs, and communications vehicles. All of them, too, need more members, supporters, donors, and spokespersons. But all of them also need administrative and organizational personnel who could be drawn, at least in part, from the ranks of skilled and enthusiastic volunteers. Could you be one? Will you be one?

DO SOMETHING!

- Compile and scrutinize a list (search the Internet or review Appendix 2) of conservative party or movement organizations in your area
- Offer your services as a volunteer at the one whose objectives and leadership most appeals to you

Of course, to make greater and better use of volunteers, conservative party and movement organizations need to improve their willingness and capacity to do so. This may involve providing better volunteer recruitment, training, and management procedures, especially for movement organizations which sometimes give the impression that they consider volunteers more trouble than they are worth.[112]

112 More on how to do so in Part 3: Human Resources Development.

The benefit of building a stronger volunteer sector for the conservative movement is more than simply getting more work done at lower cost. It is broadening the scope and reach of the movement by actively involving more people.

DO SOMETHING!

If you are an executive or manager of a conservative party or movement organization:

- Make volunteer recruitment a priority
- Provide quality training for the volunteers you recruit
- Recognize that volunteer management is a special skill
- Ensure that the management of your volunteers is assigned to someone who possesses that special skill

My own experience with political volunteers has impressed upon me the fact that it takes a very special person with special skills to effectively manage political volunteers so that they find enjoyment and fulfillment in their volunteer work, while effectively meeting the needs of the organization. On the other hand, mismanaging volunteers can do a great deal of harm, both to the organization itself and to its support base.

As the Reform candidate for parliament in Calgary Southwest, I was blessed with a campaign manager, Harry Robinson, who was a genius at assembling and managing political volunteers. Harry came from the United States where he had obtained his degrees in education and did his military service as a U.S. Marine. He and his wife Ruth moved to Calgary where he eventually became the highly-respected principal of Western Canada High School, one of the city's oldest and most prestigious high schools.

Harry had never done grassroots politics before but for some reason, when he retired, he became attracted to the Reform effort and volunteered to be the unpaid constituency campaign manager for the leader of a fledgling political party with no track record, limited resources, and fierce, deep-pocketed opponents.

When Harry started, we had only a few dozen volunteers in Calgary Southwest. But by the time the 1993 and 1997 elections rolled around, he had assembled a volunteer army of over 1,000 persons, not just names on a list, but skilled and motivated people who could do everything from organizing meetings and knocking on doors to fundraising and get-out-the-vote activities, and everything in between. What made Harry so successful were two things: his use of humor—he made political organizing and campaigning fun for everyone involved—and his leadership by example.

To campaign effectively in Calgary Southwest, we needed door knockers, hundreds of them, and Harry duly noted that many political volunteers are somewhat afraid of door knocking, especially if they have never done it before and were representing a new party that most people had never even heard about. So Harry, with the help of a group of students from a technical school, produced a short video on "how to door knock." In it, he presented various scenarios depicting what might happen at the doors and how to handle various eventualities. The whole presentation was hilarious.

In one scene, the door opened and a pit bull rushed out threatening the door-knocking volunteer and the candidate (played by Harry). What to do? In the video Harry climbs up a tree. The volunteer suggests shooting the dog but Harry strongly intervenes, saying that this would be an inappropriate response which would lose us the dog lovers' vote and recommending a more peaceful approach. In the next scene, the door is opened to reveal a "scantily clad elector" who immediately and enticingly invites the candidate (again played by Harry) to "come on in." In this case, Harry earnestly explains that it is the solemn duty of the door knocker to prevent the candidate from entering and getting into any kind of compromising situation whatsoever. And so on. The video contained much practical advice, but Harry's main point was that whatever happened, a well-prepared volunteer could handle it. The video was so entertaining that we had people coming to the campaign office and coffee parties just to see it, and Harry would then rope them into active volunteer service.

Harry also led by example. On one occasion, we held a meeting of the national executive of the party in Calgary and Harry happened to be present. As invariably happened, one of the main items on the agenda was how to increase party memberships since this was our principal source of volunteers and money. We broke off the meeting to go to lunch at a nearby restaurant, still discussing the membership recruitment issue, and Harry came along. Harry could never stand long, boring discussions. He claimed they killed enthusiasm and chased away volunteers, so he soon left the lunch table. Fifteen minutes later he came back and threw onto the table membership applications plus cash from the sale of eight new Reform memberships. While the executive had been discussing the subject of membership sales, Harry had gone off and sold two Reform memberships to the owner of the restaurant and his wife, two to the cooks in the kitchen, and four to some unsuspecting but open-minded diners at other tables in the restaurant.

Make it fun and lead by example, and if one can find a volunteer manager with such capabilities, the sky's the limit as to what can be accomplished to grow and effectively utilize a volunteer base.

Invest, invest, invest

If democracy, including the freedoms and responsibilities it represents, means anything to you, invest in democracy, financially if you can but, if not financially, at least invest your interest and your time. Invest, if not in for the benefit of your generation, for the benefit of generations to come.

Invest in measures and actions to record and learn from the lessons of our democratic past, to equip our democratic institutions and processes to meet the demands of the future, to redefine political space for millennials, to make citizen-directed democracy more competitive with state-directed governance, and invest in participants in our democratic processes and institutions who will bring character and trustworthiness to elections and elected assemblies.

And if principled conservatism, including the freedoms and responsibilities it represents, means something to you, then invest in conservatism. Invest in conservative-oriented political parties and the movement organizations that undergird them, in measures to record and learn from the history of conservatism, and in measures to make conservatism relevant to next-generation Canadians and new Canadians.

Let me be clear that none of the preceding proposals for increasing political investment in the conservative movement and other components of the political system are intended to divert political investments away from the political parties, their election campaigns, or the campaigns of individual candidates. Rather, my aim is to vastly increase the total investment in the development of political ideas, human resources, and the other organizational components necessary to strengthen Canada's democratic system and the ability of conservative-oriented parties to serve more effectively within that system.

DO SOMETHING!

- Invest in democracy
- Invest in conservatism

PART 2

DEVELOP INTELLECTUAL CAPITAL

Contemporary partisan political organizations, from constituency organizations to political parties, have become mainly marketing organizations for fighting elections. They have neither the time nor the resources for rethinking and refining basic principles, generating substantive, forward-looking ideas and policies, or producing up-to-date educational and training materials to equip their people to perform at the highest levels of excellence.

As Henry Kissinger observed in his memoir *The White House Years*, politicians in high office are consumers not generators of intellectual capital.[113] They are largely dependent on others, the civil service if they are a governing party, and movement organizations if they are in opposition, to generate intellectual capital for them.

While political parties are unable to generate adequate intellectual capital in support of their own partisan activities, they certainly have neither the time nor the resources to develop the intellectual capital required to support and advance democracy generally, that is, the refinement and restatement of basic democratic principles, the generation of ideas to assist democracy to adapt to changing conditions, and the preparation of training materials for small-d democrats whatever their partisan ideological orientation.

So what are the principal areas in which the intellectual capital of democrats and conservatives need to be replenished and increased? And who is going to finance and generate the development of such capital?

---

113 Kissinger, Henry, *White House Years*, Simon & Schuster, 2011, p.54.

With these questions in mind, the next five chapters will address the need to *Do Something!* to:

- Refresh traditional positions
- Cultivate new ground
- Strengthen relations with the science community
- Build the policy bank
- Invest in ideas.

2.1 Refresh Traditional Positions

Even fundamental concepts and excellent ideas can begin to lose their lustre and appeal with the passage of time. Unfortunately, this is true even of as important and valuable a concept and idea as democracy itself. In the western world people have heard democracy and democratic freedoms described and invoked so often, sometimes inappropriately or even deceptively, that the words associated with these concepts have lost much of their ability to inspire and motivate.

So what can be done to refresh our notion of democracy, particularly among next-generation Canadians who might generally consider any treatise, speech, blog, or tweet on democracy of little interest?

To answer this question, a more fulsome exploration and discussion is necessary and would be beyond the scope of this book. However, I have three positive suggestions which may be steps in the right direction: tell the democracy story, hold more frequent public referenda on key issues, and strongly encourage our political parties to refresh periodically themselves and their positions.

The democracy story

Democracy can be presented as a concept described in terms of principles, institutions, and practices. But it can also be described by simply telling its story, as it is one of the most fascinating and inspiring stories in the history of civilization. From its extraordinary birth in ancient Greece, through its long and painful exile in Europe when it was opposed and rejected by monarchies, aristocracies, and theocracies, to eventually finding a home in the hearts and minds of the common people of France and the British Isles, to experimentation, institutionalization, and refinement in the political arenas of Great Britain, Europe, and America, to triumphing over fascism and communism in the twentieth-century, to joining hands with growing numbers of democrats in Africa, South America, and Asia, to facing the daunting challenges of the twenty-first century and the age of social media. What a story! A story full of tragedy, failures and disappointments, but also triumphs and successes inspiring faith and hope for the future.

Telling the democracy story through literature, theatre, and music is perhaps the best way to introduce democracy to children and rekindle the enthusiasms of adults, too, especially those whose appetite for democracy has become jaded by the ravages of time and the familiarity that all too often breeds contempt.[114]

DO SOMETHING!

- If you are a parent or grandparent, learn and tell the democracy story to your children and grandchildren
- If you are a teacher or educational administrator, make sure your curriculum includes the democracy story
- If you are a gifted storyteller yourself, learn the democracy story and experiment with new and better ways of communicating it

Referenda campaigns

Most jurisdictions in Canada, federal, provincial, territorial, and most municipalities, have elections every four years. Would not our interest and enthusiasm for voting, one of the key democratic functions performed by citizens, be strengthened if we had more meaningful opportunities to do so?

I am talking about providing more opportunities for Canadians to vote, not just for the purpose of electing our representatives to democratic assemblies, but to express our opinions on other issues of real concern and interest through more public referenda. Referendum campaigns, conducted more frequently on key public issues, can perform

---

114 For an abbreviated version of the Democracy Story, see Part V, chapter 5.6.

a valuable educational function with respect to such issues, thereby refreshing the content of democratic discourse.

Critics will argue that too many referenda could have the opposite effect.[115] But, at the federal level, at least, Canada has hardly been overdosing on referenda.[116] Amendments to election laws enabling a referendum to be held only if a sufficient number of citizens petition for it, limiting the number of referenda that can be held during any election cycle, and providing for referenda to be held simultaneously with election balloting when appropriate, would be well worth enacting.[117]

DO SOMETHING!

- If you are a Canadian citizen and voter, urge the political parties and your elected representatives to amend election legislation to facilitate the greater use of referenda to secure public input and involvement in decisions on key issues

continued

115 Switzerland has had more experience with referenda than most other countries (traditionally two or three a year). The highest voter turnouts (up to 86%) have tended to be in relation to matters directly affecting individuals (property taxes, salaries of federal civil servants, social benefits, military training, and emergency economic measures.) https://docs.google.com/spreadsheets/d/1E-1J43WRE3p3zxPoLlZi4WfmyJkx5NCJAOF2reiLyVM/edit?usp=sharing

116 The three referenda initiated by the federal government were the 1898 Prohibition referendum, the 1942 Conscription referendum, and the 1992 referendum on the Charlottetown Constitutional Accord. Examples of key provincial referenda include the 1948 referenda (two of them) in Newfoundland on whether or not Newfoundland should join Confederation; the 1948 plebiscite held in Alberta (in conjunction with the provincial election) on public or private ownership of the electricity sector; the 1980 and 1995 Quebec referenda on sovereignty association; and the more recent referenda in B.C. on sales tax changes (2011) and electoral system reform (2018).

117 B.C.'s Referendum Act [RSBC 1996] Chapter 400, enables the government to order a referendum by regulation or legislation as in the case of the 2018 referendum on changing B.C.'s electoral laws. See ELECTORAL REFORM REFERENDUM 2018 ACT [SBC 2017] CHAPTER 22; http://www.bclaws.ca/civix/document/id/complete/statreg/17022_01#section2. B.C.'s Recall and Initiative Act [RSBC 1996] Chapter 398 requires 10% of the registered voters in each of the provinces electoral districts to sign an initiative petition in order for a referendum to be held. To date (2019) there have been eleven citizen attempts to initiate a referendum, only one which succeeded (resulting in the 2010 referendum to end the Harmonized Sales Tax.)

- If you are a legislator, or a member or executive of a think tank or advocacy group, with an interest in refreshing democracy, advocate for the provision of referendum legislation and for the more frequent use of referenda

Refresh the party positions

Political parties are one of the principal components of our democratic system. If political parties were abolished in Canada today, they would reappear in another form tomorrow because of the majoritarian nature of democracy. To win an election, you need to get the support of at least a plurality, if not a majority, of voters. To pass any measure in a democratic assembly, you need to get majority support for it. In order to get that support, electorally or in a legislature, people who share certain common values and objectives need to cooperate and work together in some manner. When they do so, once, twice, half a dozen times and more, you have the beginnings of a party whether it is immediately recognized as such or not.

But as parties age and express their principles and policy positions time and time again in the same language and style, like democracy itself, they begin to lose any original lustre and inspirational appeal they might once have had. The refreshing of democracy should therefore include an effort by the parties to periodically refresh themselves and their traditional positions.

Refresh traditional conservative positions

Conservatives hold to a variety of policy positions which are as valid and valuable today as when they were first proclaimed. The difficulty in communicating and increasing support for these positions is that they, too, have been held and communicated in the same language and style for so long that they have lost much of their persuasiveness, especially with the younger generation.

So this is the challenge to be addressed by conservative think tanks, academics, policy-makers, politicians, and communicators: find new and better ways of describing and communicating such positions; periodically and systematically restate, reframe, reposition, or re-energize them so as to increase their clarity and persuasiveness.

Restate in positive language

Conservatives have traditionally expressed our commitment to reducing deficits, debts and taxes by calling for limited government and achieving balanced budgets by slashing expenditures and programs. Are there not more positive and appealing ways of stating these positions, such as calling for measures to grow the non-governmental sector and to increase the productivity of the public sector, rather than always stating these propositions in the negative?

In addressing public audiences on the theme of restoring fiscal prudence, an effective way to get the discussion off on the right foot is to define the objective as securing "more bang for your tax dollar," a positive objective. A conservative politico can then hold up a ten-dollar bill and ask: "In whose hand is this bill most productive, in your hand, to spend or invest as you choose, or in the hand of a politician or bureaucrat to spend or invest as they choose?"

In other words, restate the goal of fiscal prudence and the means of achieving it differently and positively rather than traditionally and negatively.[118]

Reframe

Refreshing key conservative positions to make them more attractive and persuasive with the general public usually involves changing the language in which those positions are expressed. But often what is more urgently required strategically is a wholesale change in the conceptual framework within which that position and the issues it addresses is debated. In other words, the issues need to be reframed so as to make the conservative solution more understandable, relevant, and persuasive.

118 An instructive American example of restating a policy objective in fresh and more attractive language was the renaming the legislation providing federal aid to education as the "no child left behind" bill.

When engaging in any political debate, you may often find yourself competing within a hostile conceptual framework defined primarily by your opponents (or often, in our day, by unsympathetic media whose biases favor the positions of your opponent). Under such circumstances, your chances of winning the debate are slim unless you can reframe the issue to the advantage of your cause. This usually involves directly challenging the old conceptual framework as inadequate and seeking to replace it with one in which your arguments and cause have a better chance of succeeding.

A classic illustration of this approach comes from one of the most effective issue campaigns ever conducted in the history of British parliamentary democracy, the campaign by William Wilberforce and his colleagues to abolish the slave trade and slavery itself within the British Empire.

When this campaign began, the abolitionists had little chance of swaying public opinion or winning the argument for abolition as long as slaves were primarily conceptualized as property. Within that framework, any debate on the pros and cons of slavery would be mainly focused on its economics, not its morality or inhumanity. In other words, on the financial benefits of sustaining slavery and the financial costs of limiting or abolishing it.

From the very outset of their campaign, abolitionists sought to shift the public and parliamentary perception of slaves from property, which could be bought, sold, used, and abused as economic objects, to human beings who deserved to be recognized, appreciated, and treated as such.

In our day, when income redistribution through progressive taxation is the conceptual framework that dominates any discussion on how to alleviate poverty and economic inequality in Canada, conservatives are at a disadvantage since liberals and social democrats largely hold that ground and insist on its efficacy despite the limited success of policies based upon it.

But if pursuing a better, wider, and deeper distribution of the tools of wealth creation (economic education, improved access to capital, markets, and technology) becomes the framework for discussing the alleviation of economic inequality and poverty, conservatives are in a much better position to win with that type of policy debate and to achieve better results.[119]

119 See chapter 2.2 for a more in depth discussion of the tools of wealth creation, and Appendix 3 for an example of their application.

Reposition

Why did the Canadian cross the road? To get to the middle.

We Canadians have a penchant for finding and favoring the middle. Football, soccer, and basketball games are divided into two parts, the first and second halves. But how is our national game, hockey, divided up? Into three periods. Why? So it will have a middle.

As Pierre Trudeau once observed, we Canadians are extreme moderates. We prefer the centre. We don't like the edges. They are too far from the middle. We're afraid of falling off the edges if we get too close to them.

What this means politically is that we Canadians dislike being confronted with stark choices. "Will it be A or will it be B? Choose one or the other." We hate making definitive choices like that because there's no middle ground.

We prefer the muddle of the middle to the clarity of choice. If we're forced into these stark choice situations, we're quite likely to invent a middle by saying, "Why can't we do both?"

What this penchant for favoring and finding the middle means in the framing and presentation of policy options for Canadians, is that you will find greater public support for your policy if it is perceived by the public as being the middle course between two extremes – and is rightly so – than if it is seen as too close to either of those extremes.

In Quebec, there have always been hard-line separatists who have advocated for the complete separation of Quebec from Canada. This position attracted limited public support as it was seen as too extreme a position. However, when Rene Levesque and his successors presented sovereignty-association as a political option, Quebecers responded much more positively. Why? Because sovereignty-association was seen by many, not as an extreme option, but as the middle ground between outright separation and status quo federalism.

A mixed economy with an appropriate balance between market forces and government regulation is more appealing to the majority of Canadians than the extremes of unrestricted free enterprise or a government-dominated economy because it is the middle option. So if conservatives want to see more freedom of choice in education and health care, better to call for a mixed social-services sector with more freedom of choice between public and private services, than to simply call for greater privatization of education and health care. This legitimately repositions freedom of choice in social services as the middle way rather than as some extreme right-wing option.[120]

Re-energize

Liberal governments and supporters in recent years have worked assiduously to convince Canadians that national unity is best maintained and strengthened by recognizing and championing diversity, emphasizing and celebrating the differences among Canadians rather than their commonalities. "Strength in diversity" has become the watchword. This redefinition of national identity began by declaring that Canada was a mosaic, not a melting pot, with the emphasis on the many and diverse pieces that distinguish a mosaic. Today the identity definition is that Canada is a rainbow coalition of many hues and colors, not a dull and boring single-color identity. Furthermore, we are encouraged to become cosmopolitan citizens of the world rather than nationalists drawing our identity from history, race, and place.[121]

Without denigrating the value of diversity, conservatives should be in the forefront of re-energizing an older, more fundamental, and equally valid approach to national identity and unity. What makes a mosaic more than a hodgepodge of diverse pieces of different colors and shapes is the common background to which those pieces are affixed, the glue that binds them together, and a unifying design.

Let others emphasize and champion the diversity of the pieces; let conservatives champion what we share in common and those personal characteristics that unite rather than divide us.

Re-emphasizing and re-energizing the communication of those commonalities and unifying characteristics means recognizing and celebrating our common interests in acceptance, freedom, opportunity, security, and unity, regardless of how diverse we may be geographically, ethnically, sexually, linguistically, or demographically.

---

120 More on this in Chapter 2.2, including advocacy of a balanced approach to climate change as a middle ground between denial and hysteria.

121 A prominent exponent of this view is Michael Ignatieff, in books written before his unsuccessful sojourn as leader of the federal Liberal party (2008–11). See Ignatieff, Michael, *Blood and Belonging: Journeys Into the New Nationalism,* Farrar, Straus, and Gioux, 1995

Re-energize freedom of trade

If there is one conservative economic policy position that desperately needs to be re-energized for the benefit of Canada and new generation Canadians, it is our commitment to freedom of trade both domestically and internationally.

At one time, of course, the Conservative Party of Sir John A. Macdonald was protectionist, champion of the National Policy (introduced in the 1879 budget) which built a tariff wall between Canada and the U.S. In those days it was the Reformers and Liberals who championed Free Trade.

Regionally, national protectionism crippled the Atlantic provinces whose economies were strongest when their primary trade links were with "the Boston States." Eventually, the West came to be an opponent of the federal tariff policy as well, because when combined with discriminatory freight rates, it resulted in the charge that, because of protectionism, "the West pays more for everything she buys and gets less for everything she sells."[122]

But fast forward 110 years, and the positions of the two federal parties were reversed, with the Progressive Conservative Party of Brian Mulroney championing the North American Free Trade Agreement (NAFTA) and the federal Liberals criticizing and opposing it. The West not only strongly supported Canada-U.S. free trade, but also made a concerted effort to secure greater freedom of trade domestically, for example, via the New West Partnership Trade Agreement (NWPTA) of 2010.[123]

Fast forward once again to the present and the North American Free Trade Agreement has recently been re-negotiated. This time, the U.S. negotiators have been led by a pit-bull protectionist with extensive business experience while Canada's negotiation team was led by a former drama teacher and a journalist, neither having any previous business or trade experience at all.

Meanwhile, in the west, the NWPTA is dead, its dispute settling mechanism unused, while British Columbia blocks the movement of prairie petroleum to tidewater, and Alberta and Saskatchewan are

---

122 This became a slogan of the western based Progressive Party of Canada and farmers' parties like the United Farmers of Alberta.

123 See www.newwestpartnershiptrade.ca/

understandably tempted to retaliate with protectionist measures of their own.

If ever there was a time for Canadians and conservatives in particular to take stock and decide where we stand on freedom of trade, this is it. Are we free traders or protectionists internationally? Are we free traders or protectionists domestically? Are we economic separatists or unionists? Are we narrow provincialists or broad nationalists? Are we Big Westerners or Little Westerners? Are we Big Canadians or Little Canadians?

This phrase "Big Westerners or Little Westerners" has a history that is particularly instructive.[124] One cold winter night, December 18, 1901, in Indian Head, Saskatchewan, an historic debate was held between Rodman Roblin, Premier of Manitoba when it was still the "postage stamp province,"[125] and F. W. G. Haultain, the last and greatest Premier of the Old Northwest Territory which at that time stretched from the Canadian shield to the Rockies and from the U.S. border to the Arctic Circle. The debate was attended by some 1,500 people who came by sleigh and horseback from miles and miles around despite the severity of the season and the weather.

Roblin supported the federal Liberal position, which was to carve the great northwest into several smaller provinces, each with its own legislature, government and laws. Haultain, whose writings and speeches on constitutional matters were of the same calibre as those of Macdonald and Laurier, vehemently opposed the subdivision of the northwest. What he advocated was retaining the northwest as One Big Province, with control over its own natural resources, and constitutional equality with Ontario and Quebec. Those who supported Roblin's position, Haultain styled as "Little Westerners." Those who supported his position he styled as "Big Westerners."

In the end, the federal Liberals under Laurier were able to impose their position and the northwest was carved up into three provinces and two territories, with the powers to practice provincial and territorial

124 Lingard, Charles Cecil, *Territorial Government in Canada: The Autonomy Question in the Old Northwest Territory,* University of Toronto Press, 1946. See also, MacEwan, Grant, *Frederick Haultain: Frontier Statesman of the Canadian Northwest,* Western Producer Prairie Books, 1985

125 Geographically, the boundaries of Manitoba did not initially extend all the way to Hudson Bay. It was much smaller than the present day Manitoba and was completely rectangular in shape, like a "postage stamp."

protectionism if they chose. But it is a renewed commitment to free trade, internationally and domestically, that in my judgment, holds the promise of a brighter economic future and maintains the economic union needed to firmly bind our political union together.

Should not conservatives be in the forefront of re-energizing our commitment to free trade? And if so, where are the business, labor, community, and political leaders who will *Do Something!* to make genuine free trade an international and domestic reality going forward?

DO SOMETHING!

If you are an executive or policy development manager with a think tank, political party, or movement organization:

- Make it part of your organization's schedule to periodically examine your most traditional and long-standing policy positions to identify those needing to be "refreshed"

If you are an academic or policy researcher with a think tank, political party, or movement organization:

- Alert yourself to the need to periodically refresh policy positions adopted in the past, including those which you may have originally helped to formulate
- Be in the forefront of calling for and assisting in the refreshing of those positions, particularly those that need to be reframed or repositioned
- Initiate the process of restating, reframing, repositioning, or re-energizing those positions

If you are a communications consultant or staffer with a think tank, political party, or movement organization:

- Alert yourself to the need to periodically refresh policy positions adopted in the past including those which you may have originally helped to communicate

continued

- Be in the forefront of calling for and assisting in the refreshing of those positions, particularly those that need to be restated or reenergized.

If you are a member of an interest group or party, a candidate for public office, or an elected official committed to key policy positions of your group or party:

- Be alert to recognize which of your positions are beginning to lose traction with the public or media through which they are being communicated
- Be on the forefront of calling for and assisting in the refreshing of those positions and in communicating the refreshed versions
- Give particular attention to the necessity of re-energizing a commitment to free trade, internationally and domestically

2.2 Cultivate New Ground

The generation of intellectual capital for Canada's political class and institutions must include the generation of new and innovative ideas and policies. These new and innovative ideas are needed to improve the performance of our democratic system and the capacities of our political parties to address the many problems and challenges facing our municipalities, territories, provinces, and nation.

While the development of such ideas and policies is beyond the scope of this book and the capabilities of this author, let me at least illustrate the kind of innovative intellectual capital development which I believe would be beneficial to our democracy and politics. By "new" I do not mean the ideas discussed hereafter have never been thought of before. However, their actual adoption and implementation in the political arena would be something new and different from past practices and positions.

Cultivating new democratic ground

The implementation of such ideas as: teaching democracy by telling its story; making more frequent and creative use of referenda; and restating, reframing, repositioning, and re-energizing the traditional positions of political parties would put us well on the path to cultivating new democratic ground. In addition, so will:

- Developing a "Model Parliament for Canada" as a permanent and well-equipped working laboratory for experimenting with improvements to parliamentary processes, and providing advanced training for democratic representatives.[126]

---

126 Named *Democracy House, and* described and discussed in detail in chapter 3.5.

- Responsibly utilizing the internet, social media, data mining, and psychometric profiling to improve democratic processes.[127]

Allow me to also suggest three additional measures for increasing and improving democratic participation: rewarding democratic innovation, providing financial incentives for democratic participation, and more strongly supporting student voting.

An XPRIZE for democratic innovation

Organizations like the XPRIZE Foundation[128] design and manage public competitions intended to elicit and encourage beneficial innovations in a host of areas: human interconnectedness, environmental protection, and artificial intelligence, to name only a few. Anyone anywhere can enter and the financial rewards for submitting a winning innovation are substantial.

A recent (April 2018) story carried by the BBC and entitled "Solving the world's problems one prize at a time,"[129] described the expansion of the XPRIZE concept as follows:

> Besides well-publicized prizes staged by XPRIZE and NESTA (the National Endowment for Science Technology and the Arts), private companies such as Amazon and Netflix now set technical challenges, and a number of websites specialize in connecting problems that need to be solved with solvers interested in a cash reward.
>
> Cliff Edwards, who describes himself as an "open innovation solver," earns his living by submitting ideas to a website called InnoCentive, where he is ranked the most successful solver. Working out of coffee shops in Vancouver, Edwards has pitched ideas for everything from market strategies to utilize 5G bandwidth to ways to reassemble someone's skull after brain surgery.

So how about an XPRIZE for innovative ideas on how to improve the performance of our democratic institutions and practices?

---

127 Described and discussed in detail in chapter 4.3.
128 See https://www.xprize.org/
129 http://www.bbc.co.uk/news/stories-43787457

DO SOMETHING!

If you are a high net-worth individual or executive of a charitable foundation or corporation with an interest in supporting democratic innovation:

- Become the sponsor and organizer of the first XPRIZE for Democracy in Canada
- Share the results with interest groups, election officials, and politicians, with interests in democratic innovation

Financial incentives for democratic participation

When I was the Member of Parliament for Calgary Southwest, I once held an informal discussion among my supporters as to how we might increase the voter turnout in elections. There was the usual debate as to whether fining people for failing to vote (as is done in Australia) would be helpful, the consensus being that we should be looking for positive rather than negative ways of incentivizing democratic participation. And then someone asked, what might happen if Elections Canada was authorized to offer a grant of $500,000 or more in support of some charitable project in each of the ten federal constituencies achieving the highest voter turnout (above some floor level of, say, 80%) in the next federal election?

Many details would have to be resolved to implement such an idea. How would the charitable project be selected in advance of the election? How would the election laws have to be amended to provide for such a grant and prevent abuses in its pursuit? How would such a grant be administered? And, most importantly, how do we overcome the resistance of those in the political arena and media whose initial reaction to any innovative idea is to give a hundred reasons why it couldn't possibly work and therefore shouldn't even be tried?

While recognizing the need to answer such questions, might not such an idea be worth experimenting with if we are really serious about trying to find new and positive ways of increasing citizen participation in democratic elections?[130]

130 This idea, of course, opens up the philosophical debate about our duty as citizens. Do not each and every one of us have a duty to vote as one of the rights and

DO SOMETHING!

If you are an elected member of a democratic assembly with particular interests in and responsibilities for democratic reform, or an executive of a political party:

- Draft a proposal along these lines to provide financial incentives for increasing voter turnout in elections
- Promote your proposal among your political colleagues and election administration authority
- Introduce legislation to permit such financial incentivizing of election participation on an experimental basis and evaluate the results

Encourage and expand Student Vote

A not-for-profit organization named Student Vote[131] has been quite successful in organizing trial votes among high school students in parallel with actual municipal, provincial, and federal elections and using the process to educate participants on the importance and practices of democratic participation. A study by Elections Canada[132] found that this has

responsibilities of citizenship, without having to be paid or otherwise rewarded for doing so?

131 See studentvote.ca. Student Vote Canada is a program of CIVIX, a non-partisan, nationally-registered charity dedicated to building the skills and habits of active and engaged citizenship among young Canadians. CIVIX envisions a strong and inclusive democracy where all young people are ready, willing, and able to participate. CIVIX was born through a merger between Operation Dialogue and Student Vote, two non-partisan organizations with a significant history of engaging Canadian youth.

132 https://www.elections.ca/content.aspx?section=res&dir=rec/part/svp...index... The Student Vote Evaluation was commissioned by Elections Canada to evaluate the effectiveness of the Student Vote Program (SVP) in achieving civic participation. See.http://www.elections.ca/content.aspx?section=res&dir=rec/part/svp&document=index&lang=e Also see the evaluation by Elevate Consulting at http://www.elections.ca/res/rec/part/svp/svp_e.pdf

had a positive impact on election participation by those students once they are eligible to vote in real elections.

And so might not the Student Vote concept be dramatically expanded? With the support of provincial education departments, school administrators, and elections authorities, why not give every high school student in the country at least one opportunity to participate in a Student Vote exercise prior to becoming eligible to vote in an actual municipal, provincial, or federal election? Public, partisan, and media support for this exercise would be enhanced if the results were to be officially tabulated, aggregated, and released as an indication of the direction in which the voters of the future are trending. Again, consideration might be given to offering a substantial cash prize in each province to the school obtaining the highest voter turnout in a specified Student Vote election.

DO SOMETHING!

If you are a teacher, school administrator, education minister, or an education department official with an interest in adding the Student Vote component to the educational curriculum of your jurisdiction:

- Familiarize yourself with the existing program and evaluations of it
- Prepare and implement a proposal for instituting Student Vote in every high school within your jurisdiction
- Provide, or solicit donations toward, a cash prize for the school in your jurisdiction obtaining the highest turnout in a specified Student Vote election

If you are a high net-worth individual or executive of a charitable foundation or corporation with an interest in supporting democratic innovation:

- Offer financial support to the Student Vote organization, including a cash prize for the school obtaining the highest turnout in a specified Student Vote election

Cultivating new conservative ground

Cultivating new political ground is not just the responsibility of small-d democrats across the political spectrum, it is also an imperative for democratic political parties and movement organizations if they wish to maintain their relevance under changing conditions and attract the interest and support of next-generation voters.

Again, by "new" I do not mean "never thought of before." I mean positions strongly embraced and implemented by a political party as an alternative or successor to past positions and practices.

Allow me to propose that conservatives, going forward, vigorously champion the following:

- A new birth of freedom in Canada, in particular, championing the fundamental freedoms of conscience, religion, thought, belief, opinion, expression, assembly, and association
- Freedom of choice (as previously mentioned) in a "mixed (public and private) social services sector," as the current institutions of the welfare state, lodged in and predominantly managed by the public sector, reach the point of diminishing returns.
- A better distribution, as previously mentioned, of the tools of wealth creation, as an alternative to addressing poverty and economic inequality solely through the redistribution of income via progressive taxation.
- The recognition and entrenchment of property rights in the Canadian constitution
- The emergence and development of the sharing economy
- The re-conceptualization and promotion of the responsible development of natural resources as foundation stones and fundamental components of the Canadian economy
- The organization of a TransCanada Corridor Coalition to secure national rights of way for transportation infrastructure to move inland natural resources to tidewater and world markets
- The promotion and adoption of market-based approaches to environmental conservation
- A proactive, balanced approach to the challenge of climate change

A new birth of freedom

The Canadian Charter of Rights and Freedoms declares that everyone in Canada is guaranteed freedom of conscience, religion, thought, belief, opinion, and expression, as well as freedom of the press, peaceful assembly, and association "subject only to such reasonable limits prescribed by law as can be demonstrably justified in a free and democratic society."[133]

Because the Charter was initiated by a Liberal Prime Minister, Pierre Elliott Trudeau, whose priority was the constitutional entrenchment of linguistic and cultural rights for Quebecers, and because the courts have tended to neglect and limit the protection of freedom of conscience and religion while championing and extending constitutional protection of minority rights not originally envisioned by the framers of the Charter, conservatives have tended to take a negative and critical view of the Charter.

What is most disturbing, however, is that in the absence of a strong and determined champion these "fundamental freedoms", as they are designated in the Charter, are increasingly threatened on two fronts:

- At the federal political level, where the current Trudeau administration, in its misguided and divisive pursuit of identity politics uses its promotion of "equality rights" to circumscribe and suppress the "fundamental freedoms" of conscience, religion, thought, belief, opinion, and expression[134]
- At the universities and other institutions of higher learning, where political correctness is running rampant and threatens to erode freedom of conscience, thought, and expression, the very heart of academic freedom itself, in the one place where one would

---

133 Canadian Charter of Rights and Freedoms, s. 2, Part I of the Constitution Act, 1982, being Schedule B to the Canada Act 1982 (UK), 1982, c. 11. See https://laws-lois.justice.gc.ca/eng/const/page-15.html

134 Examples include the Supreme Court's denial of the right of Trinity Western University to establish a law school in accordance with its religious convictions. See Trinity case summary https://canliiconnects.org/en/summaries/62326 and Trinity SCC decision https://www.canlii.org/en/ca/scc/doc/2018/2018scc32/2018scc32.html. Also note the discriminatory rejection by the federal government of applications by religious institutions for participation in the Canada Summer Jobs Program. See https://globalnews.ca/news/4732603/canada-summer-jobs-attestation-change/

think these freedoms would be most vigorously championed and protected.[135]

Surely the time is long overdue for conservatives to revise our approach to the Charter: to champion the recognition and guarantee of all those rights declared by the Charter, with particular attention to restoring recognition and respect for those fundamental freedoms upon which the maintenance of all other freedoms depends. Despite the reluctance of some jurists to acknowledge it, the word fundamental in our constitution must mean something—the dictionary defining it as "serving as a foundation or basis, as basic or underlying." Fundamental freedoms are the underlying foundation of all other rights and freedoms guaranteed by the Charter and need to be recognized, championed, and affirmed as such. In other words, if and when there is a conflict between the *fundamental* rights and freedoms and other rights and freedoms guaranteed by the charter, it is the fundamental rights and freedoms that should prevail.

A "new birth of freedom," led and championed by conservatives should be characterized by an insistence that genuine freedom is *indivisible* and that it is undesirable, inconsistent, and unconstitutional, to protect and advance some freedoms while denying others. Such a selective and self-serving approach to freedom as practiced by the current Trudeau administration and by other administrations in the past is ultimately discriminatory and a threat to the freedoms of all.

Any new birth of freedom must also be characterized by a renewed acceptance of responsibility. Responsibility for the consequences of exercising our freedoms and a willingness to subject that exercise to evaluation and judgment on the basis of ethical criteria. In other words, no exercise of freedom should be exempt from ethical evaluation or divorced from the acceptance of responsibility for its consequences. A new birth of freedom must be accompanied by a new birth of accountability without which freedom eventually degenerates into license and freedom-destroying anarchy.

At the federal political level, the championing of a new birth of freedom should occupy a prominent place in the election platform

135 A championing of fundamental freedoms on a contemporary university campus in Canada means challenging the granting of privilege to individuals based on racial, cultural, religious, or gender factors. At present, many university administrations are actually engaging in this type of behavior, such as discriminating between tenured and non-tenured staff.

of the Conservative Party of Canada, and its pursuit should be a matter of high priority for any conservative government.

At the university level, conservatives should rally to the support of those, such as University of Toronto professor Jordan Peterson[136] who are seeking to champion that new birth of freedom within the institutions of which they are part. For example, since most universities are established under statutes passed by provincial legislatures, it is within the power of those legislatures to amend those statutes to more explicitly require universities to respect freedom of conscience, thought, and expression in practice and not just in theory, to acknowledge and deal with alleged violations of such freedoms, and to report annually to the public on their efforts to do so.

Because freedom is ultimately indivisible, a new birth of freedom focused initially on championing the fundamental freedoms guaranteed by the Charter will also strengthen the pursuit of other freedoms discussed hereafter, facilitating a new birth of freedom of choice in health, education, and social services and a new birth of freedom in domestic and international trade.

In this regard, conservatives also need to be consistent in our defense and expansion of freedoms, in particular the freedom of Canadians from arbitrary and heavy-handed interventions in society by the state. In our desire to increase national and personal security, for example, we must be careful not to support the placement of extraordinary or arbitrary powers into the hands of police, customs officers, and counter-intelligence agencies, state actors whom we generally support while at the same time we call for a curtailment of the arbitrary exercise of monopolistic state powers in other areas such as the trade and social services sectors.

At the end of the day, the restoration and safeguarding of fundamental freedoms is in the interest of all Canadians and should be supported by all to whom freedom is supremely important, particularly if we wish to pass the benefits and responsibilities of a truly free society on to the next generation.

136 Peterson, Jordan, *12 Rules of Life: An Antidote to Chaos*, Toronto, Penguin Random House Canada, 2018.

DO SOMETHING!

If you are an executive, researcher, or communicator with a think tank, interest group, or political party, with expertise, interest in, and a commitment to protecting and expanding the exercise of the fundamental freedoms in Canada:

- Develop your own freedom-enhancing policy suggestions and make your own policy contributions to a new birth of freedom in Canada
- Develop, communicate, and support efforts to commit conservative parties, caucuses, and governments to a New Birth of Freedom policy

If you are an executive with a philanthropic foundation or company, or a major donor to policy development institutions, interest groups, and political parties who support this objective:

- Make a significant financial contribution to those working to achieve a new birth of freedom in Canada
- Withdraw your financial support from any organization seeking to constrain or privatize the exercise of fundamental freedoms.

If you are an executive, member, or supporter of any group, a religious or educational organization, a business, or service provider, whose fundamental freedoms are being constrained or limited:

- Provide your support to think tanks, interest groups, and political organizations working to protect and expand the exercise of fundamental freedoms in Canada

If you are a Canadian citizen and voter to who freedom really matters:

- Become a champion of "freedom indivisible" and an active supporter of those who seek to restore Canada's commitment to the fundamental freedoms of conscience, religion, thought, belief, opinion and expression

Freedom of choice in a mixed (public and private) social services sector

In Canada we have primarily assigned the provision of health care, childcare, education, social assistance, old-age assistance, eldercare, and other important social services to the public sector. These welfare state services, often organized as public monopolies or near monopolies, are then financed primarily through taxation.

But this aging model of how to meet social needs is reaching the point of diminishing returns. Fewer and fewer Canadians believe that further increasing the size and complexity of the bureaucratic welfare state, and further increasing taxes to finance it, will lead to a higher quality of life for themselves and their children. There is therefore a need for a new and better alternative to the monopolistic, bureaucratic, union-dominated, and taxpayer-dependent aspects of the welfare state. The challenge for conservatives is to provide it.

If conservatives are to become champions of a new birth of freedom, one of those freedoms which needs championing, because it has been denied or curtailed by liberal and socialist administrations is freedom of choice, in particular freedom of choice in education, health care, and other social services.

How can conservatives address this need? By offering and championing the concept of a mixed social services sector.

Such a sector would offer both public and private service options and freedom of choice for the users of these services. The financing of this mixed social services sector would also be mixed through a combination of taxes, user fees, public capital, and private investment. Facilitating legislation would also need to guarantee an adequate minimum standard of care for the sector, and universal access so that no Canadian would be denied access due to inability to pay.

Would there be intense opposition to a mixed system from reactionary elements among the leadership and membership of the public service unions? Of course. What major system innovation have those elements not opposed? But let that opposition be countered by appeals to the progressive elements of the public service unions and by state-supported efforts to assist those public-service workers desiring a place in the private social-service sector to gain both employment and equity positions therein.

What province might take the lead and be at the forefront of reforming the social-services sector along these lines? On the healthcare front, the two top candidates would likely be Quebec and Saskatchewan.

Saskatchewan, as the province which pioneered medicare in Canada, has the longest history of any province with universal healthcare coverage and could conceivably be the first to acquire the social license to pioneer the next iteration of healthcare service. In doing so, it would be following the path of the Scandinavian countries which were the first in Europe to adopt a universal healthcare system but for many years now have been expanding freedom of choice as a fundamental characteristic of their healthcare systems.

To quote but one observer of this shift, "over the past twenty years, the Scandinavian healthcare model has undergone major changes. . . Choice, once seen as an unnecessary trait of a market-based system (such as that of the United States), has now been introduced in all Scandinavian countries. This reflects, in part, the fact that the information age has also come to healthcare. Patients today are conscious and demanding consumers, not simply passive recipients of healthcare. Also, choice implies recognition that increased use of market-type initiatives is an excellent way of correcting inefficiencies in a system that has been characterized by structural as well as managerial rigidity."[137]

In Quebec the Chaoulli decision of 2005[138] was a major legal step toward establishing the principle that Quebecers, notwithstanding prohibitions against private medical insurance in several Quebec statutes, are under no legal obligation to suffer and even die on the public healthcare waiting lines if private services are available.

In English Canada, Dr. Brian Day, the courageous B.C. physician who operates the Cambie Clinic in Vancouver, has been fighting for years to establish the same principle for all Canadians against the massive and well-financed opposition of defenders of the status quo, including the B.C. government.[139] Dr. Day's efforts need to be urgently

137 "The Scandinavian Healthcare System," Jon Magnussen, PhD., Professor of Health Economics at the Norwegian University of Science and Technology in Trondheim and at the University of Oslo, in *Medical Solutions*, May, 2009, www.siemens.com/healthcare-magazine.

138 *Chaoulli v Quebec (AG)* [2005] 1 S.C.R. 791, 2005 SCC 35, was a decision by the Supreme Court of Canada in which the Court ruled that the *Quebec Health Insurance Act* and the *Hospital Insurance Act* prohibiting private medical insurance in the face of long wait times violated the *Quebec Charter of Human Rights and Freedoms*. The decision applied only to Quebec.

139 Dr. Day's campaign for freedom of choice in health care is being supported by

and more strongly supported by conservatives, indeed by all Canadians desiring the benefits of a mixed social services sector.

To achieve the goal of greater freedom of choice for consumers through a mixed social-services sector would require conservatives to champion, as a minimum, major reforms to:

- The Canada Health Act, to permit greater freedom of choice in health care insurance and services
- Provincial statutes, to permit greater freedom of choice in health care, education, and childcare
- Tax laws and laws governing charities to encourage the growth of, and investments in, private charities, social enterprises, and public-private partnerships in the social services sector

By boldly tackling this challenge, conservatives will be addressing a service sector that consumes almost two-thirds of the annual budgets of most provincial governments.

It is not enough to maintain, as many progressive conservatives did in the past, that conservatives will simply manage the welfare state more efficiently than liberal or socialist administrations. Rather, conservatives should be in the fore of challenging the old welfare-state model, pointing out its financial unsustainability in the long run, harnessing private-sector entrepreneurship, management, and capital to social-service objectives, and striking that new and more productive balance between the public and private sectors which will meet the growing and changing social service needs of Canadians.

DO SOMETHING!

If you are an executive, researcher, or communicator with a think tank, interest group, or political party, with an interest in, and commitment to achieving greater freedom of choice in health care, education, and social assistance:

continued

the Canadian Constitution Foundation. Information on the progress of the campaign is available on the Foundation's website (https://theccf.ca) and much-needed donations in support of the campaign can be made there as well.

- Undertake and communicate research to further the development and implementation of a mixed social services sector
- Support efforts to persuade conservative parties, caucuses, and governments to champion such an approach

If you are an executive with a philanthropic foundation or a major donor to policy development institutions, interest groups, and political parties:

- Make a significant financial contribution to those working to achieve greater freedom of choice within a mixed social services sector

If you are involved in an interest group or NGO dedicated to improving health, education, and other social services in Canada:

- Insure that your organization investigates the limits to the continued expansion of the current welfare state and the merits of moving toward a better balance between public and private delivery of services
- Promote the adoption of the freedom of choice/mixed social services sector approach by your organization

If you are a conservative policy maker, political activist, or legislator, be in the forefront of:

- Developing a social service policy along the above lines
- Communicating it effectively to stakeholders and the general public
- Securing an electoral mandate to proceed with implementation

If you are a Canadian citizen and voter who attaches great importance to improving the quality, delivery, and availability of health, education and other social services in Canada:

- Become a personal advocate and practitioner of this approach, and an active supporter of those who champion it in the political arena

A better, wider, and deeper distribution of the tools of wealth creation[140]

The existence of poverty and economic inequality are chronic conditions in Canada that cannot be ignored or overlooked by anyone engaged in democratic politics and governance with a sense of compassion and fairness.[141] The current model for addressing poverty, heartily subscribed to by liberal and socialist administrations is primarily that of income redistribution through progressive taxation, government intervention to transfer income from the "haves" to the "have nots," and with governments taking a substantial cut from that revenue stream to support the bureaucracy required to achieve and police it.[142] The sad and inconvenient truth, however, is that this approach has yielded consistently disappointing results in terms of actually reducing poverty and income inequality.[143]

Conservatives, therefore, should develop and champion a better alternative, namely, the tools-of-wealth-creation approach which aims to better distribute the means to create wealth, rather than simply attempting to redistribute wealth itself.

With respect to poverty alleviation, too many academics, politicians, and well-meaning poverty fighters tend to dismiss the market

---

140 Harris, Mike, and Manning, Preston, "Vision for a Canada Strong and Free," The Fraser Institute and the Montreal Economic Institute. (November 2007). https://www.fraserinstitute.org/sites/default/files/VisionCanadaStrongFree.pdf

141 Former Ontario Premier Mike Harris and I endeavored to persuade Canadian conservatives of the necessity of bringing market-based instruments to bear on this challenge in *Vision for a Canada Strong and Free,* The Fraser Institute and the Montreal Economic Institute, November 2007. See: https://www.fraserinstitute.org/sites/default/files/VisionCanadaStrongFree.pdf

142 A macro-variation of this concept was entrenched in the Canadian constitution in 1982 in the name of equalization. "Parliament and the government of Canada are committed to the principle of making equalization payments to ensure that provincial governments have sufficient revenues to provide reasonably comparable levels of public services at reasonably comparable levels of taxation" (Subsection 36(2) of the Constitution Act, 1982). In 2019–20, equalization transfers to provinces and territories will amount to approximately $78.7 billion. See https://www.fin.gc.ca/fedprov/mtp-eng.asp

143 Between 1980 and 2005, the average earnings among the least wealthy Canadians fell by 20%, even as the country went through a period of sustained economic and employment growth. See http://www.wellesleyinstitute.com/wp-content/uploads/2013/06/SOHC2103.pdf

economy and the wealth-creating tools it offers as fundamentally flawed, when the reality is that the market economy is simply insufficiently inclusive.

Conservatives believe that it is not capitalism that has failed the poor, but corporations, governments, and societies that have failed to provide their citizens with greater access to its powerful tools of wealth creation. We need to abandon exclusive reliance on income redistribution and focus much more on securing a better, wider, deeper distribution of those tools which will allow the poor and disadvantaged to reduce their own poverty.

What are these tools? Five of the best are:

(1) property rights (severely limited, for example, on indigenous reserves);[144]
(2) access to capital (in particular, "micro-capital" through micro-banking and crowdsourcing)[145]
(3) development of human capital through entrepreneurial encouragement and business skills training[146]

---

144 On a better distribution of property rights, see *The Mystery of Capital: Why Capitalism Triumphs in the West and Fails Everywhere Else* (2000), by renowned Peruvian economist Hernando de Soto. Also see, *Do better property rights improve local income? Evidence from First Nations' treaties by* Fernando M. Aragon: https://www.uvic.ca/socialsciences/economics/assets/docs/seminars/Fernando%20Aragon%20paper.pdf

145 On a better distribution of access to capital, see the work of the Nobel Prize-winning, Bangladeshi economist Muhammad Yunus, who demonstrated the poverty-reducing effectiveness of micro-banking and micro-credit through his Grameen Bank. See https://grameenfoundation.org/muhammad-yunus, or examine the micro-banking, micro-credit successes of Opportunity International (OI) founded in the early 1970s by Canadian Ross Clemenger. See https://www.opportunityinternational.ca/

146 On the role of human capital development through education and training, see the role of aggressively-funded teacher training for primary and secondary schools in poverty stricken communities and post-secondary education geared specifically towards entrepreneurship and business skills. For example, the international work of Making Cents International, a for-profit social enterprise started by Canadian Fiona Macaulay, which provides training and technology curriculum for micro-entrepreneurs in approximately forty developing countries. Also see, *A Review of the Role of Human Capital in the Organization by* Mohammad Pasban and Sadegheh Hosseinzadeh Nojedeh https://www.sciencedirect.com/science/article/pii/S1877042816311338

(4) access to technology and information (in particular, through cheap mobile devices)[147]

(5) access to trade and consumer markets (often unknown and seemingly inaccessible to poor people)[148]

Time and space do not allow me to elaborate thoroughly on the application of these tools to poverty alleviation but a growing body of literature on this subject (see footnotes) supports the contention that these principles and techniques should become part of the conservative policy arsenal going forward.

My own personal experience with and enthusiasm for the tools-of-wealth-creation approach came through my twenty-year involvement with a community development company, originally named Slave Lake Developments (SLD) in an underdeveloped part of north-central Alberta.[149] It was a region specifically identified by an Alberta government study in the late 1960s as failing to prosper economically to the same extent as the rest of Alberta.

At the time, the town of Slave Lake, 150 miles north of Edmonton, was in especially rough shape with unpaved streets, a declining population, few job opportunities, increasing numbers of welfare dependents, and inadequate housing, rental accommodation, or commercial space. But on the optimistic side, it had the potential for becoming an oil-field service town as the energy industry was beginning to expand into that region.

SLD, the community development company we formed to address this situation had dual objects: undertaking projects of specific social benefit to the community and earning a reasonable return on the capital invested by its shareholders. The company became a vehicle for distributing tools of wealth creation to some 300 local shareholders, including an aboriginal band by:

---

147 On the role of technology and information conducive to wealth creation, note the potentially massive boost for productivity and growth enhancement among poor people represented by improved access to cheap mobile devices and computers.

148 Note the wealth creating role which increased access to markets can play for poor people, particularly in rural areas.

149 Goodbrand, P. & Holloway, T., *SpruceLand Developments Inc.: Social Enterprise through Real Estate Development*, Case Number 9B19M100, Ivey Publishing, London, Ontario, October 16, 2019.

- Creating access to capital through a localized share offering and joint-venturing with resource companies operating in the area
- Undertaking local real estate projects (the provision of affordable housing and commercial office space[150] in a community where little previously existed) which provided both a financial and social return
- Accessing business know-how and "connections" through systematic relationship-building with management and financial consultants, corporate executives, and government officials who shared and supported the dual objects of the company.

This innovative community development company expanded and grew (see Appendix 3 for the more complete story), paying a total of $11-million in dividends to its local shareholders over its lifespan. In 2016, its directors, with shareholder approval, decided to cash out, selling all the company's assets and distributing the proceeds to the shareholders. The result has been an additional payment of $55 million into the bank accounts of those shareholders (most of them still local) for a total wealth creation and distribution effect of $66 million, plus the value of all the payroll and local purchases made by that company over the last forty-five years.

What this one community did through this vehicle and related activities to improve local incomes, employment, and services could conceivably be replicated by local communities and indigenous groups all over the country, pursuing the reduction of poverty and economic inequality, not through exclusive reliance on progressive taxation and other government income redistribution programs, but through a better, wider, deeper distribution of the tools of wealth creation.

---

150 As an example of increasing community access to a market, the Alberta government was persuaded not to build a small government office-building in the town as it was inclined to do, but to give a twenty-year lease for 20,000-square-feet of office space to the community company (i.e. access to a rental market that previously was closed to them). The community company was then able to take that lease and get financing from a mortgage company (the first major commercial mortgage of that type in the town) which enabled it to build and operate the facility and eventually secure financing for other projects from the same source.

DO SOMETHING!

If you are an executive, researcher, or communicator with a think tank, interest group, or political party, with an interest in, and commitment to reducing poverty and economic inequality in Canada:

- Undertake and communicate research to further develop and implement a better, deeper, and wider distribution of the tools of wealth creation
- Support efforts to persuade conservative parties, caucuses, and governments to champion such an approach to reducing poverty and income inequality

If you are an executive with a philanthropic foundation or a major donor to policy development institutions, interest groups, and political parties:

- Make a significant financial contribution to those working to further develop and implement the tools-of-wealth-creation approach

If you are involved in an interest group or NGO dedicated to reducing poverty and economic inequality:

- Insure that your organization investigates the merits of the tools-of-wealth-creation approach
- Promote the adoption of such an approach by your organization.

If you are a member or leader of an indigenous community or organization concerned about poverty and economic inequality among your own people:

- Initiate an investigation of the merits of the tools-of-wealth-creation approach
- Promote the adoption of such an approach by your own community or organization

continued

If you are a Canadian citizen and voter who attaches great importance to reducing poverty and income inequality in Canada:

- Become a personal advocate and practitioner of the tools of wealth creation approach to that challenge, and an active supporter of those who champion it in the political arena.

The recognition and entrenchment of property rights in the Canadian Constitution[151]

The Canadian Charter of Rights and Freedoms[152] provides constitutional guarantees of fundamental freedoms, linguistic and cultural rights, democratic rights, mobility rights, legal rights, equality rights, linguistic-minority educational rights, and certain pre-charter rights including aboriginal rights and the rights of denominational schools. But despite the fact that millions of Canadians hold trillions of dollars of private property, and that property rights and freedom of enterprise are foundational stones of the private sector of the economy which itself requires billions of dollars of capital investment to function and provides employment for the majority of Canadians, the charter doesn't even mention economic rights, let alone property rights.

151 See http://publications.gc.ca/Collection-R/LoPBdP/BP/bp268-e.htm#ARGUMENTS for a website/paper that gives examples of arguments for and against property rights.
152 Section 26 of the Charter stipulates "The guarantee in this Charter of certain rights and freedoms shall not be construed as denying the existence of any other rights and freedoms that exist in Canada." Case law has construed this section to mean that the common law protection of property rights is at least not threatened by the Charter. Only the inclusion of property in the Charter, however, would enable an individual whose property rights had been infringed to have recourse to the enforcement section of the Charter. Subsection 24(1) states in part that "anyone whose rights or freedoms, as guaranteed by this Charter, have been infringed or denied may apply to a court . . . to obtain such remedy as the court considers appropriate and just in the circumstances."

The Canadian Bill of Rights,[153] passed by the conservative government of John Diefenbaker in 1960, and now to all intents and purposes superseded by the charter, did at least make mention of property rights, affirming "the right of the individual to life, liberty, security of the person and enjoyment of property, and the right not to be deprived thereof except by due process of law.[154] The weaknesses of this provision, however, were three fold: (1) It did not carefully define "property"; (2) It did not constrain governments from arbitrarily taking or confiscating private property (it only required that they do it "lawfully"); (3) It made no provision, unlike the property rights protection clause of the American constitution, for "just compensation"[155]for the property taken.

When the Canadian Charter of Rights and Freedoms was drafted, even this weak property rights protection clause was dropped, the Charter's reference to individual legal rights simply reading: "Everyone has the right to life, liberty and security of the person and the right not to be deprived thereof except in accordance with the principles of fundamental justice."[156]

There have been various attempts over the years, all of them unsuccessful, to strengthen the protection of property rights in Canada, including efforts to have a strong property rights protection clause entrenched in the constitution via the charter. My own experience with this effort goes back to 1969, when Harry Strom, who had succeeded my father as premier of Alberta in December of 1968, came back to Edmonton from a constitutional conference between the premiers and the new Prime Minister, Pierre Elliott Trudeau.

---

153 The 1960 Canadian Bill of Rights, which affirms the right of the individual to the enjoyment of property and the right not to be deprived thereof except by due process of law.

154 Canadian Bill of Rights (S.C. 1960, c. 44, s.1(a)).

155 The U.S. Constitution protects property rights mainly through the Fifth Amendment's Takings or Just Compensation Clause: "nor shall private property be taken for public use without just compensation."

156 The property rights reference in the Alberta Bill of Rights, passed in 1972, (RSA 2000, c. A-14, s.1(a)), has exactly the same wording with respect to property rights as the Canadian Bill of Rights and shares the same weaknesses. For example, in 2010, the Alberta government amended the *Mines and Mineral Act* to declare that: "the pore space below the surface of all land in Alberta is vested in and is the property of the Crown in right of Alberta and remains the property of the Crown in right of Alberta. . ." The amendment goes on to expressly deny any compensation, as well as the right to bring action against the government for the taking.

Trudeau was pressing for agreement from the premiers for a series of amendments to the Canadian constitution which was to become known as the Victoria Charter, and it was to include the entrenchment of certain political and linguistic rights. My father and I took Harry to lunch and asked him this question: "When the discussion got around to entrenching rights, did any of you premiers insist on the entrenchment of property rights, since the BNA Act specifically assigns responsibility for property and civil rights to the provinces?"[157]

Harry replied that the subject had come up but that there wasn't much enthusiasm for discussing it. He said that Trudeau had mentioned that in the U.S. the implementation of the property rights provision of the U.S. Constitution had been very controversial and the subject of much litigation. Discussion of the subject in Canada might better be deferred to a more propitious time. And so the conference moved on.

All of this raised alarm bells for me and my father as we watched the adoption and aftermath of the Victoria charter. We subsequently persuaded the Business Council on National Issues (BCNI) to provide us with the funds to hire a legal expert to draft a property rights protection clause suitable for entrenchment in Canada's constitution. With that clause in hand, we then undertook to try to persuade at least one of the premiers to champion it in any future constitutional discussions and negotiations with the federal government.

The legal expert we hired was Gerry Gall, a constitutional law professor at the University of Alberta whose courses I had once audited. We asked Gerry to give particularly close attention to getting the definitions of property and the enjoyment of property right for entrenchment, resulting in the following:

- "Property" was to be defined as including "the bundle of all rights, individual or in the aggregate, exercisable directly or indirectly, by persons over things, tangible or intangible, real or personal"
- "The use and enjoyment of property" was to be defined as including "ownership, possession, utility, control, management, profitability, and value of that property."

The main reason for defining property and its enjoyment in these ways was to ensure that property in Canada would be protected against

---

157 BNA Act, 1867, s. 92, ss. 13.

indirect confiscation by the state through governments expropriating the functions associated with property without actually taking ownership of it.[158]

Of course, our property rights protection clause included the provision that property could not be taken by the state "except by due process of law." However, the most important provision was that property could not be taken by law "unless that law provides for just compensation." If our clause were to be entrenched in the constitution, it would remedy the greatest weakness of the property rights protection provisions of the Canadian Bill of Rights and provincial property rights legislation.

Satisfied that we now had the right wording of a property rights protection clause, we then proceeded to contact the various premiers of the day, in particular the conservative-oriented ones, to see if we could find someone who would carry it into constitutional negotiations with the federal government and become its public champion.

The story of this attempt is a long one (summarized elsewhere).[159] And sad to say our efforts were unsuccessful. The once in a lifetime opportunity (between 1971 and 1980 when the Charter was finally adopted) to get property rights protection firmly entrenched in Canada's constitution was allowed to slip away because we were unable to find a strong political champion, not even among the conservative-oriented politicians of the day.

Nevertheless, some of the lessons learned from this exercise will be extremely helpful to those making the next attempt to achieve the same objective, and these are briefly summarized below:

1. *An effective champion must be in favor in principle of entrenching rights in the constitution, or if not enthusiastically in favor, at least believe that, if some basic human rights are to be constitutionally entrenched, property rights should be included.*

158 It was our understanding that Pierre Trudeau had studied and was somewhat enamored by "functional socialism" as practiced in several Scandinavian countries. Under functional socialism, the state may, by regulation, in effect expropriate the functions associated with property, the right to manage, control, reorganize, sell, etc., without actually taking ownership of the property itself.

159 This project was undertaken by my consulting firm, at the time named M. And M. Systems Research Ltd., and the file summarizing it is currently in my personal archives.

Unfortunately, at the time we were promoting property rights protection, all of the western premiers—Bill Bennett of BC, Peter Lougheed of Alberta, Allen Blakney of Saskatchewan, and Sterling Lyon of Manitoba—were opposed in principle to Mr. Trudeau's entrenchment efforts. Premier Bourassa of Quebec was also opposed. Because a majority of the Premiers honestly believed Trudeau's entrenchment effort would fail, they were not really open to seriously discussing what rights should be included if it did not fail.

2. *An effective political champion must strongly desire property rights protection for his/her own jurisdiction and be willing to accept the consequences of its constitutional entrenchment.*

As we quickly discovered, this was generally not the case in most, if not all, of the provinces, even in those with conservative administrations. For example, when I showed our property rights protection clause to B.C.'s constitutional minister, Rafe Mair, he took one look at it and exclaimed, "But this would make it harder for us to expropriate stuff." To which I replied, "That's exactly right. It doesn't prevent you from expropriating; but it does prevent you from doing so illegally and unfairly."

3. *To broaden the support base for the entrenchment of property rights, be prepared to consider demands for the entrenchment of other "economic rights" such as labor rights and consumer rights.*

This was suggested by several of the constitutional advisors to the premiers whom we consulted. But to so broaden the definition introduced further complications with respect to wording and determining "just compensation" for confiscation, and probably reduced the prospects of entrenching property rights rather than enhancing them.

4. *Given the transactional nature of interprovincial and federal-provincial relations, be prepared for horse-trading propositions in which support by some provinces for property/economic rights entrenchment will be made contingent upon accepting the entrenchment of other completely unrelated rights.*

For example, it was suggested that the western provinces' support for the entrenchment of linguistic and cultural rights should be made contingent on Quebec's support for entrenchment of western economic rights. Premier Richard Hatfield of New Brunswick even suggested that any possible support for property rights entrenchment by his government would be contingent on securing entrenchment of the Atlantic provinces' "right to equalization."

5. *What proved to be most influential in at least stimulating some provincial interest (if not support) for entrenching property rights, was expanding the definition of property to include "property held by the Crown in the right of the provinces."*[160]

This provision would have given the provinces constitutional protection against the direct or indirect expropriation of their natural resources by the federal government. (If such a provision had been in place in 1980, the petroleum producing provinces would have been at least partially protected from the ravages of the Trudeau government's National Energy Program which expropriated billions of dollars-worth of wealth from those provinces through confiscatory price regulation.)

Although we incorporated this definition into our later proposals for the entrenchment of property-rights protection, it was still not sufficient to enable us to find a vigorous provincial champion for the concept.[161]

---

160 Ironically, I hit upon this idea, not in my discussions with the western officials, but on a snowy night in Quebec City in discussion with Guy Joron, Rene Levesque's energy minister. In preparing for the meeting, I asked myself, "What line of argument can I possibly use to make property-rights entrenchment attractive to a socialist, separatist government?" And then the answer dawned on me: expand the definition of property to include property held by the crown in the right of the provinces, which would then provide provincial governments with protection from the federal government expropriating their resources and doing so at less than market price.

161 Perhaps our greatest disappointment in this regard, was our inability to persuade Premier Lougheed, in our home province of Alberta, of the merits of the concept. In Alberta's case we tried to persuade him to simply amend the Alberta Human Rights Act to include our property rights protection clause, and then insist at the federal provincial negotiation table that any rights previously granted by a province should be grandfathered and guaranteed by the federal Charter. This could hardly be objected to by the federal government as it had already indicated that it was prepared to grandfather such pre-Charter rights as language rights and the rights of denominational schools and indigenous peoples. We also strenuously pressed the argument that entrenching the protection of property in the Constitution, if the definition of property were to include property held by the Crown in the right of the provinces, would in effect provide Alberta protection

Nevertheless, as history sometimes tends to move in circles, I anticipate that the opportunity[162] to secure property rights protection in the constitution may well come around again and hopefully the lessons from past experience will enable those prepared to *Do Something!* on this front, to be more successful.

As time marches on, there is now an additional and even more weighty reason for urgently re-considering the necessity of strengthening property rights protection in Canada. Development and expansion of the information economy has created a situation whereby thousands of bytes of information on every Canadian now exist in digital form and can be acquired, stored, and utilized by others, including corporations, political parties, and governments, with or without the individual's consent. To whom does such information belong?[163] Surely the conservative position is that it belongs to the individual to whom it pertains and that the ownership of that information by the individual should be protected by law.

against unfair de-facto expropriation of its energy resources by the federal government. But at that time, the Lougheed government did not apparently see any need for such protection. Why was the Lougheed administration so cool to our presentation? Although it was never said, I think it was because our proposal was an indirect criticism of the inadequate property rights protection provisions of the Alberta Human Rights Act, Lougheed's very first piece of legislation of which he was inordinately proud.

162 For example, if in future there is ever a conservative government in Ottawa and one in Alberta at the same time, who jointly wish to send a signal to the capital markets that reinvestment in Canada's petroleum sector is now welcome, a province-specific provision of constitutional protection for property, at least in Alberta (similar to the province-specific protection of linguistic and education rights for New Brunswick provided by section 16 of the Charter) might be one way of doing so.

163 This question is equally applicable to such highly personal information as your personal genome. As early as 1958, in a famous paper "On Protein Sequences," Francis Crick, the co-discoverer of the structure of DNA, drew attention to the vast amounts of information that are hidden away in the protein sequences of an individual human being, and that such sequences represent the most precise observable register of the physical identity of that human being. (See Quammen, David, *The Tangled Tree,* Simon and Schuster, 2018, pages 40–41.) Who owns that information? Should it not be that individual human being, that is, you, with the right to retain ownership of it and not to relinquish it to others, including governments interested in practicing identity politics, without your consent and by due process of law?

DO SOMETHING!

If you are an executive, researcher, or communicator with a think tank or interest group with an interest in, and commitment to, the entrenchment of property rights protection in the Canadian constitution:

- Join and support efforts to persuade conservative parties, caucuses, and governments to adopt and implement such a provision.

If you are an executive with a philanthropic foundation or company, or a major donor to policy development institutions, interest groups, and political parties with an interest in this objective:

- Make a significant financial contribution to those working to achieve the constitutional entrenchment of property rights protection;
- Withdraw your financial support from any organization opposing the entrenchment of property rights protection in the Canadian constitution.

If you are an individual or company whose property rights have been circumscribed or infringed upon by governments:

- Provide your support to think tanks, interest groups, and political organizations working to entrench property rights protection in the Canadian constitution.

If you are a Canadian citizen and voter who supports the entrenchment of property rights protection in the constitution of Canada:

- Provide your support to think tanks, interest groups, and political organizations working to achieve that objective;
- Withhold your support from those who do not.

The emergence and development of the sharing economy[164]

As previously discussed, a major source of new ideas for conservatives to champion are those being embraced by next-generation Canadians. So consider the following:

Each year the Manning Centre has recruited and supported summer interns to work on projects designed to strengthen the knowledge and skills of political practitioners in Canada, especially those who subscribe to free-market values and principles. In 2016, we asked that summer's interns, what cutting edge addition to the policy arsenal of conservative-oriented political parties might have the greatest appeal to their generation?

Their answer? Championing the sharing economy as exemplified by Uber[165], AirBnB[166], and the growing number of economic sectors embracing the collaborative-consumption model.[167]

In this model, the consumer acquires access, for a price, to the assets of others (cars, houses, equipment, and much more) rather than having to personally purchase and own such assets. What has contributed to the explosive expansion of this model are the new technologies which enable asset owners and would-be consumers to identify and communicate with each other effortlessly and cheaply through the internet and a plethora of handheld devices and apps.

Why should conservatives be attracted to this model and be in the fore of promoting public policies which encourage rather than retard its development? Four reasons:

164 Gerard Lucyshyn and Lee Harding, "The Sharing Economy: A story of creative destruction and the erosion of barriers to entry," *Asper Review of International Business and Trade Law*, Volume XVIII, (2018): page 266.

165 Berger, Thord; Chen, Chinchih; Frey, Carl B., "Drivers of Disruption? Estimating the Uber Effect," (20 January 2017), Oxford Martin School. www.oxfordmartin.ox.ac.uk/publications/view/2387.

166 Zervas, Georgios; Prosperio, Davide; Byers, John W., "The Rise of the Sharing Economy: Estimating the Impact of Airbnb on the Hotel Industry," (2016) 54:5 *Marketing Research* 687–705. journals.ama.org/doi/abs/10.1509/jmr.15.0204.

167 Juho, Hamari; Sjöklint, Mimmi; Ukkonen, Antti, "The Sharing Economy: Why people participate in collaborative consumption." *Journal of the Association for Information Science and Technology* 67, no. 9 (2016): 2047–2059. Collaborative consumption is defined as the peer-to-peer-based activity of obtaining, giving, or sharing the access to goods and services, coordinated through community-based online services.

- The sharing economy is a market-based economy which works best if governments and government bureaucracies, with their tendencies to over regulate and over tax, simply get out of the way. Reliance on market mechanisms and limiting the role of government to facilitating rather than disrupting markets, are values which most conservatives already strongly endorse
- Collaborative consumption integrates economic objectives with environmental and social objectives, conserving resource consumption and reducing waste. This is an integration which twenty-first century conservatives need to more fully embrace if we desire to appeal to and represent next-generation Canadians
- On the employment side, collaborative consumption is compatible with and complementary to job sharing, another emerging trend[168] (see chapter 3.2 for further discussion of job sharing in the political sector)
- The Sharing Economy has particular appeal to next-generation Canadians, the element of the population with which conservatives need to establish stronger and lasting rapport.

DO SOMETHING!

If you are an executive, researcher, or communicator with a think tank, interest group, or political party, with expertise, interest in, and a commitment to addressing the economic preferences of next-generation Canadians:

- Develop and communicate your own policy suggestions as to how to encourage the growth and development of the sharing economy
- Support efforts to persuade conservative parties, caucuses, and governments to commit themselves to the development of the sharing economy

168 "Job sharing is a work arrangement in which two people hold responsibility for one full-time position. One position that is split in salary, benefits, and responsibilities," says Angela Spencer in "Job Sharing: A Primer," *Journal of Hospital Librarianship*, 2017, 17:1, 80–87, DOI: 10.1080/15323269.2017.1259471

If you are an executive with a philanthropic foundation or company, or a major donor to policy development institutions, interest groups, and political parties, and you have an interest in addressing the economic preferences of next-generation Canadians:

- Make a significant financial contribution to those working to achieve this objective

If you are a participant in the sharing economy and believe in its expansion:

- Provide your support to think tanks, interest groups, and political organizations working to safeguard and expand the sharing economy

If you are a Canadian citizen and voter who believes that the development and expansion of the sharing economy is in the best interests of the country:

- Become a champion of the sharing economy and an active supporter of those who seek to develop and expand it

The re-conceptualization and promotion of responsible development of the natural resource sectors as foundational to the Canadian economy.

There is an old model of the national economy, unfortunately still firmly lodged in the heads of many of our media and political class, which is also badly in need of replacement. It is in the shape of a pyramid (see Figure 4)[169] with the natural resources sectors at the bottom (in the

169 Traus, Andreas. "Estimating the Canadian GDP of the Resource Sector: An Analysis for the Manning Centre for Building Democracy." May 18, 2018. Statistics Canada Senior Economic Analyst Traus estimated that the direct, indirect, and induced impact on GDP by the resource sector in 2014 was in the vicinity of 25%.

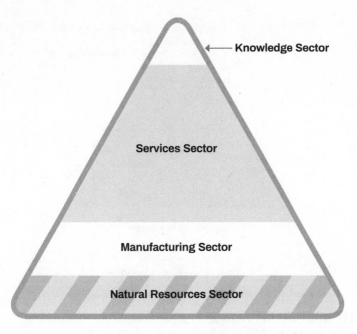

FIGURE 4 Traditional Conception of the National Economy

cellar), the manufacturing sectors on the more respectable ground floor, the service sectors on top of that, and the knowledge sectors occupying the penthouse.

Politicians, media, and policymakers whose thinking is consciously or unconsciously shaped by this model, tend to be embarrassed by and apologetic about Canada's natural resource sectors. They dismiss the founders of the Canadian economy as little more than hewers of wood and drawers of water, and tend to regard today's natural resource sectors as relics of the past, threats to the environment, and unworthy of political support. Generally speaking, these apologists are much more enamored with the manufacturing sector, and desperately anxious to move our economy into the airy heights of the knowledge economy while ignoring all the backward and forward links which tie these sectors to natural resource development.

But notwithstanding the prevalence and acceptability of this old model, there is another very different and more realistic way of conceptualizing our economy. This involves recognizing that the natural resource sectors, in particular, agriculture, fisheries, forestry, mining, and energy, are foundation stones of the entire economy on which the

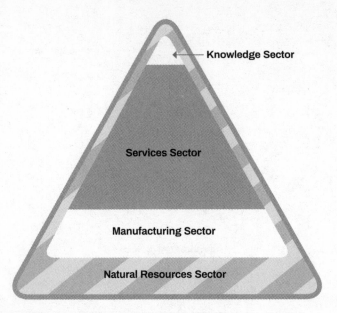

FIGURE 5 Expanded Conception of Natural Resources Sector as Foundational to the National Economy

growth, prosperity, and employment capabilities of all other sectors and the national wealth are highly dependent. (See Figure 5)[170]

The contributions to national GDP and national employment of a natural resource sector like the energy sector are not just those of the energy sector *per se*. They also include, through what the economists call backward and forward linkages, the contributions of the energy manufacturing sector, the energy services sector, and the energy knowledge sector. Likewise, for the contributions to the manufacturing, service, and knowledge sectors of all the other natural resource sectors, including agriculture, fisheries, forestry, and mining.

Remove the natural resource sectors, in whole or in part, from the Canadian economy and the negative economic impacts—reductions in incomes, employment, and the GDP—are huge. Strengthen and expand

---

170 See additional data from StatsCan showing direct, indirect, and induced contributions of the resource sectors to GDP. Traus even suggests showing the contributions to labour employment as perhaps being more relevant to the average reader.

the natural resource sectors, especially to serve the export market, and the positive impacts are also huge.

Therefore, there is an urgent need to impress these facts upon the public and our political decision-makers; to find new and better ways of communicating the absolute dependence of the Canadian economy on the health and expansion of the resources sectors; to clearly express the impacts of ignoring or restricting the resource sectors in terms of employment and income effects; and to adopt policy measures which promote, encourage, and facilitate rather than restrict the health and growth of these sectors.

Conservatives should be in the forefront of championing these natural resource sectors and reforming the conceptual frameworks and econometric models which ignore or understate their fundamental importance to the economy and the prosperity of the next generation. Guess who among the electorate is most likely to welcome such championing? Millennials.

In a recent survey conducted for the Manning Centre by a respected pollster, a national cross-section of millennials was asked whether they supported or opposed a strengthening of the natural resource sectors? Surprisingly, only 20% of the sample declared themselves somewhat or strongly opposed, while 81% of the sample declared themselves somewhat or strongly supportive of strengthening those sectors.

DO SOMETHING!

If you are an executive, researcher, or communicator with a think tank, interest group or political party with an interest in, and a commitment to, recognizing and strengthening the role of the resource sectors:

- Undertake and communicate research to demonstrate that the natural resource sectors are fundamental building blocks of the Canadian economy
- Support efforts to persuade conservative parties, caucuses, and governments to become champions of the natural resource sectors as foundational to the Canadian economy.

If you are an executive with a philanthropic foundation or company, or a major donor to policy development institutions, interest groups, and

continued

political parties – and you have an interest in encouraging the recognition and promotion of the natural resource sectors as foundational to the Canadian economy:

- Make a significant financial contribution to those working to achieve this objective
- Withdraw your financial contributions from those organizations which denigrate the natural resource sectors

If you personally work or invest in Canada's natural resource sectors:

- Provide your support to think tanks, interest groups, and political organizations who champion the natural resource sectors as foundational to the Canadian economy

If you are a Canadian citizen and voter who believes in the recognition and development of the natural resource sectors as foundational to the Canadian economy:

- Become a champion of the natural resource sectors and an active supporter of those who champion the recognition and development of those sectors as fundamental building blocks of the Canadian economy

Provision of national rights of way for unobstructed transportation infrastructure corridors to move inland natural resources to tidewater and world markets[171]

The following facts bare repeating and urgently require a coordinated response from governments, companies, and Canadians whose jobs, incomes, and living standards are jeopardized by ignoring them:

---

171 "To build pipelines, we must create coalition corridors," Manning, Preston, *Globe and Mail*. December 13, 2018; https://www.theglobeandmail.com/opinion/article-to-build-pipelines-we-must-create-coalition-corridors/

- As the second-largest nation on earth by area, Canada has roughly the second-largest store of natural resources in the world, something we should be immensely proud, not apologetic, about
- The natural resource sectors (agriculture, energy, mining, forestry and fisheries) are foundational to the Canadian economy, directly and indirectly accounting for over twenty percent of our gross national product, with the energy sector being the biggest contributor.
- Since the bulk of these resources are located inland, unobstructed, efficient, environmentally sound, transportation infrastructure corridors are required, in the national interest, to move those resources to tidewater and world markets by various modes of transportation including road, rail, and pipeline
- Canada is losing approximately $80-million per day[172] in revenues, plus thousands of jobs and billions of dollars in investment[173] because opposition to the building of pipelines to tidewater and world markets forces Canada to sell oil and natural gas to the U.S. market at discounted prices
- The immediate requirements are for corridors to the Pacific to access Asian markets and corridors to the Atlantic to replace foreign oil imports with Canadian oil. In future, corridors to the Arctic will also be required

Section 92.ss. 10 (a) and (c) of the BNA Act gives the federal government jurisdiction over:

- Lines of Steam or other Ships, Railways, Canals, Telegraphs, and other Works and Undertakings connecting the Province with any other or others of the Provinces, or extending beyond the Limits of the Province:
- Such Works as, although wholly situate within the Province, are before or after their Execution declared by the Parliament of Canada to be for the general Advantage of Canada or for the Advantage of Two or more of the Provinces.

---

172 Approximately $80 billion between August and November 2018 as per https://globalnews.ca/news/4662706/alberta-lost-revenue-counter-pipeline-delays/

173 Alberta lawyer and former President of the Canadian Petroleum Tax Society, Robert T. Iverach, has been in the forefront of documenting and publicizing the negative impacts of this situation on the Canadian economy, the Canadian petroleum industry, and national unity. See www.actionalberta.ca

The federal government needs to be urgently persuaded to use these constitutional powers to at least legislate the rights of way for transportation infrastructure corridors, some of which already partially exist. Proponents of particular transportation projects such as resource roads, rail lines, pipelines, transmission lines, etc., could then apply for licenses to build and operate facilities within the corridors subject to meeting pre-established safety, environmental, financing, and operating standards. This would still necessitate regulatory hearings and decisions, but at least the right of way would be pre-established and no longer be the subject of protracted disputes, endless adjudications, and costly delays.

Canada's inability under the Trudeau government to provide unobstructed transportation corridors from its interior to tidewater is not only crippling the energy sector but threatens to make this country the laughing stock of international infrastructure investors. In the mocking language of one such investor, "*Trans*Canada Pipelines, *Trans* Mountain pipeline . . . you Canadians can't "*trans*" anything. You can't build infrastructure across your own provincial boundaries. The Chinese can build transportation infrastructure across five countries as part of their initial Belt and Road initiative and you can't even build infrastructure across five provinces within one country."

So what will it take to pressure the federal government to use its constitutional powers to establish the required rights of way? Just as the creation of the original Canadian Pacific Railway, which bound Confederation together with a ribbon of steel,[174] required a uniting of pre-Confederation political and economic interests to achieve that nation building objective, today we need what might be called the TransCanada Corridor Coalition (TCCC) consisting of governments, companies, interest groups, indigenous people, and other citizens dedicated to creating and maintaining the transportation infrastructure corridors to the Pacific, Atlantic, and Arctic required for the twenty-first century.

At the provincial government level, both the Alberta and Saskatchewan governments are in the forefront of demanding such corridors as part of their Fair Deal Now initiative to address the underlying

---

174 *The National Dream: The Great Railway, 1871–1881,* was a 1970 bestseller by journalist and historian Pierre Berton recounting John A. Macdonald's epic drive to build the Canadian Pacific Railway, linking the new province of British Columbia to the rest of Canada.

causes of the growing separatist movement in the west. It is also especially encouraging that an ever increasing group of indigenous leaders,
bands, and companies in Canada are already taking major steps to
explore and promote transportation infrastructure corridors of their
own across indigenous lands.[175] If they too were to participate in the
TransCanada Corridor Coalition, that would significantly strengthen it
and lay to rest the canard that the majority of Canada's indigenous
people are unalterably opposed to responsible resource development
and its transportation requirements.

DO SOMETHING!

If you are an executive, researcher, or communicator with a think tank
or academic policy institute desirous of facilitating the efficient and
responsible movement of Canadian natural resources to tidewater
and world markets:

- Take the initiative in performing and publicizing research which
  will be useful to the TransCanada Corridor Coalition in advancing
  this cause
- Support efforts to persuade political parties, caucuses, and governments to enact and enforce enabling legislation

If you are an executive with a philanthropic foundation or a major
donor to policy development institutions, interest groups, and political parties:

- Make a significant financial contribution to those working to
  advance the corridor concept
- Withdraw your financial contributions from those who oppose the
  creation of such corridors

continued

175 See the website and work of The First Nations Major Projects Coalition, www.
   fnmpc.ca and the proceedings of the February 2019 Forward Summit on
   Empowering Indigenous Economies, http://forwardsummit.ca.

If you are an executive or senior manager of a mass media organization (a newspaper, a radio/television organization, or social media platform):

- Actively promote the need for policy and legislation to advance the corridor concept

If you are an executive, staffer, or member of a political party desirous of facilitating the efficient and responsible movement of Canadian natural resources to tidewater and world markets:

- Work to make the creation of the Pacific, Atlantic, and Arctic corridors a clearly stated objective of your party
- Work to include in your party's policy platform a commitment to support and advance the corridor concept

If you are a Canadian citizen and voter desirous of facilitating the efficient and responsible movement of Canadian natural resources to tidewater and world markets:

- Become a personal advocate and supporter of interest groups, candidates, and political parties committed to securing such a balance
- Withdraw your support from interest groups, candidates, and political parties whose positions contribute to polarization and imbalance on the economy-environment front

The promotion and adoption of market-based approaches to environmental conservation[176]

There is another old model of the economy firmly entrenched in the minds of many of the business and political decision-makers of my generation which is well on its way to being replaced by something different. That old model envisions the economy as a sequence of functions:

---

176 See Scruton, Roger, *How to Think Seriously About the Planet*, Oxford University Press, 2012.

extraction, processing, manufacturing, distribution, and consumption. And, oh yes, then there is the environment and environmental protection. But note that in this model, attention to the environment is usually an afterthought, a latter-day add-on and not an integral part of the economic model (see Figure 6).) Economists refer to the problem of "environmental externalities": negative environmental effects of production and consumption that are imposed on third parties, but occur outside of the market mechanism and are uncompensated.

Notwithstanding the usefulness and long-standing entrenchment of the traditional economic model that treats the environment as an add-on external to the system, many next-generation Canadians have a very different and more holistic way of conceptualizing our economy. It implicitly recognizes the tight and all pervasive inter-relationship between the economy and the environment: that the economy draws all its resources from this planet's soil, minerals, plant and animal life, water, and atmosphere, and discharges all its outputs and wastes into various ecosystems with finite carrying capacities.[177] (See Figure 7)

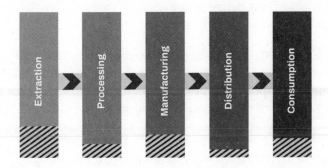

 **Environmental Protection Add-On**

FIGURE 6 The Traditional Conservative Conception of the Economy with Environmental Protection as an Add-On

177 Note that the acceptance of this conceptual framework changes our conception of what really constitutes our standard of living. The old conception was that Gross Domestic Product (GDP) per capita was an adequate economic measure of our standard of living. The new conception is that Real Standard of Living Equals Gross Domestic Product Minus the Gross National Waste. A country can have an ever increasing GDP, but if it is achieved at the cost of a serious deterioration in the quality of its water, land, and atmosphere, the real standard of living of its people may actually be declining.

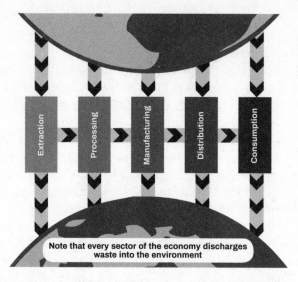

Note that every sector of the economy discharges waste into the environment

FIGURE 7 An Integrated Conception of the Economy and the Environment

The relationship between the economy and the environment is rooted in two basic physical facts:

(1) Every economic activity extracts resources from the environment, from the earth's soil, vegetation, water, and atmosphere for the production, distribution, and consumption of goods and services
(2) Every economic activity has some kind of environmental impact, including the generation of wastes from the production, distribution, and consumption of goods. These wastes are eventually re-deposited back into the environment from whence they came.

The science that best informs this linkage between the economy and the environment is not climate science but the much broader, older, and irrefutable Laws of the Conservation of Mass and Energy.[178] The total

---

178 According to the Law of Conservation of Mass (Lavoisier, 1773), matter cannot be created or destroyed (in a system closed to all transfers of matter and energy) although it can change form. According to the Law of Conservation of Energy (Mayer, 1842), later called the First Law of Thermodynamics, energy (in a closed system) can neither be created nor destroyed but can only be transformed or transferred from one form to another. These two laws have since been merged (Einstein, 1907) into the Law of Conservation of Mass-Energy which states that the total amount of mass and energy in the universe is constant.

mass/energy of what we extract from the environment will be the total mass/energy of what we discharge into the environment, our economic processes changing the form of what we extract from the environment but not the total amount.

Thus the performance of any and every economic function has environmental impacts, some of which are negative and which should be clearly identified. A commitment to environmental conservation and protection then requires us to devise measures to avoid or mitigate those impacts as best we can.

We now have three major choices as to how to implement and finance those avoidance and mitigation measures:

1. Through ever-increasing macro-regulation and micro-regulation by governments, with the costs borne primarily by taxpayers
2. Through market mechanisms, incorporating the costs of these measures in the price of the product or service responsible for the environmental impact so that the cost is primarily borne by those producing and consuming that product or service
3. Through some combination of (1) and (2).

Market mechanisms designed to avoid and mitigate environmental consequences come in two main forms. First, governments can attempt to make producers and consumers internalize the economic cost of externalities by imposing fees or taxes that compensate for the environmental damage. For example, a factory could be required to pay a fee for every unit of pollution it emits into the atmosphere. This approach is associated with the British economist Arthur Pigou. Second, the economic system can try to create a form of property rights over pollution that can be traded between individuals or companies. For example, companies could be given the right to release a certain number of units of pollution into the air, low enough to keep the total amount within environmentally acceptable limits. Companies could then buy or sell those permits or credits among themselves, allowing more efficient, lower-emitting firms to sell their permits at a profit to less efficient, higher-polluting firms, but still keeping the overall level of pollution within acceptable limits. This approach is associated with the American economist and Nobel laureate Ronald Coase. Both kinds of market mechanisms can be used as conservative policy solutions to the problem of environmental externalities.

Unfortunately, it has often been left-of-centre commentators and politicians with a predisposition toward government intervention who have seized the high ground on many environmental issues, with conservatives taking a largely defensive posture or even denying that an environmental problem exists. These left-of-centre politicians and activists will usually support command-and-control regulation as the best way of dealing with environmental challenges, and tend to be skeptical of market mechanisms. Meanwhile, conservatives who try to minimize or ignore environmental challenges aren't even bringing their market-based solutions to the table. This puts conservatives in a very disadvantageous position in addressing such issues and in securing the support of next-generation Canadians.

From a philosophical and ideological standpoint, conservatives who believe in the efficacy of markets ought to be in the forefront of championing market-based approaches, either Pigou's pollution pricing or Coase's permit trading, for environmental conservation. But, again unfortunately, left-of-centre administrations in Canada have largely been allowed to co-opt that option as well, for example, by advocating carbon pricing as the best way to mitigate the adverse environmental impacts of burning hydrocarbons.

This is particularly unfortunate since the implementation of a market-based approach (pollution pricing) to environmental conservation by politicians who really don't believe in or understand markets, results in a bungling of the implementation and a discrediting of the market-based approach. Rather than using market mechanisms as a way to nudge individuals and companies towards environmentally responsible behavior, they often see them as a way to generate new revenue for ever greater government spending programs. From a conservative perspective, a genuinely market-based carbon pricing regime should be:

- Revenue neutral, that is, accompanied by a reduction of other taxes in the amount to be raised by the carbon levy so as not to increase the overall tax burden on the taxpayer and the economy
- Subsidy free, since subsidies distort markets and send contradictory and misleading signals to consumers
- Accompanied by a significant reduction in regulations since a market mechanism is supposed to be, at least in part, a substitute for regulation
- Accompanied by ongoing negotiations with major trading partners to secure similar policies and conditions in their jurisdictions, so as to avoid rendering the more environmentally responsible party less competitive from a trade perspective

None of the carbon pricing regimes instituted in Canada, in particular, those instituted by the Trudeau regime federally, the Wynne government in Ontario, or the Notley government in Alberta[179] have come anywhere close to possessing the characteristics necessary to make a market-based approach work.[180]

While the Trudeau government's approach to carbon pricing at the federal level may be conceptually superior to that of the Wynne or Notley governments, it, too, was accompanied by the layering on of economically distortive regulations and policy decisions like that incorporated in its no-more-pipelines legislation (Bill C-69). And, constitutionally, the Trudeau government's carbon pricing regime violates the principle that the federal government should not unilaterally legislate in areas of provincial jurisdiction (such as natural resource development and conservation), or joint federal-provincial jurisdiction (such as environmental protection) unless it has the consent of the affected provinces.

There is ample ground, therefore, for conservatives to criticize and oppose any and all of these misguided regimes, and strong incentives to develop and propose superior alternatives.

In doing so, however, conservatives should be careful not to reject the basic concept of pollution pricing, because market-based solutions are surely more effective and compatible with conservative principles than the alternative, i.e., massive macro-regulation and micro-regulation and interventions by governments in the name of environmental protection.

Here, then, are three suggestions for how conservatives can take a positive, proactive stance on environmental issues and move towards a Green Conservatism as a major component of our policy platforms:

179 The Alberta carbon tax regime, for example, introduced by the NDP government, was never revenue neutral, was riddled with subsidies, and 95 of the 100 pages of the bill introducing it consisted of more regulations. Even the ostensible political reason for introducing it—to secure the "social license" for the construction of pipelines to tidewater—was a failure. All this contributed substantially to the defeat of that government in April 2019.

180 To be fair, the carbon pricing regime instituted by the Gordon Campbell and Christy Clark governments of British Columbia came closest to satisfying these conditions. But it too, in particular its original revenue neutrality, is in the process of being distorted and corrupted by the current NDP regime in BC.

- Recognize that "conservative" and "conservation" come from the same root. There is nothing philosophically incompatible between economic conservatism and environmental conservation. Conservatives by definition should be conservationists
- Expand the application of the basic principle of living within our means, the principle at the heart of fiscal conservatism, to living within our means ecologically[181]
- Since conservatives believe market mechanisms are superior to government interventions and regulations, make the harnessing of market mechanisms[182] to environmental conservation via pricing signals and financial incentives, the signature contribution of conservatives to addressing environmental issues

There is no reason whatsoever for conservatives to cede the moral high ground when it comes to environmental conservation. As the British conservative philosopher Sir Roger Scruton has written, "Conservation and conservatism are two aspects of a single long-term policy, which is that of husbanding resources and ensuring their renewal."[183] Conservatives are deeply attached to the idea of stewardship of our land and resources, seeing them as a sacred trust which should be handed down from generation to generation. It is no wonder that conservatives have often been at the forefront of conservation efforts historically, whether John A Macdonald establishing Canada's first national park at Banff, Alberta, or American Republican President Teddy Roosevelt, a lifelong hunter and sportsman, preserving 230-million acres of public land in the United States. Today's conservatives must apply these deeply conservative insights and instincts to the problems of our own era, especially around the question of energy and climate change.

---

181 "Living within our means" is actually an ecological principle. We cannot put demands on ecosystems beyond their ability to carry those demands. Thus fiscal conservatives especially should be open to rigorously applying this principle to ecosystems and to becoming champions of measures to eliminate ecological deficits and to balance the ecological budget.

182 A pure market is simply a device to efficiently bring supply to bear on demand by means of pricing signals and financial incentives. In theory, a market doesn't care whether the demand is for widgets or automobiles or oil, or whether it is for clean air, clean water, or reclaimed soil.

183 Roger Scruton, *Green Philosophy: How to Think Seriously About the Planet*, 2012.

If we apply a conservative, conservationist, market-based approach to energy production it would mean that a responsible and forward-looking position for conservatives would be:

- To recognize the absolute importance of the energy sector to the well-being of Canada and Canadians
- To identify any negative environmental impacts associated with the production of energy from any source
- To identify, cost out, and implement avoidance or mitigation measures to reduce those impacts
- To include the costs of those measures in the price of the energy through a pollution levy
- To promote and adopt other necessary and complementary policies, such as revenue neutrality, freedom from subsidies, regulatory-burden reduction, and trade compatibility, required to make the concept of pollution pricing environmentally effective, economically sound, and politically feasible
- To champion the eventual application of market-based approaches to environmental conservation and full-cost accounting to all forms of energy production (not just production from hydrocarbons) and to all economic activities, not just energy production.[184]

184 If we are going to internalize the negative environmental impacts from hydro-carbon production and consumption through carbon-pricing regimes, surely it is only logical and fair that we also internalize the negative environmental impacts of other energy sources since failing to do so will send erroneous, environmentally-insensitive, market-distorting pricing signals to consumers of those forms of energy. So if we institute a carbon tax for the petroleum producers and consumers, where is the reservoir tax for the hydro producers and consumers, who (in Canada) have flooded carbon sinks the size of Lake Ontario and use copious amounts of concrete (the production of which generates significant amounts of CO_2) to build their dams? Where is the radiation tax for the nuclear energy producers and consumers who, while they don't generate a lot of greenhouse gases, produce one of the deadliest pollutants known to man in the form of radioactive wastes which have required the expenditure of hundreds of millions of public dollars to process, transport, and store? And while we're on the subject, where is the environmental levy on the solar and wind power producers and consumers, since no form of energy production is environmentally neutral, although some forms are obviously less environmentally damaging than others and this will only be fairly reflected in a full cost accounting system that includes them all.

Does this mean that conservatives should give unqualified support to the carbon taxes being imposed for example by left-of-centre governments? As already stated, of course not. But it means that these initiatives should be critiqued and if necessary attacked, not because the concept of pollution pricing is wrong but because its implementation has been wrong and has been bungled by governments who really do not believe in the efficacy of market mechanisms and are therefore hopelessly inept at applying them.

If you are skeptical about global warming and the role of human economic activity in contributing to it, then apply this concept of market-based pollution pricing in some other area where you do acknowledge a negative environmental impact from some economic activity, for example, as a means of dealing with industrial waste, household garbage, water shortages, or traffic congestion.

In summary, in cultivating new ground there would be great merit in conservatives adopting Green Conservatism as a major component of our policy platforms going forward. And guess who among the electorate is most likely to welcome such initiatives and contribute to their further development and implementation? Next-generation Canadians whose current interests and future well-being should be uppermost in our minds.

DO SOMETHING!

If you are an executive, researcher, or communicator with a think tank, interest group, or political party with environmental interests and concerns:

- Undertake and communicate research to further develop the market based approach to environmental protection
- Support efforts to persuade conservative parties, caucuses, and governments to champion such an approach

If you are an executive with a philanthropic foundation or a major donor to policy development institutions, interest groups, and political parties:

- Make a significant financial contribution to those working to develop and promote market-based approaches to environmental conservation
- Withdraw your financial contributions from those organizations which oppose market-based approaches to environmental conservation and promote massive macro- and micro-regulation by governments

If you are a corporate board member or executive with an interest in and commitment to environmental conservation:

- Initiate a full-cycle analysis of the environmental impacts of your company if that has not already been done
- Support the adoption of market based approaches to avoiding or mitigating the negative environmental impacts identified
- Provide corporate support to think tanks, interest groups, and political organizations who champion market-based approaches to environmental conservation.

If you are an executive or senior manager of a mass media organization (a newspaper or radio/television organization):

- Initiate an environmental impact assessment of your own operations and publicize the results
- Identify and implement avoidance or mitigative measures to reduce or eliminate negative environmental impacts identified
- Incorporate the cost of those measures in your advertising and subscription rates, practicing and demonstrating, not just preaching the concept and benefits of pollution pricing

If you are a Canadian citizen and voter who attaches great importance to environmental conservation and protection:

- Become a personal advocate and practitioner of market-based approaches to that challenge, and an active supporter of those who champion that approach in the political arena

A proactive, balanced approach to the climate change challenge

In the run up to the 2019 federal election in Canada, the polls indicated that at a majority of Canadians considered climate change to be a major issue which they wanted effectively addressed by their elected representatives.

For example, a pre-election poll[185] which surveyed 3,000 French-speaking and English-speaking Canadians over the age of eighteen, with an additional oversampling of first-time voters (ages 18–21), indigenous Canadians, and new Canadians, revealed the following:

- Close to two-thirds said that our survival depends on addressing climate change or that addressing climate change is a top priority, and 65% said that the government needs to do more to address climate change. Only 6% said they did not believe in climate change
- Four in ten supported carbon pricing and just under half were opposed. A majority of those from Alberta, Manitoba, Saskatchewan and Ontario were opposed, but the majority in the remaining provinces were in support. Four in ten also said that they didn't understand the carbon tax—understanding was correlated with support
- The percentages of respondents who agreed strongly or somewhat agreed with the statement "Canada is not doing enough to fight climate change" were 76% for Quebec, 66% for B.C. and Atlantic Canada, 64% for Ontario, 54% for Saskatchewan, and 44% for Alberta

The acceptance of climate change as an urgent reality and the insistence that it be recognized and addressed appeared to be stronger among young people (18–24 years of age) than among older voters, and stronger among electors living in our major cities than among rural voters.

Three of the national political parties (the Liberals, the NDP, and the Green Party) devoted major portions of their platforms and campaigns to respond to the climate change issue. These responses included

---

185 The poll was conducted by Public Square Research and Maru Blue in partnership with the CBC, between May 31, 2019 and June 10. See http://www.public-squareresearch.ca/

castigating the petroleum sector and its supporters, committing themselves to the goals of the Paris Climate Change Accord,[186] and supporting the use of carbon taxes to reduce greenhouse gas emissions. The Conservative Party of Canada[187] opposed carbon taxes, did not address the climate change issue directly or substantively, and appeared to pay a price at the ballot box, i.e., failing to achieve the levels of support in the big urban centers and among younger voters it had hoped to secure.

Conservatives can debate the exact extent to which the federal party's position or lack of a position on climate change was a factor in the election. But surely it is safe to say that conservatives in Canada, whether we believe anthropogenic (i.e. caused by humans) climate change to be a reality or not, need to develop a proactive and substantive response to the issue if only for the democratic reason that a majority of our fellow citizens wish it to be addressed.

What then might be the particular contribution of conservative to the climate change debate at this point in time, a response rooted in conservative principles and involving a credible transition from the reactionary position of the past to one that is more positive, proactive, and credible?

My suggestion is that conservatives make a major effort to champion balance in the climate change arena which has become seriously polarized and characterized by extreme statements and positions on both sides, one camp denying that there is even a problem and the other camp declaring that the end of the world is imminent if their analyses and solutions are not immediately adopted.

Bringing balance to the climate change debate and the composition of the policy measures that flow from it is not only a conservative thing to do, it is a very Canadian thing to do. After all, as the old joke goes: Why did the Canadian cross the road? To get to the middle.

As I've mentioned in the past, Canadians were especially known for having a sense of balance, for seeking and finding the midpoint between extremes. But this is not presently the case, as finding a balance between environmental protection and economic activity increasingly eludes us.

186 See Paris Agreement (All language versions) | UNFCCC; https://unfccc.int › paris-climate-change-conference-november-2015 ›

187 See Andrew Scheer's Climate Plan—Conservative Party of Canada. https://www.conservative.ca › cpc › andrew-scheers-climate-plan The plan rested on three policy principles: (1) Green technology, not taxes. (2) A cleaner and greener natural environment. (3) Taking our fight against climate change global.

What, then, can and should be done to achieve balance on the environment-economy front? Here are seven suggestions:

- Expand consideration of the body of scientific evidence relevant to climate change to include *all the scientific evidence*. This would include any legitimate scientific evidence which challenges the global warming hypothesis,[188] or current responses to it,[189] and scientific evidence pertaining to the non-human causes of climate change[190] such as slight alterations in the earth's orbit, solar activity, volcanic activity, and the El Nino Southern Oscillation (ENSO)[191]. At the same time, conservatives need to accept that the preponderance of scientific evidence indicates that human-caused global warming is a real, verifiable phenomenon, as even skeptical, conservative leaning scientists like nuclear physicist Richard Muller have convincingly shown.[192]
- Balance efforts and expenditures to address climate change between mitigative policies and measures which constrain the human contributions thereto and adaptation policies and measures which assist society to adapt to climate changes beyond human control
- Find and implement the appropriate balance between policy-based solutions (e.g. pollution pricing and regulatory regimes) and technology based solutions (such as those currently being explored or used to dramatically reduce GHG emissions from oil-sands production).
- Since Canada is responsible for only 1.6% of global GHG emissions, aim for a much more realistic balance between efforts and

---

188 See "31,000 scientists say "no convincing evidence." http://ossfoundation.us/projects/environment/global-warming/myths
189 See Lomborg, Bjørn, *The Skeptical Environmentalist: Measuring the Real State of the World*, Cambridge University Press, 2001.
190 Human vs. Natural Contributions to Global Warming https://skepticalscience.com › graphics
191 The El Niño–Southern Oscillation (*ENSO*) is an irregularly periodic variation in winds and sea surface temperatures over the tropical eastern Pacific Ocean, affecting the climate of much of the tropics and subtropics.
192 Rohde R.; Muller R.A.; Jacobsen R.; Muller E.; Perlmutter S.. et al. (2013) "A New Estimate of the Average Earth Surface Land Temperature Spanning 1753 to 2011," *Geoinformatics and Geostatistics: An Overview 1:1. See also* Muller, Richard, "The Conversion of a Climate Change Skeptic," *New York Times*, July 30, 2012 https://www.nytimes.com/2012/07/30/opinion/the-conversion-of-a-climate-change-skeptic.html

expenditures to reduce GHG emissions at home and Canadian support of GHG emission reduction in other countries whose emission levels are much higher than our own. For example, by exporting CO_2 reduction technology and liquified natural gas (to replace coal-fired electricity generation) to countries like India, China, and Indonesia.

- Since the two main policy mechanisms for reducing GHG emissions are (1) employing market mechanisms such as carbon pricing and (2) securing reductions through macro-regulation and micro-regulation, debate and decide what is the most appropriate balance between the two, recognizing that market mechanisms are usually the most effective, lowest cost way to achieve emissions reductions.

- If we are going to require internalization of the costs of mitigating the negative environmental impacts of energy production from hydrocarbons through a carbon pricing regime, then balance requires internalization of the costs of mitigating the negative environmental effects of all other sources of energy—hydro, nuclear, solar, wind, biomass, etc.—since no energy source is "environmentally neutral." The failure to do so creates an unfair imbalance between the price of energy obtained from sources which internalize the cost of mitigating their negative environmental impacts and the prices of energy obtained from source which do not

- Continue to require honest and reliable Environmental Impact Assessments of economic activities, but, to achieve balance on the environment/economy front, also insist upon Economic Impact Assessments of major environmental protection measures including carbon pricing regimes, environmental protection regulations, and international environmental protection agreements such as the Paris Climate Change Accord[193]

This latter point is particularly important and worth elaborating on as it is a practical measure which can be immediately pursued via legislative amendments initiated by elected officials in any of our democratic assemblies.

---

193 It is unconscionable that the government of Canada would become a signatory to the Paris Climate Change Accord without first of all assessing the economic impacts of the environmental protection measures called for.

As the historical record shows, at one time economic development in Canada took precedence and priority over environmental considerations, to the serious detriment of the environment. And so, at both the provincial and federal levels, Environmental Impact Assessment legislation and regulations were adopted requiring any proponent of a major economic initiative to file environmental impact assessments with the appropriate regulatory authorities.

At first, these assessments grossly underestimated the environmental impacts of economic projects. But under the pressure of regulatory scrutiny and third-party examination, they gradually increased in scope and reliability, and in the weight assigned to them by regulators in assessing the appropriateness of the economic initiatives to which they pertained.

In physics, according to Newton's third law, for every action there is an equal and opposite reaction. But in our polarized political world, for every action there is often an opposite and unequal reaction, resulting in an imbalance. Thus, in an increasing number of cases, environmental protection now takes precedence and priority over economic development. In British Columbia, for example, this imbalance has gone so far that for a resource developer to harm a fish, an animal, or a tree is deemed an unpardonable sin, but for an environmental lobby to kill the job and income of a resource-sector worker is deemed a cause for celebration.

This imbalance was evident in the 553-page report of the National Energy Board[194] to the federal cabinet recommending conditional approval of the Trans Mountain Expansion project, the report found to be deficient by the Federal Court of Appeal in its 272-page decision.[195] In the NEB report, two summary pages and one short chapter were devoted to the economic feasibility and benefits to Canada of the project, whereas over one-third of the report is devoted to the recognition and assessment of negative environmental and social impacts. Nowhere in the report was there an assessment of the costs and economic impacts of project deferral or implementation of the hundreds of constraints demanded by interveners, or the 150-plus conditions recommended by the board.

194 https://apps.neb-one.gc.ca/REGDOCS/Item/Filing/A77045
195 Tsleil-Waututh Nation v. Canada (Attorney General), 2018 FCA 153 (CanLII), <http://canlii.ca/t/htq8p>, retrieved on 2019-05-09

Despite the NEB's extensive attention to indigenous and environ- ·mental issues, this was still found to be insufficient by the Federal Court of Appeal. That decision furthered the imbalance between economic and non-economic factors by requiring yet another round of consultations with indigenous groups and additional assessments of marine traffic impacts. Again, the court's analysis and decision-making process was focused almost entirely on the environmental and social impacts of the project, with no counter-balancing consideration of impacts on the economy, the negative impacts on energy users, investors, and work- ers if the project fails to proceed, or the costs of delays and mitigation measures.

In February 2019, the NEB then released its 680-page Reconsideration Report[196] in response to the decision of the Federal Court of Appeal. The board's overall recommendation to the federal government was that the Trans Mountain Expansion Project is in the public interest and should be approved. But the recommended approval was then made subject to the imposition of 156 conditions on the project plus sixteen new recom- mendations that fall outside the NEB's mandate, and largely focus on environmental considerations.

To be fair, neither the board nor the court can really be blamed for this imbalance. As the Appeal acourt itself pointed out, it and the board are bound by the legislative regime established by such statutes as the National Energy Board Act and the Canadian Environmental Assessment Act.

This imbalance has been made even worse by the Trudeau gov- ernment's ill-advised changes to the regulatory regime governing the energy/environment relationship. Bill C-48, passed prior to the federal election, established a moratorium on oil tanker traffic on the west coast. But it fails to provide for any assessment of the economic impacts of that measure or its extension to the east coast should that eventually occur. The Trudeau government also put forward Bill C-69 replacing the NEB with a new Impact Assessment Agency. But what are the impacts that agency is directed by the legislation to assess? Only environmen- tal impacts, with no legislated directive or mandate to assess economic impacts at all, let alone find the balance between the two.

---

196 See A98021-1 NEB—NEB Reconsideration Report https://www.neb-one.gc.ca/ pplctnflng/mjrpp/trnsmntnxpnsn/trnsmntnxpnsnrprt-eng.html

What kind of legislative action is required to establish genuine, Canadian-style balance between environmental protection and economic development?[197] Maintain the legislated requirements for environmental impact assessments but amend regulatory and environmental protection legislation to require:

(1) that the proponents of major environmental protection measures file economic impact assessments of the measures they propose
(2) that regulators and government decision makers give equal and balanced consideration to the economic and environmental impacts of the projects they evaluate. At the federal level, legislate these provisions via a Canadian Economic Impact Assessment Act,[198] the economic equivalent of legislation mandating environmental impact assessments.

If it is feared that meeting these requirements will further lengthen the regulatory hearing process, let governments also impose reasonable time limits to such hearings. Should a hearing exceed those limits, empower the regulators to allocate the costs of the extension to those deemed most responsible for causing it. As it is, the time required to arrive at binding decisions on energy projects has become so long and uncertain as to discredit the whole process and make it a subject for ridicule. As one regulatory lawyer (tongue firmly in cheek) has suggested, if Canada were to ever run out of oil and gas, we could just burn the transcripts from all the energy/environment related regulatory and court hearings and thereby extend our energy supplies for another ten years.

197 See Manning, Preston, "We must restore balance between the environment and the economy," *Globe and Mail*, October 19, 2018.
198 For an excellent primer on the principles of Economic Impact Assessments, see http://www.edrgroup.com/images/stories/Transportation/econ-impact-primer.pdf The application of these principles needs to be extended to assessing the economic impacts of major environmental protection proposals and initiatives.

DO SOMETHING!

If you are an executive, researcher, or communicator with a think tank or academic policy institute desirous of seeing balance restored between economic growth and environmental protection:

- Take the initiative in performing and publicizing Economic Impact Assessments on some major environmental protection measure currently being proposed by an environmental interest group or governmen
- Support efforts to persuade political parties, caucuses, and governments to enact and enforce Economic Impact Assessment legislation

If you are an executive with a philanthropic foundation or a major donor to policy development institutions, interest groups, and political parties:

- Make a significant financial contribution to those working to balance the current requirements for Environmental Impact Assessments with legislation requiring Economic Impact Assessments of environmental protection measures
- Withdraw your financial contributions from those organizations which oppose such legislation and related research and advocacy

If you are a corporate board member or executive of an environmental interest group which promotes environmental protection measures:

- Voluntarily undertake and publish Economic Impact Assessments of the environmental protection measures you propose
- Submit your Economic Impact Assessments to third-party and regulatory scrutiny

If you are an executive or senior manager of a mass media organization (a newspaper, a radio/television organization, or social media platform):

continued

- Actively promote the need for legislation to require Economic Impact Assessments of all major environmental protection measures and publicize the results of such assessments

If you are an executive, staffer, or member of a political party desirous of seeing balance restored between economic growth and environmental protection:

- Work to make the achievement of such balance a clearly stated objective of your party
- Work to include in your party's policy platform the requirement that proposals for manor environmental protection measures be accompanied by Economic Impact Assessments of those measures

If you are a Canadian citizen and voter desirous of seeing balance restored between economic growth and environmental protection:

- Become a personal advocate and supporter of interest groups, candidates, and political parties committed to securing such a balance
- Withdraw your support from interest groups, candidates, and political parties whose positions contribute to polarization and imbalance on the economy-environment front.

If you are a conservative skeptical about the reality or urgency of human-caused climate change:

- Do not allow that skepticism to make you an opponent of environmental conservation and protection on other fronts.
- Become a personal advocate and supporter of policies and measures to facilitate adaptation to climate changes due to factors beyond human control.
- Support efforts to make Canadian conservatism a champion of balance on the environment/economy front.

Avoid the wet blanket syndrome

Finally, let me make an appeal for a fundamental change of attitude with respect to how we Canadians generally respond to new ideas whatever their nature and source.

As someone who has been involved in pushing new ideas all my life, it has been my experience that our initial reaction as Canadians to a new or novel idea tends to be skeptical and negative. "What a weird idea!" "That will never work!" "Haven't you thought about this obstacle, that problem, etc."

In our cold climate, the predictable consequence of pouring cold water on a new idea is to immobilize ("ice") its further development.

But all is not lost. If the innovator is persistent and can hang in there long enough, we Canadians often have second thoughts which are sometimes more positive and encouraging. "Well, maybe that would be worth thinking about." "Maybe that could work if. . ." And so on. Unfortunately, in many cases, our initial negative reaction has so discouraged the innovator that he or she has given up or gone elsewhere (often to the U.S.) where the innovation climate is usually more accepting.

In my own case, two of my first short term jobs were in California. The first was a summer internship as a physics student with the Bechtel Corporation in San Francisco where my assignment was to do a paper on whether or not "light amplification by the stimulated emission of radiation" (LASER) had a commercial future. The second was as a pioneer "civil systems analyst" with TRW Systems of Redondo Beach, California.

TRW was the firm that pioneered the application of general systems theory[199] to project management in the US defense industry, in particular to the development and management of the Minuteman Missile Defense System. To diversify, TRW had then become interested in exploring whether systems analysis and management techniques, an innovation at the time, could be applied to civil systems like the organization and management of health care and educational systems.

---

199 See Bertalanffy, L. von, *General System Theory*, George Braziller, New York, 1969. Bertalanffy's conceptualization of physical and biological entities as "systems," in terms of inputs, outputs, and definable relations among their components, is applicable to understanding and managing a great variety of systems, including companies, social service organizations, and even political systems.

What I noticed with the California crowd was that their initial reaction to a new idea was usually positive. "What an interesting idea!" "You know, that just might work." "Maybe somebody should investigate that further . . . etc." Of course, in the end this did not mean unqualified acceptance, because then they would have their second thoughts. In their case, these would involve hard-headed critical analysis which might well lead to resistance to or abandonment of the new idea. But because the initial response to the new idea was positive or at least open, it often provided enough encouragement and generated sufficient resources to enable the innovator to persevere and carry the idea several steps further, rather than giving up or going elsewhere.

And so, as Canadians with a congenital predisposition to resist new ideas and give in to the Wet Blanket Syndrome, let us resolve to be more open to political and policy innovation at the outset. As conservatives, let's *Do Something!* to encourage and support the cultivation of new ground; there will be enough objections and resistance from naysayers, media sceptics, and public inertia to whatever new ideas we might embrace, without ourselves needlessly adding at the very outset to those objections and that resistance.

Finally, to conclude this chapter, if none of these illustrations of cultivating new ground are novel or relevant enough to stimulate your interest and support, I challenge you to come up with and promote your own new ideas for advancing democracy in Canada and the contributions of conservatives thereto. In any case, *Do Something!*–something positive–to significantly increase and improve the intellectual capital available to Canada's political practitioners.

2.3 Strengthen Relations With the Science Community

A personal interest

My personal (but amateur) interest in science began in high school. For some reason, I became particularly fascinated by Mendeleev's Periodic Table of the Elements. In 1870, he organized information concerning the sixty-three then-known elements into a matrix.[200] His observations of gaps in the intersections of the rows and columns of his matrix then led him to predict the existence of thirty as-of-yet unknown elements with properties appropriate to fill those gaps. In other words, by simply re-structuring known data of existing elements in matrix form, he provided guidelines for the discovery of new elements. Amazing.

At the time I was living on my parents' dairy farm east of Edmonton where we had a bunkhouse for the hired man with an extra room at one end. This I appropriated and turned into my laboratory. I borrowed hydrolysis equipment from school and began to manufacture oxygen and hydrogen which my friends and I hoped to pressure into balloons, to then be shot at with our .22 rifles, hopefully producing spectacular explosions. (This never quite worked out as planned, the fate of most of my scientific experiments.)

One December, I advised my folks that I wanted a Geiger tube for Christmas. Somehow they managed to obtain one that I then embedded in a hollowed-out broom handle and hooked to an amplifier with a long cord. I now had a homemade Geiger counter capable of detecting

---

200 "Matrix" is the Latin word for "womb," the place where a "new" being comes into existence.

radioactivity. I persuaded my father (Premier of Alberta at the time) to request some pitchblende samples (which contained radium) from the Alberta Research Council. They probably wondered why the Premier's Office was requesting pitchblende, but obliged nonetheless. I would then invite my friends to hide the samples and impress all concerned with my ability to find them using my home-made radiation detector.

Unfortunately, the hired man heard me talking darkly about doing experiments with hydrogen and radiation in my lab. He got the mistaken idea that I was just one step away from making "the bomb" and threatened to quit unless my lab was shut down. Since this would have meant that I would end up milking cows, I reluctantly agreed.

Upon graduating from high school I was interested enough in science to enroll at the University of Alberta, whose motto was "whatsoever things are true," in the honors physics program. But in pursuing truth through physics I soon found that I couldn't handle the math so I switched to economics where you can pursue truth and make the math work out by changing the assumptions. Later, of course, I got into politics, which some cynics have interpreted as an abandonment of the pursuit of truth altogether.

Having by now thoroughly impressed you with my interest in and pursuit of science, let us turn to a more serious discussion of the interface of science and politics.

Science and the founding of Canada

Most Canadians know the story of how Canada began as a country, how a few farsighted leaders pursued a vision to unite the British North American colonies into one nation under a federal constitution, integrated the colonial economies into a single national economy, and provided for future development by acquiring the vast territory and resources of Rupert's Land. They then bound the whole enterprise together by building the longest railway in the world to tie in British Columbia.

But what we often fail to appreciate today is that there was also a science-based dimension to that story. A generation earlier, the leaders and people of those same British North American colonies launched a scientific endeavor which was to contribute as much to the building of Canada as the BNA Act and the Canadian Pacific Railway. It was called the Geological Survey of Canada and it began with a £1500 grant from the legislature of the United Colony of Canada to carry out a geological survey of its territory.

After Confederation in 1867, the Geological Survey of Canada[201] was expanded to become the principal science-based endeavor of the new federal government. Under the leadership of able scientific directors such as William Logan, G. M. Dawson, Alfred Selwyn, and J. B. Tyrrell, its dedicated personnel methodically surveyed and cataloged the land, minerals, soil, climate, water, and forests of Canada, the natural resource base of the Canadian economy and the first scientific description of Canada's physical environment.

Strengthening the science-political relationship

Flash forward a century and a half and there is now no denying that science is one of the most dominant forces and influences in modern societies. The scientific method is now our chief mechanism for generating knowledge and solving problems. Science and technology are principal drivers of the economy as well as major contributors to environmental protection, improvements in human health, national defense, and the list goes on.

Science has a major contribution to make in almost every area of public policy and government service and governments are a major funder of scientific research and development. Nevertheless, notwithstanding these realities, a large and persistent gap exists in understanding and relationships between the political and scientific communities. A concentrated effort to define and reduce that gap is therefore in order, strengthening the intellectual capital of the political class by strengthening its relationships with the scientific community.

The gap defined

Politicians generally are not up on science or scientific advancements, feel little compulsion to improve their knowledge and contacts in this

---

201 The Geological Survey of Canada (GSC) was founded in 1842. It helped develop a viable Canadian mineral industry by establishing the general geological base on which the industry could plan detailed investigations.

area, and are uncomfortable with and reluctant to deal with the public policy implications of scientific advancements, especially if they raise difficult ethical and social issues. (The major exception to this point is the extent to which many contemporary politicians have become engaged with the scientific aspects of climate change policy.)

At the same time, scientists are not usually attracted to politics and the political world, feeling little compulsion to improve their knowledge and contacts in this area. They are generally uncomfortable when political and public-policy considerations are brought to bear on their work.

The knowledge gap

The ignorance of basic science among many elected officials and their political staff and their indifference to acquiring a better understanding of science and its relevance to public policy is often reflected in the speeches which political people give to scientific conferences and gatherings.

Far too often, at scientific conferences where a politician is invited to speak, it will be the politician's address which will be the weakest and least relevant of all the presentations.[202] Of course, any politician invited to address a scientific gathering could recite Mary Had A Little Lamb and still expect vigorous applause, as long as the address included a funding pledge or announcement.

The interest gap

If the gap between the political and scientific communities is to be closed, much work needs to be done to stimulate greater interest in scientific knowledge among the political class.

---

202 For example, at the 2017 Canadian Science Policy Conference in Ottawa, attended by over 800 people from the science community, many with very impressive scientific credentials, the two weakest and most self-serving addresses were delivered by whom? The federal Minister of Science and Sport, who spent the first fifteen minutes of her speech shamelessly flattering the attendees, and the Ontario Minister of Research, Innovation, and Science who spent most of his time congratulating his own government on its magnanimous support of science.

During my time in parliament (1993–2002), one of the most significant scientific breakthroughs was the successful sequencing of the human genome,[203] a development with enormous implications for everything from human health to biological warfare.

One of the Canadian medical scientists who played a significant role in that development was Dr. Tom Hudson[204] from McGill University. When several of us MP's heard that he was going to be in Ottawa to address a breakfast meeting on the subject, we asked him to also meet with members of the House of Commons to brief us on this momentous scientific advancement. Ideally, the invitation to MPs to attend this meeting should have been accompanied by an explanation of its purpose and importance and issued by the scientifically-oriented members of our parliamentary caucuses or staffs. Unfortunately (and this is part of the gap problem), there are few if any former scientists or former science administrators in the caucuses of the House of Commons or even among parliamentary staff. And so the meeting with Dr. Hudson had to be organized and promoted by MPs like myself who had an interest in the subject of the human genome but no real scientific background or knowledge of the subject.

Of the three hundred members of the House, we identified the one hundred who would most likely be interested. These were all contacted and invited personally and persistently to meet Dr. Hudson, not by outside interests or lobbyists, but by their own peers, fellow members of parliament.

When the day came for the meeting, however, only twenty MPs showed up. Ignorance of the science and its significance, indifference to appeals to become more knowledgeable, and a reluctance to come to grips with some of the issues it raised, all played a part in limiting the attendance.

203 The Human Genome Project (HGP) was an international scientific research project with the goal of determining the sequence of nucleotide base pairs that make up human DNA, and of identifying and mapping all of the genes of the human genome from both a physical and a functional standpoint. The project was launched in 1990 and completed in 2001, and at the time constituted the world's largest collaborative biological research project.

204 Dr. Thomas J. Hudson was formerly assistant director of the Whitehead Institute/ MIT Center for Genome Research. He led efforts to generate dense human and mouse genome maps. In June 1996, he founded the Montreal Genome Centre, based at the McGill University Health Centre. The Montreal Genome Centre doubles as Expertise Centre for Genome Quebec.

The credibility gap

The lack of depth on the part of the political class with respect to science and technology is nowhere more evident than when politicians begin to wax eloquent on the subject of innovation. Today, every politician has a platitudinous speech on innovation. "Innovation is the key to economic progress. We are heartily in favor of innovation. Look at all the wonderful things we are doing or proposing to advance innovation in Canada etc."

What makes these speeches so hollow and lacking in credibility is this: if members of the political class are truly committed to innovation, why don't they demonstrate it, less by speechifying on the subject and more by supporting and practicing innovation in their own sphere of influence, in the political world of parties, democratic assemblies, public policies, and elections?

The reality is that whenever any innovation is proposed for their world, the traditional party politician is usually in the forefront of the resistance to it.

Most of the innovative ideas in Canadian politics, such as, voting rights for women, universal health care insurance, monetary reform, sovereignty-association, expansion of free trade, and various proposals for electoral reform, came initially from third parties[205] or special interest groups. And what was invariably the initial reaction of the traditional political class to these proposed innovations? Vehement opposition and resistance.

The Canadian Senate is an unelected, regionally unbalanced, and ineffective institution that is one of the most anachronistic features of the Canadian parliamentary system. But every innovative attempt to reform it for the last hundred years has been resisted and repulsed by the political defenders of the status quo.

The government of Justin Trudeau, which boasts endlessly about its enthusiasm for innovation, hopelessly bungled and has since abandoned its one attempt at political innovation shortly after its election in 2015, namely replacing the current first-past-the-post voting system with something better. If a political party or government will not

---

205 For example, the Progressives, the Cooperative Commonwealth Federation, the Parti/Bloc Quebecois, the Reform Parties, and the Green Parties.

or cannot innovate in its own sphere of undisputed influence,[206] why should members of the scientific or business communities believe in its ability to foster and manage innovation in other areas where its understanding is far less complete?

The relationship gap

The gap between the political and scientific communities is fostered in part by the simple fact that most politicians have little or no contact with scientists in the normal course of their daily work. Furthermore, Canadians with strong scientific backgrounds hardly ever seek to become candidates for election to our parliament, legislatures, or municipal councils. Of those who do, even fewer are ever elected. As a result, there are few if any genuine scientists in any of the legislative caucuses or in the offices of elected officials or their parties. In other words, very few scientists go on the inside where they might champion science-related issues and causes or at least increase the knowledge and understanding of their non-scientific colleagues on such issues and causes.

When politicians are invited to speak at universities, 90% of the time the invitations come from the administration, the law faculty, the political science and economics departments, the business schools, the political clubs, the alumni associations, and occasionally the medical schools.

Those invitations hardly ever come from the basic science faculties, from the physics, mathematics, computer science, chemistry, and life sciences departments. If they did, it would oblige those politicians to get up on the work and interests of such disciplines.

Various scientists and representatives of scientific associations often sought meetings with me in my parliamentary office as did representatives of many other interests. Invariably these meetings were for the sole purpose of securing my support for increased funding of various

206 Other examples of government mismanagement of technological innovations abound, but one of the most egregious at the time of this writing pertains to the federal government abortive attempt to implement the Phoenix payroll system. The Phoenix pay system is a payroll processing system for Canadian federal government employees, run by Public Services and Procurement Canada. After coming online in early 2016, Phoenix has been mired in problems with underpayments, overpayments, and non-payments.

scientific undertakings, rarely to provide a scientific perspective on any of the other issues with which I might have been wrestling or in which I was personally interested.

Meetings, especially frequent, meaningful meetings on a broad range of subjects, ought to foster deeper relationships among the participants. But in the nine years that I was an MP, I can hardly recall one instance when a scientist sought a personal meeting with me in my constituency office. In my case, such meetings would have been more productive and conducive to relationship building than meetings in my parliamentary office, especially if the scientist was one of my own constituents to whom I would feel a personal as well as legal obligation to understand and represent.

Scientists are also conspicuously absent from party membership lists and from constituency town hall meetings attended by hundreds of other citizens, evidence to me again of indifference or even antagonism toward things political.

Meetings which are dominated by a single issue on which the participants have different positions often tend to polarize rather than foster and build solid, multi-dimensional relationships. And unfortunately, the vast majority of meetings between members of the political and scientific communities tends to be completely dominated by one issue: money. And while the funding of science is enormously important, if the only relationship of the political community to the science community is that of the milk cow to the milking machine, that relationship is too narrow, restrictive, and competitive to generate long term knowledgeability and respect. Or put more positively, if the relationship between members of the political and scientific communities could be built first on mutual interest in and respect for each other's work, on personal friendships and associations, on shared commitments to common goals such as improving the lives of Canadians, the discussion of how to adequately finance the development of science and technology would be much more productive and satisfying to both communities.

The communications gap

A communications gap exists between the political and scientific communities which adversely affects all other aspects of relations between them. To a large extent this gap is due to fundamental differences in how politicians and scientists communicate, differences which need to be better understood and accommodated if relationships between the two communities are to be significantly improved.

Most politicians, especially if they are genuine democrats, tend to be "receiver-oriented communicators." They approach the communication process by asking themselves: who is my audience? What are their attitudes and interests? What is the context in which I will address them? What is their vocabulary and conceptual framework? What is their preferred medium of communication? What competing messages are they being exposed to? And so on. Then, given all that information about the receiver of my communications, how should I frame my message so that it will resonate and generate understanding and action from that receiver?

Most scientists and science administrators tend to be "source-oriented communicators." They tend to communicate what they have to say in the way that it is most natural to them and in a manner shaped by the scientific method, that is, by starting with observations and facts, moving to hypotheses and propositions, then to descriptions of the results of experimental activity to verify hypotheses, and then finally to conclusions which are the ultimate message. The sequencing of the mental process is almost the opposite of that of the receiver-oriented communicator. Which is why, if you watch a banker or members of a parliamentary committee reviewing a briefing presentation from a scientist or scientific association, especially if it doesn't contain an executive summary, they will often flip to the back pages first trying to find out what all the preparatory lead-up is ultimately about.

When receiver-oriented communicators and source-oriented communicators get together, unless they understand, appreciate, and accommodate the difference in their modes of communicating, they can be like ships passing in the night. And the net result of their getting together may well be a widening rather than a narrowing of the communications gap between them.

When I was an MP I was once approached by some scientists at the Chalk River Laboratories of Atomic Energy of Canada who were anxious to get parliamentary support for the development of a neutron beam reactor.[207] They asked me to round up a few other MPs, if I could, and

---

207 A neutron beam is a stream of neutrons, extracted from a nuclear reactor or particle accelerator, and used to study the physical composition of samples in physics, chemistry, and biology.

bring them to Chalk River for a presentation. This I did, although once again it was difficult to stimulate much interest in this subject among my colleagues.

When we arrived, we were given a presentation by a very distinguished and knowledgeable physicist who obviously knew what he was talking about. But it was Physics 101 delivered largely in the source-oriented format. It started with what is a neutron, a neutron beam, and a neutron reactor, all from a physicist's perspective. Interesting and technically sound, but I could see some of my MP companions starting to look at the ceiling or out the window. The presentation then went on to explain, in scientific terms, how the neutron beam could be used to probe the composition of various forms of matter. Fine, but I could see my companions wondering where this was leading. Then came the cost data and the pitch for money, which is where we thought it was leading all along.

Finally, we were taken to a large room where there were samples of the various things that could be probed with the neutron beam including (the physicist only casually mentioned it), a portion of an 0-ring from a U.S. space launch vehicle like those of the Challenger spaceship which blew up in January, 1986, killing seven astronauts.

My colleagues were duly impressed, well sort of, but not enough to generate strong support. Nor were they really equipped or incentivized to repeat the main messages of the presentation to their colleagues back in Ottawa.

So how would I, a receiver-oriented communicator, have made that presentation in order to generate the enthusiasm and support that the Chalk River physicists obviously hoped to create? I would first of all have thought long and hard about my audience, the MPs. What could I possibly say to them or show them, to grab their interest and attention right from the get-go, and then link that to the physics of the neutron, the uses of the neutron beam and the need to finance the development of a neutron reactor?

First off, I wouldn't have started in the laboratory or the lecture room. I would have taken them to the theatre/video room of the Chalk River complex. On the screen would be one big word repeated several times, it wouldn't be neutron, or neutron beam, or neutron beam reactor. The word would be "stress."

Next, a dynamic shot of a tire exploding: "stress causes accidents." Then one of a bridge or a building collapsing: "stress destroys property." Then the video clip of the Challenger Space Shuttle exploding because its O-ring blew apart: "stress kills!"[208] And so on through several more dramatic examples. Stress costs money. Stress costs time. Stress costs lives.

So what is this stress, the MPs should now be wondering? We've now got them asking the right question, which we shall now answer. It's the result of forces that pull the molecules of a material structure apart when they're supposed to hold together (my layman's definition which no doubt can be improved upon). Now direct them to the neutron beam. With this neutron beam our physicists are going to tell you about, we can probe those structures at the molecular level, better understand how stress works, and hopefully find ways to render stress less costly and destructive. Having captured the full attention of my MP colleagues, the physicists can now proceed with the Physics 101 lecture and we will be all eyes and ears.[209]

Why is it essential to close the gap between the political and scientific communities?

There are a number of reasons to bring science more effectively to bear on addressing the major public issues and problems of our time, to make members of the science community more active and effective

---

208 Natural or man-made disasters—floods, fires, explosions, tsunamis, pandemics—are tragedies. But from a "communication of science" perspective, because they capture the attention of the public and the politicians, they create rare opportunities for science to explain the physical, chemical, and biological realities behind them. The science community needs to be better prepared and equipped to seize such opportunities.

209 By this illustration, I do not mean to imply in any way that there are not some excellent communicators within the scientific communicators, because there most certainly are. One of these whom I encountered during my time in Ottawa was Dr. Art McDonald, Director of the Sudbury Neutrino Observatory (SNO). Dr. McDonald, who was later to co-win a Nobel Prize for his work, also invited MPs to see his project and, in my case, I came away both enlightened and impressed. I must mention that Art had one communications strategy, although he insists that he never really did seriously employ it, that was bound to generate enthusiasm for his neutrino detection project. And that was to take us MPs two miles down into the old mine shaft where his observatory was located, lead us through a maze of tunnels to the actual SNO facility, then turn off the lights and very subtly imply that the likelihood of us getting back to the surface was somewhat dependent on our support for the project.

participants in Canada's democratic institutions and processes, and to put future public financing of the development of science and technology on a more solid, relational footing.

One of the most important reasons for closing the gap, the one most heavily impressed upon me by my time in parliament, is this: unless there is a dramatic improvement in the scientist-politician relationship, there is a high probability that our elected members and governments will bungle the application of scientific and technological advancements to public needs and Canadians will be denied the many benefits they should have received from such applications.

Consider the worst case of bungling a scientific advancement that I ever witnessed during my years in Ottawa, and one which is still going on under the Trudeau administration. It involved the response (or non-response) of the federal government and parliament to the need for a regulatory framework for assisted human reproduction and related science.[210] This is one of the most rapidly developing areas of science today and one with enormous implications for human health and well-being. It was a subject with which I was to become personally familiar as a member of the House of Commons' Standing Committee on Health in 2001.

In 1989, the Mulroney government, in response to rapid developments in genetic science, established the Royal Commission on Reproductive Technologies under the chairmanship of Dr. Patricia Baird. Four years and millions of dollars later, the commission completed its report which strongly recommended the immediate creation of a legal framework for regulating assisted human reproduction and related science, including that pertaining to cloning, stem cell production and use, egg and embryo donations, and gene therapies.

With a change of government (the election of the Chretien government) in 1993, nothing was done until 1995 when the Minister of Health announced an interim voluntary moratorium on several activities of concern such as human cloning and paying surrogate mothers for

210 "Proceed With Care: Final Report of the Royal Commission on New Reproductive Technologies," Patricia Baird, Chairperson: http://publications.gc.ca/pub?id= 9.699855&sl=0 While the Commission concluded that some reproductive technologies and some of their uses are unethical and contrary to Canadians' values, it found that others are potentially beneficial, if used ethically and responsibly. Hence the need for a system to oversee, license, and monitor activities discussed in the report.

their child-bearing services. Finally, in 1996, the Chretien government introduced Bill C-47, the proposed Human Reproductive and Genetic Technologies Act, which would have prohibited specified activities, but did not set out a clear mechanism for regulating other important activities that could be carried out under prescribed conditions. This bill died on the order paper of the House of Commons at the call of the 1997 federal election.

While genetic and reproductive science was advancing at warp speed, another four years passed during which parliament did nothing on this front. Then, in May 2001 the Minister of Health invited the House of Commons Standing Committee on Health to conduct a full review of a new draft bill containing Proposals for Governing Assisted Human Reproduction. In December 2001, the health committee, of which I was a member, tabled its report and among its multiple recommendations requested that regulatory legislation be introduced on a priority basis.

On May 9, 2002, the government introduced Bill C-56 *An Act Respecting Assisted Human Reproduction,* a bill based in part on the previous draft and modified somewhat by the health committee's recommendations. But on June 21, parliament prorogued. On October 9th, 2002, after parliament had reconvened, the government reintroduced Bill C-56, with some modifications, as Bill C-13. This Bill, believe it or not, was eventually passed by the House and moved on to the Senate in 2003. But it stalled there. Parliament again prorogued while the Liberal leadership changed hands from Jean Chretien to Paul Martin.

When Parliament reconvened, Bill C-13 was reintroduced as Bill C-6. It was deemed to have passed all stages in the House on February 11, 2004, and was subsequently passed by the Senate. On March 29, 2004, Bill C-6 was given royal assent, that is, it became law fifteen years after the Royal Commission had been struck to address this "urgent national priority."[211] But that is still not the end of the story.

---

211 Other examples exist of the long lead times for innovations to be adopted and financed whenever scrutiny and approval by government bureaucracies are involved. For example, a recent study by the Montreal Economic Institute of the bureaucratic obstacle course which innovations in the pharmaceutical field must run, reported that: "In 2015–16, the process of economic assessment (employed by provincial governments to determine whether a new drug should be included on their respective lists of reimbursed drugs) added 450 days, or some 15 months, between the moment when drugs are approved by Health Canada and the

On the very first occasion that I saw this law in draft form, it was obvious to me that in essence it was dealing with measures related to human health. Under our constitution, these are primarily matters of provincial jurisdiction. I therefore suggested to the federal health minister of the day that we might as well send the bill directly to the courts because even if it was eventually passed by the federal parliament, it would surely be challenged on constitutional grounds, most likely by the Quebec government.

And sure enough, despite all the efforts of the federal government to "shoehorn" the bill into federal jurisdiction by criminalizing certain violations of its provisions (such as the prohibition against cloning) so that it would fall under the federal power to ensure "peace order and good government," the bill ended up before the Supreme Court of Canada in 2010.[212]

Predictably the court declared, after almost twenty years of legislative attention by the parliament of Canada to this highly important and rapidly-advancing field of scientific endeavor, that whole sections of the bill were *ultra vires* (beyond the powers of the federal government to enact) and therefore invalid.

This sad tale is but one example of how utterly unprepared our elected officials are, at both the provincial and federal levels, to respond in a timely and intelligent fashion to rapid advancements in the field of science.

But wait! The story is still not over. Advances in genetic engineering such as the development and use of the CRISPR Cas 9[213] technology used for editing the genomes of human beings and other organisms, are creating new demands for federal and provincial legislative responses. Is the political class, regardless of party, any better equipped to deal with such issues today? I don't think so.

---

moment they are reimbursed by public insurers." Bedard, Mathieu, "Innovative Drugs: A Bureaucratic Obstacle Course," Montreal Economic Institute, April, 2018.

212 Assisted Human Reproduction Act , 2010 SCC 61, [2010] 3 S.C.R. 457

213 No, it's not a new form of French fry. CRISPR is an abbreviation of Clustered Regularly Interspaced Short Palindromic Repeats, a family of DNA sequences in bacteria and archaea (a domain of single-cell microorganisms having no cell nucleus.) which can be used to edit the genomes of organisms to eliminate defections responsible for hereditary diseases or to give the organism enhanced characteristics.

Bridging the gap

All of these factors, the ignorance of and indifference to science in the political community, the ignorance of and indifference to politics in the scientific community, the communications gap and jurisdictional tugs-of-war combine to mar the relationship between the scientific and political communities in Canada. They graphically illustrate the need for a major strengthening of relations between those communities. So what can and should be done to accomplish such a strengthening?

First, to address the knowledge and interest gap, we need to get more well-informed, science-oriented people into the political arena at both the elected and staff levels.

This won't happen by accident or by luck or by leaving it up to the political parties. It will only occur if the executives and members of scientific associations, science-based companies, and science faculties make a conscious decision and effort to encourage a small number of their own scientifically knowledgeable people to seek public office and support their efforts.

On the political side, three measures which could and should be pursued to overcome the deficiencies in scientific knowledge and interest among the political class:

- The recruitment and inclusion of students from the science faculties among the student interns whom many MPs and MLAs hire to work periodically in their offices. The assignment for such students should include identifying what science might have to offer on any issue being addressed by that office and to provide background on representations by scientists and their associations to that office
- For the parliament and the legislatures to follow the British example and establish a Parliamentary Office of Science and Technology (a POST office)[214] to provide elected assemblies with a non-partisan, in-house source of timely, balanced and accessible analysis of public policy issues related to science and technology
- To establish the office of the Scientist General (similar to the office of the Auditor General) attached to the parliament or the legislature, not to the executive arm of government, who would be available to

214 See https://www.parliament.uk/post

put elected members, at their request in touch with various sources
of scientific information[215]

Second, we should begin to close the communications gap between the
political and science communities by working harder and more systematically to establish more personal and collegial relationships[216] on the
part of scientists with MPs, MPPs, and MLAs and vice versa. This might
be done by:

- Significantly increasing the attendance by political people (elected
officials and their staff members) at science association meetings
and conferences such as the Canadian Science Policy Conference.[217]
Even if such conferences only schedule one event, a dinner or
breakfast, at which the presentation would be geared specifically
to non-scientific political people, this would be a step in the right
direction
- Significantly increasing the attendance of scientists at political
meetings and conferences. Rather than avoiding political party
conferences completely for fear of being too closely identified with
any one party, the approach currently taken by most scientists and
scientific associations, we should encourage scientists to take the

215 Canada's first chief science adviser was appointed in 2004 by Prime Minister
Martin. He was attached as an advisor to the executive arm of the federal government, not to the legislative arm, parliament. His advice was rarely sought,
largely ignored when given, and the position was eliminated in 2008 by Prime
Minister Harper. In 2017, Mona Nemer, a cardiology researcher and vice president
of research at the University of Ottawa, was named Canada's new chief science
adviser by Prime Minister Justin Trudeau. Nemer's office will have a $2 million
budget but, again, she will report to the executive arm of the federal government,
to the Prime Minister and the Minister of Science, not to the parliament.
216 When scientists invite elected officials to visit a scientific laboratory or project,
the scientists often put a heavy emphasis on introducing the politicos to the
equipment and apparatus of the project of which the scientists are very proud.
What the scientists in their modesty don't seem to fully realize, however, is that
often the most impressive component of the project are the scientists themselves
and their co-workers, the human components of the project as distinct from
the physical components. While I and my colleagues were duly impressed by
the magnitude and complexity of the equipment comprising Dr. McDonald's
neutrino observatory, I was personally even more impressed by the knowledge
and dedication of Dr. McDonald himself and his colleagues.
217 See: https://www.sciencepolicy.ca/

"cross partisan approach" and be represented in some way at the major political conferences of all the main parties

- Instituting regular Bacon and Eggheads[218] breakfasts and lunches, not just in Ottawa but in every provincial capital and major city in the country
- Scientists scheduling at least one, personal, once-a-year meeting with their MP or MLA or municipal councilor in the elected officials' constituency office not their parliamentary or legislative office, to update them on some scientific development relevant to the interests of that MP, MLA, or councilor
- By harnessing the *Science of Communication to the Communication of Science* through seminars and presentations which analyze the different communication styles of politicians and scientists and ways and means of overcoming the gaps

Third, give greater recognition to the role that the media[219] can play in interpreting science to politicians and vice versa. In Canada, the CBC radio program, *Quirks and Quarks,*[220] hosted by Bob MacDonald, provides political listeners with a fascinating exposure to recent scientific developments. Likewise, the CBC radio program, *The House,*[221] can provide scientific listeners with a timely exposure to political goings on at the federal level. With a little personal research, scientists and politicians can find numerous websites[222] and publications playing this intermediary communications role between the two communities. The challenge then is for members of each community to systematically avail themselves of such media.

Fourth, give serious consideration to measures that are constantly being proposed to the political community by the scientific and business

---

218 See The Partnership Group for Science and Engineering, Bacon and Eggheads Breakfast Schedule. http://pagse.org/en/breakfasts.htm
219 The word "media" comes from the same root as "mediator." Science-oriented journalists who target politicians, and politically-oriented journalists who target scientists, can play this mediatorial role.
220 https://www.cbc.ca/listen/shows/quirks-and-quarks.
221 https://www.cbc.ca/radio/thehouse.
222 In the belief (I may be wrong) that the life sciences will be to the twenty-first century what physics was to the twentieth, I personally get a daily briefing on some of the latest developments in that fascinating scientific sphere by subscribing to an online service operated by *Nature* magazine at http://www.nature.com

community, to stabilize and improve the funding of the development of science and technology, the issue which currently so dominates the relationship between politics and science.[223]

Much more can and should be said, of course, on how to address the funding issue and on how to dramatically increase the quality and timeliness of the political response to scientific advancements requiring such a response. But my contention here is that if we could at least increase the knowledgeability and interest of the political class in science, and if we could at least narrow the communication gap between the scientific and political communities, it would definitely improve the capacity of politicians and governments to respond more rapidly and intelligently to the activities and needs of the scientific community, including the need for sustainable long-term funding.

Addressing the problem of science denial

One particular problem, complicating the relationship between the science and political communities, especially on the polarized energy/environment front, is that of co-called science denial. The phenomenon occurs on both the right and left sides of the political spectrum,[224] for example:

223 For example, expanding the Scientific Research and Experimental Tax Credit (SR&ED); provisions to address the operating deficits of big science developments and research programs; and smart procurement on the part of governments.

224 While serious science denial on the right currently manifests itself in the form of denying scientific evidence of climate change, serious science denial on the left is likely to manifest itself in the future in the form of ignoring or denying the implications of scientific findings by geneticists and molecular biologists with respect to beginning of life phenomenon. When the analysis of a simple blood sample from a pregnant woman will enable scientists to predict with considerable accuracy numerous distinguishing characteristics of the human being who would result if the pregnancy is allowed to come to term, and present the parents with the potentially discriminatory choice of whether or not they want a child with those personal characteristics, it will no longer be possible to maintain the legal fiction that life and therefore personhood does not begin until birth. The courts will ultimately be faced with a second Persons Case and pro-choice liberals will be forced to decide whether or not to support some form of disclosure and regulatory measures to prevent discrimination at the molecular level based on the results of genetic testing.

- Some right-of-centre politicos and their supporters deny the validity of scientific evidence related to climate change, its existence and its causes
- Some left-of-centre politicos and their supporters deny the validity of scientific evidence indicating that pipelines, not rail cars or trucks, are the most economical, effective, and safest means of moving large volumes of petroleum long distances.

What are the implications of science denial for the political/science relationship, and what can the science community do about it?

With respect to implications, science denial corrupts the relationship between the scientific and political communities by generating disrespect of the political community on the part of scientists and making it more difficult to bring scientific findings to bear on public policy issues. And with respect to doing something about science denial, the following description of the reasons behind it may be especially helpful to those members of both the political and scientific communities willing to address it.

According to legal scholar Daniel Kahan, and referenced by Harvard psychologist Stephen Pinker in his recent book *Enlightenment Now,* "certain beliefs become symbols of cultural allegiance. People affirm or deny these beliefs not to express what they *know* but who they *are.*" As Kahan and his collaborators explain: "The principal reason people disagree about climate change science is not that it has been communicated to them in forms they cannot understand. . . . Rather it is that positions on climate change convey values . . . that divide them along cultural (and I would add, *political*) lines."[225]

More particularly, the reason some right-of-centre people deny the scientific evidence for climate change is not that they have thoroughly investigated that evidence for themselves and found it wanting. Rather, it is that to accept such evidence would convey support for and allegiance to the values and positions of its political champions (in this case the environmental lobby and the Trudeau Liberals) whom they mistrust and dislike for a variety of reasons (many completely unrelated to climate change).

Similarly, the reason some left-of-centre people ignore or deny the scientific evidence in support of pipelines is not that they have

225 Pinker, Stephen, *Enlightenment Now: The Case for Reason, Science, Humanism, and Progress,* Penguin Books, 2018, pp. 357–358

thoroughly examined that evidence for themselves and found it unpersuasive. Rather, it is that to accept such evidence would convey support for and allegiance to the values and positions of its political champions (in this case the pipeline lobby and Conservatives) whom they mistrust and dislike, again for a host of reasons, many of them completely unrelated to pipelines.

In a nut shell, what all this means for the scientific community, is that, regrettably, it is unwise to allow politicians to become the principal communicators and champions of your science in the public square. Welcome interest group and political support, preferably on a cross-partisan basis, for your scientific investigations. But you yourselves, as scientists, must increasingly become the principal communicators and champions of your science in the public square and not allow that role to be co-opted by others.

DO SOMETHING!

If you are a member of the political community, in whatever capacity, make an effort to strengthen your personal and party relationship with the scientific community by:

- Subscribing to and reading at least one general science magazine and regularly visiting one or two general science websites
- Attending at least two science conferences per year, one of which should be the Canadian Science Policy Conference
- If you are in a position to do so, recruiting and hiring at least one student intern with a science background
- Attending a Bacon and Eggheads event in your jurisdiction, or host an initial one if none presently exist
- Initiating and/or supporting the creation of a Parliamentary Office of Science and Technology for your elected assembly
- Initiating and/or supporting the creation of the position of a Scientist General for your elected assembly
- Urging the appointment of a Science Critic and/or a Science Advisor to your caucus, if you do not yet have such
- Urging the creation of a Science Policy Committee and a Science Policy, and supporting both, if your caucus is not yet so equipped

DO SOMETHING!

If you are a member of the scientific community in whatever capacity, make an effort to strengthen the relationship between your discipline, faculty, or association with the political community by:

- Subscribing to and reading at least one general political magazine and regularly visiting one or two political websites
- Joining a political party or political interest group and attending at least a few of their meetings
- Personally attending at least one political party or movement conference per year, even as an observer, and insuring that your discipline or association is represented in some way at each of the annual conferences of the major parties
- Making a point of visiting your MP, MLA, or municipal councilor once per year, in their constituency office if possible to give them an update on your scientific activities and their relevance to the public interest
- Inviting an elected official or senior political staffer to visit your science project or facility for an orientation presentation and session with your key personnel. Ensure that the presentation is receiver oriented rather than source oriented
- Attaching a Political Advisor to your science project or science association, just as you desire politicians to attach a Science Advisor to their projects and organizations
- If you are at a college or university, encouraging some of your science students to apply for an internship in a political office and report back on their experience
- Attending a Bacon and Eggheads event in your jurisdiction, or host an initial one if none presently exist. Invite a party or elected official to attend as your guest
- Advocating for and supporting the creation of a Parliamentary Office of Science and Technology for the elected assembly in your province
- Advocating/supporting the creation of the position of a Scientist General for the elected assembly in your province

- If you have joined a political party, volunteering to assist it in the creation or updating of its Science Policy and in responding to public issues with a science dimension.
- Increasingly becoming the principal champion and communicator of your science in the public square, rather than surrendering that role to interest groups or partisan politicians

Addressing the ethical challenges

There is one other factor which further complicates the politics–science relationship but which, recognized and properly addressed, may actually provide some fruitful ground for strengthening that relationship. It is the challenge of deciding what ethical criteria should be brought to bear on the conduct of research and experimentation by the scientific community and on the regulation and financing of science by the political community.

Contemporary politicians, most of whom are secular in orientation, generally dislike dealing with ethical issues and seek to avoid coming to grips with them if at all possible. This is particularly true, for example, with respect to scientific advancements which raise beginning of life issues like reproductive rights, genetic discrimination, and the prospects of "designer babies." Elected politicians are averse to dealing with scientific advancements which raise these issues because most of them don't know how to handle such issues without unleashing all kinds of public misunderstandings and political trouble.

For the Canadian politician, the simplest, most expedient way of dodging responsibility for ethical issues, especially if they have religious or moral connotations, is to hand them off to the courts. This may be done directly by reference, as in the case of the same-sex marriage reference to the Supreme Court. But far more often it is done indirectly by legislators passing statutes which appear to address the subject but deliberately fail to specify legislative intent, thereby requiring the courts to fill in the blanks.

At the same time, the science community knows that if it draws serious and prolonged attention to certain ethical issues raised by a scientific advancement, in particular the dark side of scientific advances resulting from their misuse, this may well decrease public and political enthusiasm for the funding of that science and therefore retard its development.[226]

Regrettably, it is a historical fact that there has not been any major scientific advancement, from the discovery of fire and gunpowder to nuclear fission and fusion, that has not been eventually harnessed to the science and practice of warfare.[227] The latest discoveries of how to manipulate the genomes of living organisms, from bacteria to plant and animal life to human beings, have enormous potential for good. Unfortunately, these discoveries also have a dark side. For example, they have the potential to be harnessed in the service of biological terrorism and biological warfare at much lower cost than other weapons of mass destruction. (The cost of developing a pathogen for which there is no known antidote and distributing it among a human population is only a fraction of what it costs to develop and deliver a nuclear weapon).[228]

---

226 For example, a very comprehensive 325-page publication entitled *Human Genome Editing: Science, Ethics, and Governance,* prepared by a distinguished international Committee on Human Gene Editing: Scientific, Medical, and Ethical Considerations and published in 2017 by the National Academies Press of Washington D.C, avoids any mention of the harnessing of that science to biological terrorism and warfare, the one ethical issue related to the future development of that science which is of greatest concern to political decision makers.

227 This fact was brought home to me very forcibly by Dr. Cam Boulet, at the time a Canadian Armed Forces scientist responsible for assisting Canada to cope with the future prospect of biological terrorism and warfare. For one year, I taught a course on Politics and the Genetic Revolution at the University of Toronto. Since I knew very little about genetics, I would invite plant geneticists, animal geneticists, and authorities in human genetics to address my class and to describe the various advancements in their fields. I would then discuss the political and legislative implications. Finally, at the end of the year, Cam would come. I introduced him as Darth Vader and told the students: "All those wonderful genetic insights and techniques you were told about by the previous guests? Unfortunately, all of them can and will be harnessed by unscrupulous people to biological terrorism, biological warfare, and the destruction rather than the enhancement of human life." Thus the challenge is how to encourage and facilitate the marvelously beneficial side of that science, while safeguarding ourselves and our world against its dark side.

228 From "The Economics of Bioweapons," *BMJ* 2002; 325; 727 https://doi.org/10.1136/bmj.325.7367.727 published October 5, 2002: "Bioweapons are often called 'the poor man's nuclear bombs.' The reason for this is that the cost of production of these weapons, causing comparative civilian casualties, are much less compared to the conventional weapons. The comparative cost of civilian casualties per-square-kilometer will be about $2000 with conventional weapons,

Even rogue nation-states like North Korea might hesitate to develop and utilize biological weaponry for the simple reason that it would be very difficult to protect (inoculate?) its own population against the unintended spread of a deliberately triggered biological attack upon an enemy population. But terrorists and terrorist organizations are unlikely to have any such inhibitions.[229]

If scientists draw too much attention to the potential for "unethical" misuse of an exciting scientific development, the ethical debate will quite likely decrease or at least slow the rallying of public and political support and funding for that development. But political decision-makers, especially if they are in government, cannot ignore the prospects of such misuse, as much as they might desire to do so.

The mutual reluctance of significant numbers of members of both the political and scientific communities to come to grips with the ethical dimensions of scientific developments in an open, timely, and cooperative fashion often means that these issues will become a bone of contention between the two communities later on, further straining science-political relations.

On the basis of my experience, there would be great benefit in clarifying and openly discussing, rather than avoiding, some of the differing ethical perspectives which members of each community bring to the table. For example, I have encountered scientists who assume that most politicians (myself included) are utilitarians, and that all you have to do to convince us that your project is good and worthy of support is to prove that the benefits exceed the costs. (This is usually easily done by simply expanding the definition of benefits and narrowing the definition of costs until the former outweigh the latter).

However, in the long run, this heavy reliance on utilitarian ethics to get politicians on side with respect to particular scientific endeavors can work to the disadvantage of science. The argument that basic science is invaluable and should be strongly encouraged is not supported by utilitarian ethics because it is so difficult to identify and prove the concrete benefits of basic science in the short run while the costs are substantial and obvious. Rather the case for supporting basic science is much stronger

---

$800 with nuclear weapons, $600 with chemical weapons and just $ 1 with biological weapons. Note further that chemistry kits which enable genetic editing can already be bought online for under £100."

229 See https://www.telegraph.co.uk/science/2017/04/19/bill-gates-terrorists-could-wipe-30-million-people-weaponising/

and more persuasive when it rests on what the ethicists call deontological ethics,[230] that there are certain activities and results, like basic scientific research, that are inherently good and worthwhile, regardless of whether or not you can prove an immediate benefit. And there are certain activities and results, like harnessing science to the deliberate destruction of human life, that are inherently wrong, regardless of whether or not you can prove some short-term strategic benefit from pursuing them.

Ironically, perhaps, the employment by scientists of deontological ethics in evaluating the ethical status of scientific advancements and their applications, tends to put the scientists, on such occasions, much more in the camp of ideologically-motivated politicians and religious people (including aboriginals), than in the camp of the political pragmatists. For example, the scientific insistence that long-run environmental protection is worthy of vigorous pursuit regardless of whether short-run benefits can be immediately demonstrated is on the same ethical ground as the long-time insistence of indigenous elders that the environment is sacred and to be revered because it is the work and habitation of the Great Spirit, a religious conception.

Seeking and finding the right mix of utilitarian and deontological ethics in evaluating and regulating scientific and technological developments would be a very worthwhile exercise for both the scientific and political communities in Canada. As an important part of the effort to find the common ground between them, the joint pursuit of such an exercise would be advanced by:

• Explicitly recognizing rather than avoiding or downplaying the fact that there are invariably ethical issues to be resolved with every major scientific advancement. For example, discussing ways of preventing advances in the understanding and application of genomic science from being harnessed to the practice of bioterrorism and the development of biological weaponry

230 According to deontological ethics, an action is considered morally good because of some characteristic of the action itself, not because the product of the action is good. Deontological ethics holds that at least some acts are morally obligatory, and that refraining from certain acts is also morally obligatory, regardless of the consequences of those acts for human welfare. Descriptive of such ethics are such expressions as "Duty for duty's sake," "Virtue is its own reward," and "Let justice be done though the heavens fall." https://www.britannica.com/topic/deontological-ethics

- Planning and budgeting for *Economic Environmental Ethical Social Legal (EEESL) studies*[231] in connection with major scientific development projects. Making the joint review and discussion of such studies the foundation of an ongoing and cooperative dialogue between the scientific and political communities

DO SOMETHING!

If you are a member of the political community:

- Seek and enter into discussions with members of the science community on the ethical dimensions of genetic science and its applications
- Support the commissioning of and budgeting for Economic Environmental Ethical Social Legal (EEESL) studies in connection with major scientific development projects

If you are a member of the scientific community:

- Seek and enter into discussions with members of the political community on the ethical dimensions of genetic science and its applications
- Support the commissioning of, and participate in, Economic Environmental Ethical Social Legal (EEESL) studies in connection with major scientific developments

231 It is instructive to trace the evolution of formal EEELS studies of major technological developments from (a) Moral and ethical concerns arising from the Manhattan Project which produced the world's first atomic bomb, to (b) The interest of the U.S. Department of Energy in finding an efficient way of studying long-term DNA damage caused by radiation, in particular, from the atom bombs dropped on Japan in 1945 which resulted in, (c) The eventual establishment of the international Human Genome Project. In 1993, when the U.S. Congress, established the National Center for Human Genome Research [the predecessor to the National Human Genome Research Institute (NHGRI)], it then mandated that "not less than" 5% of the NIH Human Genome Project budget be set aside for research on the ethical, legal, and social implications of genomic science.

2.4 Build the Policy Bank

Public policy proposals include principles to be applied and courses of action to be taken by governments to address particular issues and the problems and challenges which arise. In the political world, the development, promotion, and implementation of public policy is one of the primary interests and activities of participants in the democratic process.

Policy proposals for strengthening democracy are developed and promoted by a variety of entities: academics, think tanks, interest groups, political parties, and both general and specialized media. Adoption and implementation of those policies is the task of democratically elected assemblies and governments. To my knowledge, there is no one place in Canada, no library, website, institution, or depository, where all the current policy proposals for strengthening Canadian democracy are assembled and catalogued for easy reference. There should be.

Similarly, conservative public policies are courses of action, based on conservative values and principles, for consideration and debate by citizens and possible implementation by elected assemblies and governments. Again, to my knowledge there is no one place, no library, website, institution, or depository, where all the current conservative public policy proposals from A-to-Z are assembled and catalogued for easy reference by Canadians. Again, there should be.

What is required is an on-line policy bank which would be an easily-accessible catalogue of public policies, organized alphabetically, drawn from a variety of sources, and expressed wherever possible in an abbreviated form. My particular interest is in the creation of a Conservative Policy Bank—let Liberals, Social Democrats and Greens develop their own Policy Banks—but every such policy bank should include a Democracy Policy Section which would be of interest and use to any small-d democrat, regardless of their particular partisan orientation.

This proposed Conservative Policy Bank would be an online place where developers of conservative public policy—conservative think tanks, interest groups, academics, political parties, and governments—would be encouraged to "deposit" their policy proposals and outputs to insure maximum exposure and minimum duplication. In other words, it would be a major depository of much of the intellectual capital of the conservative movement.

This proposed Conservative Policy Bank would also be a depository to which anyone (a candidate, an elected official, a party member, a media person, a voter) could go, without charge, to find an answer to the question: "What is a conservative policy on X?"

Once the Conservative Policy Bank is established and adequately financed, its contents could need to be updated and enhanced over time. For example, every effort should be made to gradually insure that the catalogued policies are expressed in their "politically communicable form," however they may have been expressed originally. Some means should also be developed to indicate whether a particular conservative policy proposal has ever been implemented by a government, and if so, to what extent and with what degree of success.

DO SOMETHING!

If you are an executive or funder of a think tank or interest group involved in the development and promotion of conservative-oriented public policy:

- Convene a meeting of your peers to advance the creation, financing, and operation of the Conservative Policy Bank (CPB)
- Pledge to deposit the conservative policy output of your own organization in the CPB and encourage other developers of conservative policy to do likewise

If you are responsible for the development, promotion, and implementation of conservative public policy as a member or executive of a conservative political party or government:

- Arrange to deposit the conservative policy output of your party or government in the CPB and encourage other developers of conservative policy to do likewise

If you are interested in conservative public policy or a potential user (a citizen, candidate, party member, media person, or elected official), become a customer of the CPB and avail yourself of its resources frequently.

DO SOMETHING!

If you are an executive or funder of a think tank or interest group involved in the development and promotion of public and private policies for strengthening democracy:

- Convene a meeting of your associates to advance the creation, financing, and operation of a Democratic Policy Bank
- Pledge to deposit the democracy-enhancing policy output of your own organization in this bank and encourage other developers of democracy enhancing policy to do likewise

If you are responsible for the development, promotion, and implementation of the democratic policy section of a partisan policy bank:

- Arrange to deposit the content of your democratic policy section in the general democracy-enhancing policy bank and encourage other partisan developers of democracy enhancing policy to do likewise.

2.5 Invest in Ideas

In the preceding chapters, under the general heading of Develop Intellectual Capital, we have sought to identify some of the major intellectual capital needs of:

- Democracies (if we wish to revitalize and sustain our democratic processes and institutions)
- Conservative movements and political parties (if we wish them to succeed as vitally important players in the democratic arena)

At the same time, we have sought to identify various ways and means of more effectively meeting these needs.

Significant investments of time and money in identified organizations and activities are required to meet the particular intellectual capital needs of democracy and conservatism going forward. The purpose of this chapter is to challenge you as a citizen to carefully examine these areas needing investments, to identify those which appear most important and attractive to you, and to make a decision to invest a portion of your time and money in those areas, regardless of whether your personal resources are small or great.

Investing in activities to strengthen the intellectual capital of democracy

As proposed earlier, any Canadian who truly believes in democracy and truly appreciates the benefits we all receive from Canada's democratic freedoms, should develop a Political Investment Portfolio and allocate a portion of the time and financial resources of that portfolio to meeting one or more of the needs summarized below:

The intellectual capital needs of Canadian democracy include: the need to articulate the democracy story in fresh new ways, through literature, music, theatre, and social media, to make it meaningful to future generations; to add, if they don't already exist, substantive democratic-reform planks to the platforms of every democratic political party; to think through and articulate ways and means of harnessing social media to the strengthening of democracy and coping with their potential misuse to undermine democracy; and to develop ideas and strategies for closing the gap between the political and scientific communities.

Suggested instruments for meeting these intellectual capital needs of democracies include: offering an X-Prize for Democratic Innovation; providing financial incentives to electoral districts to increase their voter turnouts: strongly supporting organizations like Student Vote in their efforts to prepare next-generation Canadians to assume their democratic responsibilities; the passage of democratic-reform legislation by our parliament, legislatures, and municipal councils; the use of referenda campaigns to teach and exercise democratic participation skills: the convening of seminars, roundtables, and conferences specifically on the theme of strengthening the intellectual and organizational underpinnings of democracy; and adopting measures to close the gap between the political and scientific communities.

Canadians invest billions of dollars per year in maintaining the physical facilities and processes of our democracy, our parliament, legislatures, municipal councils and the elections that populate them.[232] Surely it is not too much to ask that we invest a fraction of that amount on developing the ideas and intellectual capital required to enable those democratic institutions and processes to serve us more effectively.

So what will it be? Which if any of these needs, and instruments for addressing them, appeal to you? Is it volunteering your time and money to support Student Vote? Or is it championing some democratic reform, such as freer voting in your parliament or legislature, by actively campaigning for that reform within the political party of your choice? Or is it sponsoring a session or an attendee at some conference such as the Canadian Science Policy Conference?

If you're a legislator, is it voting to invest public funds in establishing the Office of the Scientist General, or for the conduct of Ethical Economic Environmental Legal Studies (EEELS) in connection with major breakthroughs in science and technology, or something else?

232 See Table 3 from Part 1

Many of us may not have the financial resources to invest personally, although by crowd-sourcing, large numbers of people giving very
small amounts of money can achieve amazing things. Even if we do
not have financial resources to invest in strengthening democracy, do
not most of us (particularly the retiring generation) have significant
amounts of time we could invest in these activities if we truly believe
them to be important?

Whatever you decide, my hope is that you will *Do Something!* to
strengthen and sustain democracy by investing time, money or both in
measures to accomplish that objective.

Investing in activities to strengthen the intellectual capital needs of conservatism

The intellectual capital needs of conservatism are somewhat different
than those of democracy. But any Canadian who truly believes in the
values of conservatism, in its efforts to achieve and sustain freedom of
enterprise in Canada and its wealth-generating capacity, should allocate
a portion of the time and financial resources of their Political Investment
Portfolio to meeting one or more of those needs.

These include the need to:

- Restate, reframe, reposition and re-energize some of the basic tenets
  of conservatism, such as the conservative commitment to spending
  constraints, budget balancing, debt reduction, and the provision of
  tax relief
- Champion a new birth of freedom in Canada, the fundamental freedoms of freedom of conscience, religion, thought, belief, opinion,
  and expression
- Cultivate new policy ground in terms of freedom of choice in health,
  education, and social services
- Find better ways to broaden the distribution of the tools of wealth
  creation to attack poverty and economic inequality
- Recognize and treat the natural resource sectors as foundational pillars of Canada's economy
- Entrench property rights in the constitution
- Facilitate the emergence of the sharing economy
- Support the application of market-based approaches to environmen-
  tal conservation

- Make conservatism the champion of "balance" on the environment/economy front
- Secure a better grasp of science and technology and seek a stronger and more positive relationship between conservatives and the science community
- Develop the Conservative Policy Bank, a complete inventory of proposed and implemented conservative policies, so that anyone from voters to legislators can readily ascertain what a conservative position is on any public issue or concern

Meeting the intellectual capital needs of conservatism going forward will require increased investment of time and money in:

- Conservative think tanks and advocacy groups to better equip them to refresh and restate traditional conservative positions and reframe and re-energize others
- National and regional Networking Conferences to achieve greater unity of purpose and action among the various components of the conservative movement
- Professionally organized and competently run conservative-oriented social media
- Projects that demonstrate the effective harnessing of market mechanisms to environmental conservation
- Projects that demonstrate the effective harnessing of the tools of wealth creation to the reduction of poverty and economic inequalities, especially among indigenous peoples; and
- Litigation to challenge interprovincial barriers to trade and the denial of freedom of choice to the users of health care, educational, and social services

So what will it be? Which if any of these needs, and mechanisms for meeting them, appeal to you? Is it the need to finance the work of think tanks to refresh, reframe, and re-energize traditional conservative positions? Or is it the need to finance research to break new ground for conservatism on harnessing market mechanisms to environmental protection or securing a better distribution of the tools of wealth creation? Or what about investing in the development of the Conservative Policy Bank?

Canadians invest billions annually in the operations of a market economy dependent on economic freedom and the security of private property rights. Surely it is therefore not too much to ask that we invest just a tiny fraction of that amount in strengthening the ideas and intellectual capital of those who champion economic rights and freedoms in the political arena, in particular, those of the conservative movement.

Again, particularly for those of us of the retiring generation, if we do not have the financial resources to invest in these opportunities, could we not invest more of our time? Could we not volunteer to do some of the administrative and organizational tasks that conservative think tanks and research groups need to perform more effectively? Or what about actively assisting in the organization and promotion of conservative networking meetings and conferences to effectively bring the generators and users of conservative intellectual capital together?

Whatever you decide, *Do Something!* to strengthen and sustain the development of conservative intellectual capital by investing time, money or both in measures to accomplish that objective.

PART 3

DEVELOP HUMAN RESOURCES

The famous Roman Senator, Cicero, was politically ambitious from his youth and yearning to get into the Forum, the great political arena of his day. And yet, he deliberately took ten years to acquire the knowledge and skills that he would need to perform effectively there. His advice to himself and other up-and-coming politicos, recorded in his personal diary, was "Intrate Parati."[233] Enter Prepared.

The pubic life of Jesus of Nazareth, one of the best public communicators and greatest public influencers of all time, lasted a brief three years. Yet scholars tell us that before he commenced his public work he likely spent eighteen years in the carpenter shop, the synagogue and the community, observing, meeting, listening, and interacting with the people who would one day be the bulk of his audiences.

Six years of personal preparation for every year of public life. Imagine the increase in the effectiveness of our federal politicians if we required twenty-four years of preparation for one four-year-term in the House of Commons?

What does it mean to enter prepared? It means intelligent study, "intelligence" here meaning the ability to recognize and absorb that which is significant with the intent of acting upon it. It means training and it means learning by doing and experiencing, not merely book or internet learning.

233 Hendrickson, G.L. & Hubbell H.M., *Cicero: Brutus, Orator*, Volume V, Loeb Classical Library No. 342.

But before we examine ways and means of improving the capacity of our politicians to serve via training, there is one prior subject which must be addressed, that is, the need to scout and recruit our trainees, potential politicians, early on when they are still teachable. This will be our starting point in addressing the unfinished business of strengthening the human-resources component of Canada's democratic sector.

3.1 Scout and recruit

I have two sons who played competitive hockey and six grandsons who currently do so. About when they reach the Peewee level (ages eleven to twelve) we began to notice certain hockey-knowledgeable persons, with clipboards in their hands, sitting along the back row of the spectator stands of the hockey arena.

Who are these people? They are hockey scouts, some working for midget, junior, or university hockey clubs; some working for NHL hockey clubs. But all with one purpose in mind: to identify, at an early stage, players with the potential to play the national game at the highest possible levels, if they were to receive the encouragement, training, and coaching required to actualize that potential.

The network of hockey scouts in this country is wide and deep. But where is its equivalent in the political world? Where are the people, many of whom may have participated in electoral politics themselves at an earlier point in their lives, who are systematically attending public events, school assemblies, university model parliaments, debating contests, and private meetings for the explicit purposes of:

- Identifying, early on, potential candidates for public office
- Directing and encouraging those potential candidates to get the training and coaching they will need to contribute and succeed

Developing and supporting this required network of political scouts is an unfinished piece of political business which must be attended to if we are to find and adequately develop the human resources needed to improve the performance of our political parties and democratic sector.

The political watering hole analogy

Think of the House of Commons, your provincial legislature, or your municipal council as a political watering hole in the middle of the political jungle toward which thirsty political animals are drawn. As in the case of most watering holes, there are certain paths through the jungle that those thirsty creatures are most likely to take in order to get there. These include:

- The party volunteer path. The person on this path has joined a party constituency association and participates in local meetings, party conferences, and campaigns. He or she volunteers to be a door knocker, a fundraiser, the constituency president, the campaign manager, and when his or her MP or MLA retires, that person becomes the candidate to replace them.[234]
- The political staffer path. The person on this path has sought or been recruited to fill a political staff position, as a researcher, executive assistant, communications director for an elected member or a party executive. As such, they work closely with elected officials and, if and when the opportunity presents itself, they decide to seek political office themselves[235]
- The prominent person path. The person on this path has been involved in business, or community service through an NGO or some other prominent organization and has come to media and public notice by virtue of their abilities and accomplishments. Someone in the political arena feels they have a contribution to make and would strengthen the party's standing, and asks them to consider running for public office.[236] In our day, the prominent

---

234 Chris Warkentin, MP, would be an example of this path. Chris was first elected to the House of Commons in the 2006 federal election and previously served at the president of the Conservative Party Constituency Association in Grande Prairie, and prior to that had been involved, at the constituency level, with the Canadian Alliance and Reform Parties.

235 Notably, Stephen Harper took this path, first coming to the attention of the Reform Party as a bright graduate student in the economics program at the University of Calgary. He served as the Chief Policy Officer of the Reform Party and as an executive assistant to Deborah Grey, the first Reform MP elected to Parliament in a 1989 byelection.

236 Mackenzie King's War Cabinet contained a number of persons like this. Prominent lawyer Louis St Laurent; prominent business man C. D Howe, etc.

person recruited may well be a sport or entertainment celebrity whose principal qualifications are name recognition and personal charisma.[237]

- The other level of government path. The person on this path has been politically successful (or in some cases, defeated) at the provincial or municipal level and wants to run at the federal level or vice versa. Contacts, experience, and name recognition gained at one level of democratic politics are used to secure election at another level[238]

- The political family path. In this case, the political aspirant may have been raised in a political family where a parent or grandparent has held political office and may even have been groomed to pursue the same path. They have become acquainted at an early age with the requirements and trials of political office and eventually decide to seek office themselves, name recognition being their principal asset.[239]

- The civil service path. This may be the road less traveled but persons on this path will be civil servants who observe the performance of their political masters on a day to day basis and decide, "I could do that job, and probably better than it is now being performed." They, too, are drawn to the political watering hole and use their civil service knowledge and experience to get there.[240]

Other routes to the political watering hole may be identified and may vary from jurisdiction to jurisdiction. But if we are sending out and positioning political scouts to identify and recruit potential candidates for the training that will better prepare them for elected office, it is important to know where these paths are and to position our scouts along them and as far "upstream" as possible.

The point at which a potential candidate for public office is most open to preparation and training for political participation is when they

237 Of course, the 45th President of the United States, Donald Trump, is the archetypal example of the celebrity politician.

238 It should be noted that no provincial premier has ever made it from the provincial level to the Prime Minister's chair, other than Charles Tupper in 1889, and he only got to the chair for sixty-nine days.

239 Examples might include Peter Lougheed, Bill Bennett, Paul Martin, Rachel Notley, Caroline Mulroney, myself, and of course, Justin Trudeau.

240 Both Mackenzie King and Lester Pearson got to the Prime Minister's office by this route. Mitchell Sharp also came to elected politics from the civil service.

have just begun to consider the possibility. It is then that they are most insecure, most conscious that "they have a lot to learn," most willing to receive "help" if it is offered, and most open to mentorship by someone who has previously navigated that path successfully.

The closer they are to the watering hole, having managed to get well along the path on their own without much help, and now able to smell the water, the less open and available they will be to training and further preparation.

DO SOMETHING!

If you are a person with an interest in becoming a candidate for public office:

- Recognize your need for prior training and adequate preparation
- Seek out persons who can advise you on what type of training you may need and from who it might be available;
- Pursue the recommend training on your own or enroll in courses or participate in activities designed to provide it. (More on sources of such training in chapters 3.2–3.5.)

If you are on a party or constituency executive:

- Develop detailed descriptions of the job of a political scout and the type of person required to fill that position well[249]

241 The hockey scout, of course, has a very clear idea of what he or she is looking for: a clear mental picture of the combination of physical and mental attributes, knowledge, and skills required to play each position on a hockey team and to play it exceptionally well. But where again is the political equivalent, the clearly thought out description of the ideal municipal councilor, the ideal member of a provincial legislature, the ideal member of parliament, the ideal cabinet minister, or the ideal prime minister? You would think that political parties and constituency associations, some of which have been in existence for decades, would have such descriptions readily at hand. But, sadly, I have been in constituencies where more thought and work has gone into the job and candidate descriptions for the local rink manager than has gone into describing the position of an elected representative and the type of person needed to fill that position well.

- Budget sufficient funds to support a scout or scouting team and their basic activities
- Recruit and hire your scout(s) and/or recruit volunteers to perform that function
- Provide your scout(s) with detailed descriptions of the position of a candidate for public office (both as a campaigner and as an elected official) and the type of person your organization needs to fill that role well

If you are someone with personnel recruiting experience, or political experience as a candidate or elected official yourself:

- Volunteer your services to the party and constituency association of your choice to assist in candidate identification and recruitment in your home constituency and beyond.

If you are an executive with a corporation, union, or educational foundation, or a person of means:

- Establish a bursary and scholarships program to provide financial assistance to those political aspirants willing to prepare themselves for office by acquiring the education and training they need to succeed

Just one cautionary note here. If you aspire to political office, be careful from whom you seek career advice, and if your advisor is an MP or MLA who shares with you the path whereby they themselves became an elected official, recognize that this will not necessarily be the right path for you.

To illustrate, in the middle of the Depression (1929–1939), when William Aberhart was attempting to spread the Social Credit doctrine across Alberta, he assigned a fellow named Eric Poole to carry the message to the Peace River country. Poole was supposed to organize and address public meetings and take a collection to support himself. But the meetings did not go well, the donations were non-existent, and Poole found himself in desperate circumstances. And so he stole a hand car from the Northern Alberta Railway and pumped his way, in the dead of winter, all the way back to Edmonton, a distance of three hundred miles. There he was promptly arrested, charged and convicted of theft, and sent to the Fort Saskatchewan jail.

But Eric Poole's story[242] captured the imagination of the pubic who sympathized with this poor political missionary being persecuted by the big, bad railway company. His reputation was further boosted when Aberhart and his colleagues traveled in a motor cavalcade to visit him in the jail. By the time he was released, he was famous. He decided to run for the federal parliament, and was elected in the 1935 federal election. If you asked Poole, "How do you become an MP?" he would have said: "Well first you steal something from a company people hate, and then when they put you in jail you parlay the publicity from that into a candidacy, and then. . ."

Advice to be appreciated, but not to be followed.

While the focus of this chapter has been primarily on scouting to recruit candidates for public office, it should be noted that there are many other positions in the partisan political system: constituency executives, campaign managers, political staffers, etc. which also need to be filled with the most knowledgeable and skilled people possible. Many times these positions are filled by the first warm and willing body that comes along, but better that they too be filled as a result of a thoroughly planned and executed recruitment effort.

---

242 For more on the colorful and eccentric Mr. Poole, see http://www.lltjournal.ca/index.php/llt/article/download/2473/2876

3.2 Train for Political Participation

Democracy in Canada and the performance of political parties would be substantially strengthened if we could substantially increase the knowledge, skills, ethics, communications abilities, and leadership capacities of those participating directly in democratic processes such as candidate recruitment and elections, and in democratic institutions such as our elected assemblies.

Those in particular need of training include:

- Party and constituency executives
- Campaign managers, teams, and volunteers
- Potential candidates and nominated candidates for elected offices, municipal, provincial, territorial, and federal
- Elected members of our parliament, legislatures, and municipal councils
- Political staffers serving all of the above
- Young Canadians interested in any of the above.

Party Training

Most political parties attempt to provide some training to their volunteers and candidates but this is limited by several factors:

- In most cases, this training is provided just prior to an election when there is very little time for any in-depth education and the focus of the training is narrow and highly partisan. (Candidate training sessions are often confined to two-day weekend seminars, at most.)[243]

---

243 To their credit, some of the pre-election training provided by the parties is becoming more extensive and accessible. For example, in preparation for the

- The closer a party is to an election, and remember the modern political party is primarily an organization for conducting election campaigns, the more proprietary the party becomes about its training. Because the implementation of election strategy and tactics will be part of the training, the party is reluctant to have anyone present at those sessions other than its own dedicated partisans, and is usually unwilling to entrust any part of that training to outsiders regardless of what expertise they may have to offer or how dedicated they may profess to be to the cause
- Party training is almost exclusively focused on equipping a candidate to get elected, not on what to do and how to perform after being elected

In this age of polarized politics, it is especially important to note that much of the training currently provided by political parties to their people prior to an election is focused on developing competitive skills, which will serve them and the candidate well in the adversarial arena. But what is also desperately needed today in the political arena is people with the collaborative skills required to create common ground and work together with others not all of whom are of the same mind. These are skills especially required if the opposition politician and party should achieve government where the ability to reconcile conflicting interests, not simply exploit them, becomes paramount. If training for the development of collaborative skills is to be provided, this is more likely and appropriately to be delivered by movement organizations than by the parties themselves.

My own experience with attempts to secure or provide political training has led to several conclusions which should be helpful in meeting the educational and training needs of Canada's politicos. These are:

- That whatever education and training is to be provided by movement organizations, or non-partisan or cross-partisan entities also interested in providing such training, it needs to be provided as far upstream as possible from elections and whatever training the parties are endeavoring to provide

2019 federal election, the Conservative Party of Canada offered a ten-week online training program to certify Campaign Managers for the election. Each class lasted 60–90 minutes and featured some of the top conservative campaigners from across the country as instructors. See http://www.victoryschool.ca/

- That while training lectures and the study of written materials are important elements of political training, "training-by-doing" is an even more effective educational method

DO SOMETHING!

If you are a voter or taxpayer:

- Insistently demand higher qualifications and evidence of adequate preparation from candidates for public office
- Ask the candidate who knocks at your door, soliciting your support at election time, "What training have you received that qualifies you to be my elected representative?"

If you are an aspirant to public office:

- Take the initiative yourself in asking your party for training, substantive not superficial training, that will better prepare you, not only for campaigning, but more importantly, for discharging your responsibilities if and when you are elected
- If your party is unresponsive to this request as it well may be at first, take the initiative and seek and receive the training you require from other sources

If you are a party or constituency association executive:

- Become a champion of more and better training for yourself and your party's candidates, staff, and elected members
- Introduce a training resolution at the annual meeting and conferences of your association and party
- If you possess knowledge, skills, and experience which could contribute to a training program, volunteer them
- Insist on a training provision in the budgets of your party, constituency association, and campaign plan
- Assist in the fundraising effort required to finance that budget item.

Upstream training

If one can identify persons with interests in direct political involvement early, before they have become too heavily involved in partisan
activities or elections, I have found that an effective tool for pointing
such individuals to helpful, in-depth training was a simple questionnaire entitled "So You Think You Might Want to Run for Elected Office?"
(See Appendix 4)

This questionnaire invites individuals interested in becoming candidates to think through the nature of the job, the adequacy or inadequacy
of their personal skills and experience, the implications for themselves
and their families of running for public office, and the qualities and
abilities required, not only to get elected, but to render effective public
service if elected.

Going through this questionnaire, especially with the help of an
experienced counsellor, helps the individual to identify their own
strengths and weaknesses and the areas where some further preparation
would be in order.

To further illustrate the kinds of programs which are needed, consider the following examples and ask yourself, "Do not these types of
programs need to be more strongly supported, financed, and promoted?"

The Clayton H. Riddell Graduate Program in Political Management at Carleton [244]

Many Canadian universities have schools of public administration
designed primarily to train civil servants. These render useful service
and can also be helpful to someone interested in running for elected
office. But when I was active in the political arena, and involved in hiring political staff, I could not help but notice that there was no advanced
degree program at any Canadian university that specialized in training
political staff, the partisans who staff the party offices, campaign offices,
and the parliamentary and constituency offices of elected officials.

After discussions with Dr. Roseann Runte, President of Carleton
University in Ottawa at the time, Carleton agreed to initiate such a

---

244 See https://carleton.ca/politicalmanagement/ for more information about the
     program.

program. As previously mentioned, it was first suggested that the program should be non-partisan. But no one could identify the "non-partisan" party or democratic assembly that would employ these non-partisan graduates. Like it or not, for the most part the real political world in Canada is organized on a partisan basis. Proper training for participating in it, however, can put partisanship in perspective and perhaps make it less so by communicating the limits of excessive partisanship. But it is particularly for participants in the partisan political arena that we need to provide better training.

What Carleton rightly wanted to convey by the term non-partisan was that neither Carleton nor the program were in the pocket of any one party or political philosophy. In the end this objective was served by designing and designating the program as cross partisan, with each of the major partisan perspectives in Canada represented among the faculty, in the course content, and among those attending as students.

As with most innovative educational efforts, it was very difficult at first to raise funding for the program. But eventually Clay Riddell,[245] a very successful and public-spirited Calgary oil executive, generously stepped to the plate by making an initial $15-million commitment through his family foundation to launch and support the program.[246] The donor agreement under which this funding was provided specifically required that the program be results-oriented with political ethics integrated into each course offering.

Course offerings include communication, campaign management, formulating and implementing a policy agenda, crisis and issues management, political persuasion and the media, polling and opinion research, political ethics, the political policy landscape, political advocacy, managing staff and constituency offices and institutions, governance, and the proper relation between political actors and the permanent public service.

By 2019, the program had graduated over 200-trained political staffers with applications each year to take the program always exceeding its

245 Sadly, in September 2018, Clay passed away after a brief illness. His funeral service in Calgary, attended by 3,000 people, concluded with a video recording of portions of an address he gave at Carleton when he was awarded an honorary degree in 2014. See Carleton University 145th Convocation, November 15, 2014.
246 https://carletonnow.carleton.ca/june-2010/carleton-gets-15-million-commitment-to-create-canada's-first-graduate-program-in-political-management/

capacity. Conditional upon raising the necessary funding, future plans for the program include the production of a comprehensive Canadian textbook on political management, offering the program on a part time basis for political staffers already employed, the further development of political management as an acknowledged academic discipline with its own journal and annual conferences, the development of a Political Management Alumni Association, and offering the program across the country in partnership with other universities.

The objective? To strengthen the knowledge, skills, and ethics of those who staff the political offices of this country.

The Institute for Future Legislators at the University of British Columbia[247]

In 2006, I interviewed a cross section of the house officers (mainly speakers and clerks) of Canada's fourteen senior elected assemblies, those serving the House of Commons, the ten provincial legislatures, and the three territorial legislatures. In particular, I asked them: having seen many elected officials of all stripes pass through your assembly, and having listened to their speeches and seen them perform under varying circumstances, what training courses would you prescribe to enable them to enter better prepared for their work?

From the answers received, I prepared a list (see Table 6) of twenty-five potential training courses, some of which would be very short, others of which would be very substantive, that would significantly improve the performance of elected members of our democratic assemblies if they could be induced to take such training.

Shortly thereafter I was visiting with Stephen Jarislowsky, the Montreal-based financier who has generously endowed over a dozen academic chairs at universities across the country. Stephen suggested I take my list to the Centre for the Study of Democratic Institutions (CSDI)[248] at the University of British Columbia. The institute, under the direction of Professor Max Cameron, is one of the institutions that Stephen supports.

---

247 See https://democracy.arts.ubc.ca/summer-institute/ for more information.
248 See https://democracy.arts.ubc.ca for more information.

TABLE 6 Training courses for elected officials suggested by house officers of Canada's parliament and legislatures

History of Democratic Institutions
The Rule of Law
Lawmaking and Legislative Analysis
De-legislating
Budgets, Estimates, Supply Motions, Money Bills
Political Ethics
Policy Development and Analysis
Parliamentary Protocol and Procedures
Committee Work and Procedures
Caucus Work and Procedures
The Role of a Parliamentary Critic
Question Period Preparation and Participation
Speechmaking and Parliamentary Debate
House Duty
Voting
Private Member's Business
Democratic Representation
Constituency Relations and Service
Dealing with Lobbyists and Interest Groups
Party Obligations and the Limits to Partisanship
Small Office Management
Relating to the Civil Service
Relating to the Judiciary
Political Communications
Balancing Your Personal, Family, and Political Life

I subsequently did so, and to make a long story short, the CSDI organized *The Summer Institute for Future Legislators (IFL)* under the direction of Professor Cameron and Professor Gerry Baier. It operates each summer, again on a cross-partisan basis, serving forty to fifty applicants, young and old, who are contemplating running for public office. Many of the participants in this program, though not all, are particularly interested in running for municipal office.

Topics covered by the IFL include:

- Representative government: the constitution, theories of representation, rule of law and law-making;
- Constituency work: knowing your constituency, small office management and work/life balance;
- Communications: political and parliamentary communications, speeches, media relations and social media;
- Parliamentary roles and procedures: caucus, cabinet, committees, opposition, and question period;
- Legislation: private member's bills, house duty, voting on bills, budget estimates and supply bills and policy development;
- Relationships: elected officials and the bureaucracy, judiciary, lobbyists and interest groups, social movements, inter-governmental relations and conflict of interest;
- Ethics: ethical challenges and practices with respect to all of the above.

The summer program ends with a special session in Victoria utilizing the Legislative Chamber of British Columbia or the chamber of the Vancouver City Council to give the students a taste of what the real thing might be like.

As with the Carleton program, the hope is for future expansion,[249] very much dependent on securing increased funding. But again, this program is a step in the right direction, a concrete attempt to raise the knowledge and skill level of political participants in this case, young future legislators.

Student internships

Student interns may be attached to virtually every organizational unit of the political system, to constituency associations, party offices, campaign teams, parliamentary and legislative offices, Elections Canada

---

249 For a description of the planned expansion of the Institute of Future Legislators, as part of UBC's proposed School of Public Policy and *Democracy House,* see chapter 3.5

and its provincial equivalents, think tanks, advocacy groups[250]and other movement organizations.

For student internships of this kind to be effective as a training mechanism, the intern needs to be given meaningful political work, adequate compensation, access and exposure to senior staff and elected officials and substantive supervision and mentoring. As long as the programs are adequately planned, supervised and supported, so that the young people participating in them actually gain meaningful experience and training and are not merely assigned menial administrative tasks, these programs can be an important stepping stone toward a full-time political career.

My own experience has been that appeals for funds to support student internships are usually responded to very generously by potential donors, especially those with students in their own immediate circle. All that was necessary to secure the $12,000 to $15,000 to support a four-month summer internship for one student, was to present a potential donor, especially one who had previously lamented the lack of young people interested and involved in politics, with the resume of an enthusiastic applicant, a one-page description of the work program proposed for the applicant, and the assurance that the successful applicant would be properly supervised and mentored, and, *voila*, three out four potential donors would donate the required amount to finance the internship.

DO SOMETHING!

If you are an executive or administrator of a political party, think tank, advocacy group, company, union, movement organization or legislative assembly:

- Champion an internship program for your organization that develops political interests and skills for participants

250 Owing to the recognized value, the majority of conservative movement organizations host summer internship programs but all could use more financial support to expand such programs.

If you are high school, university, or trade school student with political interests:

- Check out existing political internship programs and apply

If you are a foundation or NGO with particular interests in increasing political participation by next-generation Canadians:

- Provide generous funding to political internship programs when requested to do so

Challenges

You may wonder, are the political science courses and degree programs offered by most Canadian universities sufficient to provide much of the training we are seeking for would-be politicos?

Certainly, these courses and programs can be helpful. But much still needs to be done to make them of more immediate and practical use to participants in the real political world and their political employers.

When I was in the management consulting business before I entered the political arena, mainly dealing with energy sector clients, our firm would get regular visits from the deans or representatives of the business and engineering faculties of various universities asking what more they could do to ensure that their graduates were more employable and immediately useful to future employers. But in all my political years, despite the fact that my organizations were major employers of political science graduates, I can only remember one visit from the head of a political science department asking me that question. In that case, my answer was that there is a lot more that could be done[251] to make

---

251 To be frank, our major complaint was that it took almost a year of on the job training and experience to turn the recent graduate of a four-year political science degree into an employee who was truly useful to an elected official, at an estimated cost to our parliamentary budget of $80,000-plus per such employee. Why should it take that long and that large an expenditure on our part? Could not the institutions educating these graduates render them better prepared for useful political employment?

political science graduates more immediately employable and useful to a political employer.

For example, most of the recent graduates we hired had very little knowledge about, and no field training for, dealing with constituents, interest groups, lobbyists, or media. Few had had any exposure to the rules governing party and election financing or fundraising, or the skills required to manage a small office, interpret government financial statements, or analyze a draft bill. And when it came to communications, much of their university training had focused on written communications when what we were looking for, far more often, were oral communication skills and social media dexterity.

And then there is the perennial challenge facing those of us trying to raise the knowledge and skill levels of participants in the political sector. Namely, the enormous challenge of securing adequate, long-term funding to finance political training at the depth and on the scale required to significantly improve the performance and effectiveness of Canada's political class.

If we truly desire an increase in the capacity of Canada's political class to provide good government what is most urgently required is the development of a greater resolve on the part of Canada's wealth generators and philanthropists to systematically invest more in the education and training of Canada's political class.

A political equivalent of the Institute for Corporate Directors

A number of years ago, Canada's corporate sector decided that it was necessary to significantly raise the knowledge and skill levels of the directors of public companies, if those companies were to meet the challenges of the future and more effectively command the confidence of investors.

As a result, the *Institute for Corporate Directors*[252] was formed to provide in-depth training and certification for corporate directors, in particular those serving on the boards of public companies.

---

252 See https://www.icd.ca/Home.aspx. In 2018, the institute raised and spent over $17 million, $8.9 million on training. For further information see https://www.icd.ca/getmedia/35b5925a-2c8b-4e6c-a644-8b1ca7be9ee4/2018-ICD-Financial-Statements_EN.pdf.aspx

So where is its political equivalent, a well-funded and professionally managed institute for the provision of in-depth training for the
directors and official agents of political organizations and constituency
associations,[253] including certification and refresher courses? Is not the
governance of those organizations just as important to Canada's well-
being as good governance in the corporate sector?

DO SOMETHING!

If you are an elected member of parliament, a legislature, or a municipal council:

- Identify what kind of additional training would assist you to perform your duties better and begin to lobby for programs and
  funds to meet that training requirement
- Introduce and support amendments to election and party financing legislation to increase the level of limits on donations to
  political parties for research and training purposes
- Be willing and prepared to donate your own knowledge, skills,
  and experience to political training programs once your days of
  elected service are over

If you are involved as an administrator or faculty member of a political
science department at a college or university:

- Systematically survey political employers, if you are not already
  doing so, as to what knowledge and skills they are looking for
  in hiring political science graduates, and adjust your training to
  better meet those needs

253 It should be acknowledged that Elections Canada has an online video series
for candidates, see https://www.elections.ca/content.aspx?section=pol&dir=tra/
fin&document=index&lang=e
    Both Elections Canada and its provincial equivalents also offer substantive
instruction for Official Agents but these courses cannot address the partisan
dimensions of the job. Hence the need for additional courses offered by a non-
governmental Institute which is able to recognize and treat this dimension.

- Systematically survey your graduates who have already found political employment and ask what changes and additions they would make to your program to render its graduates more immediately employable and useful to their employers
- Consider adding experienced, retired elected officials to your faculty council on a volunteer basis to provide your students with a better balance between the political theory and practice

If you are a private philanthropist or involved in a charitable foundation with educational objects:

- Provide financial help to expand the capacities of existing training effort such as those of the Riddell Graduate Program in Political Management and the Institute for Future Legislators
- Respond positively and generously to additional requests for the funding of political training as other organizations take up this challenge

If you are a corporate director who has benefited from the programs of the Institute for Corporate Directors, or an executive of that organization:

- Consider extending that program or sponsoring a parallel program, for training and accrediting political executives, starting with Official Agents

3.3 Train by Doing: Work Sharing, Election Campaigns, and Issue Campaigns

Genuine democratic politics is not a spectator sport and one of the best ways of developing the knowledge and skills required to participate effectively in it is to learn by doing.

Work sharing

Work sharing or job sharing is an employment arrangement where typically two people are retained on a part-time or reduced-time basis to perform a job normally fulfilled by one person working full time.

Many of the middle- and lower-level administrative and maintenance jobs associated with an elected assembly, a political party, or a movement organization lend themselves to job sharing. And if those jobs were to be shared with students and other young people interested in ultimately working in this sector, there is a three-fold benefit to those individuals: they would get to observe the operation of a political organization first hand; they would get the opportunity to learn by doing from a more experienced co-worker; and they would receive some income in the process which may help finance their more formal education.

DO SOMETHING!

If you are in an executive or managerial position with an elected assembly, political party, campaign organization, think tank, or advocacy organization:

- Analyze the work sharing opportunities which might exist within your organization
- If and when appropriate, institute a work sharing program particularly aimed at pairing politically interested next-generation Canadians with experienced political veterans

Election campaigns

Most political parties have some form of election campaign training for their candidates, campaign managers, official agents and volunteers, and this kind of training can always be upgraded, expanded, and strengthened.

Simply participating in an election campaign as a volunteer can be an educational experience in itself, especially if volunteers are contemplating running for office one day themselves.

One of my first political jobs as a teenaged volunteer was to visit local campaign offices in Edmonton during or immediately after a provincial election or by-election and inspect the contents of their storage cupboards and garbage cans. My father and party officials wanted to know how much of the materials, posters, pamphlets, buttons, etc., prepared by the party's central campaign office, were actually being used by the local constituency campaigns and how much was left unused or discarded.

Usually, if the local campaign was going well because the party's central campaign team had accurately assessed the issues and the material needs of the candidates, all that centrally-generated material was being directly distributed enthusiastically to voters. But if the campaign was not going well, in part because the central office had misjudged the issues and the needs of the local campaigns, much of the centrally-provided material would end up unused or in the waste bins of the local campaign offices, replaced by alternative material (not always appropriate) hastily generated by the local campaigners.

Although my volunteer political job was a relatively menial one, it exposed me at an early age to grassroots campaigning at the constituency level, a beneficial educational experience.

DO SOMETHING!

If you are in a leadership or managerial position with an election campaign team:

- Identify the specific educational and training opportunities which your campaign may include
- Designate one or more members of your team to specifically recruit and employ volunteers to engage in those opportunities[262]
- After the campaign is over, evaluate the performance of those volunteers for the purposes of continuing their involvement and employing them in future activities and campaigns.

Issue campaigns

One of the best training grounds for election campaigns are so-called issue campaigns. The two objects of an issue campaign are:

- To raise some issue like budget-balancing, electoral reform, economic inequality, or environmental concerns, so loudly and insistently among the public that it cannot be ignored by the politicians and lawmakers of the day
- To raise public interest in and support for a particular solution to the issue in question, again, so loudly and insistently that elected officials are forced by the weight of public opinion to act

254   The intention here is to in no way divert resources away from the campaign itself but to use the opportunities for training by doing which the campaign provides to help attract volunteers. "By joining our campaign, you will help us and we will help you."

The key functions that need to be performed in the conduct of such issue campaigns, such as strategizing, planning, identifying supporters, motivating, coalition building, counteracting opponents, communicating, persuading, fundraising, and mobilizing volunteers, are almost identical to those of election campaigns. Thus issue campaigns can become an effective training ground for election campaigning.

For example, in 1993 the Reform Party of Canada was a new party, with a relatively inexperienced leadership and membership, preparing to participate in a national election for only the second time. But it was our participation the year before in the 1992 referendum campaign on the Charlottetown Constitutional Accord[255] (which Reform opposed) that provided many of our candidates and constituency associations with the training and experience they needed to be effective in the 1993 federal election campaign.

In my own case, years before the creation of the Reform Party I had made a detailed study of the lessons to be learned from one of the greatest issue campaigns ever conducted in the history of British parliamentary democracy, that conducted by William Wilberforce and his colleagues to abolish the slave trade and eventually slavery itself throughout the British Empire.[256]

What are some of the lessons taught by that issue campaign that will stand one in good stead in carrying out issue or election campaigns today? Consider the following:

1. *The importance of choosing the initial campaign objective and strategy wisely, in most cases by proceeding incrementally rather than going for broke.*

Wilberforce, for example, chose to first campaign simply for the abolition of the slave trade rather than the immediate and total abolition of slavery itself. In dealing with Canadians, if the ultimate political objective is to move public and parliamentary opinion from *A* to *C*, it is usually advisable to focus the issue campaign on securing public support for *B*, a more modest and attainable objective than *C* but a move in the right direction.

---

255 The *Charlottetown Accord* was a package of proposed amendments to Canada's constitution proposed by the federal and provincial governments in 1992. It was submitted to a public referendum on October 26 and was defeated.

256 See *Faith, Leadership, and Public Life,* pages 85–112.

2.   *The need to sometimes reframe an issue within a conceptual framework better suited to advancing your cause.*

In eighteenth- and nineteenth-century England, slaves were considered to be property and their treatment was viewed as essentially an economic issue. Wilberforce had to change the framework by insisting that slaves were human beings and that their enslavement was a moral and humanitarian outrage.

In Canada, when Senate reform was conceptualized as a dry and abstract constitutional issue it was difficult to get traction with the public. But when Senate reform was re-framed as an effective way to strengthen regional representation in parliament and address regional alienation, the issue was energized.

3.   *The role of coalition building in issue campaigns and the importance of distinguishing between principled coalitions and coalitions of expediency.*

Issue campaigns provide an opportunity to bring together for a political purpose individuals and groups who may have divergent views in a number of areas but have agreed to work together politically to achieve one particular objective on which they are all agreed. Thus issue campaigns provide an opportunity, especially for the leadership, to develop the skill of coalition building and coalition management, skills increasingly required to counter the pernicious aspects of polarization politics.

Of particular importance to coalition builders is the ability to recognize the difference between principled coalitions and coalitions of expediency.

Participants in coalitions of expediency generally participate out of short-run self-interest or a reactionary predisposition to oppose for opposing's sake. Such coalitions have little capacity for moral suasion with others who do not share those interests or the opposition mentality.

On the other hand, coalitions founded on principle, demanding self-sacrifice from their supporters and committed to the pursuit of principled objectives, have a moral authority that places them in good stead when endeavoring to persuade others of the worthiness of their cause. As shown by Wilberforce and others, principled coalitions are usually far more effective in the long run than coalitions of expediency.

4. *The importance of learning to wisely and graciously manage the middle
    in seeking public support for a major initiative.*

In most issue campaigns there will be people who strongly favor the
proposal in question and people who are strongly opposed. But there
will always be those in the mushy middle who are largely indifferent to the issue or proposal or who may simply wish that either the issue
or its proposed solution would just go away. How the managers and
spokespersons of the issue campaign deal with the mushy middle is
often the key to winning or losing the campaign. This was the case in
Wilberforce's anti-slavery campaign and it is usually the case in issue
campaigns today, especially if there is a polarizing moral issue involved.

5. *Issue campaigns present an opportunity to involve people in the politi-
    cal process who have previously been marginalized or excluded from the
    process altogether.*

In Wilberforce's day, women became heavily involved in the abolition-
ist campaign, particularly in boycotting sugar produced from the West
Indies slave plantations, long before they ever got the vote. In Canada
it was the prohibition campaigns of the temperance movement in the
nineteenth and early twentieth centuries which provided significant
leadership and participation opportunities for women in politics[257] and
accelerated the granting of full political rights (including voting) to
women by the 1920s.

It is also worth noting that issue campaigns can be utilized as relief
mechanisms for channeling bottom up, populist political energy into
more constructive ends other than simply fighting the establishment.[258]

Of course all such lessons, how and when to proceed incrementally, why and how to appropriately reframe an issue, the distinction
between principled coalitions and those of expediency, the why and
how of managing the middle, the opportunity to politically involve

257 The first woman to win election to Canada's parliament (Agnes Campbell
    MacPhail), and the first woman to win election to a provincial legislatures (Irene
    Parlby in Alberta), gained their relevant experience through third parties and
    interest groups engaged in issue campaigns, not through the traditional parties
    and election campaigns in which women were initially denied the vote. The same
    is true of the members of the "Famous Five" who secured recognition of women
    as "persons" in Canadian law and the political rights that pertained thereto.
258 More on this in chapter 5.2

marginalized people through issue campaigning and/or to channel populist energy into constructive ends, can be learned to some extent from
history books and campaign seminars. But they will be absorbed more
thoroughly, remembered far longer, and practiced more effectively if
they have been learned in the real-life training school of a real-life issue
campaign.

A relevant question, therefore, is what issue campaigns might be
launched and executed *today*, to achieve worthwhile public objectives
but also to serve as that needed training ground for democratic participation, especially for various marginalized groups?

Left-of-centre politicians and interest groups have been successfully conducting such campaigns for years on such issues as gender
equality, LGBTQ rights, and climate change. Major issue campaigns conducted by Canadian conservatives were the national campaign for Free
Trade in the 1980s, campaigns both for and against the Charlottetown
Constitutional Accord in 1992, the campaign against sovereignty-association in the Quebec secession referendum of 1996, the 2018 campaign
in B.C. against the establishment of a proportional representation electoral system, and the various campaigns against deficits, debts and high
taxes which have been conducted federally and provincially from time
to time.[259]

Current issues which might lend themselves to issue campaigns,
especially by conservatives, suggest the need for:

- Yet another, but updated and renewed, Fiscal Responsibility
  Campaign targeting the astronomically high levels of public spend-
  ing, public debt, and taxes being run up by the federal Liberals and
  NDP provincial governments;
- A New Birth of Freedom Campaign to re-establish a national com-
  mitment to the fundamental freedoms of freedom of conscience,
  religion, thought, belief, opinion, and expression as defined by the
  Charter of Rights and Freedoms;
- A Campaign to Better Distribute the Tools of Wealth Creation, espe-
  cially aimed at improving the condition of, and securing greater

259 Note that with the exception of the campaign in favor of Free Trade, the conserva-
      tive position in most of these issue campaigns has been one of opposition to (i.e.
      against) some policy or course of action proposed by others. In future, conserva-
      tives need to be more proactive in launching and conducting issue campaigns to
      advance positions and policies which conservatives are for rather than against.

involvement by, economically marginalized Canadians including Indigenous Canadians and low income immigrants;

- A Campaign in Favor of the Establishment of Transportation Infrastructure Corridors to the Pacific, Atlantic, and Arctic, especially aimed at securing action by the federal government to declare the rights of way for such corridors to be "works to the advantage of Canada."
- A Campaign to Reform Canada's Equalization System, likely to be conducted in conjunction with or following the referendum on equalization proposed by Alberta Premier Jason Kenney.

DO SOMETHING!

If you are seized with a particular issue and are politically motivated to Do Something! about it:

- Consider launching or supporting an Issue campaign to advance it

If you are in a leadership or managerial position with a political party:

- Recognize that supporting an issue campaign launched by others like-minded, may be a more effective way of advancing your positions on a particular issue than launching such a campaign yourself or only campaigning on that issue in the context of an election campaign
- Consider supporting at least two issue campaigns between elections, for their own value but also as a training ground for your own members and supporters

Volunteers again

You will have noted the frequent and prominent references to the crucial role of volunteers in the preceding discussions of election, referendum, and issue campaigns. In fact, one of the fundamental measures of the health of a democracy is the extent to which citizens participate voluntarily in such democratic exercises and voluntarily join democratic organizations such as political parties and interest groups.

In May 1992, Dr. Tom Flanigan and I took a trip to Latvia, Russia, the Ukraine, and Czechoslovakia at a time when those countries were in the process of freeing themselves and from the iron yoke of communism. Our purpose was to meet with the leaders of a number of newly-formed democratic parties and exchange views on how to strengthen democracy under trying conditions. When these small-d democrats were asked what were some of the greatest difficulties they were facing, one of the most frequent answers was the difficulty of securing party members and volunteers since un-coerced party membership and freely volunteering for political action were utterly foreign concepts for people who had lived a lifetime under dictatorial communist rule.[260]

In our country, with increasing numbers of people living longer and having more leisure time, the potential size of the volunteer sector is immense and growing. In addition, the prevalence of the internet, handheld devices, and networking software and applications is making the identification and mobilization of volunteers for particular purposes increasingly easier and cheaper.[261]

Identifying the particular political interests and skills of an increasing number of Canadians, and mobilizing them for participation in Canada's political processes should be a major aspect of developing the human resources required to sustain and strengthen our democracy in the years ahead. But the key to this effort will be a willingness on the

---

260 As an increasing number of new immigrants to Canada are coming from countries where volunteering to work for political parties or interest groups is a foreign concept, there is a need to more specifically introduce, explain, and market the concept of political volunteering to these new Canadians.

261 For example, University of Toronto graduate student Andrey Khesin recognized the challenges faced by emergency services when trying to arrive quickly to the scene of medical 911 calls. He therefore developed the Zeroth app which instantly connects 911 dispatchers with a network of volunteers with certifications such as CPR and first aid. These volunteers could be off-duty firefighters or nurses and can be alerted to nearby emergencies through the Zeroth app, significantly reducing the response times to 911 calls. Since time is critical in medical emergencies these volunteer Zeroth Responders can provide care before first responders arrive. The Zeroth app identifies a specialized pool of volunteers and mobilizes their services in real time to address a particular objective: getting emergency medical care to those needing it as quickly and efficiently as possible. For more information contact zerothresponders2018@uofthatchery.ca

part of an increasing number of Canadians to volunteer for political service.

DO SOMETHING!

Volunteer for political service!

3.4 Navigate the faith/political interface wisely and graciously

Why even discuss this subject? Is it not the conventional wisdom of the media and political elites of the western world that religion has no place in modern, democratic politics, and to the extent that portions of the public still have a religious orientation, their faith should be expressed and practiced only in private, not in the public square?[262]

While this well may be the current conventional wisdom, I believe there are several good reasons for rejecting it.

First of all, the number of Canadians who hold religious convictions is simply too large to ignore. According to a 2017 Angus Reid Institute Report,[263] 51% of Canadians profess to hold certain religious convictions and engage in religious practices based upon them. Of these numbers, in Canada the religious convictions and practices of a majority (67.3% in 2011, according to *Statistics Canada's* National Household Survey)[264] are rooted in the Judeo-Christian tradition.

---

262 This chapter is an abbreviation of a longer, published work on this subject: *Faith, Leadership, and Public Life,* 2017.

263 Angus Reid Institute, *A Spectrum of Spirituality*, April 13, 2017, http://angusreid.org/religion-in-canada-150/

264 Chui, Tina, "Immigration and Ethnocultural Diversity in Canada: National Household Survey," *2011*, Statistics Canada, 2013. According to a 2018 report on the religious orientation of Canadians prepared by pollster Angus Reid (http://angusreid.org/religion-in-canada-150/) 19% of the population self-identify as non-believers, 30% as spiritually uncertain, 30% as privately faithful, and 21% as religiously committed. With respect to the religious orientation of visible minorities and immigrants: 10% self-identify as non-believers, 11% as spiritually uncertain, 17% as privately faithful, and 29% as religiously committed.

Secondly, regardless of what philosophical or religious convictions Canadians hold, the Charter of Rights and Freedoms purports to guarantee freedom of conscience and religion to all Canadians, as well as freedom of thought, belief, opinion and expression "subject only to such reasonable limits prescribed by law as can be demonstrably justified in a free and democratic society."

These particular rights do not need to be written in to the constitution by the courts; they are already in there. What is required, especially with respect to freedom of conscience and religion, is a more vigorous defense and support of them resulting in a greater respect and tolerance of them by governments, universities, media, and the public at large.[265]

Thirdly, while many Christians have seemingly acquiesced to being confined in their expressions of faith to the private square, other religious communities (notably Islamic communities) have not. Democracies therefore must learn to accept and accommodate religious expression in the public square rather than ban or suppress it, if democracy is to be seen as a preferable political option in those parts of the world where faith expression is an integral component of the identity and daily life of the population.

Having said this, let me emphasize one crucial point: if persons of faith are to enjoy full freedom to express and practice their faith in the public square, it is imperative that faith-oriented persons and communities learn to do so in a constructive and positive manner.

Irresponsible, vicious, and purely negative expressions of faith in the public square simply fuel justifiable demands for their suppression. Thus, another reason to openly explore the faith/political interface is to encourage faith oriented individuals and communities to navigate it wisely and graciously and to present practical measures for doing so.

The closet

As previously mentioned, in recent years a significant effort has been made by secularists and self-styled progressives to confine expressions of faith to the private and personal sphere and in some circumstances

---

265 The "New Birth of Freedom Campaign" proposed in Chapters 2.2 and 3.2 is one mechanism for pursuing and achieving this end.

to effectively ban public expressions of faith-based positions and policy recommendations altogether.

In certain respects, today's marginalization of those Canadians with a religious orientation is analogous to the repressive marginalization of Canadians in the past on the basis of sexual orientation, a marginalization which many religiously-oriented Canadians supported but now generally acknowledge as wrong and regrettable. It is ironic and regrettable, therefore, that liberals and social democrats who have championed the liberation of LGBTQ Canadians from the closet should at the same time appear to favor pushing other Canadians—pro-life advocates, evangelical Christians, and conservative Catholics, for example—into the closet.

The message to such Canadians appears to be, "We can't prevent you from having this religious orientation with which you are afflicted, but it is only to be expressed in private or approved places of practice. In particular, it is not to be expressed in parliament, the legislatures, the courts, the classrooms, the law societies, the academy, or the broader public square."

I personally fail to see how the pursuit of such a course results in any net improvement in tolerance or inclusiveness. It merely replaces one set of prejudices with another, the main difference between the old prejudices and the progressive ones being that the latter are more heavily tainted with hypocrisy since they are held and promoted by people who claim to be inclusive and prejudice-free.

One of the practical political problems that this intolerance of the religious creates for liberals is that the number of Canadians afflicted with a religious orientation—let us say the Judeo-Christian, Indigenous, Muslim, Buddhist, and Hindu religious communities (or JIMBH community if we wish to alphabetize community identities)—is much larger than the number of Canadians who self-identify as members of the LGBTQ community. So will the liberal policy be to substantially enlarge the closet, or to somehow reduce the number of people requiring closeting perhaps through reorientation programs of some sort?

Beyond closet confinement and marginalization

Despite the efforts of secularists and self-styled progressives to marginalize people of faith, there are large numbers of Canadians of various faiths who are strongly committed to protecting and exercising the freedom of conscience, religion, and expression supposedly guaranteed by the Charter.

The exercise of this freedom includes bringing spiritual convictions and experience to bear, positively and non-coercively on public policy, legislation, and the services of governments. Since many (but not all) of these religiously-oriented Canadians are also conservatively-oriented politically, the proper navigation of the faith-political interface represents a particular challenge to conservative parties and the conservative movement.

The exercise of this freedom also involves respecting the freedom of others to exercise their freedom of belief and expression by rejecting and opposing religious values and perspectives.[266] But if we really believe in the fundamental freedoms supposedly guaranteed by the charter, and are prepared to defend and advance them, it should be possible to freely and actively participate in the Canadian political arena:

- Without having to hide one's spiritual convictions from the public view, as in the case of Pierre Elliot Trudeau[267]
- Without having to repudiate the spiritual elements of one's cultural heritage, as in the case of federal NDP leader Jagmeet Singh[268]
- Without becoming the target and victim of anti-religious bigotry, as in the case of Conservative leader Andrew Scheer,[269] if one is

---

266 An instructive mental exercise is to speculate what might happen if God decided to establish a universal Charter of Rights and Freedoms for human kind and decided to consult Canadians on the subject since we are so experienced in such matters. In particular, suppose he were to ask whether that Charter should include the freedom to sin. 'No' would likely be the emphatic answer of both religious and secular fundamentalists, the former for fear that granting such a freedom would allow abortions, same sex marriages, and assisted suicides, and the latter for fear that granting such a freedom would permit unfettered capitalism, human rights abuses, and unlimited green-house gas emissions. But it would appear that in establishing the original constitution of the universe God rejected such thinking since the freedom we have been granted includes the freedom to do both good and evil, even the freedom to reject the author of such freedoms.

267 Gwym, Richard; English, John; Lakenbauer, P. Whitney, "The Hidden Pierre Elliott Trudeau: The Faith behind the Politics," Novalis, 2004.

268 Sikhism is against abortion and same sex unions but to escape censure over such positions, Singh simply declared himself to be "a secular Sikh," just as Justin Trudeau is apparently a "secular Catholic." This position was generally accepted without analysis or criticism by most of the media and the voting public.

269 During the 2019 federal election campaign, the Liberals, NDP, and third-party advertisers repeatedly accused Conservative leader Andrew Scheer of intending

honest and forthright enough to disclose one's personal religious convictions while pledging not to impose them undemocratically on others.

Some secularly-oriented conservatives tend to favor simply ignoring the religious component of the conservative movement and allowing its marginalization to continue. Their position is to say: "Let's not object to or oppose the liberal effort to push these Canadians to the margins. What have we got to lose? If religiously-oriented voters won't support conservative parties, they are even less likely to go to the liberals or social democrats. They really have no place to go, so don't worry about accommodating them."

But if conservatives truly believe in the value of freedom, including freedom of conscience and religion and freedom indivisible, and want to be seen as the champions of a new birth of freedom, then we simply cannot ignore or abandon the religiously-oriented members of the conservative family or the Canadian population at large.

On purely pragmatic grounds, conservatives with a religious orientation also represent too large a component of the conservative workforce and electorate to either ignore or abandon. More importantly, on the positive and proactive side, we also need to appreciate that religiously-oriented conservatives can be a substantial asset of the movement, provided they articulate and promote their perspectives, ideas, and experiences wisely and graciously.

DO SOMETHING!

If you are a Canadian citizen committed to the maintenance and expansion of freedom in all its dimensions (whether you have a faith commitment or not):

to reintroduce anti-abortion legislation, roll back gay rights, etc., despite Scheer's repeated assertions that he had no such intentions. But even prior to these focused attacks, according to the pre-election survey referenced earlier, "six in ten (voters) are concerned that Scheer will introduce abortion legislation." See p. 49 of http://www.publicsquareresearch.ca/

- Affirm your faith in a literal and holistic interpretation of the Charter of Rights and Freedoms, in particular its protection of fundamental freedoms
- Make a point of asking any candidate for the federal parliament or a provincial legislature to call and work for the new birth of freedom described earlier
- Acknowledge that it was a grave mistake, for which apologies and recompense are owed, to have closeted members of the LGBTQ community in the past
- Be in the forefront of resisting the present and future closeting of any other group, including those of particular religious convictions

The constructive alternative

The positive and constructive alternative to closeting religiously-oriented conservatives is to welcome their participation in the affairs of the parties and the movement and in elections, subject to this one important condition: that such conservatives conduct themselves wisely and graciously at the interface of faith and politics so as to make a positive contribution thereto and avoid discrediting either their faith or conservatism by foolish and intemperate words and actions.

Once again, to operationalize this important condition will require preparation and training. In particular, we need to address the following questions:

- What is it of value to politics and public policy that faith-oriented citizens should strive to bring to their parties and electoral politics?
- What are the most important guidelines that believers engaged at the interface of faith and politics need to learn and practice in order to be both politically effective and a credit, not a discredit, to their faith and political allies?

Contributions

When it is asserted that faith-oriented citizens can bring ideas and perspectives of real and positive value to the practice of democratic politics

and governance, the media and secular political class of today are generally at a loss to know what those contributions might be. The prevailing
assumption on the part of secular, liberal, and progressive opinion leaders is that the participation of faith-oriented citizens in politics will be
negative, reactionary and divisive and therefore a liability, not an asset,
to the body politic.

And when it is asserted that there are significant numbers of faith-
oriented conservatives who wish to bring their spiritual convictions
and experience to bear on public policy, legislation, and the services
of governments, the automatic assumption of the media and secular
conservatives is that the only policies, legislation, and services these
believers particularly want to influence are those that pertain to the
hot-button moral issues of abortion, same-sex marriage, and euthanasia.

It is therefore particularly important for faith-oriented citizens to
vigorously define, establish, and affirm the broader contributions that
faith perspectives, particularly those rooted in the Judeo-Christian tradition, can make to democratic practice and governance.

Three of the most important of these contributions pertain to the
rule of law, conflict resolution, and service to others. I believe that the
communication and affirmation in practice of these three concepts
should be a prominent feature of the involvement of believers, especially
Christian believers, at the faith political interface.

The rule of law

The very first assertion in the Canadian Charter of Rights and Freedom is
that Canada "is founded upon principles that recognize the supremacy
of God and the rule of law." Although the courts have declared the reference to the supremacy of God to be a "dead letter" that can only be
"resurrected" by an unlikely decision of the Supreme Court,[270] no one in
the judicial or political arena disputes that the observance and practice
of the rule of law is essential to the peace, order and good government
of our country.

In addition, at the practical level of democratic politics, if you are
ever elected to a parliament or legislature, that is, if you actually become
a legislator, you will find that you are in the business of making statute

---

270 *R. v. Sharpe*, [1999] B.C.J. no.1555 at ss.78 to 80, per Southin, J.A.

law. In fact, you and your fellow legislators are the only ones who can do so. So despite the fact that your political party probably didn't mention much about you becoming a lawmaker if elected, nor did it provide you with any training or guidance as to how to carry out that responsibility, very quickly you will need to become a practitioner of and contributor to the rule of law.

In my own case, members of our family have been in the lawmaking business for fifty-five years. My father served in the Alberta legislature for thirty-three years and the Canadian Senate for thirteen, and I myself worked with him for eighteen of those years and served in the Canadian House of Commons for nine years.

Over that time, we read volumes on the history and practice of law-making and participated in framing, debating, and voting on hundreds of provincial and federal laws. And from that experience, for what it is worth, I must say that the most profound and useful texts that I have ever read on the rule of law are those to be found in the ancient Hebrew and Christian scriptures.

In the Hebrew scriptures, we find a detailed description of a 400-year-old experiment to establish right and peaceful relations among members of a human society and between humans and the source of their being as they conceived it (i.e. God). And what was the primary mechanism whereby this establishment of peace, order and good government was to be achieved? It was the rule of law, in their case the so-called Law of Moses.

The Law of Moses was law promulgated by the highest authority known to the Hebrew people. It covered every aspect of their personal, family, economic, and political lives. It was law accompanied by prom-ises of great benefits and blessings if adhered to. It was law accompanied by dire penalties and punishments if violated and by a comprehensive enforcement regime. And it was law experienced over a long period of time, with detailed descriptions of how it worked out, the benefits it brought when adhered to and the tragedies suffered if and when it was abused or misused.

All of this is of great instruction and use to anyone involved today in governing by the rule of law. But the greatest lesson taught by this historic experiment with the rule of law and the greatest contribution that faith-oriented citizens knowledgeable and respectful of it can make to lawmaking in our time, is the conclusion it teaches with respect to the limitations of the rule of law itself. It is a conclusion and a lesson highly instructive to all rule-makers and enforcers, whether they are parents in the home, leaders in the church, executives in the workplace, or lawmakers in our parliament, legislatures, and municipal councils.

That conclusion, reached by the later prophets of the ancient Hebrews, was that laws, even laws which they believed came directly from the hand of God, were insufficient in themselves to achieve the personal peace and social justice they were intended to achieve among the people to whom they were given.

These interpreters of Hebrew history, such as Jeremiah and Ezekiel, came to believe that unless law was accompanied by an internal trans-formation of the hearts and lives it was intended to govern,[271] unless laws were inscribed on "the tables of the heart," not merely on tablets of stone, or on parchment, or in statute books, the rule of law was insuf-ficient, by itself, to achieve a just society and the personal peace of those subject to it.

In our day, when the prevailing assumption is that some action, pol-icy, or expenditure of government, authorized and implemented by law, is the universal solution to almost every problem and conflict troubling society, is not this a vitally important lesson for our policy and lawmak-ers to understand? And is not insuring that this lesson is promulgated, taught, learned, and adhered to, a major contribution that faith-oriented believers participating in the political arena should be especially well equipped and able to make?

Conflict resolution

Besides lawmaking, another vital function performed by our political processes and institutions and yet another function which political par-ties fail to adequately prepare their candidates and elected members to discharge is that of conflict resolution.

Partisan candidates running for office and politicians in opposition can get away with taking sides on a particular issue and even adding to the conflict that characterizes the public square in a free society. But once one becomes part of a government, the larger and more difficult task becomes the reconciliation of conflicting interests by non-coercive means.

---

271 Jeremiah 31:33; Ezekiel 11:19; 26–27. See similar references by New Testament
     writers, II Corinthians 3:3; Hebrews 8:10

Do faith-oriented participants in the political process, especially those with a Judeo-Christian grounding, have anything unique to contribute to the understanding of this challenge and ways of meeting it? They ought to, since reconciliation and how to achieve it is the central theme of the life and teachings of Jesus of Nazareth and the New Testament record of the origins of Christianity.

One simple way of reconciling conflicting interests is to apply the rule of law. If necessary, go to court and let the law and the judges decide. As we have seen, the ancient Hebrews tried this approach for 400 years and deemed it helpful, to some extent, but insufficient in itself to achieve the desired result of peace and reconciliation in either the vertical or horizontal dimensions.

Hence the search for a different approach to the reconciliation of conflicting interests, an approach compatible with the Rule of Law but reaching beyond it, an approach which Christians believe was provided by Jesus of Nazareth.

It should be noted that Jesus did not in any way disparage the Law of Moses itself in addressing its insufficiencies or the shortcomings of its most vigorous proponents (the Pharisees). He declared that the law would endure until its purposes were accomplished.[272] But he directed some of his most biting criticisms to those whose professed commitment to the Rule of Law was hypocritical and whose adherence to it as a means of reconciling conflicting interests was deficient, in particular, unaccompanied by love and compassion for those whose interests it was supposed to serve.[273]

Jesus approach to the reconciliation of conflicting interests? Create, find, or be a mediator, a unique mediator willing and able to practice self-sacrificial mediation. Unlike a judge who must remain distant from the parties in conflict, this unique mediator becomes intimately related to and involved with both sides. If the conflict is between God and

272 Matthew 5:18: "For truly I tell you, until heaven and earth disappear, not the smallest letter, not the least stroke of a pen, will by any means disappear from the Law until everything is accomplished."

273 Matthew 23: 1–4: Then Jesus said to the crowds and to his disciples: "The teachers of the law and the Pharisees sit in Moses' seat. So you must be careful to do everything they tell you. But do not do what they do, for they do not practice what they preach. They tie up heavy, cumbersome loads and put them on other people's shoulders, but they themselves are not willing to lift a finger to move them.".

man (the theological dimension), he presents himself as the son of God and son of man. If the conflict is between Jew and Gentile (the societal dimensions) his followers, such as the Apostle Paul,[274] positioned themselves by becoming as a Jew to the Jews and as a Gentile to the Gentiles.

Not only does this unique mediator relate to and communicate with both sides of the conflict, he or she determines what measures are required to reconcile their interests and what the implementation of those measures will cost. Then, he or she, as the mediator pays the cost of the reconciliation effort rather than requiring the offending party or parties to do so.

It is an out-of-court settlement, non-coercive, self-sacrificial mediation by a third party, motivated by love,[275] which the parties are free to accept or reject. If they accept it, the reconciliation of conflicting interests is achieved; if they reject it, as they are free to do, the conflict continues and usually deepens.

This is not the place to fully discuss the role that self-sacrificial mediation has played in addressing past conflicts. The role of William Wilberforce in resolving the slavery issue by non-violent means in nineteenth-century Britain; the role of S. D. Chown, general superintendent of the Methodist church, in reconciling the conflicting interests of different Protestant denominations in Canada to create the United Church of Canada in the early twentieth-century; the role of Mahatma Gandhi in attempting to reconcile the conflicting interests of Hindus and Muslims as India gained independence; or the role of Martin Luther King in attempting to reconcile the interests of the black and white Americans in the twentieth-century.

But in our day, when the reconciliation of conflicting interests is such a huge part of governing a country as large and diverse as Canada, and when we are constantly coming up against the limits to resolving conflicts by the rule of law alone, does not this unique, self-sacrificial approach to conflict resolution have an important contribution to make to one of the primary challenges facing our politicians and governments?

Is there not a particular role in making that contribution by people for whom the understanding and experience of that approach to reconciliation is an integral part of their own personal experience and faith commitment?

---

274 1 Corinthians 9:19-21
275 2 Corinthians 5:17-21

Service

Besides lawmaking and conflict resolution, another vital function, the performance of which ought to distinguish those directly involved in our political processes and institutions, is service, in particular, public service, not self-service, but the service of others, in particular the service of those in need.

Do faith-oriented participants in the political process, especially those with a Christian grounding, have anything unique to contribute when it comes to a service commitment and the outworking of that commitment in practice? Again, they ought to, since service to others, motivated by self-sacrificial love, is again a central theme of the life and teachings of Jesus of Nazareth and the founder of their faith.

One of Jesus' most famous stories was that of the Good Samaritan. The story of an injured man lying by the side of the road whom a Samaritan (a man of a different race and religion which the Jews particularly hated) stopped and helped. Jesus instruction to his followers, including his followers today? "Go and do thou likewise!"

This is not the place to fully discuss the role that service to others rooted in the Christian concept of self-sacrificial love has already played in Canada in meeting the needs of the injured by the side of the road, from the role of Brother Andre in serving the poor in Old Quebec to the role of J. S. Woodsworth and Tommy Douglas (both Christian ministers) in laying the foundations of the modern welfare state.

But in our day, when the numbers of injured by the side of the road are increasing day-by-day and when the overwhelmed institutions of the welfare state are passing the point of diminishing social returns, is there not a need for a fresh infusion of and commitment to the service of others among our political class, the civil service, and the population at large? And is there not a particular role in the public square for restoring and revitalizing that commitment to the service of others motivated by love for people who profess to take seriously Jesus unequivocal instruction to *Do Something!* For the injured by the side of the road and not leave it to the state or to others?[276]

276 See Kristof, Nicholas, "Evangelicals Without Blowhards," *New York Times*, Sunday Review, July 30, 2011.

Guidelines

But now suppose that we can establish that faith-oriented citizens have something of significant value such as a deep understanding of and commitment to the rule of law, conflict resolution, and public service to bring to political parties and the processes and institutions of democratic governance if allowed to do so. The suspicion will still remain that the participation of such citizens in public life will nevertheless be marred by foolish remarks and intemperate actions which will discredit their positions and any party or institution associated with them.

In one sense, such suspicions and accusations based upon them are highly unfair, as if it is only faith-oriented citizens who are capable of acting foolishly or intemperately in the public square.

But as a safeguard against such behaviours and the suspicions they arouse, and to insure responsible behavior by faith-oriented citizens at the interface of faith and politics, the preparation of such citizens for political involvement should include the learning and practice of a few practical guidelines. If we are dealing with people whose faith is rooted in the Judeo–Christian traditions of this country, there is no better source for such guidelines than the Judeo-Christian scriptures themselves which such people hold to be authoritative in matters of faith and practice.

Time and space does not allow for a full elaboration of those guidelines here (I have done so elsewhere.)[277] But let me give just one highly relevant and instructive example of such a guideline, namely the imperative for Christian believers active in the public square to be "wise as serpents and gracious as doves" in both their speech and conduct

Wise as serpents and gracious as doves

About one year after the commencement of his public life, Jesus of Nazareth gathered together his motley group of initial followers and told them he was now sending them out to do public work in his name. He then gave them explicit instructions on how they were to conduct themselves in that capacity. His instructions were recorded by Matthew, the converted tax collector, who was in attendance at that meeting. Among

---

277 Manning, *Faith, Leadership, and Public Life,* see especially chapter 1.8

those instructions were what I call "The Great Guideline" for Christians active in the public square. It is the explicit command of Jesus to such followers to "be wise as serpents and harmless as doves."[278]

He might well have added "do not be vicious as snakes and stupid as pigeons," since some of his most zealous supporters, both then and now, were and are quite capable of behaving in that way to the detriment rather than the advancement of their public work as Christians.

Jesus not only gave this instruction to his followers, he demonstrated its application in his own public conduct. When asked by his opponents whether it was lawful to pay taxes to Caesar or not, a loaded political question intended to get him into trouble with the Roman authorities or the Jewish people (who hated the Roman tax collectors) or both, he shrewdly answered, "So give to Caesar what is Caesar's and to God what is God's."[279]

On another occasion his opponents asked him yet another loaded question, this time on an issue of sexual morality, a scandalous question to be posed in public in those days and the most difficult type of question for believers to handle in today's society. On this occasion his opponents dragged before him a woman purported to have been "taken in adultery" and ask of Jesus what should be done with her.

If he answered "spare her," he would be in violation of the Law of Moses. If he allowed them to stone her, as the Mosaic Law prescribed, he would be in violation of all his own teaching on love and mercy. So what did he say? To her accusers he said, "Let any one of you who is without sin be the first to throw a stone at her." And to the woman, as her accusers slunk away, he said: "Has no one condemned you? Then neither do I condemn you. Go now, and leave your life of sin." A response to the woman as gracious as his response to her accusers was shrewd.

Christians, indeed anyone professing religious faith and participating at the interface of faith and politics today, need to be adequately prepared. And at the top of the list of preparations should be learning to put into practice The Great Guideline, be wise as serpents and gracious as doves.

278 Matthew 10:16
279 Matthew 22:21

DO SOMETHING!

If you are a faith-oriented Canadian:

- Acknowledge that in the past some faith oriented Canadians have conducted themselves in such a way as to discredit their faith and the political parties and institutions with which they have been involved
- Accept as a primary condition of securing greater acceptance in the political sector the necessity of conducting oneself wisely and graciously at the faith–political interface
- Be willing to take instruction and training as to how to conduct oneself wisely and graciously at the faith-political interface
- Offer your moral and financial support to faith-based training programs and institutions offering such training
- Vigorously define, establish, and affirm your insights and commitments to the rule of law, conflict resolution, and public service as a major faith-based contribution to peace, order and good government in Canada
- Offer your moral and financial support to faith-based think tanks and advocacy groups offering faith based perspectives and contributions on public issues
- Offer your moral and financial support to faith-based training institutions offering instruction and training of how to participate wisely and graciously in the political process.

If you are a leader or executive of a faith-based institution or organization:

- Undertake to better equip faith-based Canadians with knowledge and understanding of the contributions which faith perspectives can make to the affirmation and practice of the rule of law, conflict resolution, and public service in Canada
- Make available instruction and training for faith-oriented Canadians on how to conduct themselves wisely and graciously at the faith-political interface

If you are a leader or executive of a political party or movement organization:

- Welcome participation by religiously-oriented Canadians in the political arena, subject to the condition that such participants learn to conduct themselves wisely and graciously at the interface of faith and politics
- Make available instruction and training in for faith-oriented Canadians in political participation, with a special emphasis on how to conduct oneself wisely and graciously at the faith political interface
- Specifically invite faith-oriented Canadians to contribute to the ideological and policy resources of the party or organization, particularly in areas where their faith perspective offers historical insight and experience, e.g., in such areas as the rule of law, conflict resolution, and public service.

3.5 Build Democracy House: A model parliament for Canada

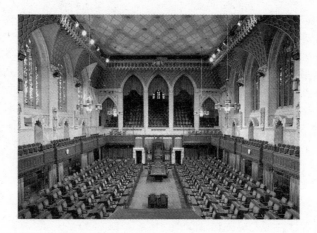

Canada's House of Commons

Every law school in the country has what is called a Moot Court, a model court where would-be lawyers learn and practice courtroom protocols, procedures and tactics before being allowed to set foot in a real court of law. Yet there is no permanent, well-financed, continuously operated model parliament in Canada where would-be lawmakers, federal, provincial, territorial, or municipal, can be exposed in advance to what it's really like to sit and work as an elected member of a democratic assembly.

As previously mentioned in Chapter 3.2, I once interviewed a cross section of the house officers (mainly Speakers and Clerks) of Canada's fourteen senior elected assemblies, those serving the House of Commons, the ten provincial legislatures, and the three territorial legislatures. In addition to asking them what training courses they might prescribe to enable elected officials to enter better prepared for their work as legislators and democratic representatives, I also asked them the following question: If the building housing your assembly was to burn down (as did the Centre Block of the federal parliament building in 1916) and you had to not only rebuild it, but also to update its procedures, what physical and procedural changes would you recommend in designing and operating its replacement?

The major suggestions received to this latter question are summarized in Table 7 below, since updated by subsequent surveying:

TABLE 7 Suggested changes to the physical and procedural features of Canada's democratic assemblies

- Alter seating arrangements – consider semi-circular formation?
- Decisions re: use of video screens, computers, hand held devices etc. in the chamber.
- Expansion of the scope and nature of the televising of assembly and committee proceedings.
- Provision of video conference capability for committees.
- Provision of child care facilities and family support services for members and staffs.
- Upgrading, including digitizing, library and information services.
- Modernize Standing Orders.
- Change Question Period schedule/format-follow British model?
- Update committee procedures, in particular method of examining expert witnesses.
- Improve budget presentations and financial reporting procedures.
- Improve debate procedures and content – especially second reading debates. e.g. discourage recitation of canned speeches prepared by staffs.
- Stiffen assembly discipline/protocols.
- Establish dispute settlement mechanism
- Expand research services and adding new support services such as a Parliamentary Office of Science and Technology (POST)

These and other consultations, intended to incorporate the very best features from the existing parliament, legislatures, and municipal councils with contemporary suggestions for improvements, have resulted in some preliminary specifications for Democracy House: a Model Parliament of Canada. They include the following elements:

- A standalone facility, with the look and feel of a real legislative building

- A 100-seat legislative chamber large and flexible enough to enable experimentation with alternative seating arrangements and also to serve as a large public meeting/conference hall when the seats are removed
- A six-to-eight week curriculum designed to provide in-depth training to people who think they want to become members of an elected assembly in such subjects as parliamentary protocol and procedures, question-period preparation and participation, throne speech and budget analysis and debates, legislative analysis and debate, the mechanics of private member's bill development and promotion, caucus meetings and critic assignments, committee meetings and committee work, and participation in media scrums
- A shorter, more general, curriculum for those unable to take the full course
- Public galleries to permit the public to attend some of the proceedings (e.g., debates on major issues) and to permit students to observe selected teaching sessions at a lower fee than that charged to full-time participants
- A media gallery to accommodate arrangements with local media and/or journalism schools to participate in mock media coverage and scrums
- Electronic and administrative capacity to provide for simultaneous translation, experimentation with electronic voting, and the video-casting of selected proceedings for teaching and promotional purposes
- Committee rooms and lobbies suitable for simulated meetings of parliamentary committees and informal caucusing
- Nearby access to accommodation, office, child care, and eating facilities for those enrolled in Democracy House sessions

The primary purpose of this institution would be to provide comprehensive, continuous, cross-partisan training for aspirants to elected office on a scale and to a depth never before attempted in Canada or any other Commonwealth country. Besides its basic training function, Democracy House could be used for several other purposes relevant to strengthening Canadian democracy. These would include:

1. Experimentation with parliamentary reform proposals

Actual parliaments, legislatures, and municipal councils are loath to experiment with alternative procedures and innovations because of the risk and potential political cost of failure. Democracy House would be subject to no such inhibitions and would therefore be free to experiment with such innovations as alternative seating arrangements (to make the legislative chamber less adversarial, structurally), alternative rules and formats for question period (the public being thoroughly disgusted with the current approach), electronic and long-distance voting (neither currently employed by our House of Commons), revisions to committee procedures (at present, archaic and totally inadequate) for obtaining and cross-examining the testimony of expert witnesses, the use of interactive websites and teleconferencing techniques by committees, and alternative approaches to structuring and televising legislative debates and proceedings to make them more interesting and relevant to the general public.

2. *Constituency days and lobby days*

A significant portion of a modern legislator's time is spent dealing with the concerns and problems of constituents and responding to pressure from interest groups and lobbyists of all kinds. To add to the realism of the experience of Democracy House participants, several well-organized constituency days and lobby days would be a valuable addition to the curriculum.

On constituency days, our would-be legislators would be exposed to a cross-section of the concerns and problems of constituents, with instruction on how to deal with these sympathetically and effectively. Some of the best instruction on how to handle constituency work will come from the experience of faithful constituency office staffs at the federal, provincial, and municipal levels who deal with a bewildering variety of real constituent interests day in and day out under all kinds of circumstances.

On lobby days, interest groups of various kinds and would be invited to make presentations and pitches to individual or small groups of our would-be legislators, with instruction provided to the latter on how to calibrate, manage, and respond to such representations critically, fairly, and ethically.

Interest groups and lobbyists, like political parties, are an integral part of our political system whether we like them or not. The responsibility of the elected official is not to avoid them but to clearly identify the interests involved, to properly assess and weigh the merits of their representations in relation to competing interests and the issue at hand, to seek out the other, and often under-represented, sides of the story, and to insist on transparency and honesty in legislator/interest group relations. To do so effectively requires both instruction and practice.

It may well be that when some of our would-be legislators discover their distaste or lack of appetite for some major aspect of elected life, such as the time and effort needed to deal with constituents and interest groups, that they will decide against pursuing a political career. So be it. Better to have discovered that "this kind of work is not for me" before seeking or attaining elected office than afterwards.[280]

One of the principal side benefits of Democracy House may well be its role in discouraging certain individuals with unrealistic expectations, conflicts of interest, or personalities un-conducive to public life from seeking elected office.

3. Training for future municipal councilors

While the concept of Democracy House was initially driven by the need to better prepare future members of parliament and of provincial and territorial legislatures for elected office, it is important to realize that more than one third of the members of those assemblies got their start in municipal politics. And contrary to the view that municipal government constitutes the third level of government in Canada, from a democratic standpoint, because it is the level of government closest to its electorate, municipal government in many respects is actually the first level of democratic government in Canada.

A modified version of the curriculum previously described in Table 6 should therefore be developed for the training of persons interested in becoming elected to municipal offices. The Democracy House chamber should also be flexible enough to be organized as a municipal council chamber, and at least one of the annual session of Democracy House per year should be devoted to the training of potential candidates for municipal office.

---

280 While I like to pride myself on having helped recruit many talented people into running for public office, I may have rendered an even more important service to democracy by persuading certain people not to run for public office.

4. Provision of special Democracy House sessions for:

- **Students:** Numerous universities, colleges, churches and service groups across the country sponsor short term model parliaments for students. These are very worthwhile endeavors as they encourage student participation in the democratic process, develop interests and skills, and are deserving of all the support they can get. Democracy House, as a permanent institution with an extensive curriculum and access to substantial parliamentary expertise, could become a major source of support for such student model parliaments.

- **New Canadians**: At least one Democracy House session per year could be dedicated to providing in-depth parliamentary training for new Canadians, in particular those coming from non-democratic traditions.

- **Seniors**: The Legislative Assembly of the Northwest Territories has experimented with an Elders Parliament in which respected elders from across the territory are invited annually to participate in a parliamentary type session to bring the wisdom of age to bear on the issues of the day. Democracy House could convene and support similar sessions which will grow in significance as Canada's population ages.

- **Virtual Participants**: From the outset, Democracy House should maintain a website and a social media presence, providing online public access to selected aspects of its curriculum, tutorials, and proceedings. These resources and the website will eventually make possible the creation of a "virtual parliament," accessible on-line to much larger numbers of people than the actual Democracy House facility itself can accommodate or serve.

5. Exporting democracy

As one of the world's oldest functioning democracies, Canada has the obligation and opportunity to export its democratic experience and technologies to emerging democracies around the world. Canada's Democracy House could make a significant contribution in this regard, by franchising the concept to democratic interests in other countries and/or by setting aside at least one session per year for the training of would-be democratic politicians from emerging democracies.

In summary, therefore, the concept of Democracy House: A Model Parliament of Canada, envisions a unique training and experimental facility designed to raise the standards of parliamentary and legislative performance at all three levels of government in this country, and to encourage more effective democratic participation by aspirants to public office including students, seniors, new Canadians, and democrats from abroad.

The business case for supporting Democracy House

The business case for providing financial support for Democracy House from governments and private donors is as follows:

Canadians currently spend just over $1.48 billion[281] annually for the support of fourteen elected legislatures, the parliament of Canada, ten provincial legislatures, and three territorial legislatures, plus hundreds of millions more for the support of the Canada's thousands of municipal councils.

In addition, each year Canadians spend hundreds of millions of dollars on:

- Permanent elections offices (Elections Canada, Elections Ontario, Elections Vancouver, etc.) in order to manage preparations for and the conduct of democratic elections
- Democratic elections themselves, at least once every four years, in the fourteen federal, provincial, and territorial jurisdictions, not to mention the elections in over 5000 municipal jurisdictions.

In other words, Canadians are investing over $1.48 billion per year on a very special service sector, the democracy sector whereby they exercise political control over thousands of lawmakers in charge of collecting and spending over $800 billion annually in taxpayers' dollars.[282]

Despite the magnitude of these figures, and the vital importance of good government to the economy and the wellbeing of Canadians, the amount of money specifically dedicated annually to the training and preparation of people for elected public office is miniscule. What

---

281 See Table 3 from Part 1. Also see https://docs.google.com/spreadsheets/d//edit? usp=sharing1ypRn3gokz7XuJ_gof-PCCJZQiRW426Vm9Lo5ucpkL7s

282 Statistics Canada. Table 10-10-0039-01. See https://www150.statcan.gc.ca/n1/ daily-quotidien/181120/dq181120b-eng.htm

else can be said but that it needs to be substantially increased if we truly desire to strengthen the practices and institutions of democracy in Canada.

A progress report

Before generating an up-to-date "to do" list for making Democracy House a reality, let me summarize what has already been done to date (fall of 2019) to advance this concept:

- The concept, based in part on the initial survey of federal, provincial and territorial assembly house officers, has been reasonably fleshed out and documented
- The University of British Columbia (UBC), because of the spaciousness, location, and climate of its Vancouver campus, has been approached as a possible home for such a facility and has expressed support conditional on the necessary financing being provided
- UBC is also in the process of planning and building facilities to house its new School of Public Policy and Global Affairs. Training for would be legislators and policy implementers will be part of its curriculum, and it is proposed that the construction of the Public Policy School complex include Democracy House as a distinguishing feature[283]
- The Centre for the Study of Democratic Institutions at UBC, through its Summer Institute for Future Legislators (IFL), has already been delivering courses for would be elected officials, similar to those recommended by the house officers, and has done so for seven years. An expanded IFL program will also be affiliated with the proposed School of Public Policy School and Global Affairs, and could utilize Democracy House as its primary training facility
- The UBC architectural consultant, assisting to design the School of Public Policy facility including Democracy House, is being encouraged to confer with the architectural consultants advising Public Works Canada on the current refurbishing of the Centre Block in Ottawa which houses the House of Commons. Thus any changes being made to modernize the House of Commons would also be reflected in the design of Democracy House

283 See https://democracy.arts.ubc.ca/ifl/

Moving forward

For Democracy House to become a reality much more still needs to be done. At the organizational and promotional level:

- Endorsement of the need for such a facility is required from the highest political levels, preferably from former Prime Ministers and Premiers across the party spectrum
- Much planning is still required to further refine the concept and provide the final design of the facility, the training curriculum, the budget, and the fundraising and marketing plan
- A major fundraising campaign, organized by UBC's Development Office, assisted by private sector volunteers, and utilizing the endorsements and planning work described above, is required to raise the necessary finances[284]
- Since financing is the biggest challenge to make Democracy House a reality, the fundraising plan with various options for donor participation needs to be carefully worked out and marketed. Requests of donors could include requests for:
- Multi-million dollar legacy pledges to build the facility, with cornerstone inscription rights being granted to legacy donors
- Support of a request-for-proposals process to find the best architect and design for the proposed facility, including a substantial prize for the winning design
- Pledges to sponsor one seat in Democracy House for multiple years, with naming rights attached, such sponsorships to be priced at $1/100^{th}$ of the annual operating costs (assuming Democracy House is a 100-seat chamber)
- Pledges to underwrite the construction of a particular room, say, a committee room, a gallery, the media room, etc., or some other physical aspect of Democracy House with naming rights attached
- Pledges to sponsor the development and delivery of one or more of the training courses to be offered by Democracy House
- Pledges to support the development of a policy position on some contemporary issue, for presentation and debate in Democracy House

---

284 Visit support.ubc.ca and/or contact Marilyn Wile, Assistant Dean, Development and Alumni Engagement, email: marilyn.wile@ubc.ca

- Pledges to support teaching fellowships for instructors providing training to students enrolled in the Public Policy School, the expanded IFL program, and Democracy House
- Pledges to sponsor a Democracy House trainee, a potential elected representative, via scholarships or bursaries plus living allowances. These are one of the most important donations required as they will support the human resource component of Democracy House
- Pledges to sponsor a distinguished lecturer or special guest to address Democracy House
- Pledges to sponsor a page, an intern, or a student observer for Democracy House sessions
- Pledges to sponsor a weekend or week-long Youth Session, Seniors Session, or New Canadians Session of Democracy House
- Pledges to sponsor a special session for training attendees from some emerging democracy
- Pledges to sponsor the establishment and upkeep of the Virtual Parliament based at Democracy House
- Pledges to sponsor special events at Democracy House, for instance, a Throne Speech debate, a Budget debate, a special debate on a hot issue
- Pledges to sponsor a Constituency Day, or Lobbyists Day, or Scrum Day at Democracy House
- Pledges to become a Friend of Democracy House, offering whatever support and input the donor is able to provide, donations big or small, in cash or in kind, so that Democracy House has that broad, grassroots support base which is an essential characteristic of any genuinely democratic institution.

DO SOMETHING!

If you are a current or former member of parliament, a legislature, or municipal council:

- Visit the Democracy House website (DemocracyHouseCanada.ca) and pledge your support to the project
- Urge the Leaders of your political party or your personal support group to support the project and to use it as a future training ground for democratic politicians

- Be prepared to donate your services on a volunteer basis as a potential instructor at Democracy House in your area of expertise

If you are an executive or manager of a charitable foundation with educational or political objectives:

- Review the various options for financially supporting Democracy House
- Pledge whatever financial support you are able by contacting the Development Office of the University of British Columbia

If you are simply a Canadian citizen who values democracy and wishes to support efforts to improve the knowledge and skills of our elected representatives

- Visit the Democracy House website (DemocracyHouseCanada.ca) and become a Friend of Democracy House
- Contribute your ideas respecting the design and operation of Democracy House
- Contribute your ideas as to what courses should be offered in order to improve the future performance of elected officials
- Pledge your personal support, however large or small, to the project

3.6 Invest in People

Democracy as Lincoln defined it, is government of the people, by the people, and for the people. People are what it is all about.

People, not ideas, money, or organizations (important as these things can be) are the greatest resource of a political party or movement.

People of all sorts–yes, leaders, candidates, elected officials, and political staff–but also rank and file citizens who volunteer, donate, and vote and to whom political leadership in a democracy is ultimately accountable.

It is therefore highly appropriate to conclude this discourse on the development of human resources for Canadian democracy and conservatism with one last appeal, even at the risk of being repetitious, for us as Canadians to significantly increase our investments in the people on whom the quality and performance and of our political movements, parties, elected assemblies, and governments are so dependent.

Let us particularly increase our investments in:

- Those people who see the necessity of entering the political arena better prepared than in the past, and indicate a willingness to better equip themselves through study and training
- Political scouts and scouting systems to identify at an early stage, people with the potential to play the democratic game at its highest levels
- Political instructors, both theoretical and practical, and the materials and programs they need to raise the knowledge and skill levels of political practitioners
- People responsible for organizing and delivering the services of political training programs already in existence, such as those of the Clayton Riddell Graduate Program in Political Management and the Institute for Future Legislators described earlier
- People responsible for organizing and delivering the services of new and improved political training programs required to meet future demand for such training

- Student interns, in training programs, in party and movement organizations, and in political work-sharing environments
- Faith-oriented citizens and the training required to enable them to
  make positive contributions to democratic politics and avoid the
  pitfalls that can so easily sidetrack and discredit their participation
- The policy researchers and developers at various think tanks and
  universities, including those soon to be brought together at the new
  public policy school at UBC
- The organizers, instructors, and trainees to be soon brought together
  in Democracy House as a Model Parliament for Canada

In the private economic sector, we have such institutions as banks and
investment firms who specialize in assembling financial resources and
investing them in economic activities of all kinds.

In the charitable sector, we have foundations and NGOs who specialize in assembling charitable dollars and investing them in humanitarian
and social service activities of all kinds.

In the public sector, we have Finance Departments, Revenue
Agencies, and Treasury Boards who specialize in collecting tax dollars
and investing them in government programs and services of all kinds.

In each of these sectors we also have consultants and advisors who
can assist Canadians of all kinds to develop investment portfolios, tax
plans, and household budgets that allocate their financial resources in
the most productive and effective manner possible.

Where are the democratic equivalents of these institutions? The
Democracy Banks? The Democracy Investment Houses? The Democracy
Financing Foundations? The Democracy Financing Consultancies? I am
talking about institutions that specialize in raising and investing funds
for investment in the essential components of our democratic system,
on which so much of the performance and success of the economy, our
social services and charities, and the public sector depends.

And where are the democratic equivalents of the public and private sector financial planners, consultants, and advisors who can assist
Canadians of all kinds to include an investment of some kind (money
or time) in the maintenance and advancement of government of the
people, by the people, and for the people?

My hope in providing this long discourse on the importance in
investing in the human resources components of our democratic system
is that such institutions, plans, portfolios, and investments will become
a prominent feature of Canadian democracy in the years ahead.

DO SOMETHING!

If you are in a corporate, governmental, charitable, or personal position with financial resources which could be invested in democracy

- Construct a Political Investment Portfolio as previously discussed
- Ensure that your Portfolio includes the various opportunities for investing in the development of the human resource needs of democracy as presented in chapters 3.1 to 3.6
- Analyze those opportunities and invest in those which you feel are most deserving of your financial support

If you are an executive or manager of a financial planning or investment counselling service:

- Develop and refine the concept of Political Investment Portfolios for presentation to your clients
- Encourage investment in such portfolios when and where appropriate

PART 4

NETWORK

Canadians who share more than a nominal and passive commitment to democracy, who are actually prepared to *Do Something!* to preserve, update, and strengthen democratic processes and institutions in this country, are scattered geographically and among different academic institutions, think tanks, advocacy groups and political parties.

Democracy in Canada would be significantly strengthened if the personal and organizational relationships among these people could be strengthened through more deliberate and effective networking, recognizing that the emergence and all-pervasiveness of social media is providing ways and means of doing so that were unknown and unavailable to previous generations of democrats.

Canadian conservatism also suffers from the fact that its constituent parts exist for the most part in silos. The conservative-oriented provincial political parties rarely associate substantively with each other or the federal party, let alone cooperate extensively on the policy making, training, or election campaigning fronts. Conservative-oriented think tanks and advocacy groups rarely sponsor events jointly, or form effective coalitions to advance their ideas and interests, each being fearful of losing donors or media attention to the others.

Surely it is true that we are stronger together than apart and there is therefore a need for a deliberate and effective effort to strengthen personal and organizational relationships among the diverse components of the conservative movement through improved networking, again aided and abetted by more extensive and effective use of the social media.

Hence the following four chapters on building the democracy network, building the conservative network, responsibly employing the social media to do so more effectively, and adequately financing this networking thrust.

One further observation before proceeding: the development of attitudes and practices conducive to democratic discourse and governance, like most of our attitudes and practices, usually has its roots in the home and one's immediate circle of relatives and friends.

If young people particularly, are given the impression that talking about politics is a risky thing to do with family and friends, for fear of causing friction over differences of views, the tendency will be to simply avoid any political conversation at all. On the other hand, if young people, particularly in the home, are shown and taught that there are ways and means of airing different views, discussing them initially with the intention of learning rather than prematurely judging the perspectives of others, and arriving at tentative (subject to future change) decisions which benefit the majority without disparaging the minority, then solid foundations for future participation in democratic discourse and governance have been well laid.

Making initial introductions to democracy in the home lighthearted and fun rather than overly serious and controversial is also not a bad idea. In our home, with three older girls and two younger boys, one of our initial democratic discussions arose over what should be Canada's national sport. All three of our girls were synchronized swimmers whereas the boys were hockey players, so when it came to a vote the girls plus their mother were able to outvote the boys and me on this important question. Democracy, however, is a long game, and as the girls acquired husbands and had children (eight boys and three girls) the voting coalition expanded in our favor, so that now the hockey party enjoys a majority position while of course, for the sake of peace in the family, still being highly respectful of the synchronized swimming minority.

On a deeper philosophical level, I also managed to politicize our early visits with the children to the zoo (Sandra is rolling her eyes) by raising the question, "Is it better to be safe or free?" Many a lighthearted but instructive discussion occurred with the children around this theme.

4.1 Build the democracy network

As previously observed, active and committed Canadian democrats are scattered geographically and among different academic institutions, think tanks, advocacy groups and political parties.

Relationships among them that need to be strengthened include the relationships between:

- Academics who research, write, and teach on the subject of democracy, and democratic practitioners in the political arena
- Advocates and supporters of democratic reforms who find themselves separated in different and competing political parties
- Older Canadians who have experienced the strengths and weaknesses of Canadian democracy, next-generation Canadians who have not, and new Canadians who often know only too well what it is like to be governed by anti-democratic regimes

Given that democratic governance is supposed to be inclusive of all members of the society and is very much about the reconciliation of conflicting interests by non-coercive means, small-d democrats should also play a prominent role in bridging the gaps between:

- Members of the scientific and political communities as discussed in chapter 2.3
- Faith-oriented and secular-oriented members of the society, particularly within the political community itself, as discussed in chapter 3.4
- Marginalized members of the society and those responsible for its governance

Mechanisms for strengthening all of these relationships include:

- Responsible and effective use of social media (more on this in chapter 4.3)
- Networking seminars and conferences whose specific objective is relationship building
- Mentoring relationships between persons experienced with the theory and practice of democracy and next-generation Canadians with democratic interests but less experience
- "You Two Should Meet" initiatives, organized by perceptive relationship builders

All of these points will be enlarged upon in the following chapter (4.2) which deals with the need to significantly strengthen relationships among the various components of the conservative movement. But before doing so, allow me to elaborate briefly on three areas of what ought to be common ground among small-d democrats in Canada that I think deserve special attention.

A democratic principles and practices curriculum for educational and training institutions.

In chapter 3.5, I proposed the creation of Democracy House as a major, permanent, dedicated institution for teaching democratic principles and practices to would be candidates for public office.

Its creation and operation must involve the development of a curriculum to teach and inculcate those principles and practices. Agreement on the need for such a curriculum, and the opportunity to contribute to its development ought to constitute common ground among democratic theorists and practitioners across the political spectrum. Developing such a curriculum and periodically updating it will also require extensive networking among the contributors and those (the political parties) with a vested interest in the outcome, thereby strengthening relationships among key players in the democratic sector.

A democratic reform agenda for members of democratic assemblies.

In each of the major political parties, and the movement organizations that support them, there are individuals who put their commitment to strengthening the application of democratic principles and practices as high or even higher on their priority lists than many of their more partisan commitments.

And, yet to my knowledge, there is no Democratic Caucus in the federal parliament or any of the provincial legislatures. Ideally, its creation should be encouraged rather than frowned upon by the leadership of the parties since all profess to be champions of democracy and public confidence in our form of democracy is noticeably slipping.

Building on the existence of this common interest in strengthening the application of democratic principles and practices among at least some legislators, might it not be possible for some political figure or some think tank or policy school to propose just one major democratic reform[285] on which those legislators could agree and which they would dedicate themselves to promoting until it was actually implemented?

As previously discussed, the Triple E Senate Committee[286] headed by Bert Brown (in later years, Senator Brown) and the Reform Party believed that insisting on the democratic election of Senators rather than their appointment by the government of the day ought to be an idea on which small d-democrats across the political spectrum could and should unite. But alas, this democratic reform proposal was strenuously resisted by many, especially the provincial premiers,[287]

---

285 Reform of the voting system, e.g. replacement of the current "first past the post" system with something else, is the one area of democratic reform where political parties are least likely to agree and are least likely to be trusted by the public. Political parties have an obvious conflict of interest on electoral system reform since each tends to favor and promote only those changes to the system which will enhance its own electoral fortunes. It was this public mistrust which forced Justin Trudeau to very quickly abandon his ill-conceived electoral reform promise naively made in the 2015 federal election. It was also this public mistrust which contributed to the defeat in 2018 of the NDP government's attempt to change the voting system by referendum in British Columbia.

286 See https://nationalpost.com/news/politics/bert-brown-senate-reform for more information.

287 To make significant amendments to the Canadian constitution requires a high degree of provincial consent: the approval of at least two thirds of the provinces

and has now been completely sandbagged by a ruling of the Supreme Court.[288]

The other democratic reform which has been vigorously advocated over the years, and might still be a good candidate for rallying small d-democrats in future legislatures, has to do with modifying the so-called confidence convention.

This confidence convention, while it is not a law nor is it even enshrined in the Standing Orders of parliament, when rigorously applied insists that the defeat of a government measure in the parliament or a legislature, even on a motion as trivial as "that the House adjourn at 5:00 pm," means the government has been defeated and must resign.

It is this convention that enables government whips to force their members to vote for measures with which those members and their constituents might strongly disagree. This puts dissenting members of the government in a very difficult position. If they vote against a government motion or bill, or even defeat a section of a bill, they run the risk of defeating the government and thereby losing their own jobs.[289]

The democratic reform which would correct this situation does not require a change in the law or the Standing Orders of our democratic

with at least 50% of the population of all provinces. The idea of amending the Constitution to make the federal Senate a more effective representative of regional interests by electing its members has generally been opposed rather than supported by many of the provincial premiers and governments who regard themselves, not some federal body, as best equipped to represent those regional interests.

Back in the days when Senator Barry Goldwater was very prominent on the American political stage, an Alberta cabinet minister explained the Lougheed government's lukewarm interest in Senate reform this way: "Everybody knows who the Senator for Arizona is. Nobody knows who the governor of Arizona is. We wouldn't want that to happen here, would we?"

288 2014 SCC 32. The court ruled that "the implementation of consultative elections and senatorial term limits requires consent of the Senate, the House of Commons, and the legislative assemblies of at least seven provinces representing, in the aggregate, half of the population of all the provinces," in effect giving the provinces a veto over any federal initiative to democratize the Senate.

289 The exceptions to the rigorous application of the confidence convention occur in minority government situations in which the minority government loses a vote but insists that it will only resign if the house passes a formal non-confidence motion (e.g. King in 1925, Pearson in 1968, Trudeau in 1983, Martin in 2005, and Harper in 2008). See House of Commons Procedure and Practice, Second Edition, 2009, "Operation of the Confidence Convention." http://www.ourcommons.ca/procedure-book-livre/Document.aspx?sbdid=a24e8688-cc45-4245-8f5c-dd32f4aa9b01&sbpid=5a1717da-cb22-4cea-9ee5-4ac5ef9a6b1a

assemblies. It only requires a twenty-second statement by a Prime Minister or a Premier to the effect that if a government motion or bill is defeated by a vote of the House, the government will not automatically resign, but will immediately cause a confidence motion to be put to the chamber. Members of the chamber will then be asked whether they actually intended to defeat the government, or was their intent simply to defeat the government measure in question?

Under this modified convention, a government member could vote against a government measure if his or her conscience or the wishes of his or her constituents demanded it, but then turn around and support the government itself on the confidence motion so that it need not resign. This reform, providing for "freer voting" in our democratic assemblies, ought to command the support of small-d democrats, especially among the back benchers, in every caucus.

DO SOMETHING!

If you are a small-d democrat and an academic or an executive or member of a think tank, advocacy group, or foundation with an interest in strengthening democracy in Canada:

- Actively network with other small-d democrats of your acquaintance
- Promote and support the inclusion of democratic reform as a subject of discussion at seminars and conferences which you organize and/or attend

If you are a small-d democrat and an elected member of a democratic assembly:

- Identify and network with other small-d democrats in your assembly across party lines
- Form a democratic caucus within your assembly to promote democratic reforms on which it is possible to secure all party agreement
- Seriously consider and promote modification of the confidence convention to permit "freer voting" in your assembly

An international initiative to promote citizen-directed democracy

In Chapter 5.4 we will more thoroughly discuss the international ide-ological competition developing between proponents of the western concept of citizen-directed democracy and state-directed governance as promoted worldwide by the Communist Party and government of China.

If Canadians decide to actively participate in this international ideo-logical competition, as we should, and on the side of citizen-directed democracy, then our small-d democrats, regardless of what domestic differences may exist among us, should come together to develop and implement the required strategy and program internationally.

The actual development and carrying out of such a strategy and pro-gram will require extensive networking among the contributors, further strengthening relationships among key players in the democratic sector.

4.2 Build the Conservative Network

Break down the silos

The various components of the conservative movement in Canada tend to be atomized and siloed: atomized in the sense of existing largely as separate and independent units, and siloed in the sense that those units generally work independently and in isolation from each other. On the other hand, left-of-centre think tanks, advocacy groups, and political parties, perhaps because of their collectivist mentality and the collectivist ("Solidarity Forever") nature of the union movement, tend to work more closely together and to coordinate their political efforts much more through interlocking directorates and integrated campaigns.

Relationships among conservatives which need to be significantly strengthened include those between:

- Conservative academics and researchers, and political practitioners. i.e. between the generators and users of conservative intellectual capital
- Conservative think tanks and advocacy groups, i.e., between the generators of conservative ideas and policy proposals and the communicators and campaigners who can popularize them
- Conservative political practitioners (constituency executives, campaign teams, candidates, and elected officials) and trainers and mentors so that the educators and trainers can impart to the practitioners the knowledge and skills they need to be more successful
- Next-generation and previous-generation conservatives, so that the former can benefit from the knowledge and experience of the latter, and so that previous-generation conservatives can benefit

from the energy and forward looking thinking of next-generation conservatives

- Conservative-oriented political parties at all levels, federal, provincial, municipal, with each other and with the other components of the conservative movement.

As previously discussed (See Figure 8), the conservative movement as a whole can be represented by a pyramid with the political parties at the apex supported by movement organizations (PACs, think tanks, communicators, training organizations, donors, etc.) underneath. Each of these components needs to be strengthened but what is especially needed is a substantial strengthening of the personal and working relationships among all the individuals and organizations involved.

A symmetric matrix (see Figure 9) may then be used to define all the first-order relationships possible among all the various organizational components of the conservative movement. If we were to shade in each square of that matrix to the extent that a strong, productive,

FIGURE 8 The Political Infrastructure Pyramid

	Political Parties	Political Media	Advocacy Groups	Political Action Committees	Think Tanks/ Academics	Training Programs/ Institutions	Mentoring Services	Fundraisers	Donors/ Investors
Political Parties									
Political Media									
Advocacy Groups									
Political Action Committees									
Think Tanks/ Academics									
Training Programs/ Institutions									
Mentoring Services									
Fundraisers									
Donors/ Investors									

FIGURE 9 The Conservative Network

working relationship exists between the component defined by a particular row (say that defining think tanks and academic institutions) and the component defined by a particular column (say that defined by political action committees), the conservative network matrix looks like a patchwork quilt, with some intersections very dark because strong relationships exist between the components in question and others being very light because the inter-relationships are very weak or non-existent. The networking challenge for the conservative movement is to maintain the strong interrelationships where they exist and establish and strengthen them where they do not.

As a practical exercise in strengthening your personal relationships with other components of the conservative movement:

- Identify the cell of the networking matrix in Figure 9 with which you most closely identify. Perhaps it's the political party cell, or the think tank cell, or the advocacy group cell, or whatever

- Then mentally move down the row or column from your cell, through every other cell, asking yourself: "Do I know anybody in this cell? Do I have a strong working relationship with anybody or any organization in this cell?

And if the answer to this latter question is "no", then add to your to do list for next year, establishing a working relationship with someone or some organization in those cells where your current relationships are weak or non-existent.

Strategies and mechanisms for strengthening all of the relationships to be discussed hereafter include:

- Networking seminars, forums, and conferences
- Coalition building, in particular for the purposes of conducting issue campaigns
- Mentoring arrangements
- Cultivation and support of mediators and relationship builders
- Developing a conservative dispute settling mechanism.

Networking seminars, forums, and conferences

To help break down the silos that characterize the conservative movement in Canada, the Manning Centre for Building Democracy has been sponsoring national networking conferences for over ten years.[290] These have been held annually in Ottawa and have grown from an initial roundtable of a few dozen people to conferences attended by hundreds of participants from across the country.

Attendees include representatives of think tanks, advocacy organizations, student groups, and conservative political parties plus general observers, media, and "tire kickers" simply interested in learning more about Canadian conservatism and its various contributors and practitioners.

These conferences are built around various themes such as Recharging the Right, New Generation Ideas and Leadership, Conservatism in

---

290 See https://www.hilltimes.com/2018/02/14/building-relationships-manning-conference-talks-reaching-outside-conservatives-base/134203 and https://www.cbc.ca/news/manning-centre-conference-recharging-the-right-1.3468198 for press from recent conferences

Transition, and Next Steps. Subjects dealt with in plenaries and break-out sessions have included, to mention only a few: Ending Project Gridlock for Resource Development, Conservatives on Cannabis, the Role of Faith in the Public Square, Scrap the CBC?, Electoral Reform, Canada & the Middle East, Pipelines and Politics, Fixing the Fiscal Mess, China, Friend or Foe?

The networking function of such conferences has been expanded and made more effective in recent years by technological and process advancements specifically aimed at facilitating relationship building. The addition of "speed networking" sessions, the provision of specific networking rooms and forums, and the use of event management software such as ATTENDIFY and collaborative applications such as Skype, Zoom, and Facetime, all enhance the networking capacity of such get togethers.

Networking conferences sponsored by movement organizations tend to be more collegial and less structured than party conferences, as there is no competition for elected positions nor are there bitterly contested votes on controversial issues. Instead the main objects are for participants to exchange ideas[291] and best practices and to enable conservatives from different parts of the movement and the country to get to know and trust one another better.

In future, it is proposed to make the relationship building aspects of these conferences even more intentional by:

---

291 Networking conferences of this type are actually more appropriate forums for exposing conservatives to new (and therefore potentially controversial) policy ideas than party conferences and conventions. At party conventions, if a new and controversial idea for "cultivating new ground" is introduced as a resolution, it usually must be debated and voted upon. The party is often obliged to take a position on it too early and is faced with media questioning as to whether it supports or opposes it. The usual default position is to "table the resolution for future consideration" but this comes across as a lame and innovation-dampening position. At networking conferences organized by movement organizations such as the Manning Centre, party representatives can attend, be exposed to new ideas, and even participate in the debate of their strengths and weaknesses. But they need not take any responsibility for the ideas debated or take any official position whatsoever upon them. If questioned by the media, they can simply say, "Well that was an interesting idea, but this is the Manning Conference, not our party conference, and we're not responsible for any of the policy ideas raised and debated here".

- Surveying representatives of conservative oriented parties, in advance of the conference, to determine those subject and policy areas in which they feel they are in need of fresh ideas and policy research
- Identifying, again in advance of the conference, particular academics or think tank personnel who could supply those ideas and carry out that research, and then ensuring that those wanting such intellectual capital and those capable of supplying it, actually meet and discuss their common interests, either informally or in structured sessions, at the conference itself
- Constantly surveying the knowledge and skill requirements of up and coming political practitioners, in particular Canadians thinking of someday seeking a conservative nomination or a position on a constituency executive or campaign team
- Continuously identifying political trainers, educators, and mentors who could provide the training required to meet those requirements
- Making special efforts to ensure that those who want to upgrade their political knowledge and skills, and those who can provide the requisite training, actually meet at the conference itself for the purposes of entering into a training or mentoring relationship

In other words, the main focus of the Manning Centre[292] as a movement organization will increasingly become the performance of this relationship building or networking function. Rather than trying (as we have in the past) to directly develop conservative intellectual capital or directly provide political training services, our particular focus will be on bringing those with specific needs and capabilities together into a working relationship so that those needs are consistently and effectively met. In other words, our focus as a conservative networking organization should be on creating an architectural forum to facilitate relationship building rather than trying to prescribe the outcomes of those relationships.

The provision of networking forums, seminars, and conferences could, of course, be vastly expanded to include regional and local

---

292 As I personally move into retirement, the name Manning will likely be dropped from both the centre organization and the annual networking conference and new names adopted. This is entirely appropriate, my hope being that the focus going forward will increasingly not be on who originally founded or supported these efforts, but entirely on the networking functions they are committed to performing and enhancing.

networking events, all contributing to the unification of conservatism in Canada by systematically breaking down the silos in which conservatives tend to find themselves at present.

DO SOMETHING!

If you are an executive of a conservative oriented political party or movement organization:

- Identify other members of the movement, beyond your immediate circle, with whom there would be benefit to you in networking with, and make the effort to do so
- In particular, identify the row and column of the Conservative Network Matrix (Figure 9) in which your organization is located, and then seek to strengthen its relationship with other key components of the conservative movement defined by the matrix
- Attend a specific conservative networking event, such as the annual Manning/Conservative Networking Conference
- Organize a networking event of your own
- Actively promote/support the periodic organization of a "What Can We Do to Help?" meeting among representatives from all conservative parties prior to any one of them facing a general election.

Coalition building

The modern political party is not a homogeneous organization in which everyone accepts and subscribes to an identical set of values, interests, and objectives. Modern parties are coalitions of people who generally share some common values, goals, and interests and have agreed to work together politically to advance them. But they may also have major ideological, demographic, and regional differences among themselves. Thus there is not only a constant need for relationship building among the diverse members of a political party itself, there is also a need to effectively maintain and manage the coalition it represents.

Within the conservative camp, for example, there are fiscal conservatives, social conservatives, democratic conservatives, libertarians, constitutional conservatives, environmental conservatives, and so on, all professing to be conservatives but distinguished from one another by adjectives important to their adherents. These ideological components of the conservative movement can very easily become isolated and even antagonistic towards one another. Networking to build understanding and relationships among them is thus a necessity if conservatism desires to be a cohesive and effective political force.

For example, when the Reform Association (predecessor to the Reform Party) was being created in the late 1980s it attracted conservatives (and some liberals) of various ideological shades from across the West. Notwithstanding their differences, what these people shared in common was a disillusionment with the traditional federal parties and a deep sense of regional alienation. This common ground, articulated and expanded by myself and others, provided the basis for a new political coalition in the form of the Reform Party.

Not only are there significant ideological differences among conservatives, but given the immense size and regional diversity of Canada, there are significant regional differences as well.

At one of the Manning Centre's annual conferences, we once assembled a panel of people representing the major regions of the country, each of whom were asked to identify the distinguishing characteristics of conservatism in their region. The Atlantic Canada representative said "tradition," the Quebec representative said, "soft nationalism," the Ontario representative said, "hierarchy and order," the Prairie representative said, "grassroots revolution," and the B.C. representative said, "polarization, and being at the right end of the pole."

All of these were self-identified conservatives, most of them members or supporters at one time of the Progressive Conservative Party of Canada. And yet the differences in regional perspectives represented,— stretching from "tradition" to "revolution" again illustrate the necessity of networking to build understanding and relationships if the "conservative coalition" in Canada is to be an effective political force capable of governing such a large and regionally diverse nation.

One of the most effective ways of advancing conservative policy ideas is through "issue campaigns". But issue campaigns also require coalition building, and coalition building requires networking among individuals and interest groups who do not agree on everything but can agree to work together to advance some particular policy objective.

It should also be noted that in an age of political polarization, even within the conservative camp itself, there is a growing need to develop what one writer has called "epistemological modesty,"[293] abandoning the notion that a single ideology, narrowly defined and vehemently applied, is the only solution to all problems at all times. Coalition building and constructive dialogue, among conservatives of different flavors or even with non-conservatives, is facilitated where such modesty exists and should be welcomed rather than regarded as a weakness.

DO SOMETHING!

If you are an executive or member of a conservative oriented political party:

- Identify other members of your party, beyond your immediate circle and with whom you might have significant ideological or regional differences, and make a special effort to understand and network with them
- Seek to identify common ground and to build upon it, perhaps through the organization of an issue campaign to pursue some jointly-acceptable goal
- Study and receive training in the art and science of coalition building

Mentoring arrangements

The need to identify political aspirants when they are young and teachable (as far upstream as possible), and the need to redefine political space for millennials, is an absolute necessity to significantly strengthening relationships between previous-generation and next-generation conservatives. This requires inter-generational networking, and one of the best ways of achieve such networking is through the establishment of mentoring relationships.

293 See Brooks, David, "A New Centre Being Born," Niskanen Centre, December 10, 2018.

In my own case, my chief political mentors were my father, who spent his entire life in the political arena, and his closest political associates. My father rarely gave me specific direction on things political but simply explained the political significance of various events, and suggested I do this and that to get a better understanding. Often he would put me in touch with others whose political knowledge and experience was insightful and useful.

A vast literature exists[294] on the subject of how to create and sustain mentoring relationships, how to identify the "mentee" and his or her needs, how to identify the appropriate mentor, how to bring them together, and how to productively manage the relationship. Suffice it to say here that the concept of mentoring, and the networking required to facilitate it, needs to be much more widely and consistently applied to the political field if we want to transmit the political knowledge and experience of the older generation to those next-generation conservatives on whom the future of conservatism depends.

DO SOMETHING!

If you are a previous-generation conservative with knowledge and experience which would be helpful to a next-generation conservative:

- Study the subject of mentoring and attend a mentorship instruction course in order to improve your mentoring capabilities, if you have not served as a mentor before
- Identify a young person within your own family or circle of acquaintances who might benefit from your knowledge and experience

---

294 See for example: Ferris, Gerald R.; Treadway, Darren C.; Perrewé, Pamela L.; Brouer, Robyn L.; Douglas, Ceasar; Lux, Sean, "Political Skill in Organizations," *Journal of Management* 33, no. 3 (June 2007): 290–320. doi:10.1177/0149206307300813; Kellerman, Barbara, "Mentoring in Political Life: The Case of Willy Brandt," *American Political Science Review* 72, no. 2 (1978): 422–33. doi:10.2307/1954102; Moberg, D. J, "Mentoring and Practical Wisdom: Are Mentors Wiser or Just More Politically Skilled?" *Business Ethics* (2008) 83: 835. https://doi.org/10.1007/s10551-008-9668-5; Chopin, Suzette M., Steven J. Danish, Anson Seers, and Joshua N. Hook, "Effects of mentoring on the development of leadership self-efficacy and political skill," *Journal of Leadership Studies* 6, no. 3 (2012): 17–32.

- Attend a "You Two Should Meet" mentee/mentor matching session at a conservative networking conference such as the annual Manning Networking Conference
- Offer your mentoring services to a potential mentee, and if accepted, establish an ongoing mentorship relationship.

If you are a next-generation conservative with an interest in being mentored by a previous-generation conservative in some particular area:

- Identify a potential mentor in your area of interest and seek a meeting to explore the prospect of a mentoring relationship
- Attend a "You Two Should Meet" mentee/mentor matching session at a conservative networking conference such as the annual Manning/Conservative Networking Conference
- Request to be mentored by a potential mentor, and if your request is accepted, enter into an ongoing mentorship relationship.

Cultivation and support of mediators and relationship builders

All of these means of strengthening relationships among conservatives—networking conferences, pre-election "What can we do to help?" meetings, coalition building, issue campaigning, and mentoring—require the cultivation and support of conservatives whose special talent is mediation and relationship building. Every constituency association needs several people with this particular talent as does every caucus, think tank, and advocacy group.

The conservative movement needs a generic job description and model of a conservative relationship builder. We also need a strategic initiative to recruit such people, place them strategically, and support them throughout the movement. And at the risk of being accused of stereotyping, it has been my experience that women seem to be better at this role than men. They tend to be quicker to perceive when and how relationships are becoming strained, more anxious to ensure harmony, and better able to build it.

A simple technique that I have found most useful in political relationship building is the writing and sending of "You Two Should Meet"
memos and emails.

To illustrate, I made the acquaintance of the finance critic for a particular provincial conservative party in opposition. He confided in me
that he needed some substantive background material on certain aspects
of debt retirement and tax reform, more than just enough to make a
speech or handle a media interview on the subject. I happen to know
an academic or think-tank researcher or former finance minister who
has studied or worked on those particular issues backwards and forwards
for years. I send the finance critic and one of these resource people a
brief "You Two Should Meet" memo giving each the background and
coordinates of the other. They meet and a working relationship is established which will become even stronger and more useful if and when
that finance critic becomes the minister of finance of his province and
needs to actually *Do Something!* about the debt and tax situation of his
province, not just talk about it.

I knew a particularly strong social conservative who was beginning
to think she had less and less in common with fiscal conservatives within
the party. I knew a strong fiscal conservative who was at least worried
about this problem and anxious to do some fence mending. I knew a
third person who was good at building personal relationships among
conservative ideologues. So I sent a "You Three Should Meet" memo to
all three giving some background and the coordinates of each. They all
eventually got together at a conservative conference, and although the
ideological differences were not totally reconciled, a personal respect for
each other developed which prevented their ideological differences from
becoming destructive to the party.

As a general rule, I find that it is usually harder for those conservatives who have actually met and spoken with each other face-to-face, to
destructively disagree over some issue, than it is for those who have had
no such personal relationship and whose knowledge of each other and
each other's positions has been gained solely through the conventional
or social media. That is why the "meet" in the "You Two Should Meet"
exercise means meet in person and is very important.

A conservative dispute settling mechanism

Nothing can be more destructive to the prospects of a conservative election win, or the performance of a conservative caucus, cabinet, or government than serious, protracted disputes within the party.[295] Because principled conservatives hold their views strongly and passionately, internal arguments over campaign strategies or policy issues can readily degenerate into destructive behaviours and damaged relationships. Nomination and leadership contests invariably generate winners and losers. Even if such contests are openly and fairly conducted, the losers may experience bitter disappointment and be unwilling to graciously accept the result. And if such contests are marred by underhanded tactics, the results may be charges and counter charges, independent candidacies, the creation of rump parties, and destructive vote splitting.

Anticipatory mediation and relationship-building can sometimes prevent such disputes and disappointments from reaching the destructive stage. But the creation and operation of a formal dispute settling mechanism might also play a role in preventing such disputes reaching that destructive point.

Conservative party constitutions could be amended to provide for the creation of arbitration panels, to be composed of the most respected and judicious conservatives the parties can find, and to which serious internal disputes could be referred for resolution. Nomination papers for constituency candidacies and leadership positions could also be altered to require each contestant to agree in advance to submit any dispute arising in the course of the nomination or leadership contest to an arbitration panel. In the end, human nature being what it is, there will still be some internal disputes and estrangements that cannot be avoided or resolved amicably. But the existence of a formal conservative dispute settling mechanism might significantly reduce their frequency and destructiveness.

---

295 I find it too painful to dwell long on specific instances of this phenomenon, but recent examples might include Maxime Bernier leaving the Conservative Party of Canada to found his own party after losing a close leadership race to Andrew Scheer, or Brian Jean and Derek Filderbrand leaving the United Conservative Party in Alberta over disagreements with UCP leader Jason Kenney.

DO SOMETHING!

If you are an executive or leader of a conservative party or movement organization:

- Identify conservatives within your organization or circle with mediation and relationship-building skills
- Be proactive in watching for and identifying potentially destructive relationship situations within your branch of the family
- Be proactive in encouraging and supporting intervention by your conservative mediator/relationship builder in such situations before they deteriorate further.
- Support the creation and operation of a conservative dispute settling mechanism as described above.

If you are a conservative with mediation or relationship building experience and skills:

- Be proactive in watching for and identifying potentially destructive relationship situations within the conservative family
- Be proactive in intervening and offering to mediate such situations before they deteriorate further
- Be willing to serve if asked on an arbitration panel to which internal disputes might be submitted from time to time.

The public policy relay race

The process whereby a public policy idea generated by the conservative movement gets from inception to implementation, can be likened to a relay race with the policy idea being the baton which needs to be passed from one runner to another. The policy researcher or developer, who may well be an academic or someone in a think tank, tends to run the first leg of the relay race. But then the policy baton must be handed off to communicators and popularizers who run the second leg. They in turn, having generated significant public interest in the idea, hand it off to the politicians who endeavor to secure the electoral support required to further advance the policy idea toward implementation. And the politicians in turn, if they can generate sufficient electoral support, will eventually hand off the policy baton to the civil servants or government contractors for that implementation.

Those who coach relay racing at the highest levels of international competition maintain that such races are usually won or lost on the smoothness and efficiency of the hand off. But the successful handoff requires a very close connection, the closer the better, between the carrier of the baton and the receiver. They need to be on the same track, with the same goal in mind, and both be at the right place at the right time.[296] Thus networking activities which strengthen the prior and current relations of policy makers to policy communicators, of policy makers and communicators to politicians, and of politicians to civil servants and other policy implementers, are absolutely essential to the smooth and effective transmission of policy ideas from conception to execution. Winning the public policy relay race with conservative ideas requires a team effort, and constant networking among the members of the conservative family is an essential part of team building.

Attention to a special relationship

Regionalism and its political manifestations are a distinctive feature of Canadian confederation and perfectly understandable since we are the second largest nation by land mass in the world. Understandable also, that various federal political parties will have deeper roots and greater appeal in some regions of the country than in others, making it especially important to give attention to networking and relationship building across regional boundaries if we desire the country to remain politically united.

---

296 To carry the relay race analogy a little further, the baton (the policy proposal itself) must be in a readily transferable form, easily and accurately transferable from policy maker to policy communicator to political promoter to implementor. If the original proposal is in a three-volume tome written in academese, the less knowledgeable communicator and promoter may not even be able to grasp it. Or they may grab it but waste precious time redesigning it to produce an overly simplistic version insufficiently instructive to the implementor. Insuring that the policy baton is substantive yet politically communicable from the outset is essential if the object is to successfully carry that baton across the finish line in winning time.

Allow me to illustrate with the following commentary, which some will immediately characterize as rooted in a prejudice toward the influence of Quebec within our federal system, but which I hope to show is quite the opposite.

In order to form a national government, the Liberal Party of Canada tends to be more dependent on votes and seats from Quebec than either the Conservative Party of Canada or the NDP. But in the twentieth-first century, as Figure 10 illustrates, this heavy dependence on Quebec for votes and seats could well prove to be the political Achilles' heel of the federal Liberals.

As Figure 10 makes clear:

- The ratio of Quebec seats to the total number of seats in the federal parliament is declining
- The ratio of Quebec's population to the population of Canada as a whole is declining
- The ratio of French speakers to non-French speakers in Canada, is declining
- The ratio of Quebec's GDP to the GDP of Canada is also declining

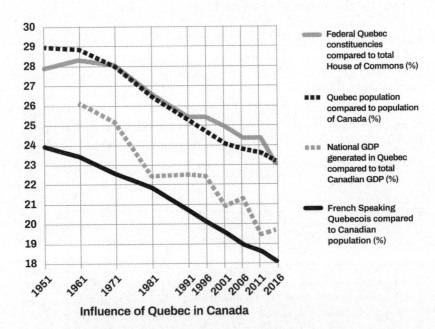

FIGURE 10 Quebec's Declining Demographic and Economic Influence

What this means is that it will become increasingly possible for a federal political party to form a majority government without winning a single seat in Quebec. This could be politically fatal to the federal Liberal Party, but more importantly it poses a future threat to Confederation itself by stimulating yet another upsurge of Quebec separatism.

There will undoubtedly be those who will mistakenly assume and vigorously assert that Western Canadians, whose interests I have long championed, will probably welcome this decline in Quebec's influence in Confederation and on the federal government. So I here want to emphatically and categorically deny that this is not the case, nor should it be.

For decades Western Canadians were in a comparable position, the identity and composition of the federal government often already determined even before the polls closed on the prairies or in B.C. on election day. It was the alienation resulting from this situation that gave rise in the late 1980s and early 1990s to the Reform Party with its cry that "The West Wants In!" It is a revival of that alienation, aggravated by the ill-advised policies of the Trudeau Liberals and the mistaken but understandable view that Quebec's potential influence in the federation is increasing rather than decreasing, that is reviving the cry that "The West Wants Out (more on this in Chapter 5.4). It is the potential alienation of Quebec from the Rest of Canada in the decades ahead, due to its declining voting strength, that may well revive the cry that "Quebec Wants Out!"

So what has this got to do with relationship building and networking within the Canadian political system? It means that in the future, Quebecers, in particular Quebec federalists, will need political allies outside Quebec more than ever before. They are going to need to build strong and enduring relationships with like-minded political people and interests in the Rest of Canada. And where are Quebecers most likely to find those allies? In western Canada, the one part of the country that most understands the frustration of political alienation from the federal system and that, like Quebec, favors a more decentralized federation, albeit for different reasons. [297]

---

297 Quebecers want a more decentralized federation primarily for cultural, social, and linguistic reasons; western Canada wants a more decentralized federation primarily for economic reasons; but the common ground is decentralization and preventing the federal government from spending and taxing in areas of provincial jurisdiction (such as natural resource development and conservation)

As already mentioned, and will be more thoroughly discussed in Chapter 5.3, western alienation is again on the rise, especially in Alberta and Saskatchewan. This in turn has generated specific Fair Deal Now demands from the premiers of those provinces with strong backing from their electorates. The effective implementation of these Fair Deal Now measures requires an ally, not an adversary in Ottawa and allies among at least some of the central and eastern provinces. Ironic as it may seem, Quebec may one day prove to be one of those allies.[298]

When we think about and discuss relationship building and networking within the Canadian political community at the macro level, it is especially important for Canadians of every political stripe to attach a high priority to networking and building strong relationships across regional and provincial boundaries. The future relationship between the western provinces and Quebec could prove to be one of the most important and impactful of those relationships.

DO SOMETHING!

If you are an executive or manager of a company, a union, an NGO, an economic institution or a political organization with an interest in maintaining and strengthening the political, economic, and cultural unity of Canada:

- Be alert to the increasing political alienation of Quebec from the Rest of Canada as its direct political influence within the federation declines
- Recognize the increasing political alienation of western Canada from the Rest of Canada as its economy is hamstrung by opposition

or joint jurisdiction (such as environmental protection) without the consent of the provinces affected.

298 While there is considerable antagonism toward Quebec in the West for its government's hostility to pipelines, its hypocritical importation of foreign oil, and its un-appreciation of a western contributions to its equalization revenues, oil patch executive and chairman of the Manning Centre Michael Binnion has developed a significant relationship with Quebec energy interests through his Modern Miracle Network. See www.modernmiraclenetwork.org.

to pipelines, governmental bungling of the energy/environment interface, and inequities in the equalization formula
- Make a sustained and increased effort to build strong and productive relationships across regional and provincial boundaries, with particular attention to strengthening the relationships between Quebec and the West

If you are a Quebecois or a resident of the Rest of Canada with a personal interest in maintaining and strengthening the political, economic, and cultural unity of Canada:

- Be alert to the increasing political alienation of Quebec from the Rest of Canada and the efforts of some members of the political class to exploit that alienation
- Recognize the increasing political alienation of western Canada from the Rest of Canada as described above.
- Make a sustained and increased effort to build strong and productive relationships across regional and provincial boundaries, with particular attention to strengthening the relationships between Quebec and the West.

Fun and friendships

The preceding sections on the importance of networking and the means for doing so: seminars, forums, conferences, coalitions, memo-ing, mentoring, arbitrating, etc. may strike some as entirely organizational and procedural. Let me emphasize therefore that perhaps the most treasured result of all such networking is the forging of closer and more meaningful friendships among people who share some common values and objectives. These are personal relationships infused with fun, laughter, disappointments, tears, and the establishment of memories and friendships which will endure long after the political circumstances that begot them have passed.

When I first ran for parliament on the Reform ticket in 1988, I ran in the huge Yellowhead riding west of Edmonton against Joe Clark who was then Foreign Affairs Minister. We had to assemble a constituency association and campaign team from people who hardly knew each other and who had never worked together politically before. But by the time the campaign was over, friendships were forged and fond memories created which lasted long after. The memories that have lasted are not about strategies, or tactics, or campaign organization. They are primarily of the camaraderie and fun we had together, of some of the hilarious experiences we shared and which still stir emotions and laughter when recalled decades later.

For example, Yellowhead was home to a fair number of cowboys, some of whom joined my team. We needed to draw attention to our campaign so one of them suggested we form a Reform Posse and ride around the constituency hunting for the notorious Joe Clark who was wanted on the charge of failing to properly represent Yellowhead in the federal parliament.

The idea generated instant enthusiasm. And when we learned that Joe was coming into Jasper from B.C. on a special train promoting Jasper National Park as a tourist destination, Jasper and Joe's visit became the target of the first public exposure of the Reform Posse.

Horses were trucked surreptitiously into the park and corralled a few miles away from the Jasper train station. Saddles, saddle blankets, and bridles were trucked in as well, along with banners identifying the Reform Posse and "Wanted Posters" featuring Joe's picture. Several CNR linemen, sympathetic to our cause, were deputized to give us the heads up when Joe's train crossed the Alberta-B.C. border just southwest of Jasper. More planning went into this endeavour than went into any of my campaign rallies, and none of my pep talks to the team generated anywhere near the enthusiasm that the Posse did.

At last the long-awaited day arrived, the day when Joe's schedule was to bring him on the train to Jasper. We saddled the horses; we unpacked the banners and posters; the Posse in full array galloped towards the station. But then the sad news came from the CNR linemen. Joe's train had developed mechanical troubles in B.C. and wouldn't be arriving as planned. So what could we do? We rode around Jasper with our banners and signs making as big an impression as we could. The CBC had positioned a reporter and a camera at the station to cover Joe's arrival, but they refused to cover our Posse so we didn't even make the evening news.[299]

299 While we failed to make the news in Canada, the Reform Posse did make the news elsewhere, in Tokyo, of all places. Months after the Jasper ride someone

What the Posse did accomplish, however, was to generate com-radery and solidify friendships. I was on the lead horse, and on my right looking like Wyatt Earp was Dale Assmus, a real outdoorsman and the husband of my campaign manager Ginny Assmus. On my left was Virgil Anderson in full western regalia, a Calgary lawyer who had sus-pended his practice and with his wife Leah came to live and work in the Yellowhead for the entire campaign. Sandra and my friendship with these two couples, formed during the Yellowhead campaign, endured long after that campaign was over. And we all had fun, lots of it, culmi-nating with a big barbecue that night to celebrate the first official ride of the Reform Posse, even though the notorious Joe Clark had escaped our grasp.

Twenty years later if you interviewed some of those Yellowhead people who participated in that Reform Campaign, they would scarcely remember the issues, the speeches, or the tactics. Some might not even remember that I was the candidate or whether we won or lost (we lost). But what they will remember with fondness and laughter is that Reform Posse. Working with others for a political cause isn't all seriousness and strain; it can be fun, exciting, and generate solid friendships and memo-ries which can last a lifetime.

sent me a copy of a Tokyo newspaper. It featured a large picture of the Reform Posse apparently taken by a Japanese tourist and explaining that this was how they did politics in Canada.

4.3 Employ Social Media, Effectively and Responsibly

Ask a millennial

The ease of understanding this chapter on the role of social media in facilitating political networking may betray the age of the reader more so than any other part of this book. Millennials and post millennials are often understood to be "native" users of social media, and so defining its uses for them may be as redundant as explaining water to a fish. It is important, nonetheless, (for those of us who still may not quite understand the difference between a "tweet" a "post" or a "live stream") to establish just what is to be discussed.

Social media, broadly defined, refers to the suite of currently available online platforms by which users share their own content and interact with content produced and recirculated by others. Popular platforms include Facebook, Instagram, Twitter, WordPress, and YouTube to name only a few.

These platforms have become some of the most popular websites on the internet. At the time of writing there are approximately three billion Facebook users. Vast numbers of individuals are increasingly living more of their lives, or the lives of their digital-proxies, through social media

What has become increasingly apparent is both the integrative and disruptive effects that the proliferation of social media have had on public participation in society and political processes over the last ten years, a very short interval of time when viewed historically. Social media have served to disrupt significant aspects of our lives (for example, disruptions to traditional news media and traditional social relationships). But social media have also facilitated a vast expansion of interpersonal connectivity and the coordinated participation of large numbers of people in public institutions and processes.[300]

DO SOMETHING!

- If you are not a user of social media but wish to be politically engaged in today's political world, make a conscious effort to become digitally literate.
- If you are already engaged with social media, particularly for political purposes, make a conscious effort to become acquainted with its positive uses and potentially negative effects.

Evaluating social technologies

Every technological development has its potential positives and negatives. The challenge in its application is to maximize the positives and minimize the negatives, which should be our objective in harnessing the social media to the operations of political processes and institutions.

On the positive side, the strengthening of individual expression

Democracy gives status to the individual and opportunity for individual participation in the political system. Both liberalism and conservatism

300 In his 2000 magnum opus, *From Dawn to Decadence, (Harper Collins, New York, 2000)* French-American historian Jacques Barzun finishes a sweeping account of 500 years of Western intellectual history with a final thought on the emergent "Demotic Life and Times" which he believes have defined the twentieth-century. Barzun draws a distinction between 'democratic' and 'demotic,' with the latter meaning 'of the people' and referring to the growth of individualism that has permeated our society following the Enlightenment. The germination of social media in the early twenty-first-century and the extent of its subsequent prolif- eration speaks perfectly to the individualistic nature of modern society: both creating a tremendous democratization of public institutions as well as increased personal focus on the opinions of individual participants in democracy.

also value the rights and role of the individual citizen in society. *The social media further strengthens the position and role of the individual person* in society and the political system by giving millions of people the opportunity and tools to personally express themselves, their opinions, their preferences, their shared values, and their differences with others, more frequently and effectively than in any other period of history.

This strengthening of individualism via the social media, carried too far, can ultimately weaken and even destroy the political community.[301] But during periods and in circumstances where the individual is ignored and devalued, where it is collectivism promoted and reinforced by the state that is being carried too far, then the role of social media in strengthening individual freedom and expression may be viewed as a positive to be valued and expanded.

On the positive side, access

The social media also facilitate increased access on the part of citizens to our political institutions and processes on a scale never before achievable. This increased capacity for electors to be able to engage with their elected officials, and vice versa, significantly strengthens democratic governance if used responsibly.

For a country as physically large as Canada, with some electoral districts larger area-wise than some European countries, the ability for constituents to interact with their elected representatives in an online and public community, with the possibility for instantaneous feedback, is again a positive benefit. That access to the public square is now at our fingertips, significantly expands opportunities to participate in our shared civic life.

Historic advancements in public communication have included the development of the Socratic dialogue in ancient Greece, the advent of the printing press, and the invention of radio and television. But the expansion of communication capacity made possible by social media exceeds these previous expansions of communications capability by a considerable margin. That Canadians are the most active users of social media in the world, indicates the extent to which that capacity is already being used; the challenge is to increase its responsible application to political discourse.

301 See Deneen, Patrick J., *The Failure of Liberalism*, Yale University Press, 2018.

On the positive side, networking

The social media also facilitate increased networking among like-minded people for specific purposes, again on a scale never before achievable. As our world becomes more complex and diversified, it is becoming increasingly difficult to establish and maintain meaningful relationships. Social media are tremendously effective in facilitating connectivity among like-minded people (from however far afield) to pursue common interests and objectives. Traditional gathering places of like-minded citizens, such as the community meeting or the local coffee shop, are being complemented or supplanted by the group chat or other digital communities, with great potential for organizing and directing collective action in pursuit of shared goals. Again, the challenge is to increase the responsible application of the networking capacities of social media to political discourse and participation.

On the positive side, the mobilization of political volunteers, donors, and voters

The beneficial operation of civil society and democratic systems is highly dependent on the participation of volunteers. Again, the social media provide powerful tools for identifying, mobilizing, and managing volunteers, on an unprecedented scale, to perform a host of important activities.

Examples include such free applications as Doodle, Ivolunteer. com, Samaritan, SignUp.com, VolunteerLocal, WhenToHelp, and YourVolunteers.

Apps for mobilizing volunteers for dozens of worthwhile purposes are being created at an ever increasing rate,[302] revolutionizing the volunteer sector to the general strengthening of the organizations and services employing them.

The application of social media to the identification and mobilization of party members, interest groups, and electors is especially relevant to strengthening democracy, and can have a dramatic impact on voter turnout.

---

302 Follow this link to see the top ten apps for managing volunteers including Volgistics, initLive, Galaxy, and more: https://www.capterra.com/sem-compare/volunteer-management-software?gclid=EAIaIQobChMI2Omu6L614QIVgSCtBh 10WwYHEAAYASAAEgJX7vD_BwE

Another primary use of social media today, by political interest groups, PACs, and political parties is, of course, for fundraising. Examples of fundraising apps include Charity Miles, Facebook Fundraiser, Prizeo, One Today by Google, Pledging, DonorPerfect, PayPal, Budge, Omaze, GiveLively, and Fundly.

Early stage political software applications such as Nation Builder and the Constituent Information Management System (CIMS) are in the process of being augmented and replaced by even more flexible and sophisticated political information management tools.

DO SOMETHING!

If you as a citizen and voter are not fully utilizing social media to connect with and influence political institutions and processes, expand your use to:

- Better and more fully express your individuality and opinions, while making sure your online profile is an honest representation of who you are as a person and what you believe
- More frequently and fully access political institutions and processes, while making sure your access and participation is legitimate and honest
- Communicate and network more fully with like-minded people and organizations, while guarding against atomization and siloing (discussed later)
- Mobilize friends, associates, and volunteers to pursue shared and benevolent objectives

On the negative side, atomization and siloing

Notwithstanding the enormous potential of social media for strengthening political discourse and participation, social media, like all technologies, have their negative side and potential to do harm—negatives and potentials which need to be recognized and strenuously guarded against.

While social media, properly used, can vastly increase the connectivity of individuals with others, they also contribute to the atomization of society by permitting those same individuals to create and sustain their own customized persona within a communications bubble increasingly impervious to the presence or influence of others. We see this every day in individuals, who in the midst of a crowd or social setting, are glued to their handheld devices and oblivious to anything and everything else around them.

The political downside of the networking function of social media is in its more efficient ability to effectively silo supporters of particular political positions, thus contributing to polarization and the insulation of political cliques or tribes from the moderating effects of productive political interaction and debate with those holding different views and positions.[303]

Social media facilitate the creation and operation of political "echo chambers"[304] which fortify antagonisms between political partisans and limit the potential for good by associating with people with whom we disagree. This siloing serves to erode the underlying humanity of the political process, the presumption that the vast majority of participants in the political process do so with virtuous intent even though they may strenuously disagree with one another.

DO SOMETHING!

Guard against and counteract the siloing effect of social media by:

- Objectively evaluating your own political information sources and associations to see if they all reflect a single perspective with which you agree, and are mutually reinforcing
- If you find yourself in an echo chamber, make a conscious effort to break out by broadening your political information sources and associations to include other points of view

---

303 See Haidt, Jonathan, *The Righteous Mind: Why Good People are Divided by Religion and Politics*, Pantheon, New York (2012) as a great exposition on why people naturally like to sort themselves into partisan teams and are increasingly allergic to hearing the other side of the debate.

304 An echo chamber is defined as an environment in which a person encounters only beliefs or opinions that coincide with their own, so that their existing views are reinforced and alternative ideas are not considered.

On the negative side, fake news

The most publicly scrutinized misuse of social media in recent years has been its role in the dissemination of "fake news."[305] The term was named Word of the Year in 2017 and refers to fabricated misinformation, spread most easily via the social media, with the deliberate intent to mislead. It is most often used to damage a person, organization, or cause to which the fabricator is opposed, or to attract attention and support to a person, organization, or cause which the fabricator favors.

Fake news has a long history, for example, in the story of the Garden of Eden the serpent is reported to have used misinformation to induce Eve to disobey her Creator. Its modern manifestations might also have been predicted when America OnLine (AOL) touted the benefits of the internet as having the world at your fingertips. The announcement neglected to mention that the world of information and communications includes, not only truth but also all the quackeries, misinformation, lies and deceits which have existed since time immemorial and continue to be generated.

What is most significant about this dark side of social media is its employment to essentially "weaponize misinformation" on a massive scale, something that ethical and discerning political participants need to be constantly on guard against.

Again, in an historical sense, the use of misinformation as a weapon is not a new concept. It is the use of propaganda (i.e. information, especially of a biased or misleading nature) to promote or publicize a particular political cause or point of view and/or to demonize the views and personas of opponents. But, whereas in the past the significant costs of a major propaganda campaign meant that only governments or the military could effectively engage in such campaigns, today the existence of social media has so lowered the costs of propaganda campaigns that virtually any organization, even individuals, can effectively conduct them.

---

305 The self-initiated misrepresentation of the true identity of an individual or organization on "Fakebook" is a another worrisome variation of "fake news".

DO SOMETHING!

Guard against being misled by fake news and counteract its dissemination by:

- Submitting political news stories and documentaries, especially those that are spectacular and attention getting, to parity checks, verification by additional sources not linked to the original source
- Gradually identifying trustworthy information sources and increasingly relying upon them for accurate information
- Refusing to share or repeat to others stories and information you suspect of being fake news
- Challenging the source and content of stories and information pieces you suspect of being fake news and reporting your suspicions/findings to others.

On the negative side, distraction

By far the greatest use of social media today is its use as a source of entertainment, young people in particular often spending hours each day being entertained by the images, music, and games offered by the online world.

Far be it from me to rail against entertainment in principle, especially as sought after by next-generation Canadians. But when the pursuit of entertainment, facilitated by social media, becomes a persistent and pathological escape from reality, distracting us from coming to grips with real life relationships, problems, challenges, and opportunities, then it has become a dangerous distraction.

History also reminds us that entertainment has been used by the political class in times past, for example, the circuses and entertainment of the Coliseum offered to the populace of Rome by the Roman Emperors, to divert the attention of the masses away from deteriorating political and economic conditions and the need for social and political reform. Digital circuses have an even greater capacity to perform this distractive function. It is possible to be entertained to death politically via social media, a possibility to be recognized and strenuously guarded against.

> ## DO SOMETHING!
>
> Guard against being overly distracted from real-life relationships, problems, challenges, and opportunities by social media use, or from becoming addicted thereto, by:
>
> - Monitoring your social media use (e.g. time spent on social media, and the percentage of time spent on particular uses, etc.)
> - Learning when and where to log off
> - Seeking professional help if there are signs that your social media use is becoming addictive

On the negative side, trivialization

Another potential negative of the proliferation of social media is in its tendency to reduce public debates to sound-bites and to amplify the most immediate and attention-capturing news items, regardless of their substance or real importance, so as to stand out amongst the high volume of information to which the social media user is subject. Long form and thoughtful reading, the in-depth lecture and academic paper, substantive public debate, all are in decline among the population at large as social media platforms increasingly favor and promote content that delivers immediate but superficial gratification through eye-catching digital images, short videos, and tweets.

Traditional media such as print and television have always had their own inherent biases when it comes to determining what is newsworthy. For example, stories that appeal to emotions are usually considered more newsworthy than those that appeal to rationality and the intellect. Negatives (especially in Canada) are more newsworthy than positives. Controversy is invariably more newsworthy than cooperation. Violence, disorder, and bad government is more newsworthy than peace, order, and good government. And short run is more newsworthy than the long run. Social media have inherited all these biases but have carried to a new level the dominance of the immediate, the abbreviated, the eye-catching, and the short run over more substantive and longer term content and considerations.

DO SOMETHING!

Guard against becoming preoccupied and satisfied by trivia disseminated and promoted by social media, and counteract any such trivialization by:

- Monitoring your social media consumption and evaluating it on a trivia/substance scale
- Balancing your social media consumption with long-form information sources (e.g. reading books, attending lectures, etc.) and real-world communication experiences (e.g. face-to-face communications with friends, attendance at family and social gatherings with real people as distinct from their digital surrogates.)

On the negative side, the use of social media for destructive purposes

One of the sad realities of history is that there has not been a single major technological advancement from the discovery of fire to the invention of gunpowder to the harnessing of nuclear energy that has not been used for destructive purposes, including war. It should not surprise us, therefore, that while social media are being used for many benevolent purposes, they have also become one of the principal weapons in the arsenal of organized crime.

Cybercriminals have taken to social media to extend and deepen their reach and to engage effectively and perniciously in identity theft, copyright trolling, cyber casing, cyber-bullying, cyber-stalking, cyber burglary—the list goes on and on.[306]

This is not the place to fully elaborate on this misuse of social media, but suffice it to say that governments and police forces the world over are seeking ways and means of detecting, confining, and combating and such misuse. The challenge will be to devise and implement such measures without unduly constraining the use of social media by law-abiding organizations and individuals.

306 See www.nw3c.org/docs/whitepapers/criminal-use-of-social-media.pdf

On the negative side, the mobilization of citizens for harm

Just as social media can be used to connect and harness citizens and volunteers to beneficial causes and activities, the dual nature and amorality of such technologies also means they can be used to mobilize people and resources for harm.

It is instructive, for example, to examine the role played by social media in Pakistan with respect to the notorious case of Asia Bibi, a Christian woman accused of insulting Mohammed. Social media were initially employed to create a national public frenzy over the incident, resulting in her arrest and public demands that she be executed by hanging. Social media were also employed to rally international support in her defense. Eventually the Supreme Court of Pakistan acquitted her of the charges[307], producing a substantive public backlash, again largely fueled by social media. While the social media were employed by both sides in this dispute, it is worrisome that the numbers of people mobilized to do harm in this case vastly exceeded the numbers mobilized in constraint of harm.

The number of persons mobilized in these instances, and the speed with which they were mobilized, illustrates just how effective social media can be as an organizing tool, whether the purpose of such organization is beneficial or malevolent.

DO SOMETHING!

Guard against the use of social media as a tool for organizing citizens for harm, and counteract this misuse, by:

- Refusing to be so mobilized or directed yourself
- Coming to the defense of vulnerable persons and groups unjustly targeted by social media campaigns
- Supporting proposed laws and regulations to constrain the criminal and destructive uses of social media

307 "Pakistan overturns Christian woman's blasphemy death sentence," https://www. channelnewsasia.com/news/asia/pakistan-overturns-christian-woman-s-blasphemy-death-sentence-10882734

The challenge which social media present for small-d democrats

Social media can strengthen democracy by strengthening individual expression, providing expanded public access to political institutions and processes, facilitating networking among like-minded individuals, and mobilizing volunteers and electors for political action and the support of worthwhile causes.

But the same social media can be used to weaken democracy by facilitating the division of electors into polarized silos and tribes, the generation and dissemination of fake news, the trivialization of political discourse, the promotion of image over substance and the immediate over the long term, the distraction of voters from political realities, its misuse by organized crime, and the mobilization of interest groups and citizens to do harm.

The obvious challenge for small-d-democrats is to promote and encourage the political positives of social media and strenuously guard against their political misuse.

A particular challenge which social media presents to conservatives

The more specific challenge, especially for conservatives, is to decide how to guard against the misuse of social media without unduly constricting freedom of enterprise and expression, values which conservatives especially cherish. In many respects, this is an old, old challenge which has faced the champions and defenders of freedom since time immemorial: how to respond to irresponsible abuses of freedom without impairing the responsible exercise of freedom itself.

When the political use of social media is in the hands of individuals, interest groups, political parties, and politicians, how is responsible use and accountability to be achieved without coercive and ideologically motivated governmental restriction of political freedom? And when social media platforms are in the hands of publicly-traded companies beholden to their shareholders, how is responsible use and accountability to be achieved without undue government interference in the economic marketplace, especially when these companies enjoy near-monopoly status?

These are again old questions in contemporary dress that have been faced before, as in how to establish the proper balance between public and private, individual and collective interests with respect to the ownership, operation, and regulation of public utilities, in particular railways, energy utilities, and telecommunications companies.

In all of these previous cases, there were those who argued that increased public ownership of transportation, energy, and communications utilities was the appropriate answer, giving birth in Canada to the Canadian National Railway, the Canadian Broadcasting Company, provincial ownership of energy utilities such as Quebec Hydro and Ontario Hydro, and (at one time) PetroCanada. And we can be certain today that this solution or some variation of it will be advocated again by left-of-centre ideologues with respect to curbing the power of social media giants such as Google, Facebook, and Amazon.

So what is the conservative alternative? Generally, the conservative answer in the past has been to focus the role of the state on the establishment and enforcement of standards of performance and behaviour and to place the burden of responsible compliance on private sector producers, distributors, and consumers. In other words, applied today, individuals and companies operating in the digital sphere should be granted as much freedom of ownership and use as they are prepared to accept responsibility for: responsibility for ethical performance and outcomes beneficial to their customers and the public while still earning a competitive return on capital invested.

More specifically, the conservative approach will likely involve the breakup up of these monopolistic social media giants, with the spin-offs remaining in the private sector but subject to increased regulation in the public interest by quasi-judicial regulatory bodies established especially for that purpose. All of this being arguably preferable to state ownership and governmental domination of the social media sector.

In any event, the proliferation and increased use of social media represents a major twenty-first century political and governance challenge. Conservative parties and governments in particular, need to decide whether or not the approach described above, some variation of it, or some different alternative is sufficient to meet the governance needs of the digital age.[308]

308 See Peppers, Don, "The Coming Big Tech Backlash," LinkedIn, December 18, 2018

Does the use of social media enhance or diminish personhood?

There is nothing new under the sun. And I have been struck by some of the parallels between the exposure of our generation to social media and the exposure of the indigenous communities of the western plains of North America to a new form of communication almost three centuries ago.

George Catlin was an adventurer, writer, and portrait painter who was fascinated by the lives, languages, and culture of the Plains Indians of North America. He traveled extensively among them in the 1830's and was the first to paint portraits of some of their most famous chiefs.

Around 1832 he visited some of the Mandan villages on the Missouri river where he persuaded several of the chiefs to allow him to paint their portraits. What then transpired he described in his journal as follows:

> "Perhaps nothing ever more astonished these people than the operations of my brush. The art of portrait painting was a subject entirely new to them, and of course, un-thought of; and my appearance here has commenced a new era in the arcana of *medicine* or mystery. . . Soon after arriving here, I commenced and finished the portraits of two of their principal chiefs . . . And when finished, it was exceedingly amusing to see them mutually recognizing each other's likeness, and assuring each other of the striking resemblance they (the portraits) bore to the originals. . ."[309]

Catlin then goes on to describe, that while the chiefs themselves seemed pleased with their portraits, they (the portraits) produced quite a different effect on the rest of the village. In particular, they provoked a very negative reaction from the women and medicine men.

"The effect upon so mixed a multitude, who as yet had heard no way of accounting for them (the portraits) was novel . . . The likenesses were instantly recognized, and many of the gaping multitude commenced yelping; some stomping off in the jarring dance—others were singing, and others again were crying—hundreds covered their mouths with their hands (a custom among most tribes when anything surprises them very much); others, indignant, drove their spears frightfully into the

309 See Catlin, George, *North American Indians*, Penguin Book, 1989, page 103

ground, and some threw a reddened arrow at the sun, and went home to their wigwams. . . The pictures seen, the next curiosity was to see the man who made them. . . I stepped forth and was instantly hemmed in by the throng. . . They pronounced me the greatest *medicine man* in the world; for they said I had made *living beings*—they said [in staring at the portraits] that they could see their chiefs alive, in two places, they said [when they looked at the portraits] they could see their eyes move—could see them smile and laugh, and if they could laugh they could certainly speak, if they should try, and they therefore must have some *life* in them. . . The squaws generally agreed, that they had discovered life enough in them [the portraits] to render my *medicine* too great for the Mandans; saying that *such an operation could not be performed without taking away from the original something of its existence. . . This curtailing of the natural existence, for the purpose of instilling life into the secondary one, they decided to be a useless and destructive operation,* and one that was calculated to do great mischief to their happy community; and they commenced a mournful and doleful chant against me as a most danger-ous man; one who could make living persons by looking at them; and at the same time, could, as a matter of course, destroy life in the same way as I chose."[310]

We in our modernity may choose to scoff at such reactions to a new technology. But the more I see of the enormous effort that increasing numbers of people, especially political people, put into establishing and enhancing their image on Facebook and other social media platforms, the more I have come to believe that the Mandan women and their medicine men may have had an insight which we would do well to appreciate.

If the persona I want people to see and pay attention to is a person-ally designed, digitally manufactured, and electronically communicated persona, is there not a sense in which the process, like Catlin's portrait painting, has taken something away from my real persona in order to create the digitized persona, especially if I myself come to believe that the digital representation is the real me whom I want others to know, "like," and trust?

And, if carried to the extreme, might not this practice, as the Mandan women suspected, have the potential to "destroy life" as well as to enhance it? Could it be, to paraphrase Catlin's documentation of their

---

310 See Catlin, pages 105–106

concern and objection, that "such an operation cannot be performed without taking away from the original person something of their existence, and that this curtailing of the natural existence, for the purpose of instilling life into the secondary one, could well prove to be a destructive operation capable of doing great harm to the community."

The parallel between the Mandans' exposure to portrait painting and our exposure to social media does not end there. Catlin goes on to describe several other reactions to his portrait painting which again have eerie parallels to the uses and abuses of social media in our time.

For example, one of the medicine men who was violently opposed at first to Catlin's portrait painting was won over completely when Catlin offered to paint *his* [the medicine man's] portrait, who was then flattered by and pleased with the result. People with reservations about the use of social media, such as its capacity for siloing, distracting, trivializing, and weaponizing the use of information, may still become champions of its use when shown how effectively it can be used to enhance their image, communicate their messages, and increase their influence in the community.

On yet another occasion, Catlin observed the following, demonstrating again that there is nothing new under the sun: "Besides chiefs, and braves, and doctors [medicine men] there is yet another character . . . familiarly known and countenanced in every tribe as an Indian *beau* or *dandy.* Such persons can be seen on every pleasant day, strutting and parading around the village in the most beautiful and unsoiled garments, without the honorable trophies however of scalp locks and claws of the grizzly bear, attached to their costume, for with such things they deal not. They plume themselves with swans-down . . . and sweet scented grass and other harmless and unmeaning ornaments, which have no other merit than they themselves have, that of looking pretty and ornamental . . . [However], these clean and elegant gentlemen . . . are held in very little estimation by the chiefs and braves and are therefore but little respected."[311]

Because these dandies were so strikingly attired, and not fully realizing in what low regard they were viewed by the chiefs and the rest of the tribe, Catlin undertook to paint the portrait of one them. He then describes the reaction:

311 See Catlin, p. 110

"I had thus progressed, with high-wrought feelings of pleasure, when two or three chiefs, who had been seated around the lodge, and whose portraits I had painted, arose suddenly and, wrapping themselves tightly in their robes, crossed my room with a quick and heavy step, and took an informal leave of my cabin. I was apprehensive of their displeasure, though I continued my work [painting the portrait of the dandy], when the interpreter came furiously into my room addressing me thus: "My God, Sir! This never will do; you have given great offence to the chiefs—they have made complaint of your conduct to me—they tell me this is a worthless fellow—a man of no account in the nation, and if you paint his picture you must instantly destroy theirs; you have no alternative, my dear Sir, and the quicker this fellow is out of your lodge the better."[312]

In our communities today, especially in political circles, there is the "political dandy"—"familiarly known and countenanced in every (political) tribe". This individual has no substance, does nothing of real value politically and has little to contribute to good government, but nevertheless "struts and parades around the village . . . in the most beautiful and attractive attire . . . having no other merit than that of looking pretty and ornamental." Unfortunately, social media can be used by a skilled campaign manager or communications director to project a most attractive image of the "political dandy," an image attractive enough to enough voters to secure the election of the dandy to a municipal council, a legislature, or a parliament. Only after the election, with the passage of time, does the electorate come to realize that this elected official—by now he or she may even be a cabinet minister or a Prime Minister—"has no other merit than . . . that of looking pretty and ornamental."

The chiefs who were prepared to demand that Catlin tear up their portraits if he was going to use portrait painting to portray and enhance the image of the dandy, were protesting the misleading use of this new medium and demanding its cessation. When political managers and communications directors today present us with the persona and candidacies of political dandies who in reality have little substance and little to contribute to democratic politics and good government, perhaps they too should rightfully be subjected to the same vigorous protests and objections which George Catlin encountered so long ago.

312 Ibid. page 112

4.4 Invest in Relationships

Building stronger and more meaningful relationships among small-d democrats in Canada, and among the various components and representatives of the conservative movement requires increased investments of time and money in networking among individuals and organizations.

Of particular importance is the investment of *time*, something which all of us have to invest in relationship building, regardless of whether or not we can also invest money.

Invest in democracy-building relationships

Every one of us benefits from the freedoms which Canadian democracy provides, including the freedom to choose, support, oppose, and replace our governments. But how much of our personal time do we actually invest in building and strengthening those relationships upon which the maintenance and strengthening of democracy depends? How much time do we invest in:

- Regularly visiting even one website or reading even one publication on a regular basis that will inform us about democratic politics in Canada in some way?
- Attending even one political event per year (a constituency meeting, a political conference, a campaign meeting, etc.) at each level of democratic government, municipal, provincial/territorial, and federal?
- Getting to know, through a telephone call, an email exchange, a personal meeting once per term, our elected municipal councilor, our member of the provincial/territorial legislature, and our member of parliament?
- Insuring that our name and those of other family members are on the appropriate voter lists?

- Networking during an election with those who can better inform us on the issues and the candidates involved?
- Social media networking for political purposes?
- Forming relationships with and encouraging next-generation Canadians with political interests?

And if we are investing even a small portion of our time in these democratic networking activities, can we not, should we not, also invest some of our financial resources in support of these activities to the extent to which we are able? Does our Political Investment Portfolio have a section for investing in democracy, especially investing in strengthening relationships among small d-democrats through cross-partisan research, conferencing, on-line collaboration, and coalition building for the advancement of democratic reforms?

Who stands on guard?

When I was in parliament, we Reformers once introduced a motion that the Speaker of the House of Commons "cause O Canada to be sung or played, once per week, at the opening of the daily session." It was rejected by the Liberal government of the day, apparently on the grounds that to do so might cause offence to some of the Quebec separatists in the chamber.

Nevertheless, and fortunately, every week, at major sporting events, hundreds of thousands of Canadians dutifully stand and sing, or listen to someone singing on their behalf, "O Canada, we stand on guard for thee."

But just suppose, in your imagination, that the Canada of whom and to whom we sing the national anthem was to respond in some audible way? What might she say in response to our declaration that we stand on guard for her?"

My fear is that she might arch her eyebrows and say: "Really? You stand on guard for me? In what respect do you stand on guard?"

And if she posed such a question how would we answer? If she posed such a question directly to you, how would you answer?

We might of course say we pay taxes to support our military and police forces and assign them to stand on guard. But then she might respond, "So you pay someone else to stand on guard for me? But I asked in what respect do you stand on guard."

For some of us, surely this means safeguarding the heritage of the past, our history, traditions, and the institutions and practices built upon them. For some it means safeguarding our public finances and protecting Canada from the ravages of reckless public spending, debt accumulation, and excessive taxation. For others, standing on guard means safeguarding the pillars of our economy and our social services system. For new Canadians, it may well mean safeguarding Canada from the abuses of freedom and human rights, all too fresh in their experiences and memories, that characterize many of those countries from which they have come. And for all of us, standing on guard must increasingly include protecting and nurturing Canada's magnificent physical environment in all its dimensions.

Rather than content ourselves with halfheartedly singing of our willingness to stand on guard for Canada, would it not be better for each of us to commit to doing some specific thing, small or great, to strengthen our country in whatever way we choose, including investing a portion of our time and financial resources in consciously networking and building relationships with others who share this objective?

DO SOMETHING!

If you are a director, executive, or manager of a corporation, small business, or an NGO, the freedom and success of which is enhanced by good, democratic governance, encourage your employees:

- To identify other individuals and organizations with interests in strengthening Canada politically, economically, socially, and environmentally
- Invest a portion of their time to networking and developing a working relationship with such individuals and organizations

If you are a director, executive, or manager of a corporation, small business, or an NGO:

- Lead by example in volunteering your own time to such networking activities

continued

- Establish and finance (as previously suggested) your organization's Political Investment Fund and earmark a percentage of that
  fund to supporting democratic networking and relationship building activities

Invest in conservative relationships

If you profess to believe in conservative values and principles and would
like to see them applied to democratic governance in Canada, how much
of your personal time do you actually invest in building and strengthening those personal and organizational relationships upon which the
political success of conservatism depends?

How much time do we invest in:

- Regularly visiting conservative websites or reading conservative
  publications that will keep us knowledgeable about "who's who" in
  the conservative family?
- Attending conservative events (a conservative constituency meeting, a conservative conference, a conservative fundraiser, etc.) at
  both the provincial and federal levels?
- Getting to know, through a telephone call, an email exchange, a
  personal meeting once per term, a conservative municipal councilor, MLA, or MP?
- Making sure that you and others within your sphere of influence
  have a membership in a conservative party and at least one conservative movement organization?

And if we are investing even a small portion of our time in strengthening our relationships with fellow conservatives and conservative
organizations, should we not also invest some of our financial resources
in support of these activities to the extent to which we are able? Does
our Political Investment Portfolio have a section for investing in the
networking and relationship building necessary for conservatism to
succeed?

DO SOMETHING!

If you are an academic or researcher engaged in generating conservative intellectual capital:

- Invest a portion of your time in establishing a personal relationship with persons engaged in the advocacy and actual implementation of conservative ideas and policies

If you are a conservative activist in an advocacy group or political party:

- Invest a portion of your time in establishing a personal relationship with persons engaged in the generation of conservative intellectual capital

If you are a conservative aspirant to political office or a staffer with a conservative organization:

- Invest a portion of your time in evaluating your personal knowledge and skill deficiencies and establishing a personal relationship with a trainer or mentor who might assist you in those areas

If you are an older-generation conservative with political experience:

- Invest a portion of your time in getting to know next-generation conservatives and offer to your mentor them

If you are an executive or elected member of a conservative party:

- Invest a portion of your time and financial resources in establishing a personal relationship with executives or elected members of another conservative party (e.g. make it appoint to attend the annual conference of another conservative party).

If you are in a position, organizationally or personally, to direct financial resources in support of conservative individuals, organizations, and activities:

- Invest a portion of your Political Investment Portfolio in strengthening conservative networking and relationship building
- Sponsor a booth, a speaker, an attendee at a conservative networking events such as the annual Manning Networking Conference
- Donate to an issue campaign which serve the purpose of bringing conservatives together to champion a particular issue
- Support a conservative mentor or a mentoring arrangement
- Support a think tank or advocacy group championing the reform of laws and regulations which obstruct relationship building among the various components of the conservative movement.

PART 5

STRENGTHEN DEMOCRACY

Democracy has been defined as government of the people, by the people, and for the people. It periodically requires a new birth of freedom and a recommitment to the protection of individual rights and majoritarian decision-making in order to survive and prosper. Strengthening democracy is therefore in the interests of all Canadians and all Canadian political parties regardless of what may divide us into competing partisan camps.

There are myriad ways in which modern democracies can be strengthened, but in this concluding section let me focus on the need to:

- Strengthen local government, the level of government closest to the people
- Treat populism as a legitimate form of democratic expression in a free society but one that requires constructive responses and wise leadership if the political energy it represents is to be directed toward positive rather than negative ends
- Apply this approach to dealing with the most recent upsurge of populism in Canada: that rooted in western alienation, which has produced an upsurge of support for separation in Alberta and Saskatchewan, and has been further energized by the results of the 2019 federal election.
- Counter identity politics, which is a threat to democracy, with unity politics
- Win the twenty-first century ideological contest shaping up between the political parties and governments of the western world and the communist party and government of China, citizen-directed

democracy versus state-directed democracy, and market-directed capitalism versus state-directed capitalism

- Communicate democracy as a 2600-year-old "story" capable of inspiring and motivating those who value freedom and democratic government today and for decades to come

5.1 Embrace the first level of government: local government

Since it is the level of government that is closest to the people, local government should be thought of as the first level of government in Canada, not the third and last.

In the older parts of Canada, local government existed before the creation of the federal and provincial governments[313] and is therefore, in this sense, the jurisdictional progenitor of the so-called senior levels of government, not their progeny.

Local government is important for another reason. It often serves as the training ground for politicians who go on to serve in the federal parliament or the territorial and provincial legislatures.

Numerically, there are over 5,000 municipal and local governments and well over 25,000 elected municipal officials in Canada (not counting elected school boards, health boards, recreational boards, etc.) compared with 760 elected provincial/territorial officials and 338 elected federal officials.

Since there are often three or more persons interested in seeking each of the 25,000-plus elected municipal council positions, this means that as many as 100,000 Canadians likely gave serious thought to running for municipal office over the last three or four years. It is therefore perverse that there are far fewer think tanks, training programs, interest and support groups explicitly dedicated to assisting these people to prepare or run for office than there are at the other levels of government.

---

313 The first legally constituted municipality in Canada was the city of Saint John in New Brunswick which received royal approval in 1785.

It should also be noted that a growing number of Canadians, namely residents of housing or condominium associations, participate in local governance structures that are "municipality-like" with the power to generate a variety of bylaws and regulations at the sub-municipal level.

Given all of this, is there not a great need to increase the amount of attention and resources we devote to strengthening that segment of the political class which operates at the local government level?

DO SOMETHING!

If you are a director, executive, manager, or donor of a think tank, advocacy group, or political movement organization:

- Analyze the past activities and outputs of your organization to determine to what extent there has been any focus at all on municipal issues and governance
- If there has been little or no such focus on your part or on the part of your organization, resolve to devote more attention and resources to municipal issues and governance in the future

If you are a Canadian voter whose political interests and focus has been primarily on provincial or federal politics:

- More fully acquaint yourself with the municipal government and municipal politics in the municipality in which you reside and/or work
- Resolve to more fully participate in the politics of your municipality by following the activities of your municipal council and participating (e.g. at least voting) in the next municipal elections

The municipal democratic toolbox

Voters in municipal elections and elected municipal councilors have access to a number of democratic tools such as regular elections, public opinion surveying, "access to information" mechanisms, the services of

municipal ombudspersons, etc. If we want to make municipal government more accountable to voters and give voters new reasons to take
interest in municipal affairs, I propose that we add two more:

- A Standard Procedural Code for Municipal Councils drafted by
  political practitioners and non-governmental agencies rather than
  bureaucrats
- Council Tracker, a program for tracking and analyzing municipal
  council performance, in particular council votes.

A standard procedural code for municipal councils

Well-codified and standardized procedures exist in Canada at the federal
and provincial levels. Parliament, for example, uses *House of Commons
Procedure and Practice* as its primary procedural authority.[314] Other sources
include Arthur Beauchesne's *Parliamentary Rules and Forms of the House
of Commons of Canada*,[315] Sir John George Bourinot's Parliamentary
Procedure and Practice in the Dominion of Canada,[316] and Erskine May's
The Law, Privileges, Proceedings and Usage of Parliament from Britain.[317] At
the federal and provincial levels in Canada, each assembly also has its
own Standing Orders,[318] and in the United States, Robert's Rules of Order
is the most widely used manual of parliamentary procedure.

At the municipal level, however, the procedural landscape is much
less clear and much more diverse. Where municipal procedural codes
exist, they vary from province to province[319] and appear, for the most

314 Bosc, Marc and Gagnon, Andre, *House of Commons Procedure and Practice, Third
     Edition,* Éditions Yvon Blais, 2017.
315 Beauchesne, Arthur, *Rules and Forms of the House of Commons Of Canada: With
     Annotations and an Extensive Index*, Canada, Parliament, House of Commons
     Canada Law Book Co., 1922.
316 Bourinot, Sir John, *Parliamentary Procedure and Practice in the Dominion of Canada,
     Fourth Edition*, The Lawbook Exchange, Ltd., July 7, 2008.
317 May, Thomas Erskine, *A Treatise on the Law, Privileges, Proceedings, and Usage of
     Parliament*, W. Clowes, 1893.
318 See for example: Standing Orders for the House of Commons http://www.
     noscommunes.ca/procedure-book-livre/document.aspx?sbdid=a3b3e81e-7578-
     4c09-899e-d64180eba3a6&sbpidx=3 Standing Orders of the Legislative Assembly
     of Ontario https://www.ola.org/en/legislative-business/standing-orders
319 For examples see Alberta Municipal Resource Handbook https://www.alberta.

part, to have been drafted by provincial bureaucrats since, in law, today's municipalities are "creatures of the provinces". And while the Federation of Canadian Municipalities offers its members an online library of useful resources, these do not appear to contain a standard procedural template for municipal councils.

Elected municipal councils could benefit from the creation of a well-researched and codified manual of standardized procedures prepared largely by political practitioners and non-governmental agencies which could then be customized to local situations by those councils themselves. Such a manual would also be useful as a training resource for candidates for municipal office.

DO SOMETHING!

If you are an executive, director, or manager of a think tank, university department, or research organization with an interest in improving municipal governance:

• Organize a project to produce, publish, and market a Standard Procedural Code for Municipal Councils in Canada

If you are an executive of or donor to a not-for-profit foundation with an interest in improving municipal governance in Canada:

• Offer to finance this project and assist in the marketing and dissemination of its output

ca/municipal-resource-handbook.aspx; Saskatchewan Municipal Guide https://www.saskatchewan.ca/government/municipal-administration/tools-guides-and-resources, Manitoba Municipal Procedures https://www.gov.mb.ca/mr/mfas/pubs/mmo/procedures_manual_2017.pdf, British Columbia Municipal Councillor's Handbook https://www.civicinfo.bc.ca/Library/Elections/Municipal_Councillors_Handbook_2008--Staples_McDannold_Stewart--November_2008.pdf, and Ontario Municipal Policy handbook https://www.strathcona.ca/council-county/bylaws-and-policies/municipal-policy-handbook/

Council Tracker[320]

If we want to encourage citizen involvement in municipal affairs we need to recognize that at the present time it is extremely difficult for citizens to understand the process of municipal decision making and to hold municipal councilors accountable for their decisions. Often it is difficult to find and access an easily understandable and accessible public record of the meetings and decisions of a municipal council, and there is rarely any organized publicly accessible database for tracking attendance at council meetings, determining who asked what questions of administrative officials, how much time was spent by council on what subjects, and who voted with whom on what subjects.

If this information were to be captured and displayed on a Council Tracker website, accessible to all citizens, it would provide voters, interest groups, and the media with a tool for monitoring council performance and holding council members more accountable for their promises, decisions and actions.

While many municipal councils in Canada profess to be non-ideological and non-partisan, analysis of "who votes with whom" over time, for example, who voted with whom to increase or constrain spending, to increase or constrain taxes, to let central planning or consumer demand drive development permitting, and so on, often reveals embryonic coalitions on council and the existence of quasi-parties with particular ideological leanings operating just below the surface of the municipal political arena.

Having said that, voting along officially recognizable party lines is the exception rather than the rule with most municipal councils and in that respect such councils are significantly different than the federal House of Commons and the provincial legislatures. A voting pattern which invariably emerges under such circumstances is often characterized by a certain number of councilors being strongly on one side of an issue, another group being strongly on the other side, and a small number being in the mushy middle who could go one way or the other. Knowing who stands

---

320 See https://www.660citynews.com/2013/09/20/how-do-your-city-councillors-vote/ for a description of the council tracker developed for Calgary City Council by Jeromy Farkas as an example of this device. (Jeromy has since become an elected member of Calgary City Council). Also see https://manningcentre.ca/content-owner/manning-foundation. Copies of council tracker have been provided to the city libraries of Calgary, Toronto, and Ottawa

where on an issue before council, but particularly knowing who is in the mushy middle, identifications made clear by Council Tracker, will be helpful to voters and interest groups, especially those wanting to push the vote on that particular issue in their preferred direction.

More importantly, in the absence of political parties and party discipline at the municipal level, properly developed and maintained Council Tracker websites would make it possible for citizens to make individual councilors more accountable for their performance. The development of a fact-based, impartial version of a Council Tracker for every major municipal council in Canada would significantly strengthen democracy at the local level.

DO SOMETHING!

If you are an executive, director, or manager of a think tank, university department, or research organization with an interest in improving municipal governance:

- Organize a project to produce, publish, and market a Council Tracker for at least one municipal council

If you are an executive of or donor to a not-for-profit foundation with an interest in improving municipal governance in Canada:

- Offer to finance a Council Tracker project and to assist in the marketing and dissemination of its output

Improve our municipal political infrastructure

There is a need in each municipal jurisdiction, especially in the larger ones affecting the lives of hundreds of thousands of citizens, for more and better municipal movement organizations to perform some of the essential functions performed by political movement organizations at the federal and provincial levels.

Such functions might include developing intellectual and human capital for the municipal arena; conducting municipal opinion surveys and polls; identifying values and principles most conducive to good municipal governance; developing and promoting policy proposals for addressing priority issues (municipal election platforms); and identifying, recruiting, and providing training opportunities for potential candidates for municipal office.

Where municipal political parties do not exist, such movement organizations might even play an active role in conducting formal nomination meetings for municipal offices; sponsoring all-candidate forums, election rallies, and get-out-the vote efforts; recruiting volunteers for municipal issue campaigns and election campaigns; supporting successful candidates between elections; and raising funds for the purposes of financing all these activities.

Municipal political parties performing at least some of these latter functions do exist in some jurisdictions such as in Vancouver,[321] Burnaby[322], and the Province of Quebec[323] where there are more than forty registered municipal parties. But those officially or informally linked to federal or provincial parties (as in the case of "green" municipal parties) tend to display the same limited strengths and more obvious weaknesses of their federal or provincial cousins, rather than offering distinctly different and superior organizational structures and governance.

The long-range challenge therefore at the municipal level is to create and support more and better movement organizations to develop the intellectual capital, human capital, and relationships so essential to good municipal governance. With the passage of time, this may even lead to the re-invention of the political party at the municipal level, a new form of political party, devoid of those self-serving and unethical features of traditional parties which voters find increasingly repugnant.

321 See website of the Vancouver 1st party at http://www.vancouver1st.ca/
     Note also the history of The Electors' Action Movement (TEAM) which was a centrist political party from 1968 to the mid-1980s at the municipal level in Vancouver. It fielded candidates for the office of mayor as well as for positions on the City Council, School Board, and Park Board. It was most successful in the 1970s when it held the majority of council seats from 1972 to 1978.
322 Burnaby Green Party https://www.burnabygreenparty.com/
323 See http://www.assnat.qc.ca/en/patrimoine/partipol.html for a list of the more than 40 municipal political parties in Quebec.

Conservative contributions to municipal politics

Each year, the Manning Foundation has conducted national and sectoral surveys to identify perceived strengths and weaknesses of the conservative movement and market-oriented political practitioners across Canada. One consistently identified area of weakness is the lack of fiscally responsible, market-oriented elected officials at the municipal level.

While conservatively-oriented municipal candidates do relatively well in rural municipalities, this is definitely not the case in Canada's urban municipalities where almost 80% of our population now resides.

While municipal politics in most provinces, with the exception of Quebec, is not generally organized along partisan or ideological lines, informal left-of-centre groups and coalitions with strong links to the NDP, the environmental movement, and public service unions tend to dominate in large urban municipalities

Seeking to organize participation in municipal politics on some basis other than the traditional partisanship which characterizes federal and political politics should in no way be interpreted as excluding people who believe in certain values and principles applicable to governments at any level from participating fully at the municipal level. But they should endeavor to do so through organizations other than the political party which they may support at the federal or provincial levels.

By ignoring and neglecting the municipal political arena, conservatives have, for the most part, surrendered this jurisdiction to left-of-centre influences often masquerading as non-ideological independents. But conservative principles and policies have as much to contribute at the municipal level, if they are intelligently and rigorously applied, as they do to the federal and provincial jurisdictions.

I am referring of course to such principles and policies as fiscal responsibility, tax relief for those who create wealth and jobs, mixed (public and private) approaches to the provision of essential services, greater use of public/private partnerships to build and operate infrastructure, a better distribution of the tools of wealth creation to cope with economic inequalities, market-based approaches (including user pay) for dealing with traffic congestion and waste treatment, and so on.

Would there not be substantial benefits to the residents and taxpayers of our municipalities if we ensured that they had conservative-oriented options to support and vote for, even though they may not be explicitly labeled conservative? Is there not an urgent need for Canadian conservatives, who have tended to ignore the municipal arena politically, to make a serious and long-term commitment to engage more thought-fully, actively, and successfully at this level?

DO SOMETHING!

If you are an executive or manager of a conservative-oriented think tank or advocacy group, consider:

- Examining what you might do to develop intellectual capital and trained human resources for the municipal level

If you are a resident and elector of a municipality and subscribe to conservative values and principles:

- Involve yourself in the formation and support of a conservative-oriented movement organizations for your municipality
- Consider standing for municipal office yourself or urging others who share your values and principles to do so
- Provide volunteer, organizational, and financial support to conservative-oriented candidates for municipal office

Reinventing democracy at the municipal level

Many thoughtful people are convinced that the introduction or expansion of traditional party politics into the municipal arena would not be a beneficial development, given the many negative and unattractive features of traditional party politics currently evident at the federal and provincial levels.

But as mentioned earlier, rather than rejecting the concept of municipal political parties altogether, might there not be merit in considering the municipal level of democratic politics as an ideal arena for re-inventing party politics: for developing the political party of the future, minus many of the objectionable features which currently render party politics unattractive?

We need to remind ourselves that democracy itself was originally invented and developed not at the empire, federation, or nation-state level, but at the city-state level in Ancient Greece. If democracy is to be reinvigorated in our time, is it not possible that this might be accomplished more readily at the municipal level than at the federal or provincial levels, if democratically-minded citizens put their hearts and minds to it?

Imagine if the speeches, legislative proposals, policy initiatives, and follow-up actions at the municipal level in our time were to attain the depth of wisdom and heights of sophistication found in those advanced by Pericles, Aristides, Alcibiades, or Demosthenes in the democratic assembly of ancient Athens. Might not such a reinvigoration or rein-vention of democratic politics at the municipal level inspire and lead by example to a reinvigoration or reinvent of democratic politics in the country as a whole?

DO SOMETHING!

If you are presently an elected municipal official:

- Strive to raise the level of and quality of your participation to new heights, to make municipal politics in your municipality the most exemplary form of democratic governance

If you are a municipal voter (and all of us should be):

- Insist that municipal candidates seeking your support raise the level and quality of their candidacies to new heights, to make municipal politics in your municipality the most exemplary form of democratic governance

5.2 Address the Challenge of Populism

Strengthening democracy in today's world means, among other things, addressing the challenge of populism, those bottom-up outbursts of political energy from rank and file people which erupt from time to time to disrupt the political status quo by raising concerns, policy issues, and leadership personalities which otherwise might not have appeared or been addressed.

Historic examples of populist uprisings in Canada include the farmers' movement of the 1920s and 1930s that created the Progressive Party of Canada,[324] and elected farmers' governments in Manitoba, Alberta and, briefly, in Ontario. These, in turn, laid the foundations for the Great Depression parties of the Cooperative Commonwealth Federation (CCF),[325] a predecessor to the New Democratic Party (NDP), and the Social Credit Party.[326] In fact, it may be argued that western Canada had more experience in the twentieth-century with populist movements, movements which expressed themselves through new political parties including the Reform Party of the 1980s and 1990s, than any other part of North America.

More examples of the populist phenomenon include the Brexit vote in Great Britain, the election of Donald Trump as president in the United States in 2016, the election of Doug Ford as premier of Ontario in 2018, the recent 2018 election of Jair Bolsonaro to the Presidency of Brazil, and the recent upsurge in separatist sentiment in Alberta and Saskatchewan.

324 Morton, W.L., *The Progressive Party in Canada*, University of Toronto Press, 1950.
325 Lipset, Seymour Martin, *Agrarian Socialism: The Cooperative Commonwealth Federation in Saskatchewan: A Study in Political Sociology*, University of California Press, 1971.
326 Irving, John A., *The Social Credit Movement in Alberta*, University of Toronto Press, 1959.

In Canada, populist sentiment and energy has also been a factor at the municipal level, for example, in the election of Rob Ford as mayor of Toronto in 2010[327] and Valerie Plante as mayor of Montreal in 2017.

A neutral starting point

Many discussions of populism today, particularly in academic circles and in the mass media, start with an a priori assumption that populism is inherently retrograde and a threat to civilized values. Populism, it is argued, grows out of the opposition of the uninformed and uneducated to changes in the modern world, ignited and sustained by would-be demagogues.

While this is seldom discussed in the academic literature, it should be noted that a completely negative view of populism is sometimes rooted in hidden but very real reservations by our political elites concerning democracy itself.

Suppose one is an accomplished and distinguished member of the political establishment, a senior executive in a prominent Canadian company, a learned professor of political science at a prominent Canadian university, a respected editorialist or commentator with a major media organization, who has devoted years to studying Canada's political issues, participating in Canada's political processes, and seeking to influence the country's politics for the better.

Such persons frankly (but secretly) resent the fact that the vote of that temporary secretary in the office next door, who knows and cares little about politics, has the same weight in an election as theirs. And they especially resent the fact that the maintenance person in the hall, with his or her large extended family that he or she strongly influences when it comes to voting, may actually command a larger voting block in an election than they do. This simply because democracy gives each member of their families and circle of influence the same voting power as members of the establishment and their friends.

What members of the establishment really resent is the equality of one person, one vote no matter how ignorant or misinformed that

327 Micallef, Shawn, *Frontier City: Toronto on the Verge of Greatness*, Penguin Random House Canada, 2017. Micallef identifies and analyzes the populist sentiments that led to the election of Rob Ford in 2010 as mayor of Toronto, Canada's largest and most diverse city.

person may be. Of course it would be dangerous, and certainly politically incorrect, to rail publicly against that feature of democracy because that would be seen as railing against equality and against democracy itself. Surely there must be something such aggrieved members of the establishment can do or say to express their resentment, but what?

Aha! Why not label any bottom-up grass roots expression of democratic egalitarianism by those rank-and-file people as populism, with all its predisposition to extremism and despotism. Then they can rail against it to their heart's content. They will especially win the applause of others in the business community, the academy, and the media who share the same antipathies and also fear and resent the democratic power of the great unwashed.

While this is often the instinctive reaction of the political establishment to the first signs of a populist uprising, in my judgment a far wiser reaction would be one of neutrality and even potential sympathy rather than an automatic negative. We should see populism, at least initially, as a legitimate form of political expression in a free and democratic society and recognize that it may well be rooted in legitimate grievances demanding attention and redress.

Yes, it has the potential to go rogue and to become a dangerous and destructive force, and that should be frankly acknowledged and guarded against. But populism also has the potential, as the history of populism in western Canada demonstrates, to force positive change and achieve beneficial results.

It all depends on how the political establishment responds to the issues and concerns that are prompting the populist uprising and how the populist movement itself is led. This, too, should be acknowledged frankly and openly.

Progressive populism[328]

Canadian populism has demonstrated both a capacity to advance progressive ideas that the establishment initially opposed and on occasion a capacity to moderate the extremism of some of its own leaders.

---

328 Former Prime Minister Harper has used the term "positive populism" to refer to this phenomenon in his recent book, *Right Here, Right Now: Politics and Leadership in the Age of Disruption,* Signal/Penguin Random House, 2018.

Here are some examples.

During the latter part of the nineteenth-century and the beginning of the twentieth, the Canadian temperance movement was largely a populist movement. Women, who at that time were denied the vote, played a particularly prominent role in this movement which sought to combat the excesses of the out-of-control consumption of alcohol.

Women gained both political skills and ambitions through that experience and then directed those skills towards strengthening women's rights to matrimonial property (dower rights).[329] Next, they demanded that women be recognized as "persons" in Canadian law,[330] with political rights, including the right to be appointed to public positions in such institutions as the senate and the judiciary, positions which were previously available only to men.

The Persons Case was championed by the "Alberta Five," later named and celebrated as the "Famous Five," five women (all Alberta based) with deep roots in western populist movements. They included:

- Emily Murphy (1868–1933), a prairie Conservative who became the first female police magistrate in the British Empire and who framed the Persons Case submission to the Supreme Court of Canada
- Nellie McClung (1873–1951), a Methodist and independent Liberal, active in the temperance movement and a leader of the campaign in Manitoba to secure women the vote (Manitoba being the first Canadian province to do so in 1916). In 1921, she became one of the first women to be elected to the Alberta legislature

329 It is significant that the first major push to advance women's rights in Canada focused on securing property rights for women (the right to matrimonial property) and that initiative then led by extension to efforts to secure political rights.

330 The Persons Case (officially *Edwards v. A.G. of Canada*) was a constitutional ruling that established the right of women to be appointed to the Senate of Canada. It was initiated by a group of prominent women activists who became known as The Famous Five. In 1928, the Supreme Court of Canada ruled that women were not persons according to the British North America Act and therefore were ineligible for appointment to the Senate. However, the women appealed to the Privy Council of England, which in 1929 reversed the Court's decision. Reference: *The Canadian Encyclopedia*. It should be noted that four of the five Canadian Supreme Court Justices who unanimously decided that women were not persons under Canadian law were Liberal appointments, one by Laurier and three by Mackenzie King. Two of King's appointments were former Liberal Members of Parliament.

- Louise Crummy McKinney (1868–1931), a teacher, temperance worker, and the first woman to be elected to a legislature in the British Empire. McKinney was elected to the Alberta legislature in 1917 as a member and representative of the populist Non-Partisan League
- Irene Parlby (1868–1965), a prominent activist in the farmers' movement, elected in 1921 to the Alberta legislature as a member of the populist United Farmers of Alberta where she served until 1935 and became the second female cabinet minister in the British Empire
- Henrietta Muir Edwards (1849–1931), the oldest of the Famous Five, independent, non-partisan founder and supporter of socially-oriented non-governmental organizations such as the Victorian Order of Nurses. Author of two law books and an early champion of matrimonial property rights for women

In addition to the Famous Five, equal recognition also needs to be given to:

- Agnes Campbell Macphail (1890–1954), the first woman to be elected to the House of Commons in 1921. Macphail, whose candidacy was bitterly opposed by the federal Liberal and Conservative parties of the day, ran as a candidate for the populist Progressive Party of Canada, later won election to the Ontario legislature as a member of the populist United Farmers of Ontario, and still later became a member of the populist Cooperative Commonwealth Federation (CCF)
- Roberta MacAdams (1880–1959), a wartime nurse and dietician and the second woman elected to the Alberta legislature in 1917. MacAdams, who had been politically active as a Conservative in Ontario, was elected as an independent member-at-large by members (largely male) of the Canadian Armed Forces engaged in the First World War
- Mary Ellen Smith (1861–1933) who came to politics through the bottom-up politics of the union movement in British Columbia. Running for the legislature first as an independent Liberal she became the first woman elected to the B.C. legislature in 1917, the first female cabinet minister in Canada, and the first female Speaker

The securing of economic and political rights for women and the opening up of elected offices to women were some of Canada's first progressive political developments. We need to recognize that these demands were first championed, against establishment opposition, primarily by women operating through populist movements and organizations.

Moderating populism

I have noted that one of the most consistent establishment criticisms of populist uprisings is that they tend, or can be easily led towards ideological extremism. We need to acknowledge this and strenuously guard against it. But we also need to recognize that in western Canada there are at least two prominent examples of the rank and file members of populist political parties themselves moderating the ideological extremism of some of their own leaders.

The Co-operative Commonwealth Federation (CCF) was the predecessor of today's New Democratic Party and first formed a government in Saskatchewan under the leadership of Tommy Douglas. It was a populist party in character and socialist in its ideology. That ideology, which had considerable appeal during the economic chaos and hardship of the Depression, called for nationalization (government ownership) of the means of production. Carried to its logical conclusion, this should have meant a government takeover of the Saskatchewan's farmlands, a position which some of the ideological extremists in the party actually advocated. But it was those common sense, rank and file farmers of Saskatchewan who very quickly made it clear that if the CCF championed that position, it would lose their support and would not be a government very long. In this case, the rank and file members and supporters of a populist party moderated its ideological extremists[331] rather than succumbing to their appeals.

In Alberta, the economic chaos and hardship of the Depression produced another populist party, the Social Credit Party under the leadership of William Aberhart. Aberhart embraced and promoted monetary reform as the answer to the Depression. He subscribed to a crude form of Keynesian economics involving the nationalization of credit and

---

331 Many years later, in 1972, NDP leader Allan Blakeney championed the creation of the Saskatchewan Land Bank Commission. In ten year, the province purchased almost 1.2 million acres of land for the land bank. As of 2001, it still held 760,431 acres.

expansion of the money supply during economic downturns to get the economy going again.

While this doctrine had considerable public appeal in the heart of the Depression and led to the election of a Social Credit government in Alberta in 1935, it began to lose its appeal as the economy recovered and when the courts ruled that monetary reform was not in any way within provincial jurisdiction. Notwithstanding that, there were ideological extremists within the party and the government who insisted that monetary reform remain its chief objective. It was again the rank and file members and supporters of the party who made it clear to its leadership that unless it abandoned this fixation and began to focus on the main responsibilities of a provincial government, it would not remain a provincial government very long. Again, as in the case of the CCF, it was the rank and file members and supporters of a populist party who moderated its tendency to ideological extremism and set it on a more constructive path.

The reaction of the establishment

The instinctive reaction to a populist uprising on the part of the political establishment and its media allies is usually to immediately denounce it and its leadership in the strongest possible terms, characterizing it as rooted in ignorance, prejudice, irrationality, emotionalism, and extremism. Sadly, this establishment reaction is probably the worst of all possible reactions because it fuels the very thing it professes to abhor. What is really required of the establishment, if populism is to be prevented from going rogue, is a sincere and concentrated effort to understand and address its root concerns and causes.

One might even go so far as to say that populist movements and leaders are, to a considerable extent, the political legacy of establishment regimes and leaders who consistently ignored or denigrated the real concerns and anxieties of rank and file citizens.

From this perspective, Rob Ford was the political legacy of David Miller, his elitist predecessor as mayor of Toronto, Donald Trump is the political legacy of Barack Obama and Hillary Clinton, and Doug Ford is the political legacy of Kathleen Wynne and her Liberal colleagues.

When the political establishment reacts to populism negatively and contemptuously, when it arrogantly ignores or dismisses the anxieties and concerns of ordinary people, it further polarizes the political arena, fuels the fires of populism even more, and makes it harder to seek common ground accommodations. To those joining the populist uprising, it provides even further proof, as if any was really needed, of how out-of-touch the establishment is with the concerns of the common people and how unsympathetic the elites are to those concerns.

So what is a better way to respond to a populist uprising?

A positive conservative response to the underlying causes of populism

In his recent book, *Right Here, Right Now,*[332] former Prime Minister Harper acknowledges the possibility of a "positive populism" which "places the wider interests of the common people ahead of the specialized interests of the privileged few."[333] He identifies the "wider interests of the common people" currently fueling populist uprisings around the world as being essentially economic, rooted in some of the negative consequences of freer trade, freer movements of capital and immigrants, and globalization, all policies which conservatives have largely championed and liberals have often imitated.

What is required then is what he calls a reformed democratic capitalism[334] requiring a realignment of conservative approaches to trade, immigration, government regulation and internationalism. In particular, this realignment should involve pursuing fair trade as well as free trade, encouraging desirable immigration while aggressively curtailing illegal immigration, creating regulatory frameworks to insure that markets (especially financial markets) work in favor of working people, and strengthening not weakening the ties of citizens to the nation state and their local communities.

The wildcat/rogue well analogy

At the political level, there is also a particularly effective way of meeting the challenge of populism, based primarily on the twentieth-century

332 Harper, Stephen J., *Right Here, Right Now,* Penguin Random House Canada, 2018.
333 Harper, p.13
334 Harper, p.5

experience of western Canada. It is relevant to both establishment leaders and the would-be leaders of populist uprisings themselves. It is best described through an analogy, drawn from the oil patch.

In the oil patch there is such a thing as a wildcat well drilled into geological formations which have not been thoroughly explored. There is also such a thing as a rogue well, also drilled into such a formation which unexpectedly unleashes so much oil and gas under such immense pressure that it blows the drilling platform off the wellhead, spews oil and gas high into the air, and sometimes catches fire.[335]

A rogue well has positive potential if its unleashed energy can be constructively harnessed and employed. But a rogue well can be dangerously destructive if unattended or mismanaged, just like populism.

One effective way of bringing the valuable energy of a rogue well under control, so it can be effectively harnessed and used, is to drill in a "relief well" from the side. But how the relief shaft is positioned relative to the rogue well is all important. If the relief shaft fails to connect directly with the rogue well at the right depth, it won't serve the purposes of diverting the flow and relieving some of the pressure. As a worst case scenario, a misdirected relief well can itself turn into a rogue well. But if the positioning of the relief well relative to the rogue well is just right, it can divert enough of the flow and relieve enough of the pressure to permit the rogue well to be brought under control and into useful production.

Western alienation and the Reform "relief well"

As already discussed, one of the root causes of populist movements is the alienation of large numbers of ordinary people from their political elites and the political processes and institutions that those elites dominate.

In the 1980s, that kind of alienation developed throughout much of western Canada. The west felt out of it, unfairly treated within confederation and not listened to by the political elites in Ottawa or Central Canada. This alienation was fueled by intense anger at the federal

335 In Canada, one of the most infamous of such blowouts occurred on March 8, 1948, just one year after the discovery of the Leduc oil field. A well named Atlantic Number 3 blew, hurling oil and debris fifty meters in the air, catching fire, burning for three days, and spewing 1.2 million barrels of oil and ten billion cubic feet of natural gas before it was finally brought under control.

Liberals over the National Energy Program which transferred $100-billion of wealth from the western petroleum producing provinces to the eastern consuming provinces and the federal treasury.

It was further fueled by deep disillusionment with the federal Progressive Conservatives for their 1986 political decision to award the twenty-year, $100 million CF-18 jet maintenance contract to Quebec-based Canadair instead of Manitoba-based Bristol Aerospace, even though Bristol was the lowest bidder and the most technically competent.

This anger and disillusionment, in turn, fueled increasing talk about and support for western separatism. This led to separatist rallies, the formation of embryonic separatist parties, and the election of a western separatist to the Alberta legislature.

This western alienation was a bottom-up, grassroots phenomenon, a populist thing, not unlike the bottom-up, grassroots populism of the farmers' movement that gave birth to the old Progressive Party of Canada, the provincial farmers' parties, and the depression parties of the CCF and Social Credit. This time it gave birth to the Reform Party of Canada with its rallying cry, "The West Wants In."

The big challenge faced by those of us involved in creating and leading the Reform movement was how to respond to and direct the populist forces which had given it birth and with which we strongly identified.

In a very real sense, what the Reform leadership tried to do in the late 1980s was drill a relief shaft into the rogue well of western alienation. We had to tap directly into it, which we did by fully identifying with much of the discontent and addressing its causes. In fact, this is the most important and essential step in responding constructively to a populist uprising, identifying and identifying with its root causes, the reasons why hundreds of thousands of rank and file people are alienated from the system, without necessarily subscribing to the remedies it initially proposes.

We believed Westerners had a right to be mad and told them so. We publicly identified with and articulated the causes of the unrest and demanded action on the part of the federal parliament and government to address them. But, rather than accepting that the appropriate response was for the West to separate and tear Confederation apart, as the Bloc Quebecois was already attempting to do in Quebec, we proposed a redirection of populist energies toward reform of the federation and the operations of the federal government so that they would work better for the West and all Canadians.

Of course, we made lots of mistakes: there is a lot of trial-and-error in taming a rogue well. But, in the end, the whole exercise worked out more or less positively. In 1993, fifty-two Reformers were elected to the House of Commons and in 1997 the Reform Party became the Official Opposition. By 2000, the movement tapped into an even larger circle of discontented electors with the creation of the Canadian Conservative Reform Alliance under Stockwell Day, broadening out again under the leadership of Stephen Harper and Peter MacKay to create the new Conservative Party of Canada in 2003. That party then formed a minority Conservative government in 2006, and finally formed a majority Conservative government in 2011—a fiscally-responsible federal government with strong western roots that lasted nine years.

Whether one agrees or disagrees with what Reform stood for, or with what the Harper administration did or didn't do, is not the main point here. What I think most Canadians can agree on is that this was a better outcome than having a full-blown separatist movement in the West at the same time as there was a full-blown separatist movement in Quebec. Had that been allowed to happen the country could well have been torn apart with unbridled, misunderstood, and mismanaged populism as a major contributing factor.

Potential sources of future populist uprisings

Populism becomes a potential factor in the politics of a country or province or city when some concern (usually an economic one) afflicts large numbers of rank-and-file voters and arouses them to some sort of bottom-up political action. If those voters believe that the political elites of the day are utterly indifferent or hostile to their concerns, they become increasingly alienated from the conventional political system and increasingly open to solutions and political actions offered by new and unconventional sources. Thus a populist movement is born.

In addition, the growing use and influence of social media makes the rapid and effective political organization of large numbers of economically and politically-alienated people cheaper and easier to accomplish than in the past. This means populist movements can spring up and grow much more rapidly today than in the past, making populism a more frequent and persistent challenge to citizen-directed democracy.

In our country, as discussed in Chapter 1.4, millennials could well become the wellspring of a populist movement if the underlying causes of their potential alienation from democratic politics are not addressed. They may be lured into political involvement temporarily by leaders and campaigns attuned to pop culture but, in the end, that approach usually disappoints, causing more alienation, and eventually falls out of favor as soon as the pop culture flavor-of-the-month changes.

Looking ahead, other potential sources of populist uprisings in Canada may include:

- Intergenerational conflict, as an aging society, with a rapidly growing and expensive class of seniors, becomes an ever-increasing tax burden on the young who work
- Tensions between the scientific and technological elites and the "lumpenproletariat" who feel threatened by scientific and technological advancements such as the replacement of human workers by robots and the increasing use of artificial intelligence
- The growing urban-rural divide, with rural Canadians feeling ignored, disrespected, and completely abandoned by the political leadership of the country
- Conflict between extreme environmentalists and those employed by or otherwise dependent on the natural resource sectors
- Identity politics run amok,[336] especially when fueled by issues involving sexual identity and practices: the LGBTQ movement,[337] the #MeToo movement, the #WeBelieve movement, and reactions thereto
- The re-emergence of Quebec separatism as Quebec's influence within the federation declines and Quebec's leadership is unwilling or unable to find political allies in other parts of the country

In the long run, one of the most likely sources of populist uprisings in Canada could be that fueled by the increasing political alienation of those Canadians who feel injured and left behind by the results of freer international trade, globalization, and the emergence of the digital

---

336 For more on this and recommendations for a conservative alternative to identity politics, see Chapter 5.3
337 See https://www.nytimes.com/2018/06/21/style/lgbtq-gender-language.html for the expansion (acronym wise) of the LGBTQ movement to the LGBTQIA+ movement and beyond.

economy, the major accomplishments of market-driven capitalism which is usually championed by conservatives.[338]

If the lessons of Canadian history concerning how to channel the disaffections and energies of past populist movements (including separatist ones) into constructive alternatives were to be learned and reapplied in this instance, what measures would they suggest? Those recommended by former Prime Minister Harper and others would be a good start. They include:

- Pursuing fair trade as well as free trade
- Encouraging legal and absorbable immigration while aggressively curtailing illegal and unmanageable immigration
- Creating just and efficient regulatory frameworks to insure that markets (especially financial markets) work in favor of working people rather than to their detriment
- Insuring that the tools of wealth creation offered by market-driven capitalism are much more broadly and evenly distributed than at present
- Strengthening not weakening the ties of citizens to the nation state and their local communities.

At present, the most recent and significant populist uprising in Canada, the one most urgently deserving of national attention, is that rooted in the re-emergence of western alienation and western separatism, especially in Alberta and Saskatchewan. The depth and scope of this populist movement, currently unappreciated and unaddressed by the Trudeau government and the rest of Canada, is such that it requires a clear and detailed description of its root causes and the measures required to address those root causes. This I have attempted to provide in Chapter 5.3 following.

338 Prime Minister Harper elaborates on this point in *Right Here, Right Now.*

DO SOMETHING!

If you are concerned about the reality of, or the potential for, populist uprisings in Canada and abroad:

- Study and apply the main lessons to be learned from Canada's past experience with populism, especially its most recent expression in western Canada

If you are in a position to respond or provide leadership to a populist uprising in Canada:

- Treat it as a legitimate expression of political discontent in a democratic society where freedom of speech and association exists and is constitutionally guaranteed
- Acknowledge and seek to understand the root causes of the alienation that fuel such discontents and uprisings, rather than ignoring or contemptuously dismissing them
- Assist in the development and communication of constructive measures to alleviate the root causes of that alienation and those discontents
- Help create structures and processes to harness the political energies of populist forces to constructive ends (i.e. employ the relief-well approach) rather than simply decrying or attempting to suppress those forces

"Inform their discretion"

Thomas Jefferson, one of the founders of the American Republic and its third President, was certainly a leading member of the political elites of his day. He knew all about the excesses to which unbridled public discontents can go and the excesses to which entrenched political establishments can go to suppress them.

Nevertheless, towards the very end of his life, he made this remarkable assertion of his ultimate faith in the political capacities of the common people when he wrote: "I can think of no safe depository of the ultimate powers of the society but the people themselves. . ."

But then, anticipating the predictable reaction from his own political class, that the people themselves, left to themselves, are neither enlightened nor qualified enough to exercise those powers wisely or in moderation, he added this important proviso: "And if we think them [the people] not enlightened enough to exercise their control with a wholesome discretion, the remedy is not to take it from them, but to inform their discretion. . ."[339]

What better way to meet the challenge of populism than to re-affirm our faith in the people themselves while redoubling our efforts "to inform their discretion" as to the choices and best means available to remedy their discontents?

---

339 "Thomas Jefferson to William C. Jarvis, 1820," in Lipscomb & Bergh, eds., *The Writings of Thomas Jefferson*, Memorial Edition, 15:27, Washington, D.C., 1903.

5.3 Address Western Alienation

Another populist uprising

In the 2019 federal election, voters in Alberta and Saskatchewan soundly rejected the leadership of Prime Minister Justin Trudeau and the Liberal candidates in all 48 federal ridings in those provinces. Liberal support in those ridings fell to a dismal 14% in Alberta and 12% in Saskatchewan, the worst showing of that party since the days of Pierre Elliot Trudeau. Among the defeated Liberal candidates were long-time Liberal cabinet minister and Trudeau apologist Ralph Goodale in his Regina riding, and the Liberal Minister of Natural Resources, Amarjeet Sohi, in his Edmonton riding, showing what voters in Alberta's capital thought of Liberal natural resource policy.

Over the previous year, a dozen pro-separation advocacy groups[340] made their appearance on the prairie political landscape, attracting thousands of supporters to their websites and on-line petitions. A public opinion survey[341] conducted by Ipsos two weeks after the October 2019 federal election, found that:

- 33% of Alberta respondents and 27% of Saskatchewan respondents agreed strongly or somewhat agreed with the statement, "My province would be better off if it separated from Canada".

340 These have included such organizations as Wexit Canada and Wexit Alberta, which claim to have 250,000-plus on-line supporters, and Action Alberta, with a reported 10,000 adherents and a heavy representation from the oil patch. The Wexit group has recently taken steps to form a separatist political party with the intent of offering a separatist platform in the next federal and Alberta elections.
341 Ipsos Press Release; Vancouver, BC; November 5, 2019.

- 65% of Alberta respondents and 62% of Saskatchewan respondents agreed strongly or somewhat agreed with the statement: "My province does not get its fair share from confederation".
- 76% of Alberta respondents and 79% of Saskatchewan respondents agreed with the statement: "Alberta and Saskatchewan have good reason to be mad about how they are treated by the federal government".

Predictably and regrettably, the reaction of the federal political establishment and central Canadian media to news of this separatist-oriented populist uprising has largely been to dismiss it as a fringe phenomenon and to completely ignore, misinterpret, or dismiss the root causes of its emergence.

In campaigning for re-election, the Prime Minister displayed no concern whatsoever for the five percent contraction of the Alberta economy over the last four years, the unprecedented job losses and flight of investment capital, the more than 50% increase in business bankruptcies between 2014 and 2018, the quadrupling of property crimes, the thousands of Albertans who have lost their homes, their small businesses and their hope, or the despair that has made the per capital suicide rate in Alberta 50% higher than that of Ontario.

When Prime Minister Trudeau delivered his pyrrhic[342] "victory speech" on election night, even though his party had just lost 40% of the federal seats in Quebec to the separatist Parti Quebecois and had been massively rejected in the prairie provinces, there was not a flicker of recognition or acknowledgement in his remarks that national unity was once again in peril and demanding immediate corrective action.

Getting to the roots

So, remembering that the first step to addressing a populist uprising is to identify, not ignore or dismiss, its root causes, what are the root causes of this western alienation, generating support for separation from

---

342 A Pyrrhic victory is a victory that inflicts such a heavy toll on the victor that it is tantamount to defeat. Someone who wins a Pyrrhic victory has also taken such a heavy toll that it negates any true sense of achievement or damages long-term progress.

Canadian confederation and the policies and personalities of the Liberal government in Ottawa?

In this case, the rise in support for separation, especially in Alberta and Saskatchewan, is rooted in:

- The galling indifference of the federal government to the depth and seriousness of the downturn in the western Canadian energy sector which has resulted in the loss of over 150,000 jobs and a massive flight of capital, companies, equipment, and talent to the United States
- The failure of the federal government to eliminate internal barriers to trade within Canada and to provide unobstructed transportation corridors to the Atlantic, Pacific, and Arctic so that the resources of the interior provinces can reach tidewater and world markets
- Resentment and growing frustration over the vetoing, canceling, or bungling of the Northern Gateway, Keystone, and Energy East pipeline projects, and the interminable delays in proceeding with the Trans Mountain Expansion Project to the west coast.
- Resentment and increasing frustration over the Trudeau government's passage of the discriminatory west coast tanker moratorium (Bill C-48) despite the Senate Committee recommendation that it be repealed, and passage of the no-more-pipelines law (Bill C-69) despite the opposition of nine provincial governments
- The active siding of the Trudeau government with anti-petroleum environmentalists, many of them funded by foreign interests, in their efforts to cripple and shut down the Canadian petroleum sector completely
- The unfairness of the implementation of the equalization principle as sanctioned by Section 36 of the constitution, whereby one province, Alberta, has contributed over $600 billion to the national coffers since 1960 and one province (Quebec) in particular, has been the continuously favored recipient of equalization payments and federal transfers in large amounts. This then compounded by the failure of the Fiscal Stabilization Fund, originally designed to provide an equalization rebate to "have" provinces if they experience a sudden and unexpected decline in revenues, to provide any relief to Alberta when its economy has suffered a serious reversal
- The intrusion of the federal government, via the unilateral exercise of its spending and taxing powers, in areas of provincial jurisdiction (such as the development and conservation of natural resources)

and areas of joint jurisdiction (such as protection of the environment) without the consent of the provinces affected. This intrusion
is particularly resented with respect to the federal government's
imposition of a carbon tax regime over the objections of a majority
of the affected provinces

- The failure of the RCMP to cope with the growing crime wave in
rural Alberta and Saskatchewan, resulting in calls for provincial
withdrawal from policing contracts with the RCMP
- General dissatisfaction with other federal policies and services in
such areas as immigration, firearms control, parole policy, housing policy, and the administration of the Canada Health and Social
Transfer, resulting in calls for substantial reforms or complete withdrawal from current federal-provincial programs in those areas
- A growing conviction that confederation, our federal institutions,
and the relationship between the federal government and the provinces are inherently flawed and biased against the interests of the
western provinces and northern territories, requiring not merely
changes in federal attitudes and policies but fundamental structural
and constitutional changes if the federation is to survive and prosper in the twenty-first century.

DO SOMETHING!

- If you are a resident of western Canada, review these root causes
of western alienation, decide whether you consider them legitimate or not and, if so, join in efforts to bring them forcibly to the
attention of federal authorities.
- If you are a resident of the rest of Canada, review these root
causes of western alienation, decide whether you consider them
legitimate or not and, if so, urge the federal government through
your member of parliament to respond positively to western
demands for action.

Fashioning a response

One obvious response on the part of a growing number of citizens in Alberta and Saskatchewan has been to consider and even embrace the separatist option. The other, favored by the current United Conservative government of Alberta led by Premier Jason Kenney and by the current Saskatchewan Party government led by Premier Scott Moe, has been three fold:

- To fully identify with and clearly articulate the root causes of the current western alienation which are causing immense pain and frustration for the citizens of Alberta and Saskatchewan and generating the call for separation
- To define and communicate to the federal government, the other provinces, and the Canadian public the key elements of a fair deal which would fully address these root causes if acted upon decisively and quickly
- To make abundantly clear to the federal government and the rest of Canada that if these requests for a Fair Deal Now are not met decisively and quickly, the country will face a full blown Independence movement in western Canada which could well begin the unravelling of the Canadian federation as presently constituted

What, then, are the key elements of a Fair Deal Now for Alberta and Saskatchewan which, if acted upon decisively and quickly, would fully address the root causes of western alienation and the current populist uprising demanding action? In Alberta, answering this question through extensive research and public consultation is the work of a special panel appointed by Premier Kenney in November 2019 (it is scheduled to report in the spring of 2020).[343] In Saskatchewan, similar research and consultations are being carried out by the provincial government under the direction of Premier Moe. And while there may be some minor differences in what constitutes a fair deal from the perspective of each province, the main elements are likely to include the following:

- A clear, honest, and public acknowledgment by the prime minister and the federal government that the concerns and grievances at the

343 https://www.alberta.ca/fair-deal-panel.aspx

root of western alienation are legitimate and deserving of national attention and redress

- Immediate action by the federal government, which now owns the Trans Mountain Corporation, to proceed with the construction and completion of the Trans Mountain Expansion Project, expanding pipeline access to the west coast
- Use of the federal government powers under sections 91(2) and 92(10) of the constitution to remove interprovincial barriers to trade and to create unobstructed transportation infrastructure corridors from the interior provinces to tidewater and world markets
- Repeal of the west coast tanker moratorium (Bill C-48) and the no-more-pipelines law (Bill C-69)
- Legislative action and the adoption of federal policies specifically designed to achieve balance[344] between energy development and environmental protection rather than the continuation of one-sided actions and policies on the environment/energy front
- Formal acknowledgment by the Prime Minister and the federal government that the current administration of the equalization principle is unfair and the formulation and adoption of specific measures to identify and remedy its inequities
- A lifting of the cap on the Fiscal Stabilization Fund, and payment to Alberta of the $1.75 billion equalization rebate it should have received had the cap not been imposed
- Entering into an administrative agreement with the provinces whereby the federal government agrees to refrain from exercising its spending or taxing powers in areas of provincial jurisdiction or joint jurisdiction without the consent of the provinces affected
- Cooperation with, rather than resistance to, provincial requests to withdraw from selected federal-provincial programs and cost sharing arrangements.
- Acknowledgment by the Prime Minister and the federal government that systemic flaws and inequities in the current structures, institutions, processes, and constitution of the federation are at the roots of

---

344 One such balancing initiative would be to continue to insist that major economic projects be required to file Environmental Impact Assessments, but to also insist that the proponents of major environmental protection measures be required to file Economic Impact Assessments of those measures so that the regulators, courts, and the government can strike an appropriate balance between environmental and economic considerations.

Canada's perennial and persistent national unity problems, and the convening of a Federal-Provincial Conference to specifically address those flaws and inequities.

DO SOMETHNG!

If you are in agreement with these Fair Deal measures to address the root causes of western alienation, urge your federal MP to call for and support immediate implementation action by the federal government.

Complementary provincial actions

While key elements of a fair deal for Alberta and Saskatchewan within confederation require an immediate and positive response from the federal government if western alienation is to be effectively addressed, there are complementary and additional actions which those provincial governments can take on their own in response to the demands of their citizens. In Alberta's case, these already include or could include:

- The launching of a public inquiry under the Inquires Act into the funding sources, especially the foreign-funding sources, behind the campaign to landlock Alberta's petroleum resources
- Pressuring the federal government to exempt Alberta from the Canada Housing and Mortgage Corporation's stress test which has put home ownership out of reach for many Albertans
- Renewal of Alberta's Senate Election Act so that Alberta will be represented in future by Senators with democratic legitimacy
- Pressuring the federal government to convert Canada Health and Social Transfers to tax points to give the province more control over how revenue is raised and spent within an area of provincial jurisdiction
- Creation of an Alberta Parole Board to take over responsibility from the Parole Board of Canada for provincial inmates
- The holding of provincial referenda on removing or amending section 36, the equalization section of the constitution; on entrenching property rights in the Charter of Rights and Freedoms; and for the

purposes of giving Albertans a chance to ratify or reject key elements of the Fair Deal proposals.

- Preparation of plans for further withdrawals from federal services such as those of the RCMP, federal programs such as the Canada Pension Plan and any ill-conceived national Pharmacare program, and the Canada-Alberta tax collection agreement so that Alberta can collect provincial income taxes directly as well as federal taxes within the province.

It should also be noted that while implementation of most of the fair deal and withdrawal measures discussed above does not require opening up the constitution, several of these measures, and other measures which might be added, have constitutional ramifications. For example:

- The removal of internal barriers to trade and the provision of unobstructed transportation corridors to tidewater requires the federal government to exercise constitutional powers on behalf of the west that heretofore it has declined to use
- The renewal of Alberta's Senate Election Act is only a partial step toward what is really required: a constitutional amendment to democratize, rebalance, and refocus Senate representation on effective regional representation once and for all
- While federal spending and taxing in areas of provincial and joint jurisdiction can be constrained by an administrative agreement, such constraint would be far more binding if it were secured through a constitutional amendment
- While provinces like Alberta have a quasi-constitution through federal statutes like the Alberta Act, the drafting of a full blown Alberta-made and Alberta-approved Constitution would be a useful and worthwhile exercise under the present circumstances.

Proposing, promoting, and securing the implementation of the measures listed above will establish a much greater degree of independence for Alberta within the federation, a prelude, hopefully, not to separation, but to a stronger and more equitable position within the reconfigured confederation of tomorrow.

Re-confederation or separation?

My father Ernest Manning was elected to the Alberta legislature in 1935 in the midst of the Great Depression. The premier, William Aberhart, immediately appointed him to the cabinet, making him the youngest cabinet minister in the country at the time. But to make sure he didn't get into trouble due to inexperience, Aberhart also assigned one of the oldest and most experienced members of the civil service to be his deputy, a man named Eddy Trobridge.

Trowbridge had once served as a clerk to F. W. G. Haultain, the last premier of the old Northwest Territory when it stretched from Ontario to the Rockies and from the U.S. border to the Arctic, and before it was carved into provinces. Trobridge had known and observed every premier of Alberta and Saskatchewan from 1905 to 1935, and he never tired of telling my father that "the greatest and best premier the west ever had was F. W. G. Haultain." He was a statesman, Trobridge maintained, of the same caliber and ability as McDonald and Laurier.

It was Haultain who foresaw that the west would be weakened if it was carved into several provinces and denied control over its natural resources as the Liberal government in Ottawa proposed. It was Haultain, who, speaking to a crowd of 1,500 people on a snowy night in Indian Head, Saskatchewan, in 1904, labelled those who sided with the federal Liberals, "Little Westerners" when what the region and the country required was "Big Westerners." Big Westerners were those who would insist that the west remain as one big province with control of its natural resources in order to counterbalance the influence of Quebec and Ontario within the federation.

In correspondence with Prime Minister Laurier, Haultain maintained that Ottawa was offending Canada's founding Constitution, the British North America Act, by failing to grant any newly-created province full jurisdiction over those aspects of governance clearly assigned by the BNA Act to provinces. By failing to do so, Haultain contended that the federal government would be creating in the west "an unwilling, inferior, and imperfect organization."

Regrettably, in the end, it was the position of the federal Liberals, not Haultain's position, that prevailed. And thus the western provinces of Alberta and Saskatchewan did in fact enter confederation in "an unwilling, inferior, and imperfect" state, a position in which those provinces still find themselves to this very day.

As Premier Kenney, who referenced Haultain in his speech[345] outlin-
ing the Fair Deal Now initiatives, so eloquently put it: "The wellspring
of modern western frustration and anger lies in the flawed articles of
confederal union. And the key to our contentment lies in repairing
those flaws. Fixing them would be easy if they were merely some act
of bureaucratic incompetence or political sabotage. But as generations
of disaffected westerners can attest, the flaws are embedded in the economic structure of the federation, our national political institutions, and
often in the complacency and condescension of the so-called Laurentian
elites."

In the aftermath of the 2019 federal election, the country has become
even more divided and weaker than it was before. Separatist sentiment
is now at an all-time high in Alberta and Saskatchewan and reviving in
Quebec. Identity politics is further accentuating the differences between
Canadians based on gender, sexual orientation, and ethnicity, rather
than building on the characteristics we share in common. Divisive
internal trade barriers persist, and foreign investors make a mockery
of the concept of "trans-Canada", arguing that we Canadians can't
even "trans" our own provincial boundaries. Environmental extremists
accuse the petroleum sector of destroying the environment, and in turn
dedicate themselves to destroying the alleged destroyer.

But wait! Maybe there is a more positive possibility than growing
division and deepening national disunity. The country now has seven
conservative-oriented provincial government with more than 50% of
the population, sufficient to fundamentally amend the constitution if
there was concurrence from the federal parliament. Just maybe some of
those elected to the 43rd parliament will come to believe that the weakness and divisiveness of the current situation calls for nothing less than
Re-Confederation: the convening of federal-provincial meetings, not
unlike those once held in Charlottetown and Quebec City, to hammer
out a new set of terms and conditions (not necessarily constitutional)
for uniting and strengthening Canada for the remainder of the twenty
first century.

Re-Confederation! Perhaps the term is too ambitious, "a bridge too
far" under the current political circumstances. Then let us find a better,

345 See "What Next," Premier Kenney's speech to the Manning Networking Conference
     in Red Deer, Alberta, November 9, 2019. Available at https://www.alberta.ca/
     release.cfm?xID=6608502355B7E-A6AE-7F2E-6A20884E613662CC

more modest objective and descriptive. But it must be a vision that is positive, inspirational, structural, remedial, and of broad rather than narrow appeal.

Members of my family have been intimately involved with Alberta and federal politics for eighty-five years. I understand and feel the pain of western alienation that is prompting separatist sentiments among many of my friends, associates, and supporters as much or more than anyone in the province or the federal parliament. Yet if forced to choose, separation or re-confederation, I vote for re-confederation and will dedicate my remaining years to help bring it about, not just for the benefit of my home province but for the lasting benefit of all Canadians.

DO SOMETHIING!

If you are supportive of remedial actions by the federal and provincial governments to address the root causes of western alienation, communicate your support of the Fair Deal Now measures to:

- Members of your own family as well as your friends and associates
- Your representative in the your provincial legislature and the federal parliament

5.4 Counter Identity Politics

Identity politics, especially as practiced by many (but not all) liberals and social democrats in Canada, has the following characteristics as briefly described in chapter 1.3:

- A group of voters is identified as a target whose support a political party wishes to secure and is defined in terms of such personal characteristics as gender, sexual orientation, race, language, or personal political status (recent immigrant, refugee, persecuted minority etc.)
- Members of the group are then offered some legal (even constitutional) recognition, a program or service of some kind, and/or financial assistance of some sort
- It is made clear to members of the group (sometimes subtly, but more often, explicitly) that the benefits they are being offered are conditional upon them supporting the political party offering them, and that if they were to support or vote for any other party these benefits would likely be taken away
- Broadening, deepening, and extending the practice of identity politics is presented, advocated, and justified in the name of pursuing equality, redressing past discrimination, and inclusiveness, and as recognizing, valuing, and strengthening the diversity of Canada
- Critics or opponents of identity politics are denounced by identity politics practitioners and their media allies as bigots motivated by prejudice against the identified group and as "un-Canadian" for their failure to recognize and appreciate the value of equality and diversity.

Identity politics is ideologically driven. As one critical observer describes it:

This ideology is [also] called "social justice," and divides up our society into "privileged oppressors," such as whites and Asians, men, heterosexuals, Christians and Jews, and "oppressed victims," such as people of colour (except East Asians), females, homosexuals, bisexuals, and transsexuals, and Muslims. In this scheme, we are no longer individuals with wishes and hopes, qualities and achievements, but ciphers in a category, and to be treated according to that category.

Allegedly, the "privileged oppressors" have unfairly taken away status and material benefits from the "oppressed victims," enjoying their ill-gotten gains. This injustice is to be corrected by "social justice," which involves reducing the "privileged oppressors" and raising the "oppressed victims." To implement "social justice," members of the "oppressed victim" categories are to be given special favours and benefits, special preferences, while members of the "privileged oppressors" categories are to be denied benefits, viewed with antipathy and aversion, and rejected. These measures are often taken under the guise of "diversity," admitting and supporting members of preferred "underrepresented minorities," while blocking and rejecting others. The majority of people, supposedly given weight and respect in a democracy, are cast in the "social justice" scheme as villains who deserve no consideration."[346]

In critiquing identity politics it again needs to be fully recognized and appreciated that there are groups of Canadians who have been, and may currently be, marginalized, victimized, and prejudicially treated by other Canadians with the concurrence of the state: women and children, indigenous people, immigrants, gays and transgender people, and most recently, people of religious faith.

Both justice and compassion demand that such wrongs be recognized and rectified to the maximum extent possible. The rationale for doing so, however, should rest not on the personal identity of those discriminated against but on the fact that they were unjustly treated. Injustice demands redress regardless of the personal identity of the victim and by ways and means that foster acceptance of people at the most fundamental level—as human beings deserving of respect and fair treatment regardless of their distinguishing personal characteristics rather than because of them.

The weakness and danger of state supported identity politics as currently practiced by the Trudeau administration and others like-minded

346 Salzman, Philip Carl, "Are Educators Enemies of the People," Frontier Centre for Public Policy, April 3, 2019.

is that it divides the population and electorate into an increasing number of minority groups distinguished mainly by their differences rather than their commonalities. This makes the reconciliation of conflicting interests and the achievement of a national or provincial consensus on anything increasingly difficult to attain.

Of course, in one sense, some form of identity politics has always been practiced in Canada. Political parties have long targeted specific groups of people whose support they hope to win by offering various ideological, policy, and financial inducements. The NDP targets union members, the Conservatives target entrepreneurs and business people, the Liberals assiduously court progressives, and all parties have designed strategies and campaigns to win the support of specific demographic, economic, cultural, and ethnic groups, especially when such groups constitute a significant portion of the electorate in particular constituencies.

But the new identity politics is taking this practice to new and disturbing depths and lengths, creating and mining databases containing vast amounts of highly-personal information on the electorate and harnessing social media to craft and target highly-differentiated messages to the targeted groups. The focus of such identity politics is not on identifying and building on what large numbers of voters have in common, but on identifying and exploiting differences, dividing the electorate, subdividing it, and sub-sub-dividing it again.

Politics is becoming too much about creating and manipulating an ever increasing number of minorities defined by ever-narrowing personal criteria—slicing and dicing the electorate in the extreme—rather than on seeking the common ground on which to build a majoritarian consensus on the most important issues of the day. The growth and feeding of this version of identity politics is becoming a threat to democracy itself by making the assembling and servicing of majorities and a majoritarian consensus on major issues increasingly difficult if not impossible to achieve.

It is no exaggeration to say that if a political party wanted to target left-handed Vancouver Island ping pong players, left or right-handedness being a very personal characteristic and ping pong being a game played by only a minority of Canadians, then identity politics technicians could find them.[347] Not only find them, but also tell the party

347 The problem would be finding a politically correct name for them. Not long ago, a group of Canadian editors seriously debated whether to ban the term "ping

exactly where they live, provide a wealth of additional information about them, precisely define the inducements required to get their support, and prescribe what media to employ to communicate appeals for their support. And if anyone should dare to criticize this targeting and wooing of the left-handed Vancouver Island ping pong players community, a plethora of countermeasures can be devised and employed to label and denounce any such critic as a bigoted opponent of equality, inclusiveness, and diversity.

The dangers of identity politics

The expansion of identity politics, especially in a country as diverse as Canada, threatens national unity since the achievement of a national, provincial, or local consensus on anything becomes more and more difficult.

By constantly defining, amplifying, and exploiting fundamental differences among the citizenry, identity politics ultimately undermines democratic governance itself by making the exploitation of conflicting interests, rather than their reconciliation, the focus of democratic politics.

In the end, identity politics even demeans the very groups it targets and professes to serve by reducing the targeted voter to a political commodity, an iconic badge of political correctness that the practitioner of identity politics can wheel out and wear at election time. In a jurisdiction dominated by identity politics, proving that one is 100% supportive of diversity and of every conceivable minority becomes the key to electoral success.

pong" in favour of the term table tennis. The line of argument, presumably derived from political correctness, apparently ran like this: "Ping pong" sounds Chinese; Asians are the largest single group of table tennis players; Asian people may think the term ping pong sounds derogatory; therefore we shouldn't use it. When it was asked whether any real, living, Asian person had ever complained about this, the editors were unable to confirm that anyone had actually done so.

DO SOMETHING!

If you are an executive, manager or researcher with a conservative-oriented think tank or advocacy group:

- Make analysis and exposure of the weaknesses and dangers of identity politics a priority

If you are a member of a group targeted by identity-politics practitioners:

- Publicly express your rejection of identity-politics tactics
- Publicly express your support for unity politics (see below) as a superior alternative

If you are a conservative-oriented candidate for public office, or the campaign manager of such a candidate:

- Offer a strong critique of identity politics as part of your campaign activity
- Offer unity politics (see below) as a superior alternative to identity politics if offered and practiced by your opponents

The dark side of the moon

I have suggested elsewhere[348] that there is merit, no matter what our ideological philosophy or position, in always taking a hard look at what might be called "the dark side of the moon." In other words, whatever doctrine or philosophy of life we may adhere to, be it religious, economic, political, or cultural, we should push it in our mind's eye to its extreme and take a hard look at what that really looks like and the results it may produce. If that image of the extreme is ugly and deformed, and the results of its pursuit are evil and dangerous as the image and products of extremism most frequently are, then that realization ought to

348 *Faith, Leadership, and Public Life*, p. 65

strongly incentivize us to back away and resist moving too far in that direction.

With respect to identity politics, the communist leadership of China is in the process of providing the world with a vivid and frightening example of what identity politics looks like when pushed to the extreme.[349] With the assistance of some of the most sophisticated high-tech firms in the world, the government of China is in the process of constructing a database containing vast amounts of specific, personal, and politically-relevant information on every one of China's 1.3 billion people. By 2020, the intention is that this database would then be mined, using the latest algorithms devised by artificial intelligence, to provide everyone in China a score that would determine their personal status in the eyes of the government, in particular, their political trustworthiness from the government's standpoint.

This so-called "social credit system" will enable the state to know the personal identity of individual persons, and to reward or punish their social, economic, and political behaviours to a degree and on a scale never before made possible until the invention of the internet, handheld communications devices, and all the technologies of the digital world (see more in chapter 5.5).

This is identity politics carried to its ultimate extreme, applied at the individual level, broadened to embrace the entire population, and harnessed to the service of a dictatorial state. If this is the destination to which the assiduous practice of identity politics by governments can lead, surely that realization should strongly incentivize us to back away and strenuously resist further movement in that direction.[350]

---

349 See references to this phenomenon in the next chapter.

350 As pointed out long ago by Francis Crick in his seminal paper "On Protein Synthesis," protein sequences represent the most precise observable register of the physical identity of an organism (including human beings). (Referenced in Quammen, David, *The Tangled Tree,* Simon and Schuster, 2018, p.41). If the current applications and extensions of identity politics are not frightening enough, consider the possibilities of their further extension made possible by advances in genetic science enabling the identification of the individual at the most fundamental level via a simple genetic test performed at birth to determine the unique protein sequence of their genome. And further imagine this information in the hands of a dictatorial government.

Unity Politics: the antidote to identity politics

While others may choose to champion ever-expanding diversity for diversity's sake, and the division of society into special groups defined by their ethnicity, gender, and other personal characteristics, let conservatives champion social cohesion, the values and characteristics we have in common and which unite rather than divide us.

In particular, let conservatives champion acceptance, freedom with accountability, security (personal, social, and economic), opportunity, and citizen-directed democracy as five of the most important pillars of unity politics.[351]

Acceptance of persons as human beings

The more freedom the people of a society have, the more diverse they often become in beliefs, tastes, vocations, behaviors, and lifestyles.

Social cohesion does not require us to endorse or practice the beliefs, tastes, behaviors and lifestyles of others but it does require us to accept the person exercising his or her freedoms in these ways. Acceptance of others because they are human, and because, in our case, they are fellow Canadians, is a fundamental precept of unity politics.

Most importantly, a clear distinction needs to be drawn between the universality of what I mean by conservative acceptance and the practice of unity politics, and the narrow and hypocritical inclusiveness of identity politics as promoted and practiced by most identitarians. For example, the inclusiveness promoted and practiced by the former NDP government in Alberta was not inclusive of all Albertans. It excluded, and in some cases even demonized, heterosexuals, males, owners and investors in corporations, the business class in general, and people of religious faith. While professing to abhor and target prejudice and

351 My own experience with new Canadians is that when you ask them what aspects of Canadian life were most meaningful to them when they first arrived, the most frequent responses were acceptance (the fact that they were accepted) and safety. Then once they became secure from an acceptance and security standpoint, they began to appreciate more the freedom and opportunity Canada offers. Canadians who have lived in Canada all their lives are far more likely to mention freedom and social/economic security as most meaningful and the values most broadly shared by all Canadians, new and old.

intolerance in others, this type of identitarianism simply substitutes its own set of prejudices for the alleged prejudices of those it attacks, all the while loudly declaring that it is prejudice free. It is this hypocritical aspect of the identitarian position that is one of its most obnoxious and repugnant features.[352]

Freedom with accountability

Has not the desire to live in freedom been the motivation which has brought generations of people from all over the globe to seek a new life in Canada from the very first settlers from France and Britain to the most recent immigrants and refugees from countries torn by war and/or ruled by dictatorial regimes? Is not the maintenance and advancement of freedom something on which we can all unite, regardless of our differences?

What precisely do we mean by freedom? How about uniting around what the Canadian Charter of Rights and Freedoms defines as fundamental freedoms,[353] in particular, freedom of conscience, religion, belief, thought, opinion, and expression.

352 One is reminded of Abraham Lincoln's comment to the effect that he would rather live in a country where they made no pretense of believing in freedom and tolerance than to live in one that professed to be free and tolerant but which in fact was not. Where people openly hold certain prejudices and try to justify or defend them, one can at least argue and reason with them in an attempt to change their minds. But where prejudiced and intolerant persons will not even acknowledge their prejudices and claim to be prejudice free, there is no starting point for addressing the issue. What Lincoln had in mind when he made this observation was an American political group named the "Know Nothings", who were strongly prejudiced against immigrants to the United States but if asked what their position was on immigration professed to "know nothing" about what the inquirer was asking about.

353 As discussed earlier, the use of the adjective "fundamental" in the Charter to describe these freedoms must mean something. According to the dictionary, fundamental means "serving as a foundation or basis" and this is the meaning we should give to these freedoms which serve as a foundation of all other rights. Liberals and some court justices may argue that we should not recognize any hierarchy of rights in the constitution, but let conservatives especially take the position that the fundamental freedoms are foundational: their recognition, preservation, and advancement underlies, but also supersedes, the recognition of all other rights, even those equality rights most often cited by the practitioners of identity politics.

How about also uniting around a concept which the Charter fails to mention but which history has shown to be inseparable from the preservation and expansion of freedom? Namely, the acceptance of responsibility for the exercise of our freedoms. This acceptance of responsibility means accepting the Rule of Law as the principal means of holding us accountable for the exercise of our freedoms.

Each of us can and should exercise our freedom of conscience, but we should be prepared to accept responsibility for doing so. If in extreme cases our conscience calls on us to break the law we should be prepared to accept the legal consequences of doing so, although a wiser course is to use our democratic freedoms to try to change the laws we consider unjust.

If the exercise of our freedom of expression permits us to slander others or propagate untruths, we should be prepared to be held to account not just by those we slander or mislead, but by the state. Conservatives should be in the forefront in insisting that society demand enforcement by the state of accountability and responsibility for the exercise of freedoms.

Physical, social and economic security

Is not the desire for physical, social and economic security something that all Canadians share, regardless of our other differences, and again something which most of our ancestors sought in first coming to Canada? Is not the maintenance and advancement of security something on which we can all unite?

By maintaining and advancing physical security, I mean supporting and strengthening law and order, our law enforcement and judicial systems, and national defense. By maintaining and advancing social security, I mean striving to achieve a basic but ever-rising level of health, education, and social-assistance services accessible to all. By maintaining and advancing economic security, I mean resisting fiscal irresponsibility on the part of governments, socially irresponsible behaviours on the part of corporations and unions, and supporting and strengthening the exercise and distribution of the tools of wealth creation which generate jobs and incomes.

Opportunity

Ask any recent immigrant to Canada what they were looking for and hoped to achieve by coming here and the likelihood is that the vast majority will mention one or more of the preceding headings, often in the following order: acceptance, security, and freedom.

But if they have or expect to have children, most often the first thing mentioned will be the opportunity for my children to experience acceptance, security, freedom and the many other benefits that opportunity makes possible.

Surely if we are progressive in the sense of looking ahead, one of the goals and pursuits which ought to draw us together, one of the most prominent principles of unity politics, should be providing opportunity for the next generation.

Citizen-directed democracy

What political system is most conducive to providing and advancing these principles of unity politics?

If the provision of physical, social, and economic security and opportunity were the only requirements, it might well be argued that an authoritarian regime with a benign dictator and an orderly succession process might outperform citizen-directed democracies. But if we want to be treated as free citizens with rights and free will and not as instruments of a huge collective run by the state—if we want security *and* freedom—then it is my belief that only citizen-directed democracy, not state-directed governance, can get us there (More on this in the next chapter).

If conservatives wish to counter the pernicious practice and influence of identity politics in Canada let us do so by offering, strengthening, and advancing "unity politics," the five main pillars of which are: acceptance, freedom with accountability, security, opportunity, and citizen-directed democracy.

DO SOMETHING!

If you are an executive, manager or researcher with a conservative-oriented think tank:

- Make strengthening the intellectual underpinnings of unity politics, the defense and advocacy of freedom, accountability, acceptance, security, and citizen directed democracy, a priority

If you are a conservative-oriented candidate for public office, or the campaign manager of such a candidate:

- Include a strong unity politics plank in your election platform
- Offer it as a superior alternative to the identity politics practiced by your opponents.

If you are a voter who prefers a political focus on what we share in common rather than characteristics that divide us; if you prefer the consensus-building function of majoritarian politics to the exploitive practice of minority politics:

- Reject leaders, parties, and candidates who practice identity politics
- Support leaders, parties, and candidates who practice unity politics

5.5 Counter international ideological competition

On the several occasions I visited China as a political leader and once as a private citizen with political interests, my visits, while organized in part by the Canadian embassy in Beijing, always involved extensive contact with the International Liaison Department of the Communist Party.[354]

For example, on my first visit as Leader of the Official Opposition in 1998, our party was met at the airport by several officials of the department, one of whom I knew well enough to test his sense of humor. Although our itinerary had been all planned in advance, he asked as a courtesy whether there was anything else or anybody else I would like to see. To which I replied, "Yes, I'd like to meet my equivalent, the Leader of the Official Opposition in China." He smiled, huddled briefly with several of his colleagues, and then replied: "We think if there is such a person he's in jail, or should be. But seriously, the one person we can think of in a position similar to yours is Mr. Martin Lee in Hong Kong." (At that time Martin Lee, someone whom I greatly admired and had the privilege of meeting on several occasions, was the founder and leader of the Democratic Party in Hong Kong and an elected member of the Hong Kong Legislative Council).

But all pleasantries aside, at every opportunity on this visit and others, our Chinese communist hosts pressed their position, sometimes vaguely, sometimes more explicitly, that a state-directed economy and state-directed governance, as organized and practiced by the Communist Party and government of China, were superior to, and would ultimately

---

354 This is a department of the Communist Party of China whose role is to establish and maintain relations with other political parties all over the world. For some reason, it took an inordinate interest in the Reform Party of Canada, likely because it assumed that, as a new party, we were more easily influenced than traditional western parties and made a major effort to be and stay in contact with us.

triumph over, market-directed capitalism and citizen-directed democracy as promoted and practiced in most of the western world.

Fast forward to October 18, 2017, to the fifty-page report by President Xi Jinping to the 19th National Congress of the Communist Party of China,[355] in which both these concepts are even further developed and more vigorously advanced today than they were when I made my first political visit to China. Both these concepts are now developed and promoted to the point where it is my conviction that the greatest ideological competitions of the twenty-first-century will be between:

- State-directed capitalism, as represented and promoted by the Communist party and government of China, and market-directed capitalism as represented and promoted by at least some of the western democracies
- State-directed democracy, again as represented and promoted by the Communist party and government of China, and citizen-directed democracy as represented and defended by the western democracies

Historically, it was the Great Wall of China that once kept China isolated and insulated from the rest of the world. Today it is the Great Web of China, woven from the silken but strong-as-steel threads of trade, finance, and government–to–government relations that extends China's influence to dozens of countries in Asia, Africa, the Middle East, and South America. In all these countries, China consistently offers state-directed capitalism and state-directed governance as superior and more stable alternatives to the market-driven capitalism and citizen-directed democracy offered by the West.

This being the case, it is therefore incumbent upon western political leaders and citizens, especially free-market liberals and conservatives and small d-democrats of whatever stripe:

- To thoroughly understand the nature of the ideological challenge which Chinese Communism represents on these two fronts, including the Chinese Communist critique of market-directed capitalism and citizen-directed democracy

355 Two sources of the report are: http://www.xinhuanet.com/english/special/2017-11/03/c_136725942.htm, http://www.chinadaily.com.cn/china/19thcpcnational congress/2017-11/04/content_34115212.htm

- To significantly bolster our own capacities to defend, strengthen, and advance our representation and practice of market-driven capitalism and citizen-directed democracy

State-directed capitalism (SDC)

In a 2010 book, political scientist Ian Bremmer[356] defines state-directed capitalism as follows:

> "In this system, governments use various kinds of state-owned companies to manage the exploitation of resources that they consider the state's crown jewels and to create and maintain large numbers of jobs. They use select privately-owned companies to dominate certain economic sectors. They use so-called sovereign wealth funds to invest their extra cash in ways that maximize the state's profits. In all three cases, the state is using markets to create wealth that can be directed as political officials see fit. And in all three cases, the ultimate motive is not economic [maximizing growth] but political [maximizing the state's power and the leadership's chances of survival]. This is a form of capitalism but one in which the state acts as the dominant economic player and uses markets primarily for political gain."

Throughout President Xi's lengthy and comprehensive Report to the 19th National Congress, he constantly uses the obligatory phrase "socialism with Chinese characteristics" to describe the guiding philosophy of the Communist Party. But when he comes to describing the accelerated efforts to improve China's economy, which he now describes as "the socialist market economy," he does so in language and terms that could have been taken straight out of the economic manifesto of any western free-enterprise party:

> "In our economic reforms, we must concentrate on improving the property rights system and ensuring the market-based allocation of factors of production, so that property rights act as effective

356 Bremner, Ian, *The End of the Free Market: Who Wins the War Between States and Corporations*, Penguin Books, 2010.

incentives . . . We will do away with regulations and practices that impede the development of a unified market and fair competition, support the growth of private business and stimulate the vitality of various market entities. . . We will promote the development of a multilevel capital market . . . and see that interest rates and exchange rates become more market-based."

This all sounds like the description of a market-based capitalistic system, with one all-important exception. The "we" who will initiate and direct all this economic activity, market-oriented as it may appear, is the state, the Chinese government under the dictatorial, ironclad, and unquestioned leadership of the Communist Party.

To again quote from President Xi's 2017 Report, which refers to "the Party" no less than 165 times: "The defining feature of socialism with Chinese characteristics is the leadership of the Communist Party of China; the greatest strength of the system is the leadership of the Communist Party of China; the Party is the highest force for leadership. . . [We must] uphold absolute Party Leadership over the people's armed forces...Every one of us in the Party must do more to uphold Party leadership and the Chinese socialist system, and resolutely oppose all statements and actions that undermine, distort, or negate them."

Some insightful political commentators such as Niall Ferguson[357] consider it an oversimplification to divide the world into market-capitalist and state-capitalist camps, and point out that all nations struggle to find the right balance between free-market forces and state-intervention/control of the economy. But from my perspective, the distinguishing political reality with respect to China is that the Communist Party and government has dictatorial powers to enforce its version of capitalism and to prohibit alternative versions, whereas the governments of the

---

357 In his article "We're All State Capitalists Now," Niall Ferguson, British historian and Laurence A. Tisch Professor of History at Harvard University, warns against "an unhelpful oversimplification to divide the world into 'market capitalist' and 'state capitalist' camps. The reality, he maintains, is that most countries are arranged along a spectrum where both the intent and the extent of state intervention in the economy vary: "...The real contest of our time is not between a state-capitalist China and a market-capitalist America, with Europe somewhere in the middle. It is a contest that goes on within all three regions as we all struggle to strike the right balance between the economic institutions that generate wealth and the political institutions that regulate and redistribute it."

western democracies do not. This is a fundamentally important distinction between the western economies and that controlled and promoted by the Communist Party of China.

Regardless of whose analysis is most accurate, state-directed capitalism, especially as promoted and practiced by the Chinese Communist government and its camp followers in the western democracies, is a major economic and political challenge to be reckoned with. And it must be conceded that its accomplishments thus far make it a formidable challenger indeed.

From 1989 to 2018, China's economic growth rate averaged almost 10% per annum, slowing to approximately 7% in 2018, but still a much higher growth rate than that of any of the more mature economies of the western democracies.[358] In the words of President Xi:

> "The [Chinese] economy has maintained a medium-high growth rate, making China a leader among the major economies. With the gross domestic product rising from 54 trillion to 80 trillion yuan, China has maintained its position as the world's second-largest economy and contributed more than 30% of global economic growth."

China can claim that its state-directed capitalism under the leadership of the Communist Party has lifted some 700-million[359] impoverished people out of abject poverty over the relatively short time period of five years.[360] It can further claim that this is a far more impressive track record than that achieved over the same time period in the rest of the world where the tools of market-driven capitalism have been employed in conjunction with western-conceived agencies such as the United Nations, the World Bank, and the International Monetary Fund and where foreign aid has often been made conditional upon the host country accepting western conceptions of democracy and human rights.[361]

---

358 See page 15 of the appendix of the WTO report at https://www.wto.org/english/news_e/pres18_e/pr820_e.pdf

359 See https://www.un.org/development/desa/dspd/wp-content/uploads/sites/22/2018/05/31.pdf

360 See https://www.un.org/development/desa/dspd/wp-content/uploads/sites/22/2018/05/31.pdf

361 An alternative perspective on these claims is as follows: "But it was China, not the U.S. economy, that prospered on Americans' spending binge. The world's most populous country grew at double-digit rates for much of the 2000s. And while

The Chinese government also points constantly to:

- The relative stability of its economy (e.g., that it was not rocked by the speculation induced 2008 financial crisis which so disrupted the western economies)
- Its ability to build infrastructure, such as highways, railways, and pipelines to move natural resources to tidewater and markets, more quickly and efficiently than in the west[362]
- Its willingness to invest heavily in such infrastructure and resource development around the world with no restrictive human rights or environmental protection conditions attached to such investments nor to its foreign aid support.

These three impressive factors, growth, stability, and the capacity to facilitate rapid infrastructure and resource development, make China's state-directed capitalism an extremely attractive model for nations with underdeveloped or very slowly developing economies. If the political systems of those nations are also susceptible to authoritarian leadership, as in much of Africa, Asia, and parts of South America, the combination of state-directed capitalism with state-directed democracy is doubly attractive. This explains, to a large degree, China's growing success in making friends and influencing people all over the globe.

the U.S. savings rate hovered around fifteen percent of GDP, China's savings rate increased from 38 percent in 2000 to 54 percent in 2006. China's savings are heavily skewed toward risk-free assets, perhaps because the Chinese are culturally more risk-averse, but also because the country's financial markets are still underdeveloped and not fully liberalized... One consolation is that the past decade of loose living in the United States and Europe has done much to lift hundreds of millions of people in China and India out of poverty. No development aid program can stake a similar claim." See https://foreignpolicy.com/2012/01/17/how-chinas-boom-caused-the-financial-crisis/

362 At the close of the 2018 China-Africa Forum for Cooperation (FOCAC) summit held in Beijing, President Xi Jinping announced that China had set up a new R900 billion ($60 billion) kitty meant for Africa's development as part of a raft of new measures to strengthen Sino-Africa ties. . . The fund, which is broken down into several parts, will be channeled to projects aligned to the Chinese government's Belt and Road Initiative covering telecommunications, construction of roads, bridges and sea ports, energy, and human capacity development. See https://www.businessinsider.co.za/here-are-150-million-rand-projects-in-africa-funded-by-china-2018-9

The challenge for the supporters of market-directed capitalism

Champions of a market-directed economy need to identify and vigorously expose the weaknesses and dangers of a state-directed economy, in particular its invariable tendency to concentrate dictatorial powers, political as well as economic, in the hands of the state.

More importantly, champions of market-directed capitalism need to remedy its weaknesses and lever its strengths to make it a more effective and persuasive alternative to the Chinese model.

In a market-driven economy the laws of supply and demand, the profit motivation of investors and entrepreneurs, and the personal satisfaction motives of consumers, drive economic decision making by economic actors and organizations which are relatively free to make those decisions. The role of government is then largely focused on creating a legal and policy framework that facilitates market-driven economic growth, constraining socially unacceptable market practices through regulation, providing services the market is unable or unwilling to provide, and redistributing a portion of the wealth generated by the market economy through taxation. This is a substantial role for government, but not nearly as all-embracing or coercive as that assumed by the Chinese government in China's economy or by governments in other countries that emulate the Chinese model.

In promoting the advantages of market-driven capitalism over state-directed capitalism we especially need to avoid the ineptitude and hypocrisy of the inexperienced Trudeau administration on this front. Last year (2019), I attended a conference of Indigenous leaders interested in the development of transportation infrastructure corridors and projects on aboriginal lands. Not surprisingly, a Chinese investment and consulting service firm was also in attendance, advising these leaders that Chinese financing was available for whatever projects they had in mind. A representative of the Chinese government was also present, so I asked him, "What is the relationship between this Chinese firm, the capital it represents, and the Chinese government?" To which he replied: "Our companies need to obey Chinese laws just as yours need to obey Canadian laws. But otherwise they are completely independent of the Chinese government." Then he added: "They are not as closely related to the Chinese government as SNC Lavalin[363] is to yours."

---

363 This at the time the Trudeau government was embroiled in controversy over the Prime Minister's office intervening in the decision of the Justice department as to whether or not to prosecute Montreal-based SNC Lavalin on charges of engaging in bribery and corrupt practices in order to secure lucrative contracts in Libya.

Time and space in this book do not permit a thorough description or analysis of the strengths and weaknesses of market-driven economies. Fortunately, however, there is an abundance of literature on this subject. Suffice it to say here that if we want to defend and promote market-based capitalism we need to nurture and grow what it does well and reform what it does not do well.

For example, we need to study and act on the writings and urgings of analysts and critics of capitalism, especially those who advocate measures to break up monopolies and increase competition, to broaden the ownership of capitalist economies, to secure a broader distribution of the capitalist tools of wealth creation, and to harness market mechanisms to environmental conservation. Strengthening market-directed capitalism should be "mission critical" for both liberals and conservatives who believe in freedom of economic thought and action. A major portion of the platforms of professedly free-enterprise political parties in the western democracies should be focused heavily on this objective.

DO SOMETHING!

If you are a political or business leader, an elected official, or a citizen who believes in the efficacy and benefits of a market-directed economy:

- Become familiar with the strengths and weaknesses of state-directed capitalism as defined and promoted by the Communist Party and government of China, and use your influence to warn against its adoption by this or other countries
- Acknowledge that there are defects and weaknesses in the scope and practices of market-directed capitalism and use your influence to champion reforms which will make it superior to, and more competitive with, state-directed capitalism

State-directed democracy (SDD)

The "People's Democratic Dictatorship"[364] was a phrase incorporated into the Constitution of the People's Republic of China by Mao Zedong, the first leader of the Communist Party of China.[365] According to this concept, the Communist party and government, by definition, represent the highest interests of the Chinese people and act on their behalf. But in doing so, both the party and the government must possess and use dictatorial powers to overcome and neutralize "reactionary" forces.

These dictatorial powers have consistently been used against Chinese citizens seeking to acquire democratic freedoms and rights more akin to those possessed by the people of the western democracies. The use of oppressive force includes the brutal suppression of the May Fourth Movement which led to the Tiananmen Square protests in 1989. It includes more recent campaigns to constrain and undermine democratic leaders in Hong Kong; to suppress Tibetan Buddhists, Muslim Uighurs of northwest China and members of the Falun Gong; and to "regulate" the activities of non-members of the Communist Party in accordance with party dictates.[366] All of this backed up by the largest and most intrusive secret police apparatus in the world.

Despite all of this, the current Chinese leadership insist that China is a democracy, but a form of democracy, fundamentally different from and superior to the citizen-directed democracy of the west.

---

364 The term "democratic dictatorship" strikes most westerners as oxymoronic. And yet within the conceptual framework of the Communist Party of China it is not regarded as self-contradictory at all. The phrase occurs again in President Xi's Report to the 19th Party Congress when he says: "China is a socialist country of people's democratic dictatorship under the leadership of the working class. . ."

365 See the Constitution of the People's Republic of China. https://www.purdue.edu/crcs/wp-content/uploads/2014/04/Constitution.pdf

Article 28 of that Constitution declares that: The state maintains public order and suppresses treasonable and other counterrevolutionary activities; it penalizes actions that endanger public security and disrupt the socialist economy and other criminal activities, and punishes and reforms criminals

366 For example, in discussing the role of religionists and intellectuals in Chinese society, President Xi says: "We will fully implement the Party's basic policy on religious affairs, uphold the principle that religions in China must be Chinese in orientation, and *provide active guidance* to religions so that they can adapt themselves to socialist society. We will *encourage intellectuals who are not Party members* and people belonging to new social groups to play the important roles they have to play in building socialism with Chinese characteristics."

In the following quotations from President Xi's Report, note the adjectives he first uses in conjunction with the word "democracy" and then the use of the word democracy itself as an adjective qualifying dictatorship and centralism:

"Steady progress has been made in enhancing *socialist* democracy, *intra-party* democracy has been expanded, and *socialist consultative* democracy is flourishing . . . China is a socialist country of *people's democratic dictatorship* under the leadership of the working class. . . The primary task of political Party building is to insure that the whole Party obeys the Central Committee and upholds its authority and centralized, unified leadership. . . We must improve and implement the systems of *democratic centralism* and *centralism guided democracy.*"

As the Chinese may well point out, western-style democracy has produced the eccentricities and instability of a Donald Trump administration in America, Brexit in Great Britain, and weak and ineffective governments in Canada and Europe, whereas the Chinese system has produced a global statesman of the caliber of Xi Jinping and one of the world's most stable and effective governmental administrations.

According to President Xi, the success of the Communist Party and government of China "means that the path, the theory, the system, and the culture of socialism with Chinese characteristics . . . [is] blazing a new trail for other developing countries to achieve modernization." Hence, as part of the Chinese government's global initiative, nation states in Africa, the Middle East, South America, and Asia are being increasingly challenged to choose between Chinese styled "democracy" and western style democracy. For many, especially those who have never known genuine, citizen-directed democracy, the Chinese model is, understandably, increasingly attractive.

State-directed democracy 2.0

As previously mentioned, there is another recently acquired feature of state-directed democracy that President Xi did not mention in his 2017 Report, but which may well prove to be its most disturbing and pernicious aspect. The October 2017 edition of *Wired* aptly described it with the headline: "Big Data meets Big Brother as China moves to rate its citizens."[367]

The magazine references a document[368] called "Planning for the Construction of a Social Credit[369] System" first published by the State Council of China in June of 2014. The plan is to provide everyone in China with a score that would determine their trustworthiness in the eyes of the government. Citizens with a high score, determined by who their friends are and who they stay away from, what they read or don't read, what they have or have not posted on social media, how they spend their incomes, whether or not they support the positions of the Communist Party, are to be rewarded by access to better educational opportunities for themselves and their children, access to better jobs and housing, greater freedom to travel, and other advantages yet to be promised. Citizens with a low score will find themselves increasingly restricted from a host of services and opportunities because their tastes, beliefs and activities have rendered them untrustworthy in the eyes of the state.

In a sense the "Chinese social credit system" will enable the state to know the identity of individual persons, and to reward or punish their social, economic, and political behaviour to a degree and on a scale never before made possible until the invention of the internet, handheld communication devices, and all the technologies of the digital world.[370]

367 Botsman, Rachel, "Big Data meets Big Brother as China moves to rate its citizens," *Wired* UK, October 21, 2017. Also see https://www.channelnewsasia.com/news/commentary/china-great-leap-forward-in-data-protection-11429624

368 See https://chinacopyrightandmedia.wordpress.com/2014/06/14/planning-outline-for-the-construction-of-a-social-credit-system-2014-2020/

369 William Aberhart, my father, and other members and supporters of Alberta's Social Credit Party would roll over in their graves if they realized how this term has been expropriated and perverted by the Communist Party and government of China.

370 It should also be noted that, at the same time the Chinese government is developing and expanding its "social credit" system, it is launching a major effort to protect the data and privacy of Chinese citizens from misuse and invasion by private companies, in particular those which are internationally based. See Chalk, William, "China's Great Leap Forward in Data Protection," Commentary, CNA, https://www.channelnewsasia.com/news/commentary/china-great-leap-forward-in-data-protection-11429624. What is conspicuously absent from these privacy protection measures is the protection of the data and privacy of the Chinese people from the invasion of their personal space by their own government.

Again, this is identity politics pushed down to the individual level, broadened to embrace the entire population, and harnessed to the service of state-directed democracy and state-directed capitalism. Let us call a spade a spade: it is monstrous. *Nineteen Eighty-Four*[371] on steroids.

Jack Ma, founder of Alibaba, the online platform with more than half a billion users, has enthusiastically pointed out: "Big Data will make the market smarter and make it possible to plan and predict market forces so as to allow us to finally achieve a planned economy."[372]

Make it possible for whom to plan and predict? The Communist party and government of China and its favored political and economic actors.

The challenge for the supporters of citizen-directed democracy

The challenge for those of us who believe in citizen-directed democracy is to remedy its weaknesses and to strengthen its institutional embodiments so as to make it more effective and attractive than its state-directed competitor. This is the primary object of the *Do Something!* proposals of the previous chapters directed to all small-d democrats in Canada whatever our other political differences may be.

Some developers of advanced technologies[373] would suggest that a major aspect of this strengthening involves harnessing big data and all the tools of the digital world to the practice of citizen-directed democracy, not as the Chinese Communists are doing with their Social Credit system, but in non-coercive ways that respect the privacy and rights

---

371 Among the seminal texts of the twentieth-century, *Nineteen Eighty-Four* is a rare work that grows more haunting as its futuristic purgatory becomes more real. Published in 1949, the book offers political satirist George Orwell's nightmarish vision of a totalitarian, bureaucratic world and one poor stiff's attempt to find individuality. The brilliance of the novel is Orwell's prescience of modern life: the ubiquity of television, the distortion of the language, and his ability to construct such a thorough version of hell. Required reading for students since it was published, it ranks among the most terrifying novels ever written.

372 Quoted in Botsman, *Wired* UK, October 21, 2017.

373 See for example, Leonard, Andrew, "Meet the Man with a Radical Plan for Blockchain Voting," Backchannel, August 16, 2018. This article explores the ideas of a political theorist, Santiago Siri of Democracy Earth, who maintains that crypto-voting can make democracy much more citizen directed than it is today.

of citizens in free societies while positively incentivizing constructive democratic involvement.[374] Only time will tell whether and how this might be done, but it is a proposition deserving of thorough and careful examination.

In competing politically with the Chinese models of state-directed capitalism and democracy, both internationally and at home, we need to more aggressively identify and communicate the weaknesses and dangers of the Chinese models and the communist regime promoting them. These include the following:

1. *The ultimate instability of dictatorial leadership and one-party states*

Dictatorships and one-party states are inherently more unstable than constitutional monarchies or democracies. China has yet to prove that a continuously orderly (non-violent) transition of leadership at the top of the Communist Party is feasible in the long run[375] or that its system has the capacity to self-correct humanely when the one-party leadership of the state itself goes off track as in the Cultural Revolution.[376]

374 At a recent conference on populism, the question arose as to how best to encourage the individual members of populist movements to direct their energies toward constructive goals and behaviours, one participant suggested that perhaps the big databases and data-mining techniques which are now readily available in democratic countries could be used to more precisely identify individual participants in populist movements and offer them rewards for actions and behaviors conducive to good citizenship as defined by western democratic standards, just as the Communist Party and government of China are using their Social Credit system to incentivize trustworthy participation by citizens in state-directed democracy. An intriguing suggestion but one fraught with both positive and negative possibilities.

375 The recent transitions have been relatively orderly and peaceful, but not the transition from Mao to his successors. And by the long run, I don't simply mean a few decades. I mean the long run in the sense Chou En Lai meant when Henry Kissinger asked him about the impact of the French Revolution, and Chou reportedly answered, "It's probably too soon to tell."

376 The Cultural Revolution, launched by Mao Zedong in 1966 and lasting ten years, ruthlessly purged anti and non-communist elements from Chinese society in order to re-establish Mao's authority after the failures his Great Leap Forward policies. The violence and disruption it unleashed, negatively affected China politically and economically for many years.

2.   The Communist obsession with uniformity and conformity

The over-emphasis on the need for uniformity and conformity which is an inherent characteristic of Chinese communism tends to ignore significant regional differences which if denied and unaccommodated can tear a large country apart.

As Canadians are well aware, no large country covering hundreds of thousands of square miles of territory with great variations in geography and demographics can grow without regional differences, some of which can become severe enough to threaten the political unity of the country itself.

Thus when Bob Mills, the Reform Party's first Foreign Affairs critic in parliament, and I visited China on our first official visit as elected MP's in 1996, we made a point of asking our hosts to what extent regional differences were a problem in China and, if so, how did the government deal with them.

We were vaguely aware that China had been torn by numerous civil wars in the past,[377] the last (1945–49) being the war between the Kuomintang-led nationalist government of Chiang Kai-shek and the Communist Party of China under Mao Zedong. But our hosts continuously asserted that there were no serious regional tensions in China at all. Chinese communist ideology acknowledged cultural and linguistic differences, but, according to our hosts, none of these threatened the unity of the state due to the universal commitment of all Chinese to "socialism with Chinese characteristics."

Being polite Canadians, we didn't argue. But a little later at lunch with half a dozen officials, Bob just happened to ask who had the best cooks, Beijing or Shanghai? At which point, a furious debate broke out at the table. No regional differences, eh?

At the same lunch, we had an opportunity to raise regional differences in Canada in the hope that this would encourage the Chinese

---

377   For example, while Canada was moving toward responsible government and confederation in the mid nineteenth-century, China was wracked (from 1850 to 1864) with total civil war between the established Manchu-led Qing dynasty and the Taiping Heavenly Kingdom under Hong Xiuquan (a self-proclaimed convert to Christianity). The conflict, which was the largest military conflict of the nineteenth-century, ranks as one of the bloodiest wars in human history with estimates of the war dead ranging from 20 to 70 million, to as high as 100 million, with millions more displaced.

to talk more freely about theirs. Our communications director, Larry Welch, who had accompanied Bob and I on our trip, inadvertently put rice in his tea cup instead of his rice bowl. Which prompted Bob to "explain" that Larry came from a culturally-challenged part of Canada called Ontario where some people didn't even know the difference between a tea cup and a rice bowl. On the other hand, Bob explained, he and I came from a more culturally advanced part of the country, Alberta, where we would never make the mistake of putting rice in a tea cup. For some reason, this exchange greatly amused our hosts, who for the rest of the trip made a point of reminding Larry of the difference between a tea cup and a rice bowl. But none of this, changed their official position that there were no serious regional differences in China.

Politically, in a large and diverse country, it is a mistake to over-emphasize regional differences, but a greater mistake to deny their existence or seriousness because the ideology and party line of the dominant political class insists on such denial. National unity, in my opinion, is not nearly as secure in China as the Communist Party and government maintain.

3. The Achilles' heel of Chinese Communist human rights

The Supreme Court of Canada insists that there is no "hierarchy of rights" established by our Charter of Rights and Freedoms: fundamental freedoms, democratic rights, legal rights, equality rights, and linguistic rights and freedoms are all of equal status and the affirmation of one category of rights cannot be used to override other rights guaranteed by the constitution. But not so with the Chinese communist conception of rights and freedoms.

One of the purposes of our first trip to China was to inquire after the fate of persons, small-d democrats, arrested at Tiananmen Square in 1989. We happened to get into a discussion of this subject, among others, with a high-ranking official of the Ministry of Foreign Economic Relations and Trade. She was relatively young, had received her higher education in the United States, and was the type of official whom you might have suspected of being at least half sympathetic to the Tiananmen Square demonstrators. She was also quite open and frank in her interpretation of events. She said she believed in "human rights" and the Chinese conception of rights and freedoms which acknowledges such rights as freedom of conscience and freedom of expression. But, as she explained, these rights are part of a hierarchy, and at the top of the hierarchy, for understandable historical reasons given China's history of famines and civil unrest, are the right to eat and the right to order.

When the Tiananmen demonstrations broke out, she said that at first her sympathies were with the student demonstrators. But as soon as the unrest started to prompt the hoarding of food, something the government and her department monitored closely, and once the exercise of freedom of conscience and political expression began to threaten the right to eat and the right to order, her sympathies swung completely over to the right of the state to take whatever measures were necessary, including the use of force, to bring such political activity to an abrupt halt.

Whether or not it is appropriate to recognize a hierarchy of human rights is a subject which can be profitably debated. But in China's case, the more prosperous the country becomes, the younger the population becomes, the more that famine becomes a distant memory, the less the right-to-eat is threatened by the exercise of freedom of conscience and political expression, the harder and harder it will become for communist officials to justify the curtailment of such rights and the easier it should become to attach greater weight to those freedoms which are the underpinnings of citizen-directed democracy, not state-directed democracy.

4.   Environmentalism as a threat to communist materialism.

My last visit to China occurred after I had left parliament and founded the Manning Foundation for Democratic Education and the Manning Centre for Building Democracy, both of which encourage participants and small-d democrats to prepare themselves for participation in our democratic processes and institutions. I had kept up my contacts with the International Liaison Department of the Communist Party and so inquired whether they would arrange for me to visit some of the think tanks and training institutes used by the Communist Party to prepare their officials for political office at the municipal, state, and national levels. Somewhat to my surprise, they agreed to do so and in July 2008, I visited several of the Party's major think-tank and training institutions in Beijing, Shanghai, and Tianjin.

This is not the place to report on all the events and findings of that trip but suffice to say, the time and effort that the Communist Party of China invests in developing the knowledge and skills of its political practitioners is far greater and far more systematic[378] than the limited and sporadic investments western political parties make in our political practitioners.

Yet another reason to plead with Canadian democrats and the supporters of market-directed capitalism to vastly increase our commitment to investments in democracy and market-based solutions to public problems if we wish to remain competitive on the world stage with the politicos of China.

At one of the think tanks I visited, I posed a rather convoluted question to a Chinese scholar which took some time to frame, and I wasn't quite sure that the translator was accurately transmitting what I was trying to ask. The essence of my question, with an explanatory preamble, was as follows. "Suppose that in the heyday of the Roman Empire, when the regime of the Caesars was the dominant world power, the leadership had held an in-depth session to determine whether there were any serious threats to the continued leadership and dominance of the Roman Emperors. The participants might have speculated that there was a possible threat from a resurgence of the Persian empire to the east; they might have worried about the growing incursions of the northern barbarians; they might even have speculated about the dangers of a rebellion from within by the growing slave population and a restless under-class. But it is highly unlikely that they would ever have guessed that a follower of an obscure religious sect in a backwater province of the Empire, the followers of a leader[379] whose public career lasted only thirty-six months before his execution, would a few centuries later come to occupy the throne of Caesar and transform their Empire into what would become known as The Holy Roman Empire."

And so, I concluded, "was it possible, that way down in the cultural depths and political weeds of China, there could be some idea or group

---

378 Of course, it should be pointed out that for a Communist party official in China, attendance at these training institutions and sessions is mandatory not voluntary. In Canada there is no mandatory requirement for any candidate for public office to receive any sort of training whatsoever, but it has been suggested that perhaps this should be changed. For example, requiring that if you want to be the official candidate of a party, you must have completed some sort of "basic training" offered and required by that party.

379 The leaders I was referring to were, of course, Jesus of Nazareth and Constantine, the first Christian Emperor of Rome.

that, with the passage of time, could actually displace the ideology and personnel of the Communist Party of China?"

The question was a rambling one and the scholar took a long time to think before answering. (I was accompanied at the time by a Communist Party official so I'm sure this created a further reason for the scholar to think carefully before replying). But when he finally did, his answer surprised me.

He said, if there was such an idea or group it might be associated with the environmental movement. But then he hastened to add that the Party was well aware of the growing interest and concern about environmental issues on the part of the Chinese people, and both it and the government were taking positive and aggressive steps to address those concerns.[380] Thus environmentalism, in whatever form it manifested itself, really posed no threat whatsoever to the rule and role of the Party or the government.

Perhaps the scholar is right, but I'm not so sure. Genuine concern for the environment and measures to insure its conservation and protection are at fundamental odds with the materialism that is at the heart of both communism and capitalism. But communism with its ideological rigidity and suppression of freedom may have even more difficulty in the long run in adjusting to the environmental challenge, and its inability to do so may be a threat to its ultimate longevity.

5.   *The rejection and suppression of theistic religions*

During another meeting on my trip to explore the infrastructure in place to develop the intellectual capital and human resources for the Communist Party of China, I raised with a Communist party official

---

380 This it certainly has. President Xi's 2017 Report contains statements (backed by major environmental protection initiatives in the real world) such as the following: "We have devoted serious energy to ecological conservation . . . the entire Party and the whole country have become more purposeful and active in pursuing green development . . . building an ecological civilization is vital . . . we must cherish the environment as we cherish our lives . . . we will continue our campaign to prevent and control air pollution . . . we will carry out major projects and restore key ecosystems . . . we will promote afforestation . . . and vigorously protect farmlands . . . we will reform the environmental regulation system . . . we must do our generations share to protect the environment."

the challenge of corruption. In this case, I mentioned that in much of the western world, the moral codes that defined and proscribed certain behaviors as unacceptable—"Thou shalt not steal," for example—had religious underpinnings. And so, had the Communist Party thought about revising its negative stance on religion in order to harness religion-based morality to the fight against corruption?

Again to my surprise, the communist party official to whom I posed this question, was quite prepared to answer it and did so in words to this effect:

> "Yes, we have thought about that. But because our Party is officially atheistic, we can't contemplate harnessing a theistic religion or a theistic moral code to our anti-corruption campaigns. But *Confucianism* is not theistic, it has deep cultural roots in China [though Mao strenuously denounced it][381] and it has a moral code that is antithetical to corruption. Thus we have been quite prepared to rethink our initial opposition to Confucianism and are supportive of its study and application not only in China but abroad."

As has been pointed out by others better versed on this subject than myself, this may have been just the personal opinion of this one particular official and is not the official line of the party. The party, however, has supported the creation and expansion of Confucius Institutes at home and abroad. This has ostensibly been done as a means of promoting the study of the Chinese language and culture, although others see other motives in this state sponsored support of Confucianism.

On the broader front, however, while the Communist Party rejects theistic religions as guides to moral behavior and the meeting of personal spiritual needs, increasing numbers of the people of China do not. Not the Buddhists of Tibet and elsewhere, not the Islamic Uighurs of the northwest, not the tens of millions of persecuted practitioners

---

381 Chiang Kai Shek had actually resurrected Confucianism as a guide to proper behavior and morality in the 1930's. But Mao denounced Confucianism as feudal, superstitious, backward, reactionary and counter-revolutionary. He is reported to have told his nephew Mao Yuanxin: "If the Communist Party has a day when it cannot rule or has met difficulty and needs to invite Confucius back, it means you (i.e. the Party) are coming to an end."

of Falun Gong,[382] and not the estimated 100-plus million Chinese[383] who are swelling the ranks of the semi-underground Christian church in China.

The societies and politicians of most African and South American countries, traditionally and even today, are much more respectful and accepting of the teachings and influence of theistic religions than North America, Europe, or Communist China. As the Communist Party of China and its government assiduously seeks to expand its influence and its promotion of state-directed capitalism and democracy in Africa and South America, its rejection of and antagonism to theistic religion may well prove to be a significant liability.

6.   *Learning from and levering the experience of others*

Australia is a citizen-directed democracy with laws and political traditions similar to Canada's. But because China is Australia's number one trading partner, the Australians have had a much more intensive relationship with China's state-directed economy than has Canada.

Australian perspectives on how to cooperate and/or compete with China's state-directed enterprises and economy, and how to respond to China's growing influence in the world, are well worth considering.

382 Falun Gong or Falun Dafa has been described as a Chinese religious practice, rooted in Confucianism and Taoism, that combines meditation and physical exercises with a moral philosophy centered on the tenets of truthfulness, compassion, and forbearance. Its practitioners have been ruthlessly persecuted by the Communist Party and government of China.

383 See Albert, Elenor. "Backgrounder: Christianity in China." Council of Foreign Relations. Oct 11. 2018. "The CCP officially recognizes five religions: Buddhism, Catholicism, Daoism, Islam, and Protestantism. The activities of state-sanctioned religious organizations are regulated by the State Administration for Religious Affairs (SARA), which manages all aspects of religious life, including religious leadership appointments, selection of clergy, and interpretation of doctrine. Christianity in China is overseen by three major entities: the Three-Self Patriotic Movement, the China Christian Council, and the Chinese Patriotic Catholic Association . . . In 2010, the Pew Research Center calculated sixty-eight million Christians in China, or approximately 5 percent of the country's population. Other independent estimates suggest somewhere between 100 and 130 million. Purdue's Yang projected that if "modest" growth rates are sustained, China could have as many as 160 million Christians by 2025 and 247 million by 2030. https://www.cfr.org/backgrounder/christianity-china

And then there is India. When I have visited with Indian politicians and they learned that I have devoted much more time and thought to relations with China than with their country, they raise this legitimate complaint which I paraphrase as follows:

"We in India, because of our colonial past, have inherited and tried to adopt, however imperfectly, such western democratic practices as the rule of law, free elections, and the Westminster parliamentary system. And yet you Western politicians are much more anxious to visit China and to ingratiate yourselves with its Communist leadership than you are to visit India and strengthen your relationships with our people and leadership. You fall all over yourselves in trying to deepen your trade and political ties with China, a country whose political system and leadership is much more contemptuous of your economic and political systems than we in India are with our more market-oriented economy and more citizen-directed democracy. Is this wise or right?"

Point well taken. In developing a strategy for competing ideologically with China on the economic and political fronts, Canada can learn much by consulting the Indian perspective, and should definitely do so.

An alternative perspective?

While I am personally inclined to believe that the Chinese communists' promotion of state-directed governance and capitalism is ultimately a threat to citizen-directed democracy and market-driven capitalism, I want to acknowledge that there is another, less pessimistic perspective.

It may be argued that the history and culture of China are so fundamentally different from that of the west, that they were bound to produce a fundamentally different approach to governance. We should therefore monitor its development and seek to better understand it, but not prematurely fear or totally oppose it.

It may also be argued that western-based corporations will simply need to learn to compete effectively with the state-linked corporations of China in the global marketplace, and that the former are not nearly as independent of the policies and interests of western governments as we profess to believe. Both China-based companies and western-based companies want to do business with each other and with each other's customers, so better to cultivate some mutual respect for our differences rather than allow them to poison our relationships.

On top of all this, the evolution of China's economy and system of governance is still very much in a state of flux, and who knows but that the future results of that evolution may be more positive from a western perspective than negative. Thus the question, "China, Friend or Foe?" may prove to be the wrong question. Or the answer may be some as-yet-unseen combination of both.

Citizen-directed democracy versus state-directed democracy, again

Returning once again to the current and future competition between these two systems of governance, where this competition is currently most intense and punctuated with violence is in Hong Kong. As can be witnessed daily on our television screens and hand-held devices, there is growing and widespread resistance, often courageously led by students, to the imposition of state-directed democracy (as conceived and insisted upon by the Communist Party and government of China) on the people of Hong Kong. But what is equally apparent is the increasingly oppressive and forceable push back by the governing communist authorities, providing a foretaste of what may be in store when conflicts between these two systems eventually arise in other countries.

The pro-democracy forces in Hong Kong, should be encouraged and supported, and in Taiwan as well. If our government is reluctant to do so for fear of damaging trade relations with the Chinese government, there is nothing stopping pro-democracy academics, NGO's, and individuals from doing so, and we should.

One final point which cannot be emphasized strongly enough is the need for an immense amount of hard work on the part of supporters of citizen-directed democracy to vastly improve the performance and credibility of that form of democracy in our own countries.

The governments and citizens of western democracies may be limited in what we can do to challenge state-directed democracy within China. But there is a great deal we can and must do to address the weaknesses and shortcomings of citizen-directed democracy at home so as to make it more attractive to our own citizens and much more competitive on the world stage.

As previously mentioned, the reputation of citizen-directed democracy has been severely challenged by the eccentricities and conduct of Donald Trump in the United States, the paralyzing polarization that has occurred in reaction to his election, and the current preoccupation of the American media and much of the American people with the efforts to impeach him.

In Britain, there is the political chaos triggered by the Brexit vote and the seeming inability of a democratically-elected government to either honor or reverse it. (With the resounding victory of Boris Johnson and the British Conservatives in the December 2019 general elections, Britain may, hopefully, be on the road to ending the uncertainty and instability associated with Brexit). The current practice of democratic politics is not producing stellar or exemplary governance in much of Europe or Australia. And then there is the Canadian example of the seeming inability of democratic governments elected on the basis of style rather than substance to even recognize let alone effectively address the major issues of the day.

The bottom line? the biggest single thing we can do to strengthen the competitive position of citizen-directed democracy in our times is to clearly identify its principal deficiencies and vigorously implement reforms to address them. In other words, *Do Something!* Do many things to make citizen-directed democracy great again, which is the principal aim of this book.

DO SOMETHING!

If you are a political or community leader, an elected official, or a citizen who believes in the efficacy and benefits of a citizen-directed democracy:

- Acknowledge that there are ways and means in which citizen-directed democracy can be improved and strengthened, and use your influence to champion reforms which will make it superior to, and more competitive with, state-directed democracy.
- Become familiar with the strengths and weaknesses of state-directed democracy as defined and promoted by the Communist Party and government of China, and use your influence to warn against its adoption by this or other countries.

5.6 Follow the Flame!

Over my many years in politics and in the years since I left the House of Commons in 2002 to promote the ideas put forward in this book, I have addressed many audiences on the importance of democracy and their participation in its processes and institutions.

In concluding such addresses, I gradually developed a short summation of the democracy story from ancient Athens to the present day, describing it as one of the greatest and most moving dramas that has ever been enacted on the human stage and inviting members of my audiences to become active participants in that drama.

Of all the public presentations I have given, and I've given many over the years, this simple telling of the democracy story is the one that has produced, not just an intellectual response, but a visceral and emotional response which is what is needed to motivate people to action and commitment.

I am not a novelist, nor a composer of music, nor a producer of stage dramas or motion pictures, and so am not capable of putting this political story into a compelling novel like Victor Hugo was able to do in his *Les Miserables*, or that Claude-Michel Schonberg and Alain Boublil were able to do in turning *Les Miserables* into a great musical, or that director Tom Hooper was able to do in turning that story into a hit film.

But somewhere in Canada there are people with such talents[384] and my concluding challenge is for you to apply those talents to putting

---

384 Suggestions concerning potential sources, made by some of those who have reviewed my generic text of the "democracy story", include the following: How might Cirque du Soleil communicate it, or the talented group that perform L'Histoire de Royaume de Saguenay each year in Lac St. Jean, Quebec? Or the suggestion from Calgary-based actress and musician, Camille Devine McCreath (daughter of former Saskatchewan Premier Grant Devine) that many of Canadian composer David Foster's love songs could readily be adapted in a stage musical to communicate the tumultuous love affair between democracy and the people over the centuries.

the democracy story into such a form with the capacity to inform and inspire next-generation democrats all over the world.

In its generic form, the story that needs to be told in a more popular and compelling fashion, is this:

In the beginning

It is a love story which began twenty-seven centuries ago, in events now shrouded in the mists of time, in a frontier settlement established to produce food for one of the Greek city states. There, the independence of the settlers, the natural equality of the frontier, and the absence of fixed institutions of governance, somehow combined to ignite the first democratic flame. It burns brightly at the centre of the village.

A beautiful young girl, we shall call her Athena, lights her torch at that fire. She draws the attention of a handsome young settler, whom we shall call Populus, who falls in love with her and zealously courts her. He is the first of a series of ardent suitors symbolizing the people who are attracted by the bearer of the democratic flame and all that she signifies.

Athena and Populus decide to carry the sacred flame back to the city of Athens where they are married amidst much joy and celebration on the Acropolis. Pericles, who has declared that "we are a democracy, for our affairs are in the hands of the many and not of the few," proposes the toast to the bride and groom and wishes them a long and prosperous future.

Tragedy and exile

But sadly, democracy has her enemies, the insidious enemies of indifference and neglect, and those who promote dictatorship, tyranny, and war. Athens is attacked by her enemies. Populous stays in a vain attempt to defend the city but urges Athena to flee. She does so, bearing the democratic torch, but soon finds herself an exile, driven from Greece to wander Europe friendless and alone.

At first, she seeks acceptance in the Roman Republic, but tyranny and war again make her a refugee. She knocks on the door of the church, but the church has embraced theocracy and rejects her. She seeks shelter in palaces, but kings and princes believe in aristocracy and they too turn her away. Try as she might, she can find no friend or partner in the Republic, the Church, or among the Aristocracy who will cherish her as Populus once did.

Acceptance by the common people

In the hearts of the common people, however, she slowly wins acceptance. Thus, whenever anyone stands up for their rights and freedoms, and against autocracy, she steps from the shadows and offers the flickering light of her torch to the signatories to *Magna Carta*, to Luther as he nails his liberating theses to the door of the church, and to the scholars of the Renaissance as they rediscover her virtues in the ancient texts.

It is in a small French village on the outskirts of Paris where Athena eventually finds refuge among the common people. Here she meets a handsome and energetic youth, Francois, who reminds her of Populus. He befriends her and they fall in love.

Revolution is in the air and tensions are high. Francois expresses his anger and frustration with the tyranny of the establishment as well as his dreams for a brighter future. His love for Athena burns brightly but so does his lust for revolution and revenge against the ruling classes.

The common people of France are boiling in anger at the inequities they see all around them. Their wishes and desires are ignored by their leaders and elites. In its anger, the mob seizes Athena's flaming torch and uses it to set fire to the palaces and churches of the hated establishment. In the struggle for her flame, Francois sides with the mob and Athena is abused and abandoned.

Once again, heart-broken, she is forced to flee, this time across the English Channel where she makes the acquaintance of a stalwart English lad named William. He befriends her and slowly nurses her back to health and strength.

Athena, bruised and hardened by her past experiences, is now reluctant to give away her affections to a new suitor. But slowly William wins her confidence and trust.

Travel to the new world

Seeking a new life together and even greater freedom than they enjoy in England, William and Athena board a ship for the new world. There in North America, where a statue of a torch-bearing woman will one day be erected in her honor at the entrance to New York harbor, she finds her most enduring home.

In America, Athena moves northward and westward. In the colonies destined to become Canada, she is at first regarded with suspicion. But Nova Scotia pioneers the creation of a democratic assembly, and in Upper and Lower Canada, government by anti-democratic cliques slowly gives way to democratic responsible government.

And among the agricultural pioneers of the western frontier where rugged independence, natural equality, and unstructured opportunities for self-government invoke memories of her ancient birthplace, she is most warmly welcomed.

Flee again or fight?

Never, not even in modern times, is Athena free from the threats of those who oppose the freedoms and values she represents. But now, when threatened by war or tyranny or the ideology of oppression, Athena and her growing company of friends do not flee but fight, against the Kaiser in World War I, against Hitler and the Nazis in World War II, against Stalin and his cold war successors, against the caste system in India, against apartheid in South Africa, against communist aggression in Asia, against ethnic cleansing in the Balkans, and against religious and political extremism in the Middle East.

At great cost, she triumphs, and lives in our lifetime to see tyrants brought to trial for crimes against humanity, to dance on the Berlin wall as it crumbles beneath her feet, to lead Nelson Mandela from his prison cell into the sunlight of a new day, and to see a genuine revival of citizen-directed democracy in the twenty-first century.

Conclusion and a final question

When we identify ourselves as followers, carriers, and re-kindlers of the democratic flame, when we feel her warmth and govern ourselves by her light, when we employ her freedoms and tools to advance ideas and common interests, when we invest our blood, sweat, tears, and wealth in nurturing and defending her, we take our place as actors in one of the greatest dramas ever staged in the theatre of civilization.

Will the bearers of the democratic flame continue to live and prosper? Or will they once again be crippled by the insidious enemies of indifference and neglect, or be abused and subjugated by the practitioners of revolution and war, or be driven into exile by the promoters of dictatorship and tyranny?

If Athena were to appear on the political stage of our country, turn to us with her arms wide open, and plead for the affections and support of this and the next generation, how will we answer her?

The answer depends on whether or not we decide to follow the flame—on whether or not we personally decide to *Do Something!* to defend and advance citizen-directed democracy in our time.

DO SOMETHING!

If you are a citizen of Canada who truly values citizen-directed democracy:

- Review the numerous proposals for strengthening democracy in the preceding pages, and choose to champion one or more of them

If you are a novelist, musical composer, or movie producer:

- Put the democracy story into a compelling literary, musical, and movie form that will inform and inspire next-generation people the world over to follow the flame

APPENDIX 1

Organizations Engaged in Strengthening Democracy in Canada

Canada Foundation for Democracy and Development: **cfdd.ca**
Centre for the Study of Democratic Institutions (UBC): **democracy. arts.ubc.ca**
Civix Canada (Sponsor of Student Vote Canada): **civix.ca**
Democracy Watch: **democracywatch.ca**
Fair Vote Canada: **fairvote.ca**
Institute for Future Legislators (IFL): **democracy.arts.ubc.ca**
Institute on Governance (IOG): **iog.ca**
Samara Centre for Democracy: **samaracanada.com**
Centre for Law and Democracy: **law-democracy.org**
Springtide Collective: **springtide.ngo**

APPENDIX 2

Major Organizations Contributing Directly or Indirectly to the Strengthening of Conservatism in Canada

Alberta Proud: **albertaproud.org**
Association for Reformed Political Action: **arpacanada.ca**
Atlantic Institute for Market Studies: **aims.ca**
BC Liberals: **bcliberals.com**
BC Proud: **britishcolumbiaproud.com**
C2C Journal: **c2cjournal.ca**
Canada Growth Council: **canadagrowthcouncil.ca**
Canada Proud: **canadaproud.org**
Canada Strong and Proud: **strongandproud.ca**
Canada West Foundation: **cwf.ca**
Canadian Constitution Foundation: **theccf.ca**
Canadian Federation of Independent Business: **cfib.ca**
Canadians for Democracy and Prosperity: **democracyandprosperity.ca**
Canadian Taxpayers Federation: **taxpayer.com**
C. D. Howe Institute: **cdhowe.org**
Cardus: **cardus.ca**
Coalition Avenir Québec: **coalitionavenirquebec.org**
Conservative Party of Canada: **conservative.ca**
Civitas: **civitascanada.ca**
Fraser Institute/Foundation: **fraserinstitute.org**
Frontier Centre for Public Policy: **fcpp.org**
Generation Screwed: **Generationscrewed.ca**

Institute for Liberal Studies: **liberalstudies.ca**
Justice Centre for Constitutional Freedoms: **jccf.ca**
MacDonald-Laurier Institute: **macdonaldlaurier.ca**
Manning Centre for Building Democracy: **manningcentre.ca**
Montreal Economic Institute: **iedm.org**
National Citizens Coalition: **nationalcitizens.ca**
New Brunswick Proud: **proudnewbrunswick.com**
Nova Scotia Proud: **novascotiaproud.org**
Ontario Proud: **Ontarioproud.ca**
Progressive Conservative Party of Manitoba: **pcmanitoba.com**
Progressive Conservative Party of New Brunswick: **pcnb.ca**
Progressive Conservative Party of Nova Scotia: **pcparty.ns.ca**
Progressive Conservative Party of Newfoundland: **pcnl.ca**
Progressive Conservative Party of Ontario: **ontariopc.ca**
Progressive Conservative Party of Prince Edward Island: **peipc.ca**
Saskatchewan Party: **saskparty.com**
SecondStreet.org: **secondstreet.org**
The Evangelical Fellowship of Canada: **evangelicalfellowship.ca**
True North: **tnc.news**
The Orca: **theorca.ca**
The Post Millennial: **thepostmilllennial.com**
United Conservative Party of Alberta: **unitedconservative.ca**
Western Standard: **westernstandardonline.com**
Yukon Party: **yukonparty.ca**

APPENDIX 3

The Slave Lake Developments/ SpruceLand Properties Story

My personal faith in the tools-of-wealth-creation approach to tackling poverty and economic inequality was born many years ago when I was in the consulting business and became involved in community economic development work in a then depressed area of north-central Alberta.

In the 1960s, the Alberta government conducted seven studies into why certain areas of the province were not prospering economically to the same extent as the rest of Alberta. One of those areas was the region along the south shore of Lesser Slave Lake, including the town of Slave Lake, 150 miles north of Edmonton in north central Alberta.

At the time, the town was in rough shape with unpaved streets, a declining population, few job opportunities, increasing numbers of welfare dependents, and inadequate housing, rental accommodation or commercial space. But on the optimistic side, it had the potential for becoming an oil field service town as the energy industry was beginning to expand into that region.

One day a group of five people came to ask my father and me to join with them in creating and managing a "community development company" for the Slave Lake region through which local people could participate directly, as investors and project initiators, in the social and economic development of their region.

The group had already gone ahead and incorporated a private company called Slave Lake Developments Limited with two stated objectives: "to undertake projects which would contribute to the social and economic development of the Slave Lake Region" and "to earn a fair and reasonable return for its shareholders on the capital invested in those projects." Today it would be called a "social enterprise" because it had a social objective as well as a financial one.

The group asked my father and me to act as consultants in helping them develop the company and its initial projects. We found their invitation appealing and very much in line with our own thinking on community development, and so we agreed.

Upon our advice, the company was re-incorporated as a public company to permit the participation of a larger number of local shareholders. An associate company, Slave Lake Developments Associates Ltd., was also created, through which we hoped to induce some of the oil companies to work and invest with us on joint ventures.

A housing project named Woodland Place, two apartment buildings and forty-six townhouse units, was identified as our first venture. It was urgently needed in the community, especially if it were to become a successful oil-field service community. Woodland Place would satisfy a socio-economic need, but its rental rates would also have to enable it to earn a reasonable rate of return.

A long-term mortgage was negotiated with Central Mortgage and Housing Corporation. A prospectus was drawn up seeking authorization to sell SLD common shares, mainly in the Slave Lake region, for $1 per share. An expanded board of directors was chosen with Leo Boisvert, the town mayor, serving as chairman and myself as president.

Although I was an officer of SLD, I really acted more as a consultant and representative of the company to the oil companies and the governments. But for the next twenty years, I travelled at least once a month to Slave Lake for meetings with SLD's board, management, and shareholders.

SLD's prospectuses, share offerings, rights offerings, letters to shareholders, project pro-formas, annual reports, and annual meetings were as much exercises in economic education as they were corporate activities. Many of our shareholders had not held a share in any public corporation before, but most were real investors, not speculators, who stuck with the company through thick and thin.

Eventually, most of SLD's common shares came to be held by about 300 families and small businesses, 75 percent of which were in the Slave Lake Region. No one shareholder held more than 10 percent of the shares, which allowed SLD truly to represent itself as a community company. The Sawridge First Nations band was one of the original shareholders with a 10% stake and Chief Walter Twinn sat on the board of directors.

My first major assignment for the company was to try to find some joint-venture partners for our Woodland Place Housing Project. We identified six oil companies operating in the area whose workers needed rental accommodation, and went after the companies for a "social investment" of $25,000 each.

One morning, much to my surprise, I got a phone call from Bill Twaits,[385] the president of Imperial Oil, asking, in a rather blunt fashion, "What's all this about you trying to get a $25,000 'social investment' out of Imperial?" I hurriedly explained the concept, that we had a group of people in Slave Lake who wanted to develop their community by private-enterprise means, that they had raised some capital through local share sales, that they needed some joint-venture partners to finance a project to house oil-field workers, and that they hoped to buy out their joint-venture partners in a short while if the project was a success.

"If it's a real estate project, why don't you just go to our real estate people?" asked Twaits.

"Because," I answered, "I know what kind of return your real estate people will be looking for, and this project can't deliver it. We want you to take a portion of your return in the form of a social benefit, better housing for your field people in Slave Lake and some community good will. That's why we call it a 'social investment.'"

"Sounds like a charity project to me," snorted Twaits, "So why don't you just go to our charity people?" I could tell he was getting impatient.

"Because," I explained, "these people don't want charity or government handouts. They're tired of that approach and don't believe it works. They want investment capital on which their project will pay a return."

"Well, Imperial doesn't have a policy on 'social investments,'" said Twaits. "I'd have to discuss it with my board. Good-bye." And he hung up.

I could hardly imagine the president of Imperial Oil in Toronto asking his board of directors to discuss an agenda item headed "$25,000 social investment in Slave Lake Developments."

---

385 For our little consulting firm to get a phone call from the President of Imperial Oil was a major event, but I had no illusions as to how it had come about. Because my father had been Premier of Alberta for such a long time he had dealt with the executives of virtually all the major oil companies. And when Twaits heard that former Premier Manning was somehow involved with this Slave Lake project, he probably felt he owed us at least a courtesy call if nothing else. On the other hand, he did make the call, took the time to hear me out, and Imperial ultimately supported our project despite his initial skepticism.

Several days later, however, he called back to saying: "I discussed this with my people and we're going to give you your $25,000. I know that you are now going to run around Alberta saying you got a $25,000 'social investment' out of Imperial Oil. But I want you to know," his voice was rising, "that as far as I'm concerned, it's charity!" And he hung up again.

With Imperial in, we got another social investment from Rainbow Pipeline (a joint venture between Imperial, Mobil, and Aquitaine). The Woodland Place project was successfully completed and soon became profitable. Within three years, Slave Lake Developments was in a position to buy out its joint-venture partners and stand on its own feet.

To celebrate this achievement, we put on a little luncheon in Calgary. The SLD Directors came down from Slave Lake, as did my father and I from Edmonton. Our special guests were Walt Dingle representing Imperial, and Ed Bredin of Mobil, representing Rainbow.

After a nice lunch and a little speechifying, Leo Boisvert handed Imperial's cheque for $25,000 to Walt Dingle. He then handed Walt another cheque representing the 6 percent return which we had promised. All of this was duly photographed with copies sent to Bill Twaits with some graphic captions: "Imperial getting its $25,000 'social investment' back." "Imperial getting its six percent return on the investment." "Thanks for everything, but this isn't charity!"

A similar set of cheques was handed to Ed Bredin of Mobil. But after the lunch he came to me and said: "This was all very nice but we have a little problem. None of us expected to get our money back. We've already written this investment off and our accountants won't know what to do with these cheques. So could you find some charitable project up there that we could donate this money to?"

After a hurried huddle with the Slave Lake directors, we advised him that the Slave Lake seniors were raising money to build a Senior Citizens' Drop-In Centre, and that they would welcome a contribution. Thus that original social investment returned to Slave Lake and went around a second time.

All of this was great fun, but there was of course a serious side to it, and Woodland Place was just the beginning. The provincial government was planning to build a small provincial building in Slave Lake, just as it had done in a scores other communities of that size. Instead of constructing their own building, we persuaded the government to grant a twenty-year lease for office space in a new building which the community development company proposed to build. This lease enabled

SLD to get one of the Town's first commercial mortgages, from an insurance company that had collected hundreds of thousands of dollar in life insurance premiums from the people of that region but had never re-invested anything back in their communities.

Other property development projects followed, an increasing number outside the Town of Slave Lake proper as the Directors wisely decided they didn't want "all their eggs in one basket." The name of the company was then changed to SpruceLand Properties Ltd.[386]

I eventually resigned from the board to pursue my political activities with the Reform Party, my last recommendation being that the company acquire more professional and experienced management, which it did. In the year I resigned, the market value of the company's assets was more than $6 million, and common share dividends had been paid every year since 1975.

The conclusion of the story? In 2016, after paying a total of $11 million in dividends to its local shareholders over the years, the directors, with shareholder approval, decided to cash out, to sell all the company's assets and distribute the proceeds to the shareholders. The result was the payment of $55 million into the bank accounts of those shareholders for a total wealth creation and distribution effect of $66 million, plus the value of all the payroll and local purchases made by that company over the last 45 years.

The real dividend for me, however, was twenty years of association with the people of Slave Lake and twenty years of experience with the trials and rewards of pursuing community economic development through a dual-object social enterprise.

What this one community did could conceivably be replicated by local communities and indigenous groups all over the country, pursuing the reduction of poverty and economic inequality, not through exclusive reliance on progressive taxation and government income redistribution programs, but through a better, wider, deeper distribution of the tools of wealth creation.[387]

---

386 See http://www.sprucelandproperties.com/

387 For a more technical, third-party description and analysis of the Slave Lake Developments (Spruceland) story, see Goodbrand, P. & Holloway, T., *SpruceLand Developments Inc.: Social Enterprise through Real Estate Development*, Case Number 9B19M100, Ivey Publishing, London, Ontario, October 16, 2019, or contact Pernille Goodbrand, Haskayne Business School, University of Calgary (pernille.goodbrand@haskayne.ucalgary.ca).

APPENDIX 4

Journal Looking
For Dirty Stories

Is the world on the verge of E-Day?

Some scientists say ecological disaster is within the lifetime of many of us. We will die from our own garbage and waste rather than under a nuclear cloud, they claim.

On Oct. 14, groups will be rallied across the nation to attract attention to the problems of pollution.

The Journal invites readers to submit type-written stories of 200 words of less about a pollution problem of which they are aware. It may be a belching smoke stack, an uncared-for dump, or a careless industry.

Take up your pens and write a dirty story. Address to Pollution, City Editor, Edmonton Journal.

Edmonton Journal, *September 12, 1970*

A Dirty Story

This is the story of an Edmonton factory. To produce, it requires raw materials. These include about 140,000 lbs. of a creamy-white cellulose material and 180 gallons of a black viscous liquid, *per day*.

The demands of this factory for raw materials substantially affect our environment. For example, to meet its demands for cellulose material, the prime vegetation on 500,000 acres of forest land must be cut and processed on a continuous basis. This processing:

- Creates a biological oxygen demand (b.o.d.) of 1–1.5 tons per day on rivers and streams into which accompanying wastes are poured.

- Produces 5–7 tons of bark per day which when burned generates 25–56 million BTUs of heat, 2.5–4 tons of carbon dioxide, and .05–.15 tons of ash, per day.

The end product of this factory also contributes to solid waste and air pollution in the City and district. Because this product becomes obsolete within 24 hours after being produced, it is rapidly discarded, often litters the streets, and accumulates in garbage cans. Eventually it is oxidized, either by direct burning at City dumps and incinerators, or through slow decomposition. Oxidation of one day's production may generate up to 1000 million BTUs of heat (sufficient to adequately heat 1000 Edmonton homes in the middle of winter), 110–140 tons of carbon dioxide, .7–2.8 tons of ash, and .3 tons of smoke, *per day*.

In summary, therefore, this factory is directly and indirectly responsible for generating daily:

- 1–1.5 tons of b.o.d. on streams and rivers
- More than 1000 million BTUs of heat
- 110–145 tons of carbon dioxide
- 1–3 tons of ash
- .3 tons of smoke

Not to mention indeterminate but significant amounts of sulphur compounds, oily wastes contained in the black viscous liquid, and other chemical residues.

To appreciate the magnitude of the environmental effects of this factory's operations over a ten-year period (production rates and processes remaining as is), multiply the above figures by a factor of 3000.

These figures, and the contribution to environmental deterioration which they represent, could be substantially reduced if the enterprise in question would alter its purchasing policies, the volume and methods of its production, and the existing provisions for disposal of its product. To plan and implement such alterations, it is essential that the enterprise in question:

- Recognize that production and pollution are inseparably related within a definable "material balance framework"
- Analyze its own production activities and their environmental effects within that framework

Whether this enterprise has the concern or the will to make the required analysis and alterations, particularly if these should affect its profit margins, is at present questionable. To date, spokesmen for the enterprise have been more interested in pointing the finger at other polluters than in analyzing and cleaning up their own industry.

To conclude, let us identify this enterprise and its products. The creamy white cellulose material is newsprint. The black viscous liquid is printer's ink. The product which becomes a waste problem within 24 hours of its production, a daily newspaper. The enterprise responsible for this stream of pollutants – the *Edmonton Journal*. The moral of this story, "physician, heal thyself."

Preston Manning,
General Manager,
M. & M. Systems Research Ltd.

APPENDIX 5

SO YOU THINK YOU MIGHT WANT TO RUN FOR ELECTED OFFICE?

THE ROMAN SENATOR CICERO TOLD THE AMBITIOUS YOUNG POLITICOS OF HIS DAY: *INTRATE PARATI - ENTER PREPARED.* HOW PREPARED ARE YOU?

BY PRESTON MANNING

 WATCH THE FULL TALK
MANNINGCENTRE.CA/SOYOUTHINK

1. WHY DO YOU WANT TO DO THIS?

The media asks every candidate this. Is it personal ambition? Do you have a particular vision for how your municipality, province, or country should be governed? If you get elected, one day you'll be under a lot of stress and you'll need to be able to remind yourself why.

2. HOW MUCH DO YOU KNOW ABOUT...

	NOTHING	A BIT	A LOT
THE ROLE OF A CANDIDATE/ ELECTED OFFICIAL	☐	☐	☐
REPRESENTING AND SERVING CONSTITUENTS	☐	☐	☐
MAKING PUBLIC POLICIES AND LAWS	☐	☐	☐
BUDGETS AND FINANCIAL STATEMENTS	☐	☐	☐
THE EFFECTS ON HEALTH AND STRESS	☐	☐	☐
LAWS GOVERNING ELECTIONS	☐	☐	☐
IMPLICATIONS FOR YOUR FAMILY	☐	☐	☐
IMPLICATIONS FOR YOUR FINANCES	☐	☐	☐
IMPLICATIONS FOR YOUR REPUTATION	☐	☐	☐
YOUR PROBABILITY OF SUCCESS	☐	☐	☐

One way to learn more is to spend time shadowing an elected official you know. The more you know, the more likely you'll be satisfied when elected.

A lot of the job involves scrutinizing financial statements and determining how public funds should be spent.

You should develop a health and exercise regimen to withstand the stress and long hours.

Being an elected official is a joint venture!

How would you handle personal attacks? Do you have any skeletons in your closet? Better to be upfront about past mistakes than have them discovered by your opponents.

If you have marital, financial, or substance abuse issues, get them under control before running. These problems will only get worse once elected.

3. WHAT MORAL AND ETHICAL STANDARDS DO YOU ADHERE TO?

Democracy is an adversarial system where you aren't expected to make the other guy's case. But you want to be truthful. Also, there is a difference between attacking the position rather than the person.

You are a trustee of public money. Are you aware of any conflicts of interest you might have (e.g. are you or your family doing business with government)?

4. WHO WILL YOU REPRESENT WHEN YOUR VIEWS CONFLICT WITH THOSE OF YOUR PARTY OR CONSTITUENTS?

YOUR OWN PERSONAL CONVICTIONS ☐

YOUR PARTY'S POLICIES ☐

THE WILL OF YOUR CONSTITUENTS ☐

What will you do when these come into conflict?

In reality, you will likely represent all three – but you need to consider this BEFORE you run for office.

5. WHICH PRINCIPLES AND POLICIES DO YOU STAND FOR?

SOME CONSERVATIVE EXAMPLES:

"Government should support individual initiatives first rather than always trying to provide its own solutions"

"Most of the time, efforts to rehabilitate criminals don't work"

"Government should live within its means"

Do you have an ideology? If you are in a party, look at its statement of values point by point. Even though you may disagree with some points, remember that parties are coalition of interests.

Which issues concern you? Which issues are your constituents interested in? If you have nothing in common, it might be hard to earn their trust. On the other hand, voters can detect an opportunist.

Are you a single-issue candidate? This can be dangerous: the higher up you get, especially in government, you will likely have to reconcile conflicting interests on an issue.

STILL THINK YOU MIGHT LIKE TO RUN? GET IN TOUCH!
YOU CAN REACH US AT MIKEMARTENS@MCBD.CA OR MANNINGCENTRE.CA

WATCH THE FULL TALK
MANNINGCENTRE.CA/SOYOUTHINK

MANNING
CENTRE
FOR BUILDING DEMOCRACY

APPENDIX 6

The Conservative Challenge

1. Some favor the strengthening and expansion of governments and government bureaucracies.

   - Let conservatives champion the strengthening and expansion of the non-government sector of civil society and the economy.

2. Some favor the continuous expansion of government spending, debt, and taxation.

   - Let conservatives champion spending restraint, debt reduction, and tax relief.

3. Some favor ever-expanding diversity and the division of society into special groups defined by their ethnicity, gender, and other personal characteristics.

   - Let conservatives champion social cohesion based on values and characteristics we have in common and which unite rather than divide us.

4. Some favor constant government intervention in the lives of citizens and communities—interventions that restrict freedom.

   - Let conservatives champion restrictions on state intervention to protect and expand freedom.

5. Some favor the reduction of poverty and economic inequalities through the redistribution of income by progressive taxation.

   - Let conservatives champion the reduction of poverty and economic inequalities through a broader distribution of the tools of wealth creation, economic education, technology, access to markets, and access to capital.

6. Some favor government and civil service monopolies in health care, education, and social services.

   • Let conservatives champion diversity and freedom of choice in health care, education, and social services.

7. Some favor increased government macro and micro regulation of production and consumption in the name of environmental protection.

   • Let conservatives champion the harnessing of personal responsibility, entrepreneurship, and market mechanisms to the challenge of environmental conservation.

8. Some favor the centralization of political power and responsibility in the hands of national governments and institutions.

   • Let conservatives champion the decentralization of political power and responsibility into the hands of regional and local authorities and institutions.

9. Some conceptualize society as a social contract among the living only.

   • Let conservatives conceptualize society as a trust relationship in which the living have charge of traditions and assets inherited from the dead, which they in turn must pass on to those yet unborn.

10. Some see politics primarily as an instrument for mobilizing the powers and resources of the state toward the achievement of certain goals.

    • Let conservatives see politics as primarily a means of representing and reconciling conflicting interests so as to facilitate the achievement of shared goals.

SPECIAL THANKS TO THE FRONTIER CENTRE FOR PUBLIC POLICY

The Frontier Centre for Public Policy (FCPP) is an independent Canadian public policy think tank with offices in Alberta, Saskatchewan, and Manitoba.

FCPP research aims to analyze current affairs and public policies and develop effective and meaningful ideas for good governance and reform.

The author wishes to especially thank FCPP Vice President Research, Gerard Lucyshyn for his valuable and much appreciated assistance in fact checking, footnoting, and proofing the text of *Do Something!*

The observations, opinions, and proposals put forward in *Do Something!* are entirely those of the author and are not to be attributed to the Frontier Centre. Any errors in the presentation or interpretation of facts are also the sole responsibility of the author.

The author also wishes to sincerely congratulate FCPP President Peter Holle and FCPP staff for their own significant and substantial contributions to public policy research and dialogue in Canada. Canada needs "more Frontier."

ACKNOWLEDGMENTS

Since *Do Something!* contains ideas and insights collected over a political lifetime, it is virtually impossible to properly acknowledge and appropriately thank the hundreds of people to whom I am indebted for its contents.

But besides the "unsung heroes" of my own family to whom I have already paid tribute on the very first page of this volume, allow me to acknowledge with deep appreciation and thankfulness the special contributions of others, namely:

- My closest political friends and advisors, Cliff Fryers, Rick Anderson, Ian Todd, and Andre Turcotte, for their invaluable support and guidance over many years and in many diverse and stressful political situations.
- Colleagues and friends associated with the Reform Party of Canada, the Canadian Conservative Reform Alliance, the Conservative Party of Canada, and the various conservative oriented provincial parties, in particular the United Conservative Party of Alberta.
- Colleagues and friends associated with Canada's major conservative-oriented think tanks, in particular, the Fraser Institute, Frontier Centre, C. D. Howe Institute, Montreal Economic Institute, and Atlantic Institute for Market Studies.
- The directors and staff members, past and present, of the Manning Foundation for Democratic Education and the Manning Centre for Building Democracy for their selfless dedication to strengthening democracy in Canada and conservative contributions thereto through research, training, and networking.
- The faithful donors, large and small, and the numerous volunteers, who have generously donated their knowledge, time, energy, and financial resources to my political work and the work of both the Manning Foundation the Manning Centre and our numerous projects.
- Among and in addition to all the above are members of various families across the country whose personal contributions to the wellbeing of our country have been an inspiration to me and whose support has been deeply appreciated, even though they might sometimes disagree

with some of my political actions or some of those recommended in this book. These include (and forgive me for unintended omissions) the Jackmans, Eatons, Ecksteins, Mitchells, and Petersons; the Reimers and Semples; the Dohertys, Piries, Mannixes, Grays, Mackenzies, Mathesons, Hunters, Arnells, McNeils, McCaigs, Mathesons, Nixons, Hearns, Jacobsons, Eltons, Churches, Copithornes, Riddells, Bonnycastles, Farrells, and Southerns; the Winspears, Allards, Pooles, Milners, Byfields, Wusyks, Meltons, Fergusons, and Weibes: and the Stephensons, Todds, McEwens, Pattisons, Littles, Arnolds, Shaws, and Morgans.

- Colleagues and friends associated with the annual Canadian Science Policy Conference, in particular its CEO Mehrdad Hariri, for providing me with numerous opportunities to strengthen my relations with the scientific community.

- Colleagues and friends associated with Regent College, Trinity Western University, Ambrose University, the Laurentian Centre, Cardus, and "Context with Lorna Dueck " for their interest and support of my exploration of the faith-political interface.

- The shareholders and directors of Slave Lake Developments (later renamed Spruceland Properties Ltd.) for providing me with twenty years of practical experience in combatting underdevelopment through a better distribution of the tools of wealth creation.

- Faculty, directors, and students associated with the Clayton H. Riddell Graduate Program in Political Management at Carleton University, and with the Centre for the Study of Democratic Institutions and the Institute for Future Legislators at the University of British Columbia, for their interest and support of my efforts to secure better, more practical training for Canadian politicians and their staffs.

- Cal Wenzel, Jay Westman, Avi Amir, Chris Kolozetti, Gerry Baron, Glynn Hendry, Scott Haggins, Peter McCaffrey, and Jeromy Farcas for their interest and support of my efforts to strengthen democratic government at the municipal level and the application of conservative principles thereto.

- Dr. Erick Schmidt for his long-time friendship and contributions to my understanding of the nature of bureaucracy and ecology; Andy Melton for his support of efforts to redefine political space for millennials; and Mark Cameron for his assistance in fleshing out a positive, market-oriented approach to environmental conservation.

With respect to the specific task of completing, publishing, and marketing this book, I owe a huge debt of gratitude to:

- Sutherland House and Ken Whyte for his willingness to publish this volume and the application of his editorial skills to improve its relevance and readability.
- Troy Lanigan, CEO of the Manning Centre, and his assistant, Zoe Ashton, for their administrative support and marketing efforts.
- Milan Szabo for his excellent work in designing and drafting the figures and tables.
- John Barr, for early stage editorial review and advice.
- Gerard Lucyshyn, of Mount Royal University and the Frontier Centre, for research support and advice on virtually every subject covered in the preceding pages.

Lastly, while not wanting to give offence by playing favorites, I do want to single out one particular person for special acknowledgment and tribute: my long-time friend and fellow political warrior, Cliff Fryers.

Those of us who are directly involved in politics receive media and public attention, whether we deserve it or not and, for better or for worse, we end up with a visible public legacy. But there are those who make equal or even greater political contributions to democratic politics and governance largely behind the scenes, and thus their contributions often go completely unnoticed and unappreciated, or may even be mistakenly attributed to the more visible political actors whom they support

Cliff Fryers is one such individual. His behind-the-scenes efforts and activities have included managing a party, chairing innumerable meetings and conventions, trouble shooting, raising money, settling disputes, offering sound advice, hiring and firing, advancing ideas, controlling damage, telling me what I need to hear, not what I may want to hear, and the list goes on and on.

He and others like him who serve behind the scenes have a political legacy, not highly visible but just as worthy and perhaps even more worthy of recognition, appreciation, and tribute as the more visible legacies of those in the public eye.

I therefore close this acknowledgement with a special heartfelt salute to Cliff Fryers and all those like him who serve Canadian democracy and all it represents behind the scenes. Citizen-directed democracy could not survive without your unseen service and unsung devotion.

Preston Manning
Calgary, Alberta
January 2020

INDEX